HARVARD EAST ASIAN MONOGRAPHS

32

PROTESTANT AMERICA AND THE PAGAN WORLD

THE FIRST HALF CENTURY OF THE AMERICAN BOARD

OF COMMISSIONERS FOR FOREIGN MISSIONS, 1810–1860

PROTESTANT AMERICA AND THE PAGAN WORLD: THE FIRST HALF CENTURY OF THE AMERICAN BOARD OF COMMISSIONERS FOR FOREIGN MISSIONS, 1810-1860

by

Clifton Jackson Phillips

Published by
East Asian Research Center
Harvard University

Distributed by
Harvard University Press
Cambridge, Mass.
1969

The East Asian Research Center at Harvard University
administers research projects designed to further
scholarly understanding of China, Japan, Korea, and
adjacent areas. These studies have been assisted by
grants from the Ford Foundation.

FOREWORD

This publication breaks new ground not only because it is one of the first academic appraisals of a major missionary body but also because it is a thesis reproduced for a wider audience without first being reworked. Both these points call for clarification.

The remarkable backwardness of American historians in dealing with Christian missions abroad is perhaps a tribute to the success of missionary writers in describing their own work. Certainly they have done their part in giving us a very full record of missionary activity. The neglect of this record by academic researchers has apparently been due to an America-oriented as opposed to an overseas-oriented cast of mind within the historical profession. The focus of American history has been America. The European influences upon America have of course received steadily increasing attention, but the influences resulting from the American missionary experience in non-European lands have been largely overlooked.

Professor Phillips produced this Harvard doctoral dissertation in 1954. James A. Field called it to my attention in 1968. The interest it has for us now--as a study that suggests the role of overseas missions in American life of the early nineteenth century and moreover puts China missions in the context of the worldwide movement--is a measure of our newly arisen concern for American-East Asian relations. American righteousness embattled in Asia in the 1960's seems to hark back to our evangelical strivings of a century and a half ago. This Center is indebted to the Harvard History Department's Committee on American Far Eastern Policy Studies for assistance in publishing Dr. Phillips' study.

Partly because the author is fully occupied with other interests and duties, but mainly because of the excellence of his original dissertation, we are publishing it by simple reproduction. A few typographical errors have been corrected, an index has been supplied, and the author has kindly rewritten his preface. Even without "up-dating" by reference to more recent publications, we believe Dr. Phillips' work can lead us forward.

John Fairbank
East Asian Research Center

February 1969

v

PREFACE

This is a study of the early thrust of American Protestantism into the non-Christian world, as revealed in the operations of a single large benevolent corporation, the American Board of Commissioners for Foreign Missions. The ABCFM was founded by New England Congregationalists and eventually became a strictly denominational body, but for a time it represented Presbyterian and Dutch Reformed Constituencies as well as Congregational constituencies and thus reflected the attitudes of a broad spectrum of evangelical Protestant churches in the United States. Even after rival denominational organizations entered the foreign mission field, the American Board long remained the leading institution of its kind. It played a major part in expanding the vision and sympathies of the religious public who supported the various Bible, tract, temperance and similar societies which came into existence in the early decades of the nineteenth century.

This book treats briefly the social and intellectual setting from which the American foreign missionary movement sprang. It then describes the occupation of the Board's mission fields in British India and Ceylon, Hawaii and the islands of the Pacific, the lands of the eastern Mediterranean and the Middle East, East Asia, and Africa, as well as certain parts of North and South America. Here I am concerned not with the missionary impact on alien societies but with the motivations and methods, the strategy and tactics of the American Board and its agents in each area, together with some of the "reflex influences" upon American attitudes and thinking about the non-Christian world. The last chapters deal with the overall character of the missionary undertaking in this period.

During these years of American continental isolation in the early nineteenth century, only maritime commerce vied with foreign missions in the range and scope of their overseas activities. Yet missionaries were generally readier with pen and voice than shipmasters or merchants, and so they captured a larger share of the popular imagination. Their reports from the field, which were regularly publicized through ecclesiastical channels, probably did more to form the American images of the outside world than any other source. Residing in regions where the American diplomatic presence was often minimal, the Board's representatives became the chief interpreters of remote lands and peoples to their fellow countrymen.

This volume originated as a doctoral thesis prepared under the direction of the late Professor Arthur M. Schlesinger, Sr., of Harvard University, who provided many helpful suggestions during the course of my research and writing. For permission to use the manuscript reports of the American Board Commissioners for Foreign Missions I should like to express my thanks to the Harvard College Library, to the American Board, and to Mary Walker, former librarian and research director of the American Board, which is now merged in the United Church Board for World Ministries. I am also grateful to my wife for typing the original manuscript.

Clifton J. Phillips

Seoul, Korea
January, 1969.

CONTENTS

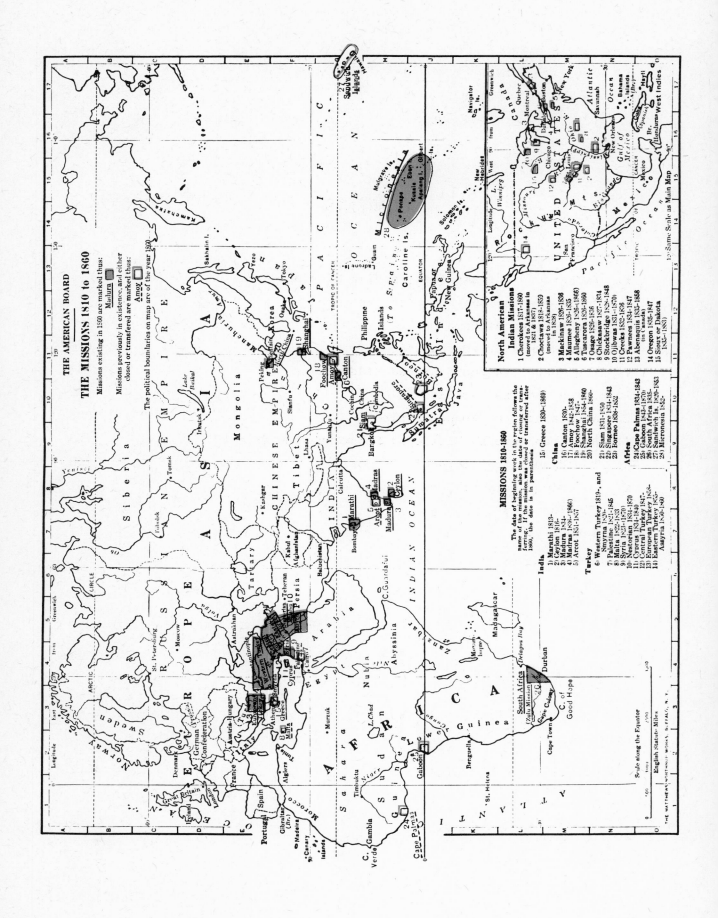

THE AMERICAN BOARD

THE MISSIONS 1810 to 1860

Missions existing in 1860 are marked thus:
Madura ☐

Missions previously in existence, and either
closed or transferred are marked thus:
Amoy ☐

The political boundaries on map are of the year 1860

North American Indian Missions

1 Cherokees 1817-1860
  (moved to Arkansas in
  1821 & 1827)
2 Choctaws 1818-1859
  (moved to Arkansas
  in 1828)
3 Mackinaw 1826-1836
4 Maumee 1826-1835
5 Allegheny 1826-(1965)
6 Tuscarora 1836-1860
7 Osage 1826-1836
8 Chickasaw 1827-1834
9 Stockbridge 1828-1848
10 Ojibwas 1831-(1870)
11 Creeks 1832-1826
12 Pawnees 1834-1847
13 Abenaquis 1835-1858
  (in Canada)
14 Oregon 1835-1847
15 Sioux or Dakota
  1835-(1883)

MISSIONS 1810-1860

The date of beginning work in the region follows the
name of the mission; the second date is of closing or transferring. If the mission was closed or transferred after
1860, the date is in parenthesis

India
1) Marathi 1813-
2) Ceylon 1816-
3) Madura 1834-
4) Madras 1836-(1866)
5) Arcot 1851-1857

Turkey
6) Western Turkey 1819-, and
7) Smyrna 1820-
8) Palestine 1821-1845
9) Malta 1822-1833
10) Syria 1823-(1870)
11) Nestorian 1834-1870
12) Cyprus 1834-1840
13) Central Turkey 1847-
14) European Turkey 1858-
   Eastern Turkey 1855-1860
   Assyria 1850-1860

15) Greece 1830-1869)

China
16) Canton 1830-
17) Amoy 1842-1858
18) Foochow 1847-
19) Shanghai 1834-1860
20) North China 1860-

21) Siam 1831-1850
22) Singapore 1834-1843
23) Borneo 1838-1852

Africa
24) Cape Palmas 1834-1843
25) Gaboon 1843-(1870)
26) South Africa 1835-
27) Sandwich Is. 1820-1863
28) Micronesia 1852-

CHAPTER I

BACKGROUNDS OF AMERICAN FOREIGN MISSIONS

On a midwinter Thursday in February, 1812, while much of the nation talked of war, an event which looked toward greater conquests than Canada took place quietly in the little seaport town of Salem, Massachusetts. On that day five young men of "highly respectable talents and attainments" were ordained as "Missionaries to the heathen in Asia." Common curiosity and a concern for the extraordinary purpose of the occasion attracted an unusually large assembly to the otherwise familiar Congregational service in Tabernacle Church. "A season of more impressive solemnity," ran the official report, has scarcely been witnessed in our country."[1]

Other sources confirm the unique character of the event. A young schoolboy who walked to Salem in the bitter cold with other students from Phillips Academy and the Theological Seminary in Andover testified in later years to the air of excitement that prevailed.[2] From the well-known engraving of the ordination scene in the possession of the Tabernacle Church of Salem one can still catch something of its impressiveness. The unknown artist has depicted the moment when five ministers of the New England churches concluded the simple sacrament by laying their hands upon the heads of the kneeling candidates in the midst of a sober, intent audience. Although, as this picture vividly shows, all

---

[1] American Board of Commissioners for Foreign Missions, Third Annual Report (Boston, 1812), 3; Panoplist, n.s., IV (1812), 425.

[2] Recollections of William Goodell, cited in E.D.G. Prime, Forty Years in the Turkish Empire (New York, 1875), 43-45.

the hopes and doubts of the religious community may have centered that day upon the young men being marked out for a novel and uncertain enterprise, it was the ordaining fathers who best symbolized the union of evangelical forces which made possible the launching of foreign missions.

Samuel Worcester of Salem and Samuel Spring of Newburyport represented the Hopkinsian strain in New England theology, with its peculiar emphasis on Christian duty which Samuel Hopkins had enunciated in the doctrine of "disinterested benevolence."[3] Deriving from an earlier theological impulse were the Old Calvinists and Moderate Edwardeans, represented in this case by the aggressive editor of the Panoplist, Jedidiah Morse, who had sounded the initial alarm against Unitarianism in 1805, when Harvard College was in the process of being captured by the liberals.[4] These constituted the major elements of New England orthodoxy, but they had only patched up their own inner quarrels as late as 1808, with the co-operative founding of Andover Theological Seminary, from which the great majority of the first missionaries was to be recruited. Leonard Woods, as Abbot Professor of Christian Theology at that institution and one of those most responsible for the peaceable union among orthodox Congregationalists in Massachusetts, fittingly delivered the ordination sermon.[5]

---

[3]O. W. Elsbree has delineated this peculiar concept in "Samuel Hopkins and His Doctrine of Benevolence," New England Quarterly, VIII (1935),

[4]For Morse's position and activities in the theological controversies of the period, see J. K. Morse, Jedidiah Morse, a Champion of New England Orthodoxy (Columbia University, Studies in American Culture, 2, New York, 1939).

[5]Leonard Woods, A Sermon Delivered at the Taberncle in Salem (Boston, 1812). For a good account of these theological divisions and Wood's own efforts on behalf of unity, see his History of the Andover Theological Seminary (G. S. Baker, ed., Boston, 1885), 27-132.

Hopkinsians and other Calvinists had joined forces chiefly in order to stem a rising tide of religious liberalism sweeping through eastern Massachusetts. In Boston and its vicinity in particular, in the very citadels of Puritanism, Unitarianism was emerging as a dangerous rival in the struggle for theological supremacy. To combat this heresy the Congregational churches of New England sought assistance and support from their fellow-Calvinists to the south, the Presbyterians of the Middle States. This accounts for the presence on that momentous sixth of February, 1812, of the fifth of the ordaining quintet, Edward Dorr Griffin, who had left a parish in New Jersey for a post in Andover Seminary and, more recently, the leadership of the new Park Street Church in Boston, a bulwark of the faith against Unitarian inroads. Clearly, this thing was not done in a corner. Five public men who stood for leading forces in the nation's spiritual life annointed the first ambassadors of the American churches to the heathen world.

The American foreign missionary enterprise, moreover, arose out of the special religious conditions of a single section of the country at the beginning of the nineteenth century. This is true in spite of the fact that the roots of the evangelical mind ran deeper, and the missionary impulse of that period was broader, than contemporary New England Protestantism. Not only did the initial organization of overseas missions take place in that region where cultural homogeneity was matched by a religious and intellectual maturity, but New England was to remain the leader in these undertakings long after the churches of other sections and denominations of the United States dispatched their own foreign evangelists. Thus the first and a large part of the continuing American religious contacts with distant lands—India, Turkey, Hawaii, and China—were made by New Englanders, supported by a New England constituency which ranged as far west as upper New York and the Ohio Valley. It was not only foreign commerce but foreign missions which made Boston a representative name for the New World in Smyrna, Canton, Honolulu, or Bombay.

I

To understand the intellectual backgrounds of the missionary enterprise as well as to appreciate the type of personality through which these formative contacts were made, it is necessary to explore some of the influential lines of religious thought and practice which preceded this great outreaching of American Protestantism. In the first place, the program of overseas evangelism took form within the matrix of a larger religious movement in Great Britain and the United States, known generally as the Evangelical Revival in the former, and the Second Great Awakening in this country.[6] This spiritual quickening became evident in the last years of the eighteenth century, when the churches began reporting frequent seasons of religious excitement. By 1800 the sober revivals breaking forth in village communities in New England were paralleled by the unrestrained camp meetings of the whole Western frontier.[7]

The evangelical temper which nurtured the revivalistic piety of this period went back to that remarkable outburst of religious enthusiasm which produced Wesleyan Methodism in England and the Great Awakening in America in the first half of the eighteenth century. Separating the two periods of religious renewal lay an interval of a generation or more of spiritual inertia—or so it seemed to exponents of the later

---

[6] A good description of the religious renewal in a single state is found in C. R. Keller, The Second Great Awakening in Connecticut (New Haven, 1942).

[7] The Western analogue of the New England awakening is described in Catherine C. Cleveland, The Great Revival in the West, 1797-1805 (Chicago, 1916).

awakening, who looked upon the immediate past as a time when doctrines repugnant to Puritan Christianity captured the popular mind. Rationalism and deism, however, only submerged and did not destroy evangelical devotion in New England. In the years after 1790 the older Edwardean piety recovered itself, and Protestant orthodoxy launched a supreme effort to regain the ground lost to infidelity and latitudinarianism in the Revolutionary era. Foreign missions provided a convenient outlet for, as well as gained an important dynamic from, the tremendous release of evangelical energies accompanying this radical readjustment of American religious life which has been called the Protestant Counter-Reformation.[8]

Of the theological currents that fed American evangelicalism in this period, none was so influential as that deriving from Jonathan Edwards. Systematized by Samuel Hopkins and other disciples of the great Northampton divine, the "New England Theology" laid the foundations for the magnificent flowering of religious philanthropy in the first half of the nineteenth century. Its historian made scarcely too sweeping claims when he wrote:

> It became the dominating school of thought in New England Congregationalism, and this denomination took the initiative in the greatest forward movement of American Christianity in all its formative years. In foreign missions, in home missions, in the founding of theological seminaries, in the planting of colleges, in revivals, in denominational co-operation, Congregationalism, during the period of supremacy in its midst of the Edwardean theology, took the unquestioned lead among American churches. Its practical labors grew directly out of its theology, just as its theology grew directly out of its practical problems.[9]

Other theologies, Lutheran Pietist and Wesleyan as well as Calvinist, and Calvinist rather than specifically Edwardean or Hopkinsian,

---

[8] E. B. Greene, "A Puritan Counter-Reformation," American Antiquarian Society, Proceedings, n.s., XLII (1932), 17-46; D. R. Fox, "The Protestant Counter-Reformation in America," New York History, XVI (1935), 19-35.

[9] F. H. Foster, A Genetic History of the New England Theology (Chicago, 1907), 3-4.

also contributed to the world-wide expansion of Protestant piety in this period. In fact, the whole movement was oriented toward the active religious life and stressed adherence to the simple evangelical doctrines of the Bible rather than dependence upon a particular theological system. But it was the special intensity of the Hopkinsian version of New England Calvinism which fired much of the humanitarian and missionary zeal of Protestant America. Hopkinsianism, with its ideal of disinterested benevolence, presented "a view of the religious life which called for an instant and unreserved consecration to the service of God."[10]

Samuel Hopkins and others infused a new activism into a theology which had suffered from the spiritual complacency into which Calvinism with its emphasis on divine rather than human agency so easily declines. The revivals beginning about 1790 and continuing at least sporadically until the Civil War were both a product of the new Calvinistic piety and its abettors; for the revivals precipitated out the ardent youth who were to man missionary outposts around the world. "It was not romance," Elsbree writes, "nor was it primarily the spirit of adventure that impelled them to leave friends and kindred and go to inhospitable lands, there to suffer privation and perhaps martyrdom. Their idea of duty was the real impelling force. They were under obligations to act, not in accordance with their own interests, but in harmony with the spirit of disinterested benevolence."[11] The spirit engendered by Hopkinsian theology is indeed the key to much of the whole humanitarian crusade: antislavery, temperance, and world peace, as well as the missionary program of distributing tracts and converting a pagan world. In New England at least, missionary and humanitarian benevolence were born at

---

[10]Williston Walker, Ten New England Leaders (New York, 1901), 354.

[11]O. W. Elsbree, The Rise of the Missionary Spirit in America, 1790-1815 (Williamsport, Pa., 1928), 152.

the same moment and of the same enthusiasm—the Calvinist concern for a practical faith and morals. Often antagonistic to each other, the two movements actually ran along parallel most of the time, aiming at complementary ends, the salvation of souls both in this world and the next.[12]

Yet theology does not explain all. The evangelical movement in England and America was borne on an even broader current of religious piety. The crusade against infidelity and Unitarian liberalism was itself a force tending to unite all evangelical Christians; but more than this, beneath theological and denominational differences was a solid core of emotional romanticism which found expression under a variety of religious forms in the drive toward social reform and soul salvation.[13] There existed not only a spirit of interdenominational co-operation in the early missionary operations, but also a strong tendency toward non-denominational association in the whole benevolent program. Some of the most significant elements in the intellectual climate of the evangelical revival were common to all Protestant factions. Chief among these, perhaps, was the expectation of the early advent of the millennium, or the thousand-year reign of Christ.[14]

The missionary spirit—in common with the whole evangelical movement of the first years of the nineteenth century—was deeply steeped in the millennial ferment of the turn of the century. It would be difficult to understand the urgency behind the drive to convert the world in

---

[12]E. C. Moore, West and East: The Expansion of Christendom and the Naturalization of Christianity in the Orient in the XIXth Century (New York, 1920), 76.

[13]Ralph Gabriel, "Evangelical Religion and Popular Romanticism in Nineteenth-Century America," Church History, XIX (1950), 45-47.

[14]See A. M. Schlesinger, Paths to the Present (New York, 1949), 259-262, and I. V. Brown, "Watchers for the Second Coming: The Millenarian Tradition in America," Mississippi Valley Historical Review, XXXIX (1952), 441-452.

a single generation without pondering the note of chiliastic expectancy clearly and impressively sounded in innumerable sermons of the day. It was a Connecticut minister speaking on missions in 1815 who announced confidently: "We have now entered upon that period which is immediately preparatory to the Millennium; a period which must be filled with wonders of grace. For as the time shortens the work will be hastened. And though we may not live to see the Millennium itself, we may see, and many of us shall see those great events, those decisive tokens of its approach, which will fill every benevolent heart with joy."[15] The very commotions of the time—the wars of Revolutionary and Napoleonic France, and the lamentable progress of infidelity and rationalism—seemed to augur the arrival of a new dispensation.[16] But in the midst of these evil signs appeared the faint glimmerings of millennial light in the progress of religious revivals and the growth of a missionary spirit, especially in Great Britain, where overseas evangelism had already commenced by 1793. A Baptist preacher in New England was echoing a common belief when he declared that "the glorious revivals of religion we have witnessed in our own happy land, and the news of the triumphs of grace which have saluted our ears from foreign climes, are auspicious precursors of the coming of the Son of Man."[17] Just as Jonathan Edwards over a half-century before had thought he could make out the faint early dawn of millennial rejoicings in the Great Awakening, New Englanders

---

[15] Joseph Harvey, A Sermon before the Foreign Mission Society of Litchfield County (New Haven, 1815), 9.

[16] For samplings of this sentiment, at a twelve-year interval, see John Mason, Hope for the Heathen: A Sermon, Preached in the Old Presbyterian Church (New York, 1797), 36; Samuel Worcester, The Wisdom of God. A Sermon Delivered . . . in Boston (Boston, 1809), 36-37.

[17] William Collier, Sanctuary Waters; or, the Spread of the Gospel (Boston, 1806), 19.

were tempted to see in the revivals around the year 1800 the inauguration, or at least a foreshadowing, of the coming millennium.

The chiliastic strain in New England theology runs back to Edwards and beyond; but the later Edwardeans and the revivalists restored and enlarged upon it, Samuel Hopkins going so far as to dedicate his Treatise on the Millennium to those future generations who "will live in that happy era, and enjoy the good of it in a much higher degree, than it can now be enjoyed in the prospect of it."[18] Perhaps only a "consistent Calvinist" could make that kind of gesture. It was an English divine, however, who delineated the prophetic meanings of the French Revolution and the rise of Napoleon in a millennial interpretation which was widely accepted on both sides of the Atlantic. George Stanley Faber, in two works written in 1805 and 1808, explained how the Antichrist was to be identified with godless Revolutionary France--and possibly with Napoleon himself.[19] The union of the Antichrist with the Man of Sin-- the Papacy--was at hand, and their mutual destruction could be expected shortly thereafter. These events were necessary antecedents to the thousand years of peace, which Faber was mathematically certain would begin in 1866, a computation arrived at by close scrutiny of the book of Daniel.[20]

---

[18]Samuel Hopkins, A Treatise on the Millennium (Boston, 1793), iii.

[19]Both of Faber's writings were soon available in American editions: A Dissertation on the Prophecies (2 v., Boston, 1808) and A General and Connected View of the Prophecies (Boston, 1809).

[20]Faber is cited in numerous sermons of the time. See for example: Elijah Parish, A Sermon, Preached . . . in Boston (Newburyport, 1807), 18-21; Timothy Cooley, The Universal Spread of the Gospel (Northampton, 1808), 12-13; E. D. Griffin, A Sermon, Preached . . . at Sandwich, Massachusetts (Boston, 1813), 23-24. Outside of Napoleon, no name was "more frequently heard in religious circles than that of Faber," according to the recollections of David L. Parmelee at a missionary celebration in 1861. Semi-Centennial of the Litchfield Co. Foreign Missions Society (Hartford, 1861), 12.

Although not everyone agreed with Faber and his imitators as to the exact date of the millennial advent, similar convictions in the minds of college presidents and village pastors produced an air of expectancy which hung around missionary activities in the first quarter of the nineteenth century. Few preachers proceeded with the caution of Samuel Miller of Princeton, who told a congregation assembled for a missionary ordination:

> Perhaps my hearers will expect me to say something more particular than I have yet said, as to the time in which the glorious day of which I have been speaking, shall be ushered in. On this subject, I profess to know so little, and feel myself so little entitled to speak with confidence, that I shall, of course, forbear to pronounce positively. That it will arrive, and before a long lapse of time, I have no more doubt than I have that the judgment of the great day will arrive. . . . Possibly some of your children's children may see it, if not in its meridian glory, yet in its early dawn.[21]

The belief that the years were hastening on toward the millennium prophesied in Scripture directly affected foreign missions. Before the last trumpet should sound, Israel must be restored from her apostasy and all nations converted to Christ. A sense of urgency, if nothing more, promoted American evangelism in the early nineteenth century. One minister, who anticipated the distant date of 1999 as the year of delivery, expressed this clearly in 1817: "Before the commencement of the Milennium the Gospel must be preached to every creature. . . . And should the whole Christian world immediately engage in this glorious work with all their might, one hundred and eighty-two years would be time short enough to accomplish it."[22] Millenarianism also encouraged the incipient missionary enterprise by its reminder that divine and human agency were working together toward the inevitable triumph of evangelical

---

[21]Samuel Miller, *A Sermon, Delivered in the Middle Church, New Haven, Con.* (Boston, 1822), 27-28.

[22]Samuel Whitman, *Blessedness of Those Who Shall Ascend to Glory without Dying* (Northampton, 1817), 19.

religion. According to the usual interpretation of the signs of the times, the two greatest antievangelical forces--the Papacy at Rome and the Mohammedan power in Turkey--were on the verge of dissolution.[23] A successful missionary venture might dislodge them altogether. President Timothy Dwight of Yale spoke of both the millenarian hope and the evangelistic objective when he envisioned a future, "when the Romish cathedral, the mosque, and the pagoda, shall not have one stone left upon another, which shall not be thrown down. . . ."[24]

Although foreign missions eventually outgrew millenarianism, its influence was important even beyond the formative stage of the enterprise. Goals were set up which soon proved unrealistic yet were not easily surrendered. Much energy was expended in persistent attempts to convert the Jews as a preliminary to their restoration to Palestine in literal fulfilment of Biblical prophecy. The adventist hope also tended to make missionaries impatient of the slow normal process of cultural assimilation and to look for a sudden flocking of the heathen to the Christian banner as soon as the Gospel was proclaimed. However, by the time that chiliastic speculation had descended from the Timothy Dwights to the Millerites, foreign evangelism had no further need of this stimulus. Experience in the mission field also helped to chasten the evangelical imagination.

Widened and generalized, millennial thinking influenced the missionary undertaking in another manner. The vision of a better, holier society to be achieved in the future qualified desire for the salvation of heathen souls by adding a note of concern for the social conditions of pagan humanity. In a missionary report for 1827, for example, the object

[23]See for example Timothy Cooley, The Universal Spread of the Gospel, 13.

[24]Timothy Dwight, A Sermon . . . before the American Board (Boston, 1813), 26.

of foreign missions was defined as "no less than the moral renovation of a world. Wars are to cease. All the domestic relations are to be sanctified. Every village is to have its school and its church; every family its Bible and the morning and evening prayer. The tabernacle of God is to be pitched among men."[25]

II

The missionary movement demonstrated, more strikingly than any other phase of the evangelical revival, the continuing cultural relations between Great Britain and America in spite of the severing of political ties. Although the religious awakening occurred in both countries almost simultaneously, it fruited in foreign missions first in England. Evangelistic enthusiasm in the New World, therefore, nourished itself upon the exploits of the motherland in the earliest years. When American Protestants finally entered the field, it was to join an enterprise already well begun by their British brethren. In the midst of an unpopular war, one New England preacher demanded peace between the "two Englands" on the grounds of their mutual religious interests. "Like a parent and child, they have united together to promote the glorious gospel. Shall they not, like the two luminaries of heaven, continue to aid each other in giving light and glory to the world?"[26]

From colonial times British Nonconformists and New England Puritans formed almost a single religious community. Provincial Americans read the works of Dissenters and followed closely theological developments abroad. But the interchange of ideas across the Atlantic was not merely a one-way affair. If Watts and Doddridge were eagerly

---

[25]American Board, Eighteenth Annual Report (Boston, 1827), 159.

[26]Elijah Parish, A Sermon . . . before the Society for Propagating the Gospel among the Indians and Others in North-America (Boston, 1814), 25.

studied on this side of the water, Jonathan Edwards commanded a large public in both England and Scotland. It was a pamphlet of the latter written in 1747 to promote the efforts of a group of Scottish ministers to organize regular "concerts of prayer" for the revival of religion which, when republished in Britain in 1789, was a major influence in the formation by the Baptists of the first English foreign missionary organization in 1792.[27] Furthermore, William Carey, one of the founders and the first evangelist sent forth by that society, acknowledged that the lives of the American apostles to the Indians, John Eliot and David Brainerd, were an important source of inspiration to him.[28] Congregationalists and Presbyterians in America were even more sympathetic to the news of the founding of the London Missionary Society in 1795, chiefly by merchants and clergymen of the Independent Churches.

Nothing indicates more clearly the solidarity of British and American Protestants than the eagerness with which reports of English missionaries were published and read in the United States. From India Carey corresponded regularly with friends and supporters in this country, and large sums of money were collected and sent to his aid.[29] Evangelicals in America followed closely the early disappointments and the growing success of the London Society in evangelizing the South Sea islands over which the account of Captain James Cook's discoveries had cast so romantic a spell. In the first years of the nineteenth century Anglo-American religious ties were further strengthened when the restrictions of the East India Company forced the directors of the L.M.S. to

[27]Elsbree, Rise of the Missionary Spirit in America, 135-136.

[28]George Smith, The Life of William Carey, D.D., Shoemaker and Missionary (London, 1885), 40.

[29]Connecticut Evangelical Intelligencer, VII (1807), 270-271; Leighton and Mornay Williams, eds., Serampore Letters (New York, 1892).

dispatch their representatives to India and China by way of New York. In this way the first Protestant emissary to the Celestial Empire, Robert Morrison, helped raise fresh enthusiasm for missions in the United States when he landed here in 1807 en route to Canton. Protected by a letter from Secretary of State James Madison to the American consul in that port, he later sailed from New York on an American vessel procured through the good offices of local churchmen.[30]

It was England, too, which forged the main instruments of the evangelical awakening--in particular the tract and Bible societies, both of which became important allies of the missionary enterprise. Within a decade of the organization of the London Tract Society (1797) and the British and Foreign Bible Society (1804), their American counterparts were in existence. Especially significant for the emergence of American foreign evangelism was the missionary propaganda carried on in England. "If Horne, with trumpet tongue," declared Professor Porter of Andover in 1820, "had not roused the slumbering church;--if Buchanan had not lifted the pall of death that covers the millions of India, your Millses and your Warrens would never have set foot on pagan ground."[31] Foremost in their influence upon American evangelicals was the work of the two Anglican chaplains, Melvill Horne in Sierra Leone, Africa, and Claudius Buchanan in India. Both directed ardent missionary appeals to England and succeeded in arousing Christians in the United States as well. Horne's Letters on Missions were reprinted in this country as early as 1797, and Buchanan's famous sermon, The Star in the East ran through at

---

[30]Mrs. Robert Morrison, Memoirs of the Life and Labours of Robert Morrison, D.D. (London, 1839), I, 126-128.

[31]Ebenezer Porter, A Sermon . . . on the Anniversary of the American Education Society (Andover, 1821), 13.

least ten American editions in two years.[32] Although Buchanan published
other influential missionary tracts, this sermon delivered in Bristol in
1809 made his a household name in America.

Besides the publication of tracts and sermons, the evangelical
revival found a powerful instrument in the periodical press. Created in
England, the evangelical magazine was transplanted across the Atlantic,
where it flourished and grew prodigiously. The editors of one of these
journals in New England explained their purpose thus in their first
issue:

> And what has contributed more to awaken and diffuse that noble
> missionary spirit, which now warms the hearts of all denomina-
> tions of Christians, than those pious, pertinent, pathetic
> publications on the subject of missions, which have had such
> a rapid and extensive circulation? . . . They have transmitted
> from Europe to America, and from America to Europe, and thence
> to the remote corners of the earth, the most useful informa-
> tion, not only concerning the deplorable condition of the hea-
> then nations, but concerning the view, and the feelings, and
> exertions, of the Christian world, to promote their best
> interests for time and eternity.[33]

One of the first of these "pious, pertinent, pathetic publications" in
America was the Theological Magazine, published in New York from 1795 to
1799. In 1800 the Connecticut Evangelical Magazine began publication,
in recognition, as its editors pointed out, of "a growing confidence in
the abilities of American writers and divines to equal their European
brethren in evangelical discussion."[34] A large part of the religious
press concerned the growing missionary movement, especially the far-
flung operations of the English societies.

---

[32]Melville Horne, Letters on Missions; Addressed to the Protestant Minis-
ters of the British Churches (Schenectady, 1797); Claudius Buchanan,
The Star in the East; a Sermon, Preached in the Parish-Church of St.
James, Bristol (Boston, 1809). Before the year 1811 editions of the
latter were published in New York, Portsmouth, N. H., Newark, N. J.,
Hudson, N. Y., and Danbury, Conn.

[33]Massachusetts Missionary Magazine, I (1803), 4.

[34]Connecticut Evangelical Magazine, I (1800), 5.

Many periodicals incorporated the missionary outlook into their titles as well as their contents. Besides the New York Missionary Magazine which succeeded the Theological Magazine in 1809, there was the Hopkinsian Massachusetts Missionary Magazine which began in 1803, the Presbyterian General Assembly's Missionary Magazine (1806) and the Massachusetts Baptist Missionary Magazine (1803). In addition a number of smaller state and local societies in New England published journals for a time, including the Piscataqua Evangelical Magazine of New Hampshire (1805-1808) and the Advisor; or Vermont Evangelical Magazine (1809-1815). Each of these printed detailed accounts of English missions during the years before the American churches established their own overseas operations. Most important of all was Jedidiah Morse's Panoplist; or, the Christian's Armory, first issued in 1805 as part of his campaign against Unitarianism. Under the later editorship of Jeremiah Evarts, the Panoplist became the chief organ of the missionary movement in New England, combining in 1808 with the Massachusetts Missionary Magazine, and finally changing its title to the Missionary Herald in 1821.

Communicated to provincial America through a variety of media, English missionary endeavors quickly produced a spirit of emulation in this country. In the fall of 1796, as reported in the Theological Magazine, "a number of Ministers, in the city of New-York, being informed of the exertions which were then, and had been for some time, making in Great-Britain, to spread the knowledge of the Gospel among the heathen, became impressed with the duty of making a similar attempt in America."[35] The result was the formation of the nondenominational New York Missionary Society, composed largely of clergymen of the Presbyterian and Associate

---

[35]Theological Magazine, III (1798), 260.

and Dutch Reformed Churches. Like other early societies in the new republic, however, the New York organization confined its efforts to the
Indian aborigines on this continent.

While praising England for her evangelism in the far corners
of the world, Americans were satisfied to look first to the conversion
of non-Christian races at home. The whole missionary tradition in this
hemisphere was bound up with a concern, real or alleged, for the salvation of the pagan Indians. The New World was explored and colonized by
Europeans who claimed religious motives for pre-empting jurisdiction over
both land and people. In spite of endemic Indian wars, the missionary
idea continued and grew in English America, producing famous apostles to
the Indians like John Eliot and the Mayhews, as well as a score of lesser
known figures. The Church of England's Society for Promoting Christian
Knowledge and Society for the Propagation of the Gospel in Foreign Parts
both employed agents among the Indians and Negroes of America but eventually directed their chief efforts to the white colonists. More effective for the Indian work was the Society in Scotland for Propagating
Christian Knowledge, usually called the Scotch Society to distinguish
it from the Anglican S.P.C.K., which set up a Board of Commissioners in
Boston and supported American evangelists like David Brainerd and
Eleazer Williams. At the same time the Pennsylvania Moravians conducted
their own efficient Indian missions from the middle of the eighteenth
century.[36]

Although the American colonists ordinarily shared the same
missionary views as their brethren in Great Britain and seldom looked
for Christian conquests beyond the continent, some New England Puritans
showed an interest in more distant fields. Boston's Cotton Mather

---

[36]A brief account of Indian missions in the American colonies is found
in Elsbree, Rise of the Missionary Spirit in America, 7-24.

corresponded with A. H. Francke in Halle and his Pietist disciples in the Danish mission at Tranquebar, India. In a sermon before a short-lived New England missionary society in 1721 he boldly advanced the hope of the future conversion of both the Indies, East and West.[37] The presence of Negro slaves in America also suggested missions to Africa, and in 1773 Samuel Hopkins and Ezra Stiles of slavetrading Newport, Rhode Island, published a circular advocating the training of blacks for African evangelism. The outbreak of war called a halt to such ambitious ventures.

In 1762 a group of New England ministers applied to the royal authorities for a charter for a Puritan counterpart to the S.P.G. The appeal was rejected, however, through the intervention of the Archbishop of Canterbury, and not until 1787 did the American Society for Propagating the Gospel among the Indians and Others in North-America come into existence. Within a score of years a half dozen other missionary societies made their appearance. All suffered from the same conflict of aims as had the colonial evangelism of the Church of England. Under frontier conditions missionary strategy was a divided one, directed partly toward the heathen Indians, and partly toward white colonists. At the turn of the century, New England was particularly sensitive to this problem, finding the aborigines gradually disappearing from her own borders, and drawn also to the task of supplying her own westward-moving population with Christian institutions. The organization of numerous state and local associations in this period reflect the dual objective. In 1789 the Missionary Society of Connecticut was formed "to christianize the

---

[37]Cotton Mather, India Christian. A Sermon, Delivered unto the Commissioners for the Propagation of the Gospel among the American Indians (Boston, 1721), 62-87. For Mather's relations with the German Pietists, see Ernst Benz, "Pietist and Puritan Sources of Early Protestant World Missions (Cotton Mather and A. H. Francke)," Church History, XX (1951), 28-55.

Heathen in North America, and to support and promote Christian knowledge in the new settlements."[38] The next year witnessed the founding of the Massachusetts Missionary Society with a similar purpose, and in another decade Rhode Island, New Hampshire, Vermont and Maine had their own organizations.[39]

Addresses and sermons at the annual convocations of these associations, however, kept alive in the religious community the vision of a greater goal. Jacob Norton spoke out boldly before the Massachusetts Missionary Society in 1810:

> Is the expectation, my brethren, visionary and unfounded, that the time is not far distant, when, from the United States, missionaries will "go into all the world and preach the gospel to every creature?" Yes, my brethren, when men in the benevolent spirit and with the holy ardour of an Eliot, a Brainerd, a Tennent, will, under the patronage of the Massachusetts Missionary Society, go forth into every region of the habitable globe, with the everlasting gospel in their hands, in their hearts and upon their tongues, accompanied with the fervent prayers of thousands for their success.[40]

Without suspecting that just such an undertaking was near at hand, Norton tempered his plea in conclusion: "But should these suggestions with respect to extending the sphere of missionary labours be judged premature and impracticable, it is most devoutly to be wished that they may stimulate to greater diligence and exertion to promote the culture of a less extended field."[41]

A consciousness of having aimed too low was apparently felt by many in New England. As early as 1804 the Massachusetts Missionary

---

[38]*Connecticut Evangelical Magazine*, I (1800), 13-14.

[39]Elsbree, *Rise of the Missionary Spirit in America*, 56-71.

[40]Jacob Norton, *Faith in the Son of God Necessary to Everlasting Life. A Sermon Delivered before the Massachusetts Missionary Society* (Boston, 1810), 25-26.

[41]*Ibid.*, 28.

Society amended its statement of purpose to read, "to diffuse the Gospel among the people of the new-settled and remote parts of our country--among the Indians of the country, and through more distant regions of the earth, as circumstances shall invite and the ability of the society shall admit."[42] Nevertheless, American foreign missions did not stem directly from the older societies organized for Indian and domestic evangelism. The fresh impulse which led to overseas endeavor demanded new channels and a different organization.

III

For Protestants the nineteenth century was pre-eminently the missionary century. Yet in America it required a special effort of the imagination to launch the overseas enterprise. The new republic, with less than four million inhabitants in 1790 and its population just beginning to overflow the Alleghanies, had many tasks at home. American destiny clearly pointed to the West. There stretched a whole continent tenanted by uncounted hordes of pagan aborigines whose salvation lay heavily on the evangelical conscience. To look to the east and outward to more ancient heathen civilizations for benevolent expansion ran counter to the strongest currents in the New World.

In the first decade of the century in New England, however, forces were set in motion which created the first foreign missionary organization and turned the eyes of American Protestants abroad. On June 27, 1810, in the village of Bradford, Massachusetts, four students from Andover Theological Seminary--or Divinity College as it was then called--appeared at a meeting of the General Association to present a brief petition to the assembled Congregational clergy. They stated first

---

[42]Quoted in S. M. Worcester, The Life and Labors of Rev. Samuel Worcester, D.D., (Boston, 1852), I, 238.

that "their minds have long been impressed with the duty and importance of personally attempting a mission to the heathen . . . and that, after examining all the information which they can obtain, they consider themselves as devoted to this work for life, whenever God, in his providence, shall open the way." The special purpose of their presence at that time, they added, was to make certain inquires of their fathers in the church and to solicit their opinion and advice. These carefully formulated questions were:

> Whether, with their present views and feelings, they ought to renounce the object of missions, as either visionary or impracticable; if not, whether they ought to direct their attention to the eastern or western world; whether they may expect patronage and support from a Missionary Society in this country, or must commit themselves to the direction of a European society; and what preparatory measures they ought to take, previous to actual engagement.[43]

The four names signed to this paper were Adoniram Judson, Jr., Samuel Nott, Jr., Samuel J. Mills, and Samuel Newell. Two others—James Richards and Luther Rice—were omitted from fear that a larger number would alarm the Association.[44]

The appearance of the seminarians with their singular proposal was not a complete surprise to all those present. Two members, Samuel Worcester and Samuel Spring, together with a prominent layman and editor, Jeremiah Evarts, had met the day before with the students and their professors at Andover. From this solemn conference issued the decision to lay the weighty question before the general gathering of Congregational pastors in the state.[45] As a result, the petition was quickly referred

---

[43]American Board of Commissioners for Foreign Missions, "Minutes of the First Annual Meeting," First Ten Reports, 9-10.

[44]S. M. Worcester, "The Origin of American Foreign Missions," American Theological Review, II (1860), 720.

[45]S. M. Worcester, Life and Labors of Samuel Worcester, II, 99-100.

to a committee of the Association, which reported the following day a plan of organization for a new missionary society. In spite of the conservative caution and initial opposition of some of the ministers, the report was adopted unanimously. The General Association proceeded to choose nine members of an "American Board of Commissioners for Foreign Missions," five from Massachusetts and four from neighboring Connecticut, who were instructed to meet as soon as possible to devise a constitution and elect officers.[46] The ambitious but rather awkward title carried echoes of the old Board of Commissioners established in Boston by the Scotch Society in the eighteenth century.

The action of these young men provided the immediate stimulus for the inauguration of American missions abroad, though it had not come unheralded. The evangelical community, stirred up by the outpouring of the spirit in the revivals of the Second Great Awakening, observing the work of the English pioneers in the foreign field, and less than satisfied by domestic efforts, had been preparing for this moment for at least two decades. What had hitherto been lacking, however, was a supply of men willing to commit themselves personally to the task.

It opposed the flow of American life, then and later, for the youth of the nation to march east and not west. From the farms and villages of New England young men had already begun to emigrate in large numbers to the Western valleys. But others, equally discontented with limited horizons, took ship at Portsmouth and New Bedford and a dozen other ports to carry the American flag to the seven seas and the exotic coasts of Asia and Africa. For New England faced in two directions: inland toward the trans-Appalachian country and overseas from its busy coastal towns. Salem already had its East India Marine Society and Museum,

---

[46]American Board, "Minutes of the First Annual Meeting," 10-13.

and many New Englanders esteemed the products of China and the East Indies which Yankee skippers had brought home.[47] In addition, the travels of Mungo Park in Africa, Vancouver and Cook in the Pacific, and many others had opened up new worlds proclaimed in the religious press and missionary sermons alike.[48] One son of New England, John Ledyard, turned from his Dartmouth training for a domestic Indian mission to become a celebrated global traveler, visiting the Sandwich Islands with Captain Cook and dying in Africa in 1788 on a final exploring adventure.[49]

Christian duty and romantic adventure both called forth the first student volunteers. The biographer of one of them afterward noted how certain books of travel stirred the young Adoniram Judson with their "glowing and overwrought pictures" of the East.[50] All four of the original subscribers to the Bradford memorial had graduated from different colleges, and each had apparently come to his decision independently. Most, however, shared in the common evangelical excitement of the time and took part in the revivals which swept through the colleges in this period. The divinity school at Andover was hardly three years old when the missionary spirit descended upon it. Judson, Nott, Mills and Newell, as well as Rice and Richards, all belonged to a secret fraternity called the "Brethren," whose members pledged themselves to undertake the work of foreign missions. Although this society persisted at Andover until shortly after 1870 and furnished over two hundred candidates to the

---

[47]Cf. Ping Chia Kuo, "Canton and Salem," New England Quarterly, III (1930), 420-442.

[48]Panoplist, II (1806), 95, 292; Parish, Sermon before the Massachusetts Missionary Society, 7-8.

[49]Jared Sparks, The Life of John Ledyard, the American Traveller (Cambridge, 1828), 6-7, 35-36, 323-324.

[50]Francis Wayland, A Memoir of the Life and Labors of the Rev. Adoniram Judson, D.D. (Boston, 1853), I, 37.

American Board, its existence was unsuspected for years and never fully revealed to the public.

Organizations of this nature were not unknown at American colleges. At Harvard as early as 1785 and at Yale in 1797 there were religious groups which enjoined secrecy upon their members but had no missionary purpose.[51] Evangelical students probably banded together covertly to avoid the opprobrium of ostentatious piety unfashionable during an era when rationalism and deism prevailed in the nation's institutions of higher learning. Current interest in the Illuminati, Free Masons, and other secret societies may have been a factor also.[52] In later years one of the charter members of the Brethren explained that the possibility of failure and the fear of popular disapproval of the novel undertaking made caution necessary. "Under these conditions," he wrote," modesty required us to conceal our association lest we should be thought rashly impudent and so we should injure the cause we wished to promote."[53]

Samuel J. Mills was the real founder of the Brethren as an undergraduate at Williams College, whence he and his associates transferred its activities to Andover early in 1810. The story of Mills and the origins of student missionary enthusiasm is shrouded in the legends which soon grew up around the man whom later generations proclaimed the "father of American foreign missions." His first biographer described

---

[51]C. P. Shedd, Two Centuries of Student Christian Movements (New York, 1934), 18-26.

[52]In a letter to a classmate, Samuel J. Mills suggested that the Brethren model their methods after the Illuminati, whose alleged subversion of Christian institutions had caused a great uproar in New England a few years before. S. J. Mills to John Seward, March 20, 1810, cited in Ibid., 54.

[53]Ezra Fisk to E. C. Bridgman, Goshen, N. Y., June 24, 1829. Brethren Papers, Andover-Newton Theological School Library.

Mills as the center of a group of Williams men who began thinking of their duty to the heathen while meeting for prayers in a meadow near the college, "by the side of a large stack of hay."[54] By reason of the well-kept secrecy of the Brethren and the accumulation of folklore surrounding the "haystack prayer meeting," the actual sequence of events cannot yet be reconstructed with perfect accuracy.

The plan of the secret missionary fraternity seems to have arisen from a series of religious gatherings and conversations among a handful of Williams undergraduates under the influence of the revivals of the early years of the century. According to an Andover professor's recollections, they had no specific object and thought of both home and foreign evangelism: "Sometimes they talked of 'cutting a path through the moral wilderness of the west, to the Pacific.' Sometimes they thought of South America;—then of Africa."[55] In the spring of 1808 the Brethren was formally organized, with a constitution written in cipher in order to preserve an atmosphere of mystery.[56] The society imposed stringent qualifications on its membership, though several of its number failed to become missionaries. Many who joined in later years, after the transfer to Andover, were dropped from the rolls when their purpose wavered. One of these, interestingly enough, was the founder of the Oneida Community, John Humphrey Noyes, who withdrew in 1834 because he had "embraced such doctrines as he thinks the Board would not wish to diffuse among the heathen."[57]

---

[54]Gardiner Spring, Memoirs of the Rev. Samuel J. Mills (New York, 1820), 30.

[55]American Education Society, Quarterly Register and Journal, II (1830), 211.

[56]In 1818 the society assigned a member to translate the constitution and early records from the original cipher. Constitution and Record Book of the Andover Brethren, 34. Brethren Papers.

[57]Record Book of the Andover Brethren, 72. Noyes had meanwhile transferred to Yale, where he attempted without success to start another chapter of the fraternity.

At Williams the Brethren considered establishing branches of the fraternity in other New England colleges. The only serious attempt made, at Middlebury, failed completely. It was finally decided that graduate seminaries offered likelier recruiting ground than other schools, and branches of the Andover society were accordingly organized in the succeeding years at Princeton, Auburn, Lane, and elsewhere. An extensive correspondence among these student clubs effectively disseminated the missionary spirit among potential candidates for the overseas ministry. Andover Theological Seminary remained at the center of this movement, however, and contributed from first to last the greatest number of evangelists to the heathen.

One of the initial objects of the Brethren was to "operate on the public mind so as to lead to the formation of a missionary society."[58] Among various expedients they approached several prominent clergymen, including Samuel Worcester, Edward D. Griffin, and Jedidiah Morse, all of whom played important roles in the founding of American missions. As one member recalled years afterward, Dr. Worcester was the first to respond and the Andover professors among the last.[59] The fraternity republished two famous missionary sermons, one by Griffin in 1805 before the Presbyterian General Assembly, and the other addressed to the New York Missionary Society by John H. Livingston of the Dutch Reformed Church.

They fed their minds on the literature of English missions and were especially impressed with the austere admonitions of Melvill Horne, who advised celibacy for foreign missionaries. Samuel Mills, who in spite of "an awkward figure and ungainly manners, and an unelastic and

---

[58]H. G. O. Dwight to W. G. Schauffler, Blooming Grove, N.Y., Jan. 27, 1829, Society of Inquiry Archives.

[59]Dwight obtained this information from an interview with Ezra Fisk of Goshen, New York, in 1829. Ibid.

croaking sort of voice"[60] furnished enthusiastic leadership to the Brethren, revealed the spirit of youthful self-denial in a letter from New Haven:

> I have not formed many acquaintances in town. Among the fair
> I know but 3 or 4. These are eminently pious, and have so much
> of that unaffected loveliness, and simplicity of manners so
> truly captivating. Don't be alarmed B/rother/ R/obbins/, I
> am not yet caught in a evil net. But in truth our hearts need
> steeling, to give up all hopes of domestic happiness, the only
> bliss (as says the Tract) which has survived the fall. But
> let us remember what Mr. Horne says, that man is not fit for
> a M/issionary/ who sighs for the delights of a lady's lap.[61]

Mills himself never wavered, and died a bachelor. But within a few years the Brethren had forsworn Horne's principle, and were beginning to seek proper material for wives. One of them reported from Hartford in 1812:

> I have seen and heard of many ladies of respectability,
> talents, and piety, who would gladly go among the heathen.
> I trust no one of your number is disposed to regard this
> observation with levity. A more awful responsibility never
> lies on a minister of Jesus, than when seeking a companion
> for life. This is especially true of one who goes as a
> missionary to the Heathen.[62]

With all the sobriety of young men having most serious ends in view, the Brethren continued their secret activities even after the accomplishment of their first objective, the formation of the American Board in 1810. Furthermore, Mills and others in 1811 organized a second group at Andover, the Society of Inquiry. This fraternity, which operated publicly rather than covertly, appealed to a broader membership, to all students interested in missions whether or not called to a personal commitment. Like its predecessor, this society quickly spread to other institutions, providing another important channel of missionary information and zeal. The Brethren, moreover, used the sister association as

---

[60] Timothy Woodbridge, The Autobiography of a Blind Minister; Including Sketches of the Men and Events of His Time (Boston, 1856), 83.

[61] S. J. Mills to R. O. Robbins, New Haven, Dec. 22, 1809. Brethren Papers.

[62] John Frost to Missionary Society (Andover), Hartford, July 12, 1812. Brethren Papers.

a facade for other activities, long maintaining its own members in the offices of president and corresponding secretary, as well as chairman and secretary of the committee on foreign missions.[63]

Both societies constituted a potent force in the early missionary endeavors of the American Board. At least one case is recorded in which an applicant rejected by the Board was later accepted upon the recommendation of the Andover Brethren.[64] Within the immediate circle of missionary candidates this student fellowship exerted tremendous pressures. One measure employed was "mutual criticism," involving the free discussion of the faults and vices of individual members in closed meeting. Noyes borrowed this technique and introduced it into his Oneida Community, where it served as one of the chief means of government.[65]

The ferment of missionary enthusiasm among New England youth in the first third of the nineteenth century produced a constant stream of men willing and eager to carry the Gospel overseas. This was self-consciously a New England movement, moreover, although it spread slowly westward with the movement of population and the growing momentum of the missionary idea. Students at Williams, Yale, Middlebury, Amherst, and Dartmouth felt that their geographical position imposed special responsibilities on them, as this letter from an Andover seminarian to a friend at Amherst indicates:

> Our Southern and Western colleges are, (so far as they are devoted to the ministry,) to supply the South and West. So with our Theo/logical/ Seminaries. Indeed, many of our N/ew/ England scholars will go that way. But who shall—who will go from hence to the gentiles? The South will not. Few—

---

[63]C. M. Clark, The Brethren: A Chapter in the History of American Missions, 16. MS Thesis in Andover-Newton Theological School Library.

[64]Ibid., 34.

[65]Ibid., 30. See Noyes's "Mutual Criticism," The Congregational Quarterly, XVII (1875), 272-281.

very few from the West. Who then shall go? Men must go from N/ew/ England.[66]

Although other sections of the nation made large contributions, both financially and personally, to foreign missions, New Englanders—and those of New England stock in other districts—predominated in the early stages of the enterprise. The table below indicates the institutions which supplied the largest number of American Board missionaries before 1840:[67]

	Colleges	Foreign	Indian
New England:	Williams	18	4
	Amherst	19	2
	Yale	20	1
	Dartmouth	15	4
	Middlebury	14	4
	Others	2	3
	Total: 106	88	18
New York and Ohio:	Union	14	1
	Hamilton	4	0
	Ohio University	3	0
	Others	2	1
	Total: 25	23	2
Middle States and South:	New Jersey (Princeton)	5	3
	Rutgers	7	0
	Jefferson	2	3
	Dickinson	2	1
	North Carolina	2	0
	Centre (Kentucky)	2	0
	Others	2	1
	Total: 30	22	8
	Grand Total: 170 (including 9 unknown)	133	28

[66] E. C. Bridgman to Asa Bullard, Andover, June 20, 1828. Brethren Papers.

[67] American Board, Statistical View of the Officers, Missions, and Missionaries (n.p., n.d.).

The missionary candidates came from the heart of evangelical America. The majority of them were natives of small towns and villages in central and western New England and upstate New York. This early frontier region engendered a powerful evangelistic zeal, not only to carry religious institutions to the "moral wastes" of the West, but also to the heathen overseas. Not many from the cities and coastal towns felt impelled to plant the standard of the cross abroad. Rather it was the farm boy and villager who dreamed in their homes in the Berkshires or the Mohawk Valley of the evangelical conquest of distant shores. The case of Samuel Mills of rural Litchfield County, Connecticut, provides a characteristic image. "While toiling at the plow," his pious biographer wrote, "was his heart touched with compassion for the heathen world, and he bid adieu to his farm, to obtain an education on purpose to carry the Gospel to millions who perish for lack of knowledge."[68]

Foreign missions naturally made the greatest appeal in those regions where Calvinist orthodoxy retained its hold most successfully. Much of eastern Massachusetts, for example, was lost to the faith when Unitarianism spread over Boston and its environs in the very years of the gestation of the missionary spirit. Although the Protestant Counter-Reformation won back important segments of the population, the seat of evangelicalism remained the rural countryside—a factor which imposed on American Protestantism a pattern persisting through most of the eighteenth century. As late as 1828 mission board directors were highly suspicious of city-bred candidates, a fact revealed by the reaction of the secretary of the American Board to the application of a young native of Philadelphia. This individual, he wrote disparagingly, "has been brought up with city

---

[68]Spring, Memoirs of Samuel J. Mills, 18-19.

habits /and/ has rather a fashionable air and polished manners."[69] The youth was not accepted. A large part of the New England clergy at this time came from humble life. When the American Education Society was formed in 1815 to assist pious, deserving youth to obtain training for the ministry, its directors did not neglect those preparing for a foreign station. A preacher before the Society in 1820 pointed out that nearly all missionaries of the Board up to that time were charity students during some period of their college and seminary years.[70]

---

[69]Jeremiah Evarts to Rufus Anderson, Philadelphia, March 4, 1828, ABC:11, 107. In American Board of Commissioners for Foreign Missions Papers, Houghton Library, Harvard University. Further references to these papers will cite only the initials, serial and volume number, and page or letter number, as above.

[70]Ebenezer Porter, A Sermon . . . on the Anniversary of the American Education Society (Andover, 1821), 25n.

CHAPTER II

THE FIRST VENTURE: INDIA AND CEYLON

Within two years of the formation of the American Board of Commissioners for Foreign Missions at Bradford, Massachusetts, in 1810, its executive, or "prudential," committee dispatched the first missionaries to British India. In the meantime the Board organized itself under the presidency of a former governor of Connecticut, John Treadwell, and set about raising funds for the work. Although originally conceived as hardly more than a local, denominational society, the A.B.C.F.M. soon accepted Presbyterian support and in 1812 elected eight commissioners from New York, New Jersey, and Pennsylvania.[1] The American Board was now, as its name implied, a national organization.

I

With little knowledge of appropriate openings for missionary labors and a yet unfilled treasury, the directors of the new enterprise turned to their British friends for assistance and advice. Since the youthful candidates from Andover were impatient of delay, Adoniram Judson was commissioned to go to England to confer with the London Society on a plan of joint action. After a difficult passage during which his vessel was captured by a French privateer and he spent several days in prison in Bayonne, France, Judson arrived in London in May, 1811, in time for the annual meeting of the English society. But the results of his conferences there were disappointing to the hopes of the American Board. The officers of the L.M.S. hailed the formation of the new.

---

[1] American Board, <u>Third Annual Report</u> (Boston, 1812), 3.

organization and suggested stations in various parts of Asia, but offered
to employ the four young men themselves rather than attempt a scheme of
co-operative support with their trans-Atlantic fellow Christians.[2]

National jealousies, moreover, plus a $30,000 legacy left to
the Board by a wealthy merchant's widow in Salem, which, though still in
litigation, held forth hope for the future, helped to hasten action by
the prudential committee. The impetuous Judson, who was ready and willing to accept the alien offer in order to get to the mission field, had
even earlier pressed upon his colleagues the notion of accepting English
service. Samuel Mills's immediate reaction expressed the spirit of independence and growing awareness of nationality which inaugurated the era
of American foreign evangelism:

> What: is England to support her own Missionaries and ours
> likewise? O for shame. If he is prepared I would faine /sic/
> press him forward with the arm of Heracles if I had the
> strength. But I do not like this dependence upon another
> nation, especially when they have already done so much, and
> we nothing.[3]

The Board proposed to commence missionary operations at the
earliest opportunity. After some research the prudential committee
decided upon Burma as the most favorable location for its first station.
This country, adjacent to the Asian possessions of Great Britain, seemed
to offer unusual advantages to American efforts for the reason that it was
outside the limits of that empire, and "therefore not so much within the
proper province of the British Missionary Societies."[4]

---

[2]American Board, First Ten Annual Reports, with Other Documents (Boston,
1834), 19-22.

[3]Mills to Gordon Hall, New Haven, December 20, 1809 /error for 1810?/.
Brethren Papers.

[4]American Board, First Ten Annual Reports, 23-24.

The candidates were still four in number, but Gordon Hall had replaced Samuel Mills, whom his classmates apparently persuaded to remain behind to promote missionary spirit at home.[5] In January, 1812, Hall and Newell, who had been hearing medical lectures in Philadelphia, returned to Boston with the news that accomodations could be secured to Calcutta on a ship leaving the Pennsylvania city in a few weeks. Shortly afterwards the wealthy Pickering Dodge of Salem offered passage on another vessel destined for the same port.[6] While making final preparations for the departure of the evangelists, the prudential committee discovered that a fifth Andover graduate desired to accompany them. With some misgivings on account of the low state of the treasury, the committee added to the group Luther Rice--one of the two whose names had originally appeared on the Bradford petition-- and arranged for the ordination of the five pioneers.[7]

This service, which took place in Samuel Worcester's Tabernacle Church in Salem, attracted large notice, as we have seen above, and brought a flood of financial contributions which enabled the Board to fit out the whole missionary company--which included the wives of three: Samuel Newell, Samuel Nott, and Adoniram Judson--before the ship Harmony and the brig Caravan sailed two weeks later. The company divided, Hall, Rice, and Mr. and Mrs. Nott leaving from Philadelphia, and Judson and

---

[5]The reasons for Mills's removal from the list of candidates are unclear. He may have given up his place to Hall out of modesty, or in obedience to a mysterious decision of the Brethren, who may have thought his genius more adapted to domestic missionary promotion. T. C. Richards, Samuel J. Mills, Missionary Pathfinder, Pioneer and Promoter (Boston, 1906), 77-78.

[6]William Bentley, the scholarly liberal minister of Salem, claimed that Dodge offered his ship because of the influence of his pious wife whom the Hopkinsians had brought into their camp. Bentley, Diary (Salem, 1911), IV (February 2, 1812), 82.

[7]American Board, First Ten Annual Reports, 34-35.

Newell with their newly acquired young wives embarking at Salem, all without fanfare. The instructions of the prudential committee admonished them to perfect their own personal religious life, maintain fraternal ties with missionaries of other societies, and to form themselves into a church and community as soon as possible. Although the committee recommended that they settle in some part of Burma, the evangelists were permitted to use their own discretion as to suitable location of the mission after reaching India.[8]

The infant enterprise encountered two difficult obstacles immediately: the radical opposition of the Honorable East India Company to all evangelism within its domains, and the outbreak of war between the United States and Great Britain. Upon their arrival at Calcutta in the summer of 1812, the missionaries were first ordered to return to America and later threatened with deportation to England.[9] Further discouragements soon befell them. Seeking a station outside British authority, Newell sailed to the Isle of France with his nineteen-year old wife, Harriet, who gave birth to a daughter during the passage and fell a martyr with her child soon after arrival. Luther Rice and both the Judsons astonished their comrades by defecting to the Baptists and resigning from the service of the American Board.[10] Since Burma seemed closed because of current wars, the faithful remnant determined to attempt to remain in British India. By successfully evading the vigilance of the East India Company's servants, Hall and Nott, with the latter's wife,

---

[8]American Board, First Ten Annual Reports, 34-35.

[9]See the Panoplist, VII (1813), 334, 373-377, 561-562.

[10]On receiving the news, the Board quickly dissolved its relations with Judson and Rice and voted that the prudential committee should examine closely all future candidates for its service. American Board, First Ten Annual Reports, 55.

managed to find temporary refuge on the west coast, in the city of
Bombay.

In Boston the departure of the missionaries left the Board
with many still unsolved problems. In February, 1812, Jedidiah Morse
and Samuel Worcester, on behalf of all the commissioners, petitioned
the Massachusetts General Court for a charter. The Democratic majority,
led by Benjamin W. Crowninshield of Salem, later secretary of the navy
under President Madison, who argued against missions from his own experience as a merchant in the Orient, opposed the measure, and it failed to
pass.[11] In May a Federalist governor and house came into office but the
senate remained in control of the party of former Governor Elbridge Gerry because of the "gerrymander" bill of the previous session. After heated
debate, however, the legislature approved the charter and the Board
finally acquired a legal existence on June 20, 1812, two days after
Congress declared war on Great Britain.[12]

Party rivalries in time of war complicated the whole New England
scene. William Bentley, Jeffersonian radical pastor in Salem rejoiced
in the news of the unfriendly reception of the American Board's missionaries in Calcutta. In his diary he vented his spleen against the political and ecclesiastical opposition:

> They who questioned the religious obligation of the plan
> were reprobated. They who questioned the political pru-
> dence of propagating religion in a foreign country against
> the obligations of treaties & without asking the consent

---

[11]The Congregational clergy, of course, was strongly Federalist in sympathy. Rufus Anderson suggested that the opposing Democrats were influenced more "by the fact that the petitioners and their clerical
supporters in the Commonwealth were generally on the other side, than
by feeling of hostility to missions." Anderson, Memorial Volume of the
First Fifty Years of the American Board of Commissioners for Foreign
Missions (Boston, 1861), 74-75.

[12]Ibid., 77-78.

of the dominant power, were thought to be Deists, and represented enemies of Britain. No art has been too small to
aid the cause & render odious its adversaries. It is now
in a state of suspicion, not to say danger of a total defeat.
The matter of the Salem legacy is yet depending in a Court
of Justice, & that loss would be the greatest to the mis-
creants at the bottom of this Money plot of Hypocrisy.[13]

In this last sentence Bentley was referring to Mrs. John Norris's

$30,000 legacy to the A.B.C.F.M. His hopes of its defeat proved prema-

ture. The contesting of the will aroused strong feelings on both

sides, but the American Board employed the well-known Federalist leader,

Harrison Gray Otis, as its attorney and won a favorable verdict after

long and expensive litigation.

In a time of flourishing theological controversy in New England,

the defection of Judson and Rice rankled in the hearts of the orthodox

and may have caused some to lose faith in the enterprise.[14] But the

chief problem was the war itself. The corresponding secretary of the

A.B.C.F.M. wrote to its departed emissaries that the "deplorable war

between this country and Great Britain" made necessary special care on

their part to avoid offending the British Government in India.[15]

America's entry into the field of foreign missions, however, seemed to

cement the ties of evangelical friendship linking the two countries more

firmly, despite the current hostilities. Timothy Dwight, president of

Yale and also one of the commissioners of the American Board, expressed

the sentiments of his fellow Federalists and Congregationalists when he

---

[13]Bentley, _Diary_, IV (December 13, 1812), 138.

[14]As late as 1818 Professor Moses Stuart of Andover Seminary thought
it necessary in an ordination sermon for another group of missionaries
to depreciate the loss and attempt to restore confidence in the Board's
operations. Stuart, _A Sermon Preached in the Tabernacle Church, Salem_
(Andover, 1818), 22-23.

[15]Samuel Worcester to Adoniram Judson, and others, Salem, November 19,
1812, ABC:1.01, I, 6.

declared in August that "the British nation and ourselves, although dissenting concerning some other subjects, are harmoniously engaged, and cordially laboring, to promote the mighty work of spreading the gospel through the world."[16] One ardent clerical partisan argued against the whole conflict as inimical to religion because it dissolved the "sacred union of efforts, now making by the good people of Britain and America, to spread the triumphs of the Cross in Asia."[17]

The war almost completely isolated the Board from its agents in India at a critical juncture of events there and brought resort to a rather questionable means of communication. A group of Salem merchants who desired to get in touch with their stranded factors in Calcutta offered to carry dispatches to the mission on the schooner Alligator, which belonged to the same Pickering Dodge whose Caravan had carried out one group of the first company of evangelists. Urging the peaceful object of the voyage, Secretary Worcester obtained from the British admiral at Halifax a letter of protection for the vessel.[18] On its arrival in India in May of 1813, the authorities seized the Alligator on the charge that it had violated its missionary character by cruising off the Cape of Good Hope for six weeks to warn American merchantmen of the declaration of war.[19] The English now had greater cause for suspicion than ever.

[16]Timothy Dwight, A Discourse . . . on the National Past (2nd ed., Boston, 1813), 58.

[17]Parish, A Protest against War (2nd ed., Newburyport, 1812), 19.

[18]Worcester to Judson, and others, November 20, 1812, ABC:8.1, IV, no. 5. The story of this remarkable incident is partially told in Joseph Tracy, History of the Board of Commissioners for Foreign Missions (2nd ed., Boston, 1842), 40-41, and Anderson, Memorial Volume, 195-196.

[19]Samuel Nott and Gordon Hall to Worcester, Bombay, October 12, 1813, ABC:16.1.1, I, no. 38.

In Goa, on his way to join his brethren at Bombay after stopping for a time in Ceylon, Samuel Newell warned the prudential committee against any unwise action lest the missionaries be accused of being "political emissaries of Buonaparte or Madison."[20]

In Bombay Gordon Hall and the Notts had not yet secured permission for permanent residence. Fortunately, with the assistance of English friends and by means of their own eloquent appeals to the governor of the presidency, Sir Evan Nepean, the Board's agents managed to avoid deportation.[21] As a result Samuel Newell was persuaded to leave Ceylon where he enjoyed the protection of the English governor and join his Bombay compatriots. As it happened, the appearance of the American evangelists in British India coincided with the struggle of the Evangelicals in England to liberalize the antireligious regulations of the East India Company. That battle was apparently won when the new charter of 1813 opened the country to British missionary societies; however, this concession did not apply to the citizens of any other nation. In August, 1814, Jedidiah Morse and Jeremiah Evarts wrote to William Wilberforce to ask his assistance in obtaining a formal decision authorizing the Americans to remain.[22] The subject shortly arose before the governing body of the Company, and Wilberforce's friend, Charles Grant, prevailed upon his colleagues on the court of directors to issue them a permit. In wartime, through the agency of a handful of young missionary pioneers from the United States, the door to a great land in Asia swung

[20]Samuel Newell to Worcester, Goa, February 26, 1814, ABC:16.1.1, III, no. 37.

[21]Most of the long correspondence between the missionaries and the British authorities is found in American Board, First Ten Annual Reports, 92-108

[22]Wilberforce's replies, in which he termed the Anglo-American war "unnatural and monstrous," were published in part in the Panoplist, XI (1815), 181-182.

further outward. As the first historian of the American Board has written, "this was the real opening of continental India to Christian missions. In what they had contributed towards its accomplishment, the Board and its missionaries had done a great work, and had earned the everlasting gratitude of India and of the Christian world."[23]

II

The American churches were beginning their work in India just as a new era was opening for Christian missions in that country. As recently as 1808 and 1809 Sydney Smith had ridiculed the Baptist missionaries in Serampore as "a nest of consecrated cobblers" in the powerful Edinburgh Review, and important segments of British opinion long opposed the introduction of Christianity into India in the belief that it would undermine the rule of the East India Company. Wilberforce, Grant, and their fellow Evangelicals struggled against difficult odds in parliament, losing the battle over the charter of 1793, but finally succeeding twenty years later and inserting a clause officially tolerating missionary activities. The bold and unilateral efforts of the Americans to obtain a foothold in Bombay in 1813 and 1814, however, offended even some of their allies in Britain. The influential Christian Observer—a champion of evangelicalism followed closely in the United States—accused the Board's agents of "lowering the missionary character, where it was of utmost moment it should be held high, and alienating their best friends without a rational hope of succeeding in their designs; for in what part of India would they reasonably expect to be allowed to fix themselves after such a transaction."[24] Again Charles Grant came to the rescue and publicly

---

[23]Tracy, History of the American Board, 47.

[24]Christian Observer, XIV (1815), 888.

vindicated the American society.[25]

Hoping to press home its advantage, the A.B.C.F.M. lost no time after the end of the war in 1815 in sending reinforcements to India. Five more Andover graduates who had volunteered some time before were ordained in June in a ceremony attended by a great assembly. Their embarkation at Newburyport four months later, unlike the hurried departure of the first group in 1812, was a festive event:

> The day was very pleasant. A large concourse of people assembled on the wharf at which the vessel lay, and on the adjoining wharves, and at other places which commanded a near view of the scene. The deck of the vessel was filled with visitors, mostly females, the particular friends of the missionaries, assembled to bid them a final farewell. . . . The utmost stillness and solemnity prevaded the attentive multitude. A missionary farewell hymn was sung to the tune of Old Hundred. Many were deeply affected and bathed in tears. After the hymn, the visitors on deck immediately stepped on shore; the brig left the wharf, spread her sails to the breeze, and quietly entered on her course, followed by the gaze of many deeply interested spectators.[26]

Since Samuel Newell had found the British authorities in Ceylon friendly to the idea of an American mission there, this second company proceeded to that island. One of their number, Horatio Bardwell, went on to Bombay to employ his printing experience in the press soon to be established there, but the rest commenced work in the district of Jaffna in northern Ceylon. This island was traditionally the location of the Garden of Eden, the home of Adam and Eve, and had enjoyed the proselyting labors of first the Catholic Portuguese and then the Protestant Dutch in centuries past. Curiously enough, a correspondent in the Netherlands once informed Cotton Mather that it was the example of John Eliot and other New England apostles to the Indians in the seventeenth century that had inspired the Dutch to attempt the conversion of Ceylon and

[25]Worcester to Charles Grant, Salem, December 15, 1816, in S. M. Worcester, Life and Labors of Samuel Worcester, II, 397-398.

[26]Panoplist, XI (1815), 533.

their other possessions in the East Indies.[27] Now under British rule, the island, or a significant portion thereof, fell to the evangelicals of the New World.

In Bombay the pioneer missionaries found a heterogeneous society—English merchants and servants of the Company, retired and disabled soldiers of European armies, many Portuguese, half-castes, and a mixed population of Hindus and Mohammedans. Their first impulse was to commence English-language instruction for this assorted community.[28] In addition they set up a series of vernacular institutions taught by non-Christian schoolmasters under the general superintendence of members of the mission, and employing the monitorial system so popular at that time in America through the influence of its English exponents, Joseph Lancaster and Andrew Bell. Thus, ironically, one of the first acts of the missionaries was to return this educational device to the country of its origin.

The organization of such schools in India caught the imagination of the evangelical community in America. Although somewhat apprehensive at first of the employment of unconverted native assistants, the Board encouraged its agents in this work and in 1816 set aside a special "Fund for Education of Heathen Youth."[29] The lively interest in the project coincided with the first stirrings of the common-school revival in the United States and indicated perhaps that American benevolence was willing to extend the ideal of universal education beyond the nation's limits. The annual report of the A.B.C.F.M. for 1817 required eight pages to record donations to the school fund alone, and the next year

---

[27]Tracy, History of the American Board, 6 and note.

[28]Panoplist, XII (1816), 34-35.

[29]American Board, Seventh Annual Report (Boston, 1816), 9.

slightly less than $11,000 was contributed for that purpose.[30] Even in the South, almost untouched by the educational awakening at home, several individuals gave money for the support of three schools in Bombay, to be named after their donors' native cities: Charleston, Savannah, and Augusta.[31]

Another kind of pedagogical philanthropy created an even more intimate bond between Americans and their East Indian wards. The missionaries at Bombay suggested a plan of gathering non-Christian children into their own families for instruction in English and a closer superintendence of their daily lives. Money was raised in the United States for the support of these virtual boarding schools for the training of native converts and future leaders of Christian communities in India before it was discovered that the mission found it next to impossible to secure the necessary students. As a result the Board transferred the growing funds to the Ceylon stations where no such difficulty was encountered.[32]

The plan proved extremely successful and became a model for later missions of the A.B.C.F.M. in other parts of the world. The children in missionary homes received names suggested by their American benefactors, who paid from fifteen to thirty dollars a year for their support. Thus the pages of reports from the field bristle with familiar New England cognomens like Mather, Brainerd, and Edwards. One child in Ceylon received the unusual favor of being christened "Jordan Lodge" after a society of Free Masons of the same title in Danvers, Massachusetts.[33]

---

[30]American Board, Eighth Annual Report (Boston, 1817), 41-49; Ninth Annual Report (Boston, 1818), 29.

[31]American Board, Twelfth Annual Report (Boston, 1821), 30.

[32]Worcester to B. J. Meigs and Daniel Poor, Salem, June 5, 1819, ABC: 1.01, III, 184.

[33]Panoplist, XV (1819), 318.

The students liked their new and foreign-sounding names. Furthermore, the missionaries themselves enjoyed this reminder of home in the midst of a pagan land. "What, dear sir," they wrote to the Board in 1819, "can be better,

> what in our minds, can be so good a substitute for the society of beloved brethren, sisters, and friends, whom we have left behind, as the prescence of a circle of males and females, bearing their names, snatched from the ignorance, and misery of idolatry, thro' their instrumentality, and placed in circumstances favourable for cultivating the same virtues, which our brethren and friends possess?"[34]

In education the Americans also ventured into an area still a matter of discussion and debate among the English authorities and the Evangelicals. A Scottish missionary, Alexander Duff, was the leading proponent of English-language schools in India and helped to build a vast network of them.[35] The struggle between the Orientalists, who demanded colleges based on Hindu learning, and the Evangelicals and Utilitarians, who hoped to introduce all "useful knowledge" to India by the medium of English language and literature, ended only in 1835, when Thomas Babington Macauley's "Minute on Education" recommending the whole-sale adoption of the latter method was adopted by the government.[36] When the Ceylon mission proposed to establish a college in 1823, the British authorities refused the institution a charter.[37] In its place, however, the Americans erected a high school with instruction in both the English and Tamil languages. In this academy, later called Batticotta

---

[34]James Richards, and others, to Worcester, Jaffna, November 13, 1819, ABC:16.1.5, I, no. 30.

[35]D. J. Richter, A History of Missions in India (S. H. Moore, tr., Edinburgh and London, /1908/), 123-124, 173-180.

[36]See E. H. Cutts, "The Background of Macauley's Minute," American Historical Review, LVIII (1953), 824-853.

[37]Plan of a College for the Literary and Religious Instruction of Tamul and Other Youth (Columbo, 1823); American Board, Fifteenth Annual Report (Boston, 1824), 149-163.

Seminary, the men of the Board taught mathematics, natural philosophy, and theology, in what was undoubtedly the first American center of higher learning in the "underdeveloped areas" of the world.

In the first years, at least, the Board's educational and informational program was more successful than direct evangelism. Its agents set up presses in both Bombay and Jaffna, Ceylon, from which tracts and Bible translations commenced to pour forth. In 1832 the American Bible Society and the American Tract Society greatly enlarged this work by beginning to subsidize these publications.[38] The printing establishment of the Board's mission in Bombay was for years the largest in India and from 1830 to 1835 issued an impressive English-language journal, the Oriental Christian Spectator, under joint British and American sponsorship.[39] In the vernacular languages—Tamil and Maratha— the stations in India and Ceylon produced a whole library of volumes, including dictionaries and lexicons, as well as translations of tracts and the Scriptures.

By 1824 the A.B.C.F.M. considered its mission permanent enough to agree to the purchase rather than rental of buildings and land in Bombay.[40] In Ceylon such a step was unnecessary because the government made available free of charge the broken-down parish churches and glebes in the Jaffna district formerly belonging to the Dutch. In America interest remained high in the work in India, despite the fact that few

[38]American Board, Twenty-third Annual Report (Boston, 1832), 25-26.

[39]The Oriental Christian Spectator (Bombay, 1830-1835). Although the prudential committee in Boston later regretted the expenditure of its missionaries' energies in the English-language publications, in 1830 it congratulated the Bombay mission for its journal and suggested that other stations follow this example. American Board, Twenty-first Annual Report (Boston, 1830), 33.

[40]Anderson to Hall, and others, Boston, June 23, 1824, ABC:8.1, IV, 35.

converts were produced. The Board sent forty missionaries, including wives, to Bombay and Ceylon before 1833, when a new charter of the East India Company opened the country freely to all who wished to enter. After that date began the occupation of India by other American societies: the Old School Presbyterians in 1834, the same year in which they withdrew from the constituency of the Board, the Free-Will Baptists—a small but vigorous sect—in 1838, the main body of Baptists two years later, and the Methodists as late as 1858.[41]

Meanwhile the agents of the Board expanded their work as reinforcements augmented their numbers. From the little island on the western coast on which Bombay stood, they extended their schools and preaching tours to the adjacent communities on the mainland. Finally, in 1831, a new station was organized in the interior of the Maratha country at Ahmadnagar, a military center of the East India Company in a region won by the British only in the first decade of the century.[42] Using these cities as bases the missionaries made extensive tours through the Bombay Presidency and parts of the Deccan.[43] The journal of two of these, Hollis Read and William Ramsay, was the first American book of travel in the subcontinent published.[44] In Ceylon the evangelists gradually occupied seven stations in Jaffna, a northern peninsula of the island. There they labored among a Tamil-speaking people—Hindus rather than Buddhists as were most of the rest of the Singhalese—closely allied to the inhabitants of the southeastern coast of India. Since the continent seemed to offer a larger and attractive field, the prudential committee

[41]Richter, History of Missions in India, 199-201, 211.

[42]American Board, Twenty-ninth Annual Report, 38-39.

[43]Missionary Herald, XLIV (1848), 305-307.

[44]William Ramsay, Journal of a Missionary Tour in India (Philadelphia, 1836).

of the Board, after conferring with Miron Winslow, who had left Ceylon for a brief visit to the United States, decided to commence operations there. Accordingly, some members of the Jaffna mission were detached for service in Madura in 1835, and the next year Winslow and John Scudder, the first physician of the A.B.C.F.M. in India, opened a station in the important city of Madras, soon to become a third great publishing center for the American Board in India.[45] Not until 1851 was a fifth and final station occupied. This was located west of Madras, in the North Arcot district, and staffed by members of a single family: the five sons and one daughter of Dr. Scudder, all born in India. Six years later, however, the Reformed Dutch communion, to which these evangelists belonged, withdrew from the Board and assumed complete responsibility for this mission.[46]

The A.B.C.F.M. made no attempt to plant stations outside English territory in India. Although its mission in Bombay was the first ever organized in that city, British societies soon entered also, and in almost every other region agents of the two nations worked amicably side by side. The Americans generally enjoyed good relations with English residents and received monetary contributions for schools and churches from many of them.[47] Bengal, the region centered upon Calcutta at the mouth of the Ganges where British missionaries operated extensively, the Board had no wish to occupy. The prudential committee's

[45]American Board, Twenty-fifth Annual Report (Boston, 1834), 84-85; Twenty-seventh Annual Report (Boston, 1837), 72-73.

[46]Anderson, History of the Missions of the American Board of Commissioners for Foreign Missions in India (Boston, 1874), 236-240.

[47]United States Naval Surgeon William Ruschenberger discovered on a visit in 1835 that the English in Bombay declared the Board's missionaries "far more active and successful than their own countrymen." W. S. W. Ruschenberger, A Voyage round the World; Including an Embassy to Muscat and Siam, in 1835, 1836, and 1837 (Philadelphia, 1838), 127.

early strategy, which was never fulfilled, pointed toward the Mohammedan
countries to the northwest. The pioneers in Bombay, for example, at
first hoped to expand their work into the Persian gulf and to Arabia
and Iran.[48] In 1836, moreover, the corresponding secretary of the Board
spoke of "a chain of posts, extending from Ceylon, through the Tamul
nation of Southern India, the Mahrattas, the Rajpoots, and Afghanistan,
Persia, Armenia, and Asia Minor to Constantinople, and into European
Turkey."[49] Although some of these last-named objectives were reached
from the western flank of Asia, no direct overland line of communications
ever connected the Board's stations in the Middle East and India.

III

A Massachusetts merchant who acted as the financial agent of
the A.B.C.F.M. in Calcutta warned a member of the Bombay mission in 1823
to exercise great care not to publish anything unacceptable to the British
authorities. "Remember too," he wrote, "you are in want of two requisites,
to obtain favor in India—you are a Missionary /and/ you are a Foreigner."[50]
While later years brought an easing of restrictions on missionaries,
American citizens served in the India missions under special handicaps.
Their labors depended in large part on the sufferance of friendly
officials of the East India Company or, as in Ceylon, the English colonial government. Fortunately, the latter was singularly favorable to
the missionaries. Sir Alexander Johnston, a former president of His

---

[48]Hall and Newell to Worcester, Bombay, July 6, 1816, ABC:16.1.1, I,
no. 64.

[49]Rufus Anderson to David Abeel, Boston, January 6, 1836, ABC:1.01,
XIV, 175.

[50]E. A. Newton to /a Bombay Missionary/, Calcutta, August 23, 1823,
ABC:13, I, no. 113.

Majesty's council in Ceylon introduced a resolution in 1832 before the Oriental Translation Society in London praising the work of the Americans.[51]

According to local law and custom, however, missionaries' children born abroad were considered British subjects, for the United States government had not yet arrived at a formal method of conferring citizenship in such cases.[52] The American Board's servants were also anxious about the proper education of their sons and daughters growing up amidst foreign and pagan influences. Blessed with large families, the members of the Ceylon mission were the first to raise the issue. In 1822 a joint letter described their situation:

> We have now fifteen children. Five of them have begun to read, and some of them are at an age in which the habits of study ought to be fixed by constant application. . . . Nothing could be more deeply affecting to our feelings than the thought that some future traveller would see in our children or their descendents what we now see in the descendants of Europeans in this District—men, women and children as much more wretched than the heathen as their ancestors were more elevated.[53]

The missionaries suggested that their children be sent to the

---

[51] His resolution stated in part: "It must be a matter of congratulations to the friends of religion and civilization in every part of the world, to see the citizens of the United States and the subjects of Great Britain in the Island of Ceylon, mutually recollecting, under the immediate protection of the British government, their common origin and their common sympathies; but mutually forgetting, under the peaceful influence of the Christian religion their former jealousies and their national animosities, and co-operating with equal zeal and prudence in spreading the English, the common language, into every part of India, in instructing the understanding and improving the morals and social feelings of the Natives of every Caste and religious persuasion, and in rendering applicable and advantageous to their present situation all those moral and political institutions which . . . invariably secured the life and liberty of the subject, the authority of the government and the prosperity of the nation." Sir Alexander Johnston to A. Vail, London, September 22, 1832, ABC:14, I, no. 40.

[52] American Board, Thirty-second Annual Report (Boston, 1841), 37-38.

[53] B. C. Meigs and others to Evarts, Jaffna, October 26, 1822, ABC:16. 1.5, I, no. 81.

United States for education at some time between the ages of eight and fifteen and, if possible, enrolled in a special school established for that purpose by the Board. Totally unprepared for this unanticipated dilemma, the prudential committee refused to sanction such a plan. In 1825, after persistent application from Ceylon, the Board formally rejected the proposal at its annual meeting in Northampton.[54] The A.B.C. F.M. up to this point had hoped that each mission would form a more or less permanent colony, setting before the heathen an example of Christian family and community life. But the ties between foreign agents and their homeland were not to be broken so easily. One of the oldest members of the stations in Ceylon, Benjamin C. Meigs, who had eight children of his own—five of them girls—continued to press for a solution.[55] In 1830 the committee accepted a compromise plan, agreeing to make an annual allowance for the education of children returned to this country, provided the parents or friends assumed the costs of transportation.[56]

Though a radical departure from the original pattern of missionary procedure, this practice was soon extended to all fields. Four years later the Board permitted children to travel to the United States at its expense and set annual allowances at a maximum of fifty dollars for boys and forty for girls, to be payable until the age of eighteen.[57] The first foreign-born youngsters arrived in the thirties, the precursors of hundreds of others who left missionary ground to seek an education and career in the land of their parents' nativity. Sometimes they created

---

[54]Anderson to Hall, and others, Boston, February 18, 1826, ABC:8.1, IV, 58.

[55]Meigs to Evarts, Jaffna, January 22, 1830, ABC:16.1.5, II, no. 1.

[56]American Board, Twenty-first Annual Report, (Boston, 1830) 18.

[57]American Board, Twenty-third Annual Report, 21-22. In 1846 the allowances were increased to a maximum of sixty dollars for boys and fifty for girls. Thirty-seventh Annual Report (Boston, 1846) 56.

difficulties, as when the son of Daniel Poor of Ceylon shocked the people of Danvers, where he found a foster home, by his tales of the many servants and tropical luxuries enjoyed in his parents' mission station.[58] But on the whole their presence in New England towns and colleges must have been a leaven, augmenting interest in the Board's foreign operations and opening a door to the outside world. A few returned to the field as missionaries, but the majority remained in America.

A second unforeseen problem arose in connection with the Board's maiden enterprise in India. The tropical climate and poor sanitary conditions took a heavy toll of the early evangelists. Within the first few years two families were forced to return because of enfeebled health—thus destroying the original assumption that the foreign ministry required lifetime exile from home. Soon a regular procession of returning missionaries—some permanently removed to this country and others on furlough—took place. Both Hall and Newell succumbed to cholera in the first decade, and the extremely high mortality of Americans in India created a growing body of widows and orphans dependent upon the largess of the Board's constituency in the United States.[59] The career of Mrs. Clarissa Frost, who accompanied her husband to Bombay in 1824, illustrates one solution of this problem: upon the decease of Edmond Frost in 1825, she married Henry Woodward, a missionary in Ceylon, who lived until 1834; two years later she took as her third husband William Todd of the Madura mission, but survived this marriage only a single year.[60]

[58]Anderson to Daniel Poor, Boston, February 26, 1831, ABC:2.01, I, 305-307.

[59]The A.B.C.F.M. did not fully admit its responsibility for disabled missionaries, widows, and children until 1830, when it established a special fund for their aid. American Board, Twenty-first Annual Report, 18-19.

[60]See the vital statistics of missionaries to India in Anderson, History of the Missions in India, 409-413.

At least until the construction of a railroad network across
India in the fifties, the evangelists in western and southern India were
unusually isolated from the main currents of American commerce. In the
first decades of the century Boston and Salem merchants carried on an
extensive trade with Calcutta but the flag of the United States seldom
appeared in Bombay and even less often in the southern ports.[61] The
tariff of 1816 hurt the importation of cotton textiles, and the East
India traffic--despite Frederic Tudor's ice trade--declined considerably
in the succeeding years. The United States was represented by a consul
at Calcutta from 1794 to 1796, but not again until 1843.[62]

Few Americans appeared in that part of the world to judge and
report home the activities of the Board's agents. A Yankee wanderer who
had been converted by the Hawaii mission turned up in Bombay, where he
joined the church and offered to help construct a type foundry.[63]
Preacher-hating Nathaniel Ames, son of the stubborn old New England
Federalist, Fisher Ames, visited India in the early years and published
an account of his voyages in which he spoke of a shipload of American
missionaries as "obnoxious" cargo and reported that he could see nothing
of the alleged victories in the "battle between Calvin and Vishnoo."[64]
After the great Sepoy Mutiny of 1857 brought British India to the

---

[61]Ruschenberger, who touched at Bombay as an officer of the ship carrying Edmund Roberts on his embassy to Muscat and Siam, estimated that
only six or eight American vessels a year landed at that port. Voyage
round the World, 106.

[62]S. E. Morison, The Maritime History of Massachusetts, 1783-1860
(Boston, 1921), 282-283; Tyler Dennett, Americans in Eastern Asia (New
York, 1922), 28-29.

[63]Poor health, however, quickly sent him back to Massachusetts. American
Board, Twenty-first Annual Report, 32.

[64]/Nathaniel Ames_/, A Mariner's Sketches, Originally Published in the
Manufacturers and Farmers Journal, Providence (Providence, 1830), 55-56.

forefront of world concern, some American travelers made tours into the interior of the subcontinent and commented in published accounts--chiefly favorable--on the philanthropic labors of their fellow countrymen.[65]

The isolation of the missionaries, moreover, raised a demand at Boston for a complete study and re-evaluation of policies and practices. The result was the dispatch of a special deputation to India and Ceylon in the years 1854-1855. Secretary Rufus Anderson, who led the visiting group, had long questioned the utility of an English-language press and schools and called for thorough reports from the missions on past and present activities. Out of a series of conferences held at the various stations of the Board came a long report calling for a drastic reduction in all educational activities, a new emphasis on vernacular instruction, and a greater attention to preaching and less to the press and schools.[66] A proposal for an English high school in Bombay was discarded and existing seminaries dropped their English-language courses-- and with them large numbers of their students who wanted only to prepare for government positions.[67] Some loyal servants of the Board demurred at the deputation's proceedings and appealed directly to the public.[68] The report, however, was accepted in America. The demand for a more restrictive missionary policy derived in part from a sentiment in favor

[65]R. B. Minturn, From New York to Delhi (New York, 1858), 215-217; J. R. Ireland, Wall-Street to Cashmere (New York, 1859), 239.

[66]Deputation to the India Missions, Report Made to the American Board of Commissioners for Foreign Missions (Boston, 1856).

[67]In Ceylon, however, in little more than a decade a new English-language educational enterprise began under the auspices of the Board's mission. This was Jaffna College, the history of which belongs to a later period. Anderson, History of the Missions in India, 362-363.

[68]Miron Winslow, Hints on Missions to India: with Notices of Some Proceedings of a Deputation from the American Board (New York, 1856); R. G. Wilder, Mission Schools in India of the American Board of Commissioners for Foreign Missions (New York, 1861).

of financial retrenchment in the overseas enterprise around the middle of the century and signaled the end of the first great expansion of American evangelical benevolence.[69]

The deputation also had the opportunity to re-emphasize the specifically American quality of the Board's work in India. Surrounded by the representatives of English mission boards and other subjects of the crown, missionaries tended to lose their national character and become part of colonial life in the British Empire. A committee from Bombay suggested a policy of more frequent furloughs in the United States:

> We are apt, with all our care, to fall behind the times. Living in a land of bullock carts and tents we can hardly realize the conception of a long line of rail road, and a crystal palace. We get further and further away from the healthy influences and social life at home. We need reanimation. We get into narrow views, and insensibly become one-sided. We need to mingle in other society, to exchange views with other minds than any we can meet here,—to have our souls warmed and all our religious life stirred up, by breathing the atmosphere of a home revival.

Continuing, the committee drew a word picture of the evangelists who come out to India young in life and inexperienced:

> They allow their feelings to run in the ordinary current of India life, and thus get often far removed from American ideas and practices. In such cases it is not easy to over-estimate the importance of bringing the man into contact with fresh American life, of shewing him by the opportunity for actual observation, the progress made in temporal and spiritual things. The missionary is also a representative of America. He should not remain too long removed from his home land, or he will cease to be a true representative, and become an echo of the ideas afloat around him.[70]

---

[69]A special meeting was held in Albany in March, 1856, to discuss the report and a "Committee of Thirteen" selected to explore charges brought against the deputation from Ceylon. At the next annual meeting of the Board in the autumn, however, the committee found for the deputation. American Board, Forty-seventh Annual Report (Boston, 1856), 29-67;

[70]American Missionaries of the Bombay Presidency, Minutes of the General Meeting (Bombay, 1855), 52.

Though not prepared to grant this argument complete satisfaction, the deputation warned the members of another mission against the danger of being swallowed up in the preponderance of British establishments in India and especially those of the newly aggressive Church of England. Advising them to "preserve your nationality unimpaired," the visiting committee stoutly declared:

> Let your mission, then, be distinctly and characteristically national; following out its own principles and plans with independence; but with no vain pretensions, and in full charity towards the principles and plans of your neighbors, and with constant endeavors to maintain peace by the exercises of all the amenities and reciprocities appertaining to our common religion. Let there be no schools depending upon British bounty; no preaching for English audiences; no common property with them in houses of worship; no trusteeships where they might claim the right of censuring your proceedings.[71]

This did not mean, however, that the American missionaries repudiated British life and authority. Anglo-American ties founded on both blood and religion—reinforced by exile in a racially alien and heathen land—stood the test of philanthropic rivalries. The outbreak of the Sepoy Mutiny in 1857 found the Americans wholeheartedly behind the government, with no lingering doubts of the justice of the English cause. The Board's agents fortunately escaped the full fury of the native uprising but watched the strife from a safe distance and beheld in it the means of opening India "still more widely to the influences of the gospel."[72] "I do not think," wrote Charles Harding from the Bombay Presidency, "our friends at home should be greatly concerned for our

[71]Madura Mission, Minutes of the Special Meeting (Madras, 1855), 124.

[72]Letter of John Rendall, Madura, July 17, 1857, Missionary Herald, LIII (1857), 348. Mr. and Mrs. Royal G. Wilder departed for the United States from their post in Bombay Presidency shortly before the outbreak, which caused some loss of life at that station. Anderson, History of the Missions in India, 273-274.

safety, or for the interests of these missions. It is but a struggle between the kingdom of Christ and the powers of darkness. The result is not doubtful."[73]

One result of the Mutiny was Queen Victoria's famous proclamation of 1858, by which she assumed direct rule over British India. The Honorable East India Company was no more. After the initial contest for the right of entry and permanent residence, the American Board's emissaries fitted comfortably into the Company's regime and watched its passing with some sadness. Actually, as far as missions were concerned, little changed when the old governor-general became the new viceroy of the Queen.

---

[73]Letter of Charles Harding, Seroor, July 28, 1857, Missionary Herald, LIII (1857), 349.

CHAPTER III

THE HEATHEN AT HOME: NORTH AND SOUTH AMERICA

When James Garrett, a printer employed by the American Board,
arrived in Ceylon in 1820 to superintend the mission press, the British
authorities refused him entry on the ground that the government and the
private agencies of England were adequate to the evangelization of the
island. Furthermore, the lieutenant-governor gratuitously suggested
that in the future Americans should stay at home in order to care for
the heathen tribes on their own continent.[1] Though Garrett went on to
Bombay, and British policy was eventually relaxed in that quarter of the
world, the Englishman's argument embarrassed the infant missionary enterprise of the American churches. In 1816, while preparing to initiate its
work among the Indians of the New World, the prudential committee admitted
that it was "fully aware, that many friends of missions, not only in this
country, but also in Europe, have thought it strange, that while so much
has been doing for the distant heathen of India, so little should have
been done for the not less destitute tribes on our continent, and within
our borders."[2]

At the outset of the Board's operations, however, the directors
argued in correspondence with the London Society that the discouragements
of past Indian evangelistic endeavors, as well as unsettled conditions
in South America, pointed them to the more promising field of the Eastern
Hemisphere.[3] Another inducement to overseas missions was the superior

---

[1]Missionary Herald, XVII (1821), 179.

[2]American Board, Seventh Annual Report, 10.

[3]Worcester to George Burder, Salem, January 3, 1811, American Board,
First Ten Annual Reports, 18.

numerical strength of Oriental paganism. This missionary strategy, as outlined in some detail in Gordon Hall's farewell sermon in Philadelphia just prior to his embarcation for Calcutta in 1812, stressed the "five hundred millions" of pagans in the East compared with the scattered tribes of Indian aborigines in the West. "Could a man know," the young missionary asked, "that inevitable ruin was coming down upon a kingdom, would he not haste to the capital, and lift up his warning voice among the multitudes, rather than bend his course to a few depopulated villages."[4] Even at that, many in New England had an exaggerated notion of the number of aborigines in the country. Thus, Samuel Newell in Ceylon, discouraged with the prospects of entering India in 1813, wondered "whether we did right in leaving the hundred millions of pagans on the western continent and coming to this distant region."[5] A few years later, one of the founders of the A.B.C.F.M., Jedidiah Morse, more correctly estimated the number to be fewer than 500,000 in his Indian report to the secretary of war.[6]

I

Although the long-standing efforts to convert the Indians in America which dated from the work of John Eliot in Massachusetts had declined somewhat by the beginning of the nineteenth century, the evangelical revival stirred up a strong sense of guilt in the religious community and reanimated the enterprise. Edward Griffin, in his famous and often-reprinted missionary sermon before the Presbyterian General Assembly in

[4]Hall, The Duty of the American Churches in Respect to Foreign Missions (2nd ed., Andover, 1815), 16.

[5]Newell to Worcester, Columbo, December 20, 1813, ABC:16.1.1, III, no. 31.

[6]Jedidiah Morse, A Report to the Secretary of War of the United States, on Indian Affairs (New Haven, 1822), appendix, 375.

1805 struck this note when he declared that "we are living in prosperity on the very lands from which the wretched pagans have been ejected; from the recesses of whose wilderness a moving cry is heard, When it is well with you, think of poor Indians." [7] Not that American evangelicals considered the red man unjustly dispossessed of his land. In a later discourse Griffin admitted that white colonists had a right to bring civilization and religion to "this uncultivated wilderness." But it was the duty of Americans to exercise a true spirit of benevolence. "In mercy to the poor hunter, whose deer have fled or fallen, we ought to take him into our fields and teach him to cultivate the ground."[8] This was the sentiment which inspired the work of the numerous state and local missionary societies which commenced active Indian missions in the early years of the century. In 1817 two of these joined in New York in the organization of the United Foreign Missionary Society, which in spite of its name operated only within the borders of the United States.[9] As early as 1803 the Presbyterian General Assembly began supporting an Indian agent, Gideon Blackburn, whose work among the Cherokees of Tennessee first brought this remarkable nation to the attention of New England and the American Board.[10]

---

[7]Griffin, The Kingdom of Christ (Philadelphia, 1805), 27.

[8]Griffin, Foreign Missions. A Sermon . . . at the Anniversary of the United Foreign Missionary Society (New York, 1819), 20.

[9]In so organizing, the directors of the society, which represented the Presbyterian, Reformed Dutch, and Associate Reformed Churches of New York, noted the existence of the A.B.C.F.M. in Boston, but reasoned that "a small section, containing scarcely more than a fortieth part of the territory belonging to the United States, could not be expected, however populous and respectable, to manage the missionary concerns of the whole." United Foreign Missionary Society, An Address of the Board of Managers, to the Three Denominations United in This Institution (/New York, 1817/), 6.

[10]Tracy, History of the American Board, 68.

The managers of the latter institution, while turning their attention to distant enterprises, did not neglect the heathen race at home. The first endeavor in that direction, however, was fruitless. In 1811 the prudential committee took under its direction the education of Eleazer Williams, descendent of an Indian chief and Eunice Williams, one of the Deerfield captives of 1704. This young adventurer, who later achieved a measure of fame by claiming to be the lost dauphin of France, was appointed to labor among his fellow Iroquois tribesmen in northern New York and Vermont and across the border in Canada, but the outbreak of hostilities in 1812 and his personal idiosyncrasies prevented fulfilment of this plan.[11] Although the Board's records disclose a request for teachers from the Delaware Indians in 1814, as well as plans to explore possible mission fields near St. Louis, neither of these proposals were apparently acted upon.[12] To answer some questions raised by the wording of the Massachusetts charter, the commissioners voted that in their opinion the pagan aborigines came within the description of the inhabitants of "heathen lands."[13]

The first forward step was taken in 1816, when Cyrus Kingsbury, an agent of the Connecticut Missionary Society, undertook to investigate

[11]American Board, First Ten Annual Reports, 26, 32, 37, 56. An extract from a letter addressed to Williams by the corresponding secretary in 1814 reveals the source of some of the difficulties as well as the paternalistic attitude of the directors toward the first non-Caucasion agent employed by them: "If by being too much in haste, by giving yourself up too much to the direction of youthful ardour, by an overwhelming confidence on your own judgment, or by yielding to influences or excitements arising from the state of war, you should be induced to despise or disregard good counsel, and should enter into any engagements, or go into any courses, or do anything by which you should lose confidence in your white fathers and friends, and finally separate you from them, it would no doubt hereafter be a great grief to you. But your grief may come too late. Worcester to Eleazer Williams, Salem, April 26, 1814, ABC:1.01, I, 18-19.

[12]American Board, First Ten Annual Reports, 80, 117.

[13]Anderson, Memorial Volume, 79-80 and note.

conditions in the Cherokee Nation for the Board. Visiting Washington on his journey to Tennessee, Kingsbury succeeded in obtaining from the secretary of war a promise of financial assistance in the education of Indian youth.[14] The next year the American Board began a mission at Chickamauga, just within the northern limits of the Cherokee Nation, and erected the first buildings with government aid. Kingsbury, who operated the station with the help of two lay teachers trained in Lancastrian methods, reported to Boston that Indian evangelism was likely to prove even more arduous than foreign:

> The Indians are extremely jealous of white people's settling
> in their country. They have been often imposed on, and it
> is difficult to communicate to them the idea of disinterested
> benevolence. . . . The establishment of missions in the West
> is attended with difficulties of a very different nature from
> those in the East. These ignorant people must see the good
> fruit of them before they will permit them to any consider-
> able extent.[15]

After a single year, the pioneer missionary left the newly created station in the hands of others and plunged into the wilderness four hundred miles to the southwest, where he established a similar mission among the Choctaws in Mississippi.[16]

The adventures of these courageous evangelists and their entourages, which included wives and children as well as unmarried young women teachers who frequently accompanied them, form a brilliant, but practically unknown, chapter in the history of the American frontier. Few of the overseas explorers of the Board traveled greater distances or endured more formidable hardships. On horseback, by wagon and keelboat,

---

[14]W. H. Crawford to Cyrus Kingsbury, War Department, May 14, 1816, ABC:10, II, no. 142.

[15]Kingsbury, and others, to Worcester, Chickamauga, November 25, 1817, ABC:18.3.1, II, no. 99.

[16]American Board, Ninth Annual Meeting (Boston, 1818), 23-24.

they made their way into nearly trackless regions to plant schools and churches in Indian territory. They sat down at great councils of the Choctaws and Cherokees with the representatives of the United States government when treaties were drawn up.[17] At one of these meetings, a segment of the Cherokee Nation was prevailed upon to move to the Arkansas River, west of the Mississippi, and the Board agreed to furnish mission schools in that distant region. In 1820 two New Englanders, Cephas Washburn and Alfred Finney, reached the Arkansas after almost incredible sufferings and returned to bring on their families the next spring, when they commenced a mission at Dwight, in the sprawling Indian Territory far beyond the line of white settlement.[18] That same year, prompted by bad advice, a large company of reinforcements, male and female, made an extraordinary journey down the Ohio and the Mississippi from Pittsburgh to the Choctaw Nation on a raft of the large variety common to emigrant travel of the time, known as an "ark," and toilsomely ascended the Yazoo River by batteau.[19]

The missions in the Old Southwest enjoyed early success. From the station at Chickamauga in Tennessee, which was christened Brainerd in honor of the famous apostle of the last century, the Board's evangelists expanded southward into that part of the Cherokee Nation within the limits of the State of Georgia. Both the Choctaw work at such stations as Eliot and Mayhew in Mississippi and the better-known Cherokee missions to the east attracted the attention of the world through the publications of men like the British traveler, Adam Hodgson, who spent

[17]Major General Andrew Jackson, who was destined later, as president of the United States, to play an important role in missionary questions, represented the government in the Cherokee council of 1816 at which Kingsbury was present and completed arrangements for the Board's first mission. Tracy, History of the American Board, 64.

[18]American Board, Twelfth Annual Report, 71-76.

[19]Tracy, History of the American Board, 109-110.

several weeks in the 1820's visiting the Board's posts in the Southwest-ern wilderness.[20] The appealing nature of the more adaptable Cherokees and the easier accessibility of Brainerd, not far off the main routes of travel in Tennessee, made these missions among the best known of all the Board's enterprises. Following the example of the Moravians who had long operated a station at Spring Place in the Cherokee Nation, the mission-aries organized a complete community at each outpost, with farms, schools, and chapels. Not only ordained preachers, but physicians, farmers, and blacksmiths and other artisans composed the "missionary families" sur-rounded by Choctaw and Cherokee wards which the prudential committee con-ceived as pilot plants of the Christian society into which all the Indians of the continent would some day be initiated. Jedidiah Morse, who made an exhaustive survey of the aborigines in 1820-1821, recommended to the secretary of war that the government extend to the whole aboriginal population a system of similar settlements, which he preferred to call "education families," as less likely, he wrote, to "offend the opposers of Missions."[21]

English-language schools were the first order of the day at each station. Borrowing the methods of the Bombay and Ceylon missions, the evangelists gave their young charges Christian names supplied by benevolent patrons in the East. Congress appropriated $10,000 for Indian education and civilization, a substantial allocation of which the Amer-ican Board received annually for its work in the Southwest.[22] The Monroe

[20]Adam Hodgson, Letters from North America, Written during a Tour in the United States and Canada (London, 1824), I, 226-239, 276-280.

[21]Morse, Report on Indian Affairs, 78.

[22]The A.B.C.F.M. unquestioningly accepted this partnership with govern-ment and even petitioned Congress for additional aid in 1824. American State Papers. Class II. Indian Affairs (Washington, 1834), II, 446-448.

administration through Secretary of War John C. Calhoun co-operated
closely with the missionaries, and Secretary Worcester invited the president himself to visit Brainerd.[23] In May, 1819, the chief executive
of the nation appeared suddenly at the door of the mission and after a
thorough inspection of the premises personally authorized further United
States funds for expansion.[24] Missionaries sent regular reports to
Washington, and the Board enjoyed friendly relations with the capital
through the administrations of both Monroe and John Quincy Adams. However, land hunger of frontier settlers in the region and the ambiguous
policy of the federal government toward its Indian wards caused great
restlessness in the Choctaw and Cherokee Nations; over the apparent calm
of daily affairs in the missions could be sensed innumerable warnings of
the storm to break shortly upon the Board's enterprises.

II

The Indian evangelism of the A.B.C.F.M. bore an important
relation to the overall program of foreign missions. A single board of
managers directing undertakings in both hemispheres did not distinguish
closely between the American and overseas stations. The subjects of
both were pagans, or at least nonevangelical Christians, requiring the
same Gospel and the same salvation. In the Indian missions the Board
had the best possible opportunity to test the implications of the superiority of Western Christian civilization. For there, if anywhere,
could be seen the onward rolling tide of white Protestant conquest. A
considerable proportion of the Cherokee Nation was of mixed blood and
had already adopted many of the customs and practices of civilized

[23]Worcester to James Monroe, Salem, April 23, 1819, ABC:1.01, III, 136.
[24]Tracy, History of the American Board, 83.

society, including the institution of Negro slavery. It was from among this partly assimilated group that the missionaries received their first converts and firmest friends. The question of the precedence of civilization or Christianization which plagued all the missions of the Board came to its crisis first in the Indian work.

The initial strategy of the evangelical friends of the red men pointed toward their absorption into American life as the best hope of survival against the encroachment of frontier society. Before the first station was established, Samuel Worcester, the first great missionary statesman of the Board, rejected any plan of evangelism which would perpetuate the dying Indian tongues.[25] In 1816 the prudential committee declared its intention of making the children of the forest "English in their language, civilized in their habits, and Christian in their religion." "Assimilated in language," the report continued, "they will more readily become assimilated in habits and manners to their white neighbors; intercourse will be easy and the advantages to them incalculable."[26] In 1822 Board member Jedidiah Morse went so far as to urge intermarriage as a desirable outcome of the missionary and governmental program of Indian education. In that way, he argued, "the end which the Government has in view will be completely attained. They would then be literally of one blood with us, merged in the nation, and saved from extinction."[27] Although his fellow New Englanders were hardly prepared to follow this startling advice, at least one male member of the Cherokee mission married the daughter of a chief.[28]

---

[25]Worcester to Jeremiah Evarts, Salem, July 1, 1815, ABC:1.01, I, 23.

[26]American Board, Seventh Annual Report, 11-12.

[27]Morse, Report on Indian Affairs, 75.

[28]Milo Hoyt, Princeton-educated son of an ordained missionary at Brainerd, married Lydia Lowry and with his "pious and intelligent" wife opened a

Following out Worcester's policy, the missionaries sent some of their brightest graduates of the boarding schools to New England, where the American Board conducted a unique institution for heathen youth from all over the world. This was the Foreign Mission School in Cornwall, Connecticut, where Cherokee and other Indian students pursued English-language courses in collegiate subjects with other young men from Asia and the Pacific islands. Two Cherokee converts, David Brown and the namesake of the great New Jersey philanthropist, Elias Boudinot, made excellent records at Cornwall and even spent some time in study at Andover Theological Seminary—the evangelical community's living proofs of the potentialities of Indian Christianity and the correctness of the civilizing policy.

The Connecticut academy, however, put American racial attitudes to a severe testing. In 1823 one of the Cherokee students married Sara Northrup, daughter of the institution's steward. When a second such match was announced the next year—between the handsome Boudinot and Harriet Gold—a tempest struck the little New England town.[29] The agents of the Board in charge of the school, headed by Lyman Beecher of nearby Litchfield, denounced "this outrage upon public feeling,"[30] and the young

---

mission school near Fort Armstrong. Tracy, _History of the American Board_, 91. A bachelor evangelist at the same station, moreover, kept a private diary in which he recorded his temptations concerning the beautiful Catherine Brown, one of the first Cherokee converts, who died shortly afterwards. "My love to her is all spiritual," he protested in the journal. "When my mind is carnal, her loveliness disappears. It is only as a lamb—a tender lamb that I would lay her in thy sacred bosom, and pour out floods of tears in her behalf." Private Journal of D. S. Butrick, ABC:18.3.3, IV (1820).

[29]The episode is treated briefly in Marion L. Starkey, _The Cherokee Nation_ (New York, 1946), and related in some detail in R. H. Gabriel, _Elias Boudinot, Cherokee & His America_ (Norman, Okla., 1941), 60-92.

[30]Lyman Beecher, and others to the public, Litchfield County, June 1, 1825, printed in the quarterly report of the Foreign Mission School, June, 1825, ABC:18.8, I.

men of the village burned the two offenders in effigy. Although the marriage was duly celebrated in 1826, and the newlyweds departed for a mission station in the Cherokee Nation with the Board's blessing, the anguish in the Puritan community over the issue of miscegenation helped destroy the educational experiment.[31]

The missionary policy of Indian assimilation had reached a crisis. In an attempt to undo the damage the news of the tumult caused in the Cherokee missions, Jeremiah Evarts, who had replaced the deceased Worcester as corresponding secretary of the Board, wrote a long letter of explanation and apology to John Ross, one of the principal chiefs; but at Brainerd and other stations the missionaries heard murmurings against New England hypocrisy.[32] Although the prudential committee missed its chance to take a strong public stand against racial prejudice, the stalwart Evarts severely reprimanded the Cornwall agents for their un-Christian opposition to the Boudinot-Gold nuptials. In a magnificent letter which explored the whole question of race relations in its bearing upon the missionary enterprise, he demanded:

> How does it appear to be the will of God, that individuals of different tribes and nations should not intermarry? Is there anything in the Bible, that asserts or implies, that man and wife should be precisely of the same complexion, or members of the same clan, or descended of parents in the same circumstances, or whose ancestors had lived precisely in the same state of civil and moral improvement? . . . Does it not tend strongly to irritate the young men, who have been educated at Cornwall, not only in the Cherokee nation, but wherever else they live, will it not strike their minds as equivalent to a declaration that their people are doomed to perpetual inferiority; and that every attempt to rise to an equality with the whites is impudent and criminal?

[31]Some writers, notably Gabriel and Starkey, overlooking the Board's official attitude, which condemned the agents, tend to lay the blame for the school's closing directly upon this incident.

[32]Jeremiah Evarts to John Ross, Boston, September 17, 1825, ABC:1.01, V, 391-392. For the reaction among the Cherokees, see Starkey, Cherokee Nation, 73-74.

The angry secretary concluded his letter, speaking officially for the prudential committee, with the request that "no measures will be taken to prevent fulfillment of a contract lawfully made; and that Boudinot, should he visit Cornwall, will be treated as becomes a Christian and civilized community to receive a youth educated among themselves and professing a faith in the Gospel of our common salvation."[33]

Although the ambiguity in the evangelical attitude toward heathen races as evidenced in the furor over miscegenation certainly prejudiced the Board's program of assimilation, the Cherokees made rapid progress under missionary guidance and the leadership of the predominant mixed-blood element. In 1827 they fulfilled some of the hopes of their white patrons by becoming a "Christian nation" with a written constitution so theocratic in nature that it provided that no one who denied the existence of God or a future state of rewards and punishment could hold office.[34]

The invention of a Cherokee syllabary by the gifted George Guess--otherwise known as Sequoya--hastened the process of civilization and influenced the shift of the prudential committee's policy away from a strictly English-language approach. Some of the early missionaries, it is true, had attempted to learn the Indian languages in order to eliminate the necessity of interpreters, but they found it difficult to render the peculiar structure and sounds in a written form. The A.B.C.F.M. was interested in the system of John Pickering of Salem, who had

[33]Evarts to Timothy Stone, Boston, August 26, 1825, ABC:1.01, V. 359-360. In a similar letter to a member of the Board, Evarts added the remark that: "As to any unpopularity which might attach to the school, through prejudice, ignorance, or misapprehension, I should think it much less to be dreaded, than that the agents or teachers of the school should act upon principles which the Christian world will not justify." Evarts to Calvin Chapin, Boston, July 5, 1825, in E. C. Tracy, Memoir of the Life of Jeremiah Evarts, Esq. (Boston, 1845), 223.

[34]Missionary Herald, XXIV (1828), 193-194.

designed a standard orthography to put into writing the aboriginal tongues as an aid to the work of missions.[35] The talented Cherokee convert, David Brown, who as a student at Andover had lent his services to Pickering in preparing the famous essay on the spelling of the Indian language, collaborated with the Salem philologist in producing a Cherokee grammar.[36] After some hesitation and debate, the Board recognized the superior merit of the new syllabary over Pickering's system, and co-operated with the chiefs of the Cherokee Nation in procuring a press and specially designed type for a vernacular printing establishment in the Indian capital at New Echota.[37]

David Greene, domestic secretary of the A.B.C.F.M., brought the press from Boston in 1829, and Elias Boudinot began publishing the famous Cherokee Phoenix, half in English and half in Guess's odd-looking syllabary. Although the newspaper was strictly an Indian affair, Samuel A. Worcester, an exceptionally able missionary and nephew of the Board's first secretary, worked closely with the mission-educated Cherokee editor, who helped him prepare translations of the Scriptures and religious tracts.[38] While English-language instruction continued to some extent in the missions, the prudential committee was now ready to use the native

---

[35]John Pickering, An Essay on a Uniform Orthography for the Indian Languages of North America (Cambridge, 1820), 10.

[36]Ibid., 15. The grammer was partially completed in 1825 or 1826, when the growing enthusiasm for Sequoya's syllabary halted its publication. M. O. Pickering, Life of John Pickering (Boston, 1887), 336-337. The unfinished text, printed but unpublished, lies now in the library of Harvard University.

[37]American Board, Sixteenth Annual Report (Boston, 1825), 51-52; Missionary Herald, XXII (1826), 47-49; XXIII (1827), 212-213. Although Sequoya bore no relation to the Board's missions, Jeremiah Evarts interviewed him in Washington in 1828 to learn his reasons for inventing the unusual syllabary. Missionary Herald, XXIV (1828), 133-134.

[38]A good biography of Worcester is Althea Bass, Cherokee Messenger (Norman, Okla., 1936).

tongues of the Indians wherever possible. Since the Cherokee syllabary proved useless for the Choctaw language, the Board's missionaries--one of whom, Cyrus Byington, was preaching successfully in Choctaw by 1824[39]-- used Pickering's orthography for the translation of religious materials for their stations. The great experiment was over. In subsequent Indian missions the American Board's evangelists labored to present their message chiefly in the native tongues. At the same time, in 1826, the Foreign Mission School in Cornwall closed its doors, in recognition of the virtual defeat of the plan to civilize the Indians through the English language and the greater expediency of educating heathen youth in the vernacular on missionary ground.[40]

During these same years Indian affairs in the Old Southwest moved toward a greater crisis. The Monroe policy of recognizing treaty rights, which guaranteed the holdings of the Five Civilized Tribes below the Ohio River in perpetuum, gradually weakened under the weight of constant frontier remonstrances. In 1818, when the Cherokees were negotiating a new treaty with Calhoun giving up a part of their ancestral domains in exchange for new lands on the other side of the Mississippi, the Board's secretary hurried to Washington and helped insure the inclusion of a clause granting the Indians perpetual rights to their remaining tracts in the South.[41] In the twenties increasing pressures were brought to bear upon the Cherokees and Choctaws, along with others of the Southern tribes, to induce them to move westward. The American Board's missionaries, though cautioned against political interference of any kind, could not refrain from expressing sympathy with the Indians and were soon

[39]American Board, Sixteenth Annual Report (Boston, 1825), 62.
[40]American Board, Seventeenth Annual Report (Boston, 1826), 103-109.
[41]S. M. Worcester, Life and Labors of Samuel Worcester, II, 413-417.

deeply involved in the struggle of the Cherokees to remain in the Old Nation.[42] An anonymous letter addressed to the secretary of war accused Samuel A. Worcester of being the "real and ostensible Editor" of the Cherokee Phoenix, and responsible for that newspaper's virulent attacks upon the State of Georgia—a charge probably half true, for Worcester and Boudinot, the actual editor, were notoriously close associates.[43]

When the Georgia legislature in 1828 attempted to extend its jurisdiction to the Cherokee settlements, the prudential committee supported its representatives in the field by taking a firm stand against Indian removal, though the views of the president-elect, Andrew Jackson, were well known in favor of Georgian claims. Jeremiah Evarts in particular showed himself a vigorous champion of the rights of the aboriginal tribesmen. In the lobbies of Washington and in the public prints he began a powerful campaign to thwart the demands of Georgia and her defenders in the national capital. In addition to organizing public meetings of protest in Eastern cities—in which the Indian question was aired alongside the anti-Sunday mails agitation—Evarts published under the pseudonym of William Penn an effective series of articles in the National Intelligencer, which were reprinted by other papers and cited in Congressional debates.[44] The climax came in 1830 when, despite tremendous efforts of Senator Theodore Frelinghuysen and other spokesmen of evangelical interests, Congress passed President Jackson's bill for Indian removal.[45]

---

[42]In 1818 the secretary of war was assured that missionaries were instructed to "withhold themselves sacredly from every colour of interference." Worcester to Calhoun, Salem, February 6, 1818, ABC:1.01, III, 22.

[43]Letter dated Cherokee Nation, November 22, 1828, enclosed in T. L. McKenney to Evarts, Washington, December 11, 1828, ABC:13, I, no. 21.

[44]Evarts's articles were also published in pamphlet form as Essays on the Present Crisis in the Condition of the American Indians (Boston, 1829).

[45]Evarts also edited a collection of speeches made by Frelinghuysen and other Congressional opponents of Jackson's bill. Speeches on the Passage of the Bill for Removal of the Indians (Boston, 1830).

The Cherokees still refused to sell their lands, and in December the American Board's missionaries held a meeting at New Echota which a-dopted a series of resolutions against the proposed removal.[46] The next year, when Samuel A. Worcester and Dr. Elizur Butler were imprisoned for refusing to recognize Georgia's authority, the prudential committee up-held their stand and supported their appeal to the Supreme Court. In presenting the case, the religious community joined forces with the polit-ical opposition to Jackson, William Wirt appearing for the missionaries before the highest judiciary. On March 3, 1832, Chief Justice John Mar-shall in his famous decision in Worcester v. Georgia declared the Cherokee Nation to be a distinct community outside the jurisdiction of the State of Georgia and ordered the prisoners dismissed from the indictments. As is well known, Jackson refused to enforce the judgment.

The case of the jailed evangelists dramatized the cause of missions in the country. In the fall of 1831, before bringing the issue to the Supreme Court, the prudential committee had petitioned President Jackson to use his office to free Worcester and Butler from prison. A few days later Secretary of War Lewis Cass forwarded to Boston his chief's answer rejecting the memorial on the grounds that state legislatures "have the power to extend their laws over all persons living within their boundaries . . ."[47] Next year, after the Marshall decision, however, the opposition newspapers published copies of a spurious letter purporting to be Jackson's personal communication to the American Board. This document, which has deceived some writers, concluded with these angry words: "I do

---

[46]Two Moravians and one Baptist missionary also attended. Missionary Herald, XXVIII (1831), 80-84.

[47]Lewis Cass to William Reed, War Department, November 14, 1831, ABC:13, I, no. 4. The memorial and Cass's reply are printed in American Board, Twenty-third Annual Report, appendix, 169-174.

not wish to comment upon the causes of the imprisonment of the missionaries alluded to in the memorial; but I cannot refrain from observing
that here, as in most other countries, they are, by their injudicious
zeal (to give it no harsher name) too apt to make themselves obnoxious
to those among whom they are located."[48] Whatever the chief executive's
real sentiments about the missionary enterprise, in an election year he
could hardly have afforded to speak in such a manner.[49] According to
Martin Van Buren, the Jackson ticket lost from eight to ten thousand
votes in the 1832 election in New York State alone as a result of the
false letter.[50]

Meanwhile South Carolina had raised the issue of nullification
and there was fear that Georgia--along with Mississippi and Alabama,
which were placed in similar positions---if pressed by the federal government would league with its sister sovereignty in resisting the United
States. The governor therefore offered to pardon the missionaries if
they dropped legal proceedings. Since they saw no hope for the Cherokees
however their own case might go and wished also to save the country from
a civil war with the nullifiers, Worcester and Butler decided to withdraw
from a lost cause.[51] They returned to their stations among the Indians,

[48]Cited as genuine by Seymour Dunbar, A History of Travel in the United
States (Indianapolis, 1915), II, 597. This error was repeated in Charles
Warren, The Supreme Court in United States History (Boston, 1922), and,
more recently, Starkey, Cherokee Nation.

[49]The spurious character of the letter was first shown by Bernard Steiner
in "Jackson and the Missionaries," American Historical Review, XXIX
(1924), 722-723. Even with the aid of the secretary of the American
Board, however, Steiner was able to find neither the original letter nor
the printed copy in the annual reports and had to be content with a hand
copy of Cass's communication in the Board's archives.

[50]Martin Van Buren, Autobiography (J. C. Fitzpatrick, ed., American
Historical Association, Annual Report, Washington, 1918), II, 293.

[51]Missionary Herald, XXIX (1833), 183-186; Tracy, History of the American
Board, 280-282.

where their colleagues had continued to labor from bases in Tennessee and Alabama, outside the authority of the Georgia Guard. Jeremiah Evarts, who had fought long and heartily for the cause, was now dead, and the American Board was ready to bow to the inevitable.

As early as the summer of 1830 the Jackson administration cut off the Board's annual appropriation of $2560 for education in the Southwest, on the grounds that present policy required the use of government funds only in the territories west of the Mississippi.[52] In that same year the Choctaw chiefs signed a treaty giving up their lands and moved westward, the missionaries following shortly afterwards.[53] The Cherokees alone refused to surrender. But a majority of the Board's agents among them, led by Worcester, whose influence was decisive at Boston, came to favor removal as the only hope for the survival of Indian civilization under the circumstances. It was the mission-trained Elias Boudinot, editor of the Cherokee Phoenix and a leader with John Ridge of a minority faction among the Nation, who was one of the chief signers of the controversial New Echota Treaty of 1835, which dispossessed the Cherokees in the South and provided for new homes on the Western frontier. Worcester had already joined the Arkansas River mission, but in 1838 the other missionaries faithfully accompanied the Indians on their "Trail of Tears" to the West.[54]

An era was ending. All over the country the pressure of white settlement was pushing the Indian tribes out toward the frontier, where

---

[52]McKenney to Evarts, War Department, June 7, 1830, ABC:13, I, no.29.

[53]Missionaries of other societies did not always maintain the same position againt Indian removal as did those of the Board. It was the Methodists who helped persuade the Choctaws to sign the treaty. Tracy, History of the American Board, 239.

[54]The standard account of the removal of the Southern Indians to the West is Grant Foreman, Indian Removal: The Emigration of the Five Civilized Tribes of Indians (Norman, Okla., 1932).

the federal government set aside the lands embraced by the so-called Indian Territory. The American Board had no alternative but to admit defeat in the Southwest and rebuild its shattered missions in the West.

In 1826 the Board had received seven Indian missions from the United Foreign Missionary Society, which dissolved its separate existence in uniting with the New England organization. These stations were scattered from New York State to the region west of Missouri.[55] In the thirties the prudential committee also extended its operations to the Ojibways at the foot of Lake Superior and the nearby Pawnees and Sioux. Of these, the Sioux mission was the most successful, having been founded by two brothers from Connecticut, Samuel and Gideon Pond, who went out independently to the Indian country in what is now Minnesota and settled near Fort Snelling. In 1835 the Board dispatched its own missionaries to the area and eventually joined with the Pond brothers.[56] By that date, the A.B.C.F.M.'s missions, with the exception of the work in a few enclaves of tribesmen on Eastern reservations, were out beyond the limit of white settlements.

The whole concept of Indian evangelism, moreover, had changed. In instructions to its agents among the Ojibways in 1832, the prudential committee explained that past experience taught the lesson that the high expense of Indian missions in comparison to foreign did not bring commensurate returns; in the future there would be no boarding schools, no large secular establishments, and no English-language instruction.[57] In general, the directors of the enterprise had become discouraged. The

---

[55]Tracy, History of the American Board, 193-198.

[56]American Board, Twenty-eighth Annual Report (Boston 1837), 115-116.

[57]American Board, Twenty-third Annual Report, appendix, 163-165.

governmental policy of removing the aboriginal remnants ever westward broke up stations from year to year, and the ensuing confusion ruined the morale of missionary and Indian alike. At the annual meeting in 1838, the prudential committee wearily concluded a report to the membership on this pessimistic note:

> Were it certain that these missions would, for ten years to come, remain in as unfavorable a state as they have been in for the ten years just past, it could hardly be wise to detain men in the field only to have their efforts paralysed, and for all the labor, property, and life expended, to reap little else than disappointment.[58]

III

In 1813 the Board directed the prudential committee to make inquiries respecting a mission in Brazil.[59] Although this resolution came to nothing at that time, it revealed the intentions of the commissioners to draw within the scope of their operations the whole western, as well as eastern, hemisphere. Outside New England there was an even greater interest in South America. The managers of the United Foreign Missionary Society declared in their 1817 prospectus that "as soon as the Southern forests yield to the hand of cultivation, our limits will extend to Mexico; and the whole region of death from the river Del Norte to Cape Horn, including more than one quarter of the circumference of the globe, will reach from our door."[60] In the second decade of the century, moreover, the series of revolutions in that continent encouraged Protestants in the United States to look southward. In an address before the U.F. M.S. in 1819, Edward Griffin pointed to the new South American republics

---

[58]American Board, Twenty-ninth Annual Report (Boston, 1838), 138.

[59]American Board, First Ten Annual Reports, 56. The restless Samuel Mills offered to undertake a missionary tour to South America about the same time. Richards, Samuel J. Mills, 181-182.

[60]United Foreign Missionary Society, An Address of the Board of Managers, 6.

as a rich field for evangelical endeavors:

> To the Christian and philanthropist, that is at present one
> of the most interesting spots under the sun; where mighty
> nations are struggling into existence, where man is rising
> in his might to burst the chains of the most unrighteous
> and degrading oppression, and stretching after the majesty
> and happiness of freedom. In the name of humanity and
> religion, let them succeed. They will succeed, and in
> their course the fetters will drop from their mind. . . .
> And when toleration and free inquiry are introduced, you
> may pour in your instructions until the capacity is full.
> . . . Let us stand ready to enter as soon as a door is
> opened.[61]

The American Board, though occupying dozens of stations in the
United States and abroad, was the first to respond by sending two men to
the Argentine capital in 1823.[62] One of them, Theophilus Parvin, remained in Buenos Aires for two years, opening a school and ministering
chiefly to Englishmen and other resident foreigners. Finding the work
of education among this class of people more rewarding than attempting
to reach the native population, which was largely Catholic, he finally
decided to make a private venture there as a teacher in the foreign community.[63] His colleague, John C. Brigham, undertook an extensive exploring tour for the Board, crossing the continent to visit Chili and Peru,
but returned to New York in 1826 to enter the service of the American
Bible Society.[64] Brigham's report was not optimistic enough to warrant

[61]Griffin, Foreign Missions, 18-19.

[62]American Board, Fourteenth Annual Report (Boston, 1823), 129-130.
Five years earlier, the young Rufus Anderson visited Brazil on a private journey and recommended against a mission there. From information
available to him there he suggested Buenos Aires, Argentina, as a more
likely location. Anderson to Worcester, Rio de Janeiro, February 1,
1819, ABC:10, I, no. 111.

[63]On his second venture he was apparently supported to some extent by
the Philadelphia Presbytery, but later took a position as professor of
English and Greek at the university. Ashbel Green, A Historical Sketch
of Compendious View of Domestic and Foreign Missions in the Presbyterian
Church of the United States of America (Philadelphia, 1838), 89-93.

[64]American Board, Seventeenth Annual Report, 100-102.

the prudential committee's entering the field, yet he berated the North American churches' lack of concern for the inhabitants of the southern continent: "We hear petitions for Asia, Africa, and the islands of the sea; for Jews, Greeks, 'the dwellers in Mesopotamia, and Judea;' but who prays for the millions of Spanish Americans in their critical situation?"[65]

The Board's only other attempt to evangelize South America in this period was made at the southern tip of the continent, among the pagan Patagonians rather than Catholic Christians. In 1832 Captain Benjamin Morrell published an account of a voyage along the western coast of that region in which he described the inhabitants as numerous and peaceful and suggested that a mission among them might be successful.[66] As a result, Secretary Anderson corresponded with the author, and in 1833 accepted the offer of a New York merchant, Silas E. Burroughs, to provide free passage for missionaries in a schooner being fitted out for a sealing trip near the Patagonian coast. Titus Coan and William Arms accepted the Board's commission and landed at Gregory's Bay in the fall. Unable to reach the west coast, they visited the interior and found the country poor and sparsely populated. Friendly New England shipmasters brought them home the next spring, where their report discouraged the Board from further efforts in that direction.[67]

No other society was any more successful in carrying the Gospel to South America before the Civil War. Although the objective appealed

---

[65]Missionary Herald, XXII (1826), 343-344.

[66]Benjamin Morrell, A Narrative of Four Voyages, to the South Seas, North and South Pacific Ocean, Chinese Sea, Ethiopic and Southern Atlantic Ocean, Indian and Antarctic Ocean, from the Year 1822 to 1831 (New York, 1832), 159.

[67]Tracy, History of the American Board, 280. Years later, Titus Coan retold the story of the abortive expedition in his Adventures in Patagonia: A Missionary's Exploring Trip (New York, 1880).

strongly to American Protestants in a time of developing anti-Catholic sentiments, the obstacles imposed by the new regimes' religious intolerance seemed too great. The Presbyterian leader, Ashbel Green, summarized the prospect in 1838:

> It was, for a time, confidently expected by the friends of Orthodox piety in the United States, as well as in Europe, that the Revolution in South America would open a door for the propagation of the Protestant religion; and sanguine hopes were entertained of the happy effects that were speedily to result, from the free circulation of the Bible, and the unobstructed labours of missionaries, in that extensive region; in which the Romish superstition had so long and so oppressively prevailed. Time and experience, if they have not entirely blasted these hopes and expectations, have proved that the period at which they are to be realized is yet future.[68]

The object of "foreign" missions was also conceived as encompassing the American Far West in a period when the nation's western borders reached only to the Rocky Mountains. The Pacific shores of the North American continent early attracted the interest of missionary promoters in New England, especially that part above the forty-second parallel and outside Spanish jurisdiction by the treaty of 1818. The profitable Northwest coast trade, pursued since the time of Captain Robert Gray, discoverer of the Columbia River, had made that region particularly well known both in Boston and Honolulu, where the Board's Sandwich Islands missionaries had many opportunities to converse with skippers engaged in the Canton-Oregon traffic.[69] As early as 1822, a student at Andover Theological Seminary read a long paper on the Northwest before the Society of Inquiry and called for the establishment of an evangelical mission there. This essay, based in large part on letters from an unnamed traveler, received a larger audience when it was published in

[68]Green, A Historical Sketch of Domestic and Foreign Missions in the Presbyterian Church, 89.

[69]Missionary Herald, XVII (1821), 280; XVIII (1822), 204.

two installments in the Boston Recorder, a weekly religious newspaper which devoted much space to the foreign missionary enterprise.[70] In the same year the Board learned of a request for teachers from an Indian chief living near the Columbia. "That it is the duty of the American public," reported the prudential committee, "to make the experiment /of sending a mission to Oregon7 there can be no doubt; and nothing is wanting in order to make it within a short time, but pecuniary resources."[71]

Not until 1827, the year of the treaty with Great Britain extending indefinitely the joint occupation of the Oregon territory, did the Board discuss the question seriously. In an address to the public in that year, the prudential committee outlined an ambitious and far-sighted program for a missionary and colonizing venture:

> The tide of emigration is rolling westward so rapidly, that it must speedily surmount every barrier, till it reaches all the habitable parts of this continent. How desirable then that the natives of the wilderness should hear the Gospel, before they are prejudiced against it by the fraud, injustice, and dissolute lives of men, who give up the blessings of Christianity that they may not be troubled with its restraints. How noble an object is here; and how worthy of American enterprise;—to convey the inestimable treasure of divine truth to pagan tribes, scattered over a vast extent of territory, and to prepare the way for future settlers from the Atlantic coast and the valley of the Mississippi. In this manner, early provision will be made for the religious wants of the adventurous voyager and the fearless man of the woods, who shall meet in these remote regions; and thus will a foundation be laid for churches, schools and colleges, and all that bright array of moral influences, which accompany Christian institutions, and form a well organized civil community. In a word, thus may be sent forth another Plymouth Colony, enlightened and happy men, through successive ages to the end of the world . . .
>
> Though such a colony, as has been briefly described, would be founded in religious principles and undertaken from

---

[70]This evangelical newspaper is mistakenly described as part of the "secular American press," by editors A. B. and D. P. Hulbert, who reprinted these articles, along with many other early missionary documents, in The Oregon Crusade: Across Land and Sea to Oregon (Overland to the Pacific, V, n.p., 1935), 7-20.

[71]American Board, Thirteenth Annual Report (Boston, 1822), 71.

religious motives, yet it would be a secular establishment,
governed by its own constitution, and not under the direction,
or at the expense, of any Missionary Society. The mission to
the natives, closely united with the colony in affection and
motive, would derive essential aid from it; and thus both enterprises would strengthen and encourage each other.[72]

This remarkable proposal was made two years before the propagandist,
Hall J. Kelley, had organized his "American Society for Encouraging the
Settlement of the Oregon Territory," although John Floyd of Virginia and
others in Congress had already debated the possibility of a United States
expedition and colony on the Columbia.[73]

The Board's first approach to this region, however, was not
overland, but around Cape Horn and by way of its mission already established and prospering in Hawaii. Thus in 1827 the prudential committee
deputed Jonathan S. Green, one of the members of that year's reinforcement to the Islands, to make an exploring tour of the Northwest Coast at
the earliest opportunity.[74] In the meantime the directors in Boston
made every attempt to learn more about the Oregon country—Secretary
Evarts even receiving private information from Congressman Floyd while
on a visit to Washington in the spring of 1828—and expressed their hopes
that the United States government would take measures to remove the prevailing uncertainty about the region.[75] Unable to secure passage from
Honolulu until 1829, Green made a nine-months' voyage in which he visited
both the Mexican territories to the south, stopping at San Francisco and
Monterey, and the Russian settlements in the north, where he was warmly
received by the authorities at New Archangel.[76] Unfavorable winds

[72]Missionary Herald, XXIII, (1827), 397.

[73]Hulberts, eds., Oregon Crusade, 22-23, 26-27.

[74]American Board, Nineteenth Annual Report (Boston, 1828), 111-112.

[75]Missionary Herald, XXIV (1828), 25-254.

[76]Excerpts from Green's journal were printed in the Missionary Herald,
XXVI (1830), 343-345, 369-373; XXVII (1831), 33-39, 75-79, 105-107.

prevented him from reaching the Columbia River region and his report to the prudential committee was a discouraging one. "There is no classick ground here," he wrote. "The land does not flow with milk and honey, nor are there wanting the sons of Anak."[77]

In the thirties new interest in the Rocky Mountains and the lands beyond produced the expeditions of Captain Benjamin L. E. Bonneville, William Sublette, and Nathaniel J. Wyeth, and awakened the zeal of missionary societies for the welfare of the mountain and plains Indians. In 1834, the same year that the Methodist Jason Lee and a small company crossed the Rockies with Wyeth on his second venture, the American Board commissioned the Rev. Samuel Parker and two assistants from Ithaca, New York, to survey conditions "among the Indians near or beyond the Rocky Mountains."[78] Since financial deficits still inhibited the Board's operations in that direction, the Presbyterian and Reformed Dutch churches of Ithaca advanced the funds for the tour. After poor calculations brought the party to St. Louis a month too late to catch the caravan in which the Methodist expedition set forth, Parker returned to the East leaving his companions behind to begin work among the Pawnees on the Platte River.[79]

The next year another New Yorker, Dr. Marcus Whitman, joined Parker in a second attempt to reach the Oregon country. They made their way as far as the traders' rendevous at Green River where Whitman extracted an arrowhead from the back of the famous hunter and guide, Jim Bridger, and a band of visiting Northwest Indians invited the missionaries to settle among them.[80] Whitman retraced his steps eastward to secure

---

[77]J. S. Green to Evarts, Honolulu, November 13, 1829, ABC:19.1, III, no. 171. Printed in part in the Hulberts, eds., Oregon Crusade, 79-80.

[78]American Board, Twenty-fifth Annual Report, 119.

[79]Tracy, History of the American Board, 301-302.

[80]Hulberts, eds., Marcus Whitman, Crusader, I (Overland to the Pacific, VI, n.p., 1936), 22-23.

additional laborers while Parker accompanied the aborigines into Oregon to select mission sites. The latter did not remain to greet the expected reinforcements, however, but accepted the Hudson's Bay Company's offer of free passage to Hawaii, and thence sailed around the Cape to New London, Connecticut, and published in Ithaca a full account of the tour and detailed descriptions of the Columbia River country and its aboriginal inhabitants.[81] Meanwhile, Dr. Whitman and a new colleague, Henry H. Spaulding, accompanied by their wives—the first white women to cross the Rockies—and an unmarried assistant, made the long and arduous journey by wagon over the "Oregon Trail." Rather than join the Methodists in the Willamette Valley, they settled among the Kayuses and Nez Perces on the Walla Walla River. Dr. John McLoughlin and other agents of the Hudson's Bay Company welcomed them in friendly fashion and offered them the facilities of the Company's ships for the transportation of supplies via Hawaii.

From the beginning, the mission in the Pacific Northwest maintained close connections with the stations of the Board in the Hawaiian Islands. In 1838 two converted Sandwich Islanders arrived to assist the missionaries on the Columbia River, and the next year the First Church of Honolulu contributed a printing press, on which Edmund O. Hall, who accompanied the press from Hawaii, published the first book printed west of the Rockies.[82] Several years later, when the Board was not satisfied with the progress of the Indian work in Oregon, missionary reinforcements intended for that post were held over in Hawaii, and one couple was transferred there from the Northwest for reasons of health.

[81]Samuel Parker, Journal of an Exploring Tour beyond the Rocky Mountains, under the Direction of the A.B.C.F.M. (Ithaca, 1838).

[82]Missionary Herald, XXXVI (1840), 230.

Although the members of the mission learned the vernacular languages and established schools, they were not notably successful in evangelizing the wild and wandering savages. In 1842 the first large American emigration arrived over the Oregon Trail, and the missionaries began thinking more in terms of the future white population of the territory. In addition, they encountered the intense competition of Catholic priests from Canada—a circumstance particularly grievous to militant American Protestants whose mission stations in other parts of the world suffered the strains of similar rivalry. In fact, the Board's emissaries in the Northwest manifested a much greater hostility toward the Roman Catholics than to the British. Their relations with the latter were unusually amicable in spite of the fact that the Hudson's Bay Company's tolerant attitude toward the Jesuits as well as the direct support afforded priests ministering to the large number of its Canadian employees made the Americans slightly uneasy. In a letter of 1843 Whitman deprecated the work of the Jesuit, Father P. J. de Smet, and warned Boston of the need for reinforcements to hold "the only spot on the Pacifick coast left where Protestants have a present hope of a foothold. It is requisite that good pious men and Ministers go to Oregon without delay, as Citizens or our hope there is greatly clouded if not destroyed."[83]

Much has been written about Whitman's famous winter trip of 1842 to Washington and Boston, a hurried journey allegedly made to save Oregon for the United States.[84] The evidence brings to light only the

[83]Marcus Whitman to David Greene, St. Louis, May 12, 1843, ABC:18.5.3, I, no. 99. Printed in Hulberts, ed., Marcus Whitman, II (Overland to the Pacific, VII, n.p., 1938), 303-304.

[84]C. M. Drury, who made full use of the A.B.C.F.M. archives, has written what is perhaps the most balanced account of this episode in his Marcus Whitman, M.D., Pioneer and Martyr (Caldwell, Idaho, 1937), 294-320. Most of the documents also appear in the Hulberts, eds., Marcus Whitman, Crusader, II, 131-331.

fact that he left his mission at Waiilatpu on the Walla Walla River primarily to persuade the Board to change its decision to reduce the work in
Oregon. One of the factors of the Hudson's Bay Company, against the
machinations of which Whitman was supposedly working in his attempt to
secure the Columbia River for American settlement, wrote to the Board
at the same time an eloquent appeal for the extension rather than diminution of the mission.[85] Unquestionably, however, the large-scale
colonization of Oregon changed the character of the missionary task there.
Whitman, who was unsuccessful in his attempt to secure additional laborers
for the mission but led out a part of the 1843 emigration on his return
to Oregon, wrote back to Boston a few months later urgently requesting
teachers to come out as colonists.

> There can be no doubt that this upper country will soon be
> settled; and we very much need good men to locate them-
> selves, two, three, or four in a place, and secure a good
> influence for the Indians, and form a nucleus for religious
> institutions, and keep back Romanism. This country must be
> occupied by Americans or foreigners; if it is by the latter,
> they will be mostly papists.[86]

Although Whitman and his colleagues did not influence the event directly,
the permanent establishment of the American flag in the Columbia Valley
in 1846 confirmed their hopes of Protestant hegemony in that region.

A final catastrophe struck the mission's Indian work in 1847,
when a band of hostile savages massacred Dr. Whitman and his whole family,
together with a number of emigrants enjoying the hospitality of the
Waiilatpu station.[87] Although the remaining evangelists endeavored for

---

[85]Archibald McDonald to David Greene, Columbia River, March 15, 1843,
ABC:18.5.3, I, no. 14.

[86]Whitman to Greene, November 1, 1843, in Missionary Herald, XL (1844),
177.

[87]H. H. Spaulding's account of the massacre appeared in the Missionary
Herald, XLIV (1848), 237-241.

a few years to restore the usefulness of the mission, the Board grew discouraged and soon left the ground to the agents of the American Home Missionary Society. Thus Oregon Territory changed in hardly more than a decade from a field of foreign, to one of domestic evangelism. A Protestant publicist described the pleasing prospect in 1849, after California too had come into American hands, in terms of an evangelical "manifest destiny":

> Home and foreign missions have struck hands on the Pacific.
> Bible and tract operations have girdled the globe. Anglo-
> Saxon civilization will spread along the Pacific, building
> cities, founding colleges, and schools, and churches, set-
> ting up printing-presses, making railroads, and propelling
> steamships. The commerce of the far east will seek the marts
> of our far western ports, and find its outlets through the
> channels formed by American enterprise across our continent.
> May it not be, that the causes which have thronged the Atlan-
> tic states with European immigrants, will crowd the Pacific
> shores with the teeming population of the Asiatic nations?
> And as Germany, France, and Ireland have been leavened, in a
> measure, with republican and evangelical principles, and will
> be in a greater degree by the reflex influence of their emi-
> gration; so, may it not be that China, India, and even Japan,
> shall receive missionaries, in due time, from the converts
> among their native emigrants to the American coast? Thus it
> may be, and doubtless is the design of God to turn the flank
> of heathenism, and from a new and unexpected quarter, with
> all the advantages of contiguity and facilities of inter-
> course, to assail the kingdom of darkness.[88]

Although the American Board continued its work among many aboriginal tribes of the continent until the Civil War and, in some cases, several years beyond, missionary statesmen gradually came to realize the increasing hopelessness of merging the primitive tribesmen into Christian civilization, or even of salvaging Indian life before the irresistible tide of white settlement. If assimilationist methods had failed to prevent the primitive American aborigines from melting away before a superior Christian society, it suggested a lesson to the

---

[88]Home Evangelization: A View of the Wants and Prospects of Our Country, Based on the Facts and Relations of Colportage (New York, /1849/), 142-143.

directors of the overseas enterprise, who toward the middle of the century began to alter their course away from the Western-style, English-language educational policy of the sanguine early years. The decline of Indian missions, at one time employing as many as half the total number of the A.B.C.F.M.'s missionaries, committed American Protestantism even more wholeheartedly to the work abroad. The United States having reached its full continental expansion, the managers of foreign missions could pursue a strategy of driving their main forces ahead into unconquered territory overseas, leaving the reduction of small pockets of resistence behind to the domestic wing of the evangelical crusade.

CHAPTER IV

THE ISLANDS OF THE PACIFIC

While the first American foreign missionaries were entering
Asia by sailing eastward to India and Ceylon around the Cape of Good
Hope, others of their countrymen plied an enterprising commerce to the
west of Cape Horn which touched at the Pacific Islands, the mouth of
the Columbia River, and the roadsteads of the Far East. Not many years
after Captain James Cook's famous exploring voyage, Yankee skippers were
making port in Hawaii, or Owhyhee, as the intrepid English navigator
transcribed the native word for the largest of the islands which he re-
named for his patron, the Earl of Sandwich. Northwest fur traders on
their way to the Canton market stopped at Hawaii to refresh their crews
and subsequently found an abundance of the sandalwood so much prized in
China. This discovery laid the basis for a vigorous American traffic
in the Pacific connecting the Sandwich Islands with Boston, Canton and
the Columbia River country.

One result of this intercourse was the appearance in New England of a number of natives of Hawaii, brought by indulgent shipmasters.
The first, clad in the gay plumes and feathers of Polynesian costume,
arrived in Boston as early as 1790, in the company of Captain Robert Gray,
who was returning from his adventurous voyage to the Columbia.[1] By the
middle of the second decade of the nineteenth century, the presence of
these heathen lads had so quickened the imagination of the religious
community that benevolent individuals were planning to educate them as
missionaries to their benighted fellow islanders.

[1]Morison, Maritime History of Massachusetts, 43-44.

I

The story of the American Board's Hawaiian mission really be-
gins in the year 1809, when Samuel J. Mills, fresh from Williams College,
visited New Haven in order to enlist Yale undergraduates in his secret
missionary fraternity, the Brethren. Though unsuccessful in that venture,
Mills got his first glimpse of an overseas pagan in the young Sandwich
Islander, Henry Obookiah, whom a New Haven student had discovered some
time before, sitting tearfully on the steps of the college.[2] A Connecticut captain had carried the Hawaiian boy, orphaned by a tribal war in
his homeland, to the United States. Struck with the missionary opportunity the presence of the homesick heathen youth suggested, the founder
of the Brethren wrote to a classmate at Williams:

> What does this mean? Brother Hall, do you understand
> it? Shall he be sent back unsupported, to attempt to reclaim
> his countrymen? Shall we not rather consider these southern
> islands a proper place for the establishment of a mission?
> . . . We ought not to look merely to the heathen on our own
> continent, but to direct our attention where we may, to human
> appearance, do the most good, and where the difficulties are
> least.[3]

Already, then, before the growth of missionary enthusiasm at
Andover Seminary, and before the formation of the American Board of Commissioners for Foreign Missions, there were set in motion the forces
which eventually led to the establishment of one of America's most influential religious enterprises. Mills transferred Obookiah, who was living
in the house of the Yale president, Timothy Dwight, to his father's
parsonage in Torringford, Connecticut. There, in rural Litchfield County

[2]Obookiah's discoverer was a postgraduate ministerial student at Yale,
Edwin W. Dwight, who later wrote the popular and pious account of the
strange life of the Hawaiian convert in the Memoirs of Henry Obookiah,
a Native of Owyhee, and a Member of the Foreign Mission School (New
Haven, 1818).

[3]Mills to Gordon Hall, New Haven, December 20, 1809, in Spring, Memoirs
of Samuel J. Mills, 50.

in the northwestern part of the state, his Hawaiian protégé, slightly bewildered at first by the rigid Puritan society but gradually accepting his new life, soon professed conversion to New England's religion. Later, Obookiah accompanied the younger Mills to the theological school at Andover, where he spent two years in work and study in the fellowship of the mission-minded students at that school of the prophets and planned the redemption of Hawaii with his enthusiastic patron.[4]

After the A.B.C.F.M. in 1812 dispatched its initial overseas mission to Calcutta, a veritable rage for "heathen education" swept the orthodox communities of Massachusetts and Connecticut. Litchfield County, where one of the earliest auxiliary missionary societies had been formed as early as 1811, had more than its share of this spirit. Under the patronage of local clergymen and several interested laymen, three additional Hawaiians stranded in this country were soon receiving an evangelical education in the county. In 1815 the American Board officially assumed responsibility for them, but committed their immediate care to the Connecticut sponsors. The next year the prudential committee authorized the establishment of an institution for the regular training of the heathen young men and named ex-Governor John Treadwell, Timothy Dwight, Lyman Beecher, and three other agents for the undertaking.[5] The committee now had four likely prospects as native missionaries, and a fifth, "Prince" Tamoree', son of an Hawaiian chief, was to join the others as soon as he could be released from the United States Navy, in which he served as a common seaman during the War of 1812.[6]

4/E. W. Dwight/, Memoirs of Henry Obookiah, 26-36.

5American Board, Seventh Annual Report, 4.

6A Narrative of Five Youths from the Sandwich Islands Now Receiving an Education in This Country (New York, 1816), 30-35. This tract was published by the Connecticut agents to publicize and raise money for the

In the same revival-ravaged county where Judge Tapping Reeve conducted his famous law classes, another educational innovation, the Foreign Mission School, took form in the sleepy Puritan village of Cornwall, Connecticut. The local townspeople, proud to receive the strange academy in their midst, donated an empty schoolhouse near the green, where the first classes commenced in May, 1817. Besides the original five Hawaiians, seven others joined the student body, giving a decidedly cosmopolitan coloring to the enterprise—two more Sandwich Islanders, two youths from British India, one Canadian Indian, and even two white Americans. The Board's agents in Litchfield County erected two additional buildings, one for the principal and another to house the foreign students, and the New England community settled back to watch the unique experiment.[7]

At the very outset the undertaking was clouded by tragedy. Before the school year was over, the talented Henry Obookiah—the pride and joy of the missionary party in New England—came down with typhus fever and died on February 17, 1818, "with a heavenly smile on his countenance and glory in his soul," according to the inscription on his tombstone in the village graveyard.[8] In a funeral sermon at Cornwall, Lyman Beecher consoled the school's supporters by predicting that, rather than defeating their hopes of Hawaii's salvation, the young convert's

proposed institution. Because of Tamoree's exalted rank, it was first suggested, apparently by Samuel Mills, to send him to West Point under the sponsorship of the federal government. This the A.B.C.F.M. declined to do, perhaps with a regard to his possible usefulness in securing a welcome for future missionaries to Hawaii. Worcester to James Morris, Salem, February 10, 1816, ABC:1.01, I, 99-100.

[7]"Report of the Agents of the Foreign Mission School," in American Board, Eighth Annual Report, 23-27.

[8]E. C. Starr, A History of Cornwall, Connecticut: A Typical New England Town (New Haven, 1926), 140.

death would advance the cause. It will afford, he claimed, "notoriety to this institution--will awaken a tender sympathy for Owhyhee, and give it an interest in the prayers and charities of thousands who otherwise had not heard of this establishment, or been interested in its prosperity."[9] The great Litchfield preacher was right. Obookiah's name became a household word in New England, and his Memoirs, published the year he died, and eventually running through twelve editions, reached into tens of thousands of homes to stir up a missionary spirit throughout the land.

Meanwhile the school prospered. In the ten years of its existence nearly one hundred students--including Chinese, Malayans, Greeks, and other foreign nationals, as well as Hawaiians and American Indians-- attended its classes. Among its first fruits was the establishment of a Protestant mission at the Sandwich Islands, in fulfillment of Mills's and Obookiah's great design. In September, 1818, the Cornwall agents wrote to the Board urging immediate dispatch of a missionary company, to be composed of several students of the academy and led by their first instructor, Edwin W. Dwight.[10] Not until the latter part of 1819, however, was such an expedition organized, which eventually numbered twenty-two persons--two ordained ministers, a physician, a farmer, and teachers, wives, and children, in addition to three Hawaiian converts and Prince Tamoree. The latter was not a member of the mission, but accompanied it as a bearer of good will from New England to his "royal" father.

---

[9]Lyman Beecher, A Sermon Delivered at the Funeral of Henry Obookiah (New Haven, 1818), 33-34.

[10]James Morris and Joseph Harvey to the A.B.C.F.M., Goshen, September, 1818, ABC:12.1, II, no. 53. Apparently Dwight was unwilling to go, or unacceptable to the Board. The prudential committee also requested Joseph Harvey, one of the school agents, to take the leading post in the proposed mission, but that gentleman declined for family reasons. Joseph Harvey to Worcester, Goshen, February 26, 1819, ABC:12.1, 11.

The American Board made preparations for the missionaries' departure in as public a fashion as possible in order to arouse the maximum interest of the evangelical community. Before a large gathering in the little town of Goshen, Connecticut, which all the Cornwall foreign students attended, a Litchfield County ministerial association ordained the mission's leaders, Asa Thurston and Hiram Bingham, both recent graduates of Andover and members of the Brethren. In his ordination sermon, entitled "The Promised Land," the Rev. Heman Humphrey expressed New England's millennial expectations in the unusual enterprise:

> This is a new scene in Connecticut;--if, indeed, it be a reality, and not a heavenly vision of future times, kindly vouchsafed to increase the faith and give a new fervency to the prayers of the Church. It is, it is a blessed reality. Here we behold a little consecrated band, ready to go forth in the name, and under the banners of the Saviour, to claim the Sandwich Islands, as the rightful possession of the Church. A spectacle so novel and so interesting, is calculated, for the time, to occupy the whole field of vision. We think much of this expedition, and certainly, when we take into view all the circumstances connected with its origin and progress, we may well inquire, "what hath God wrought?"[11]

In October, the adult members of the mission formed themselves into a church in Boston and entered a round of religious celebrations which culminated in a great sacramental service at Park Street Church before a multitude of spectators, almost six hundred of whom received communion with the missionaries. A few days later the mission family embarked on board the brig Thaddeus, while weeping friends on Boston's Long Wharf bade them tender farewell.[12] Evangelical New England's emissaries to the Pacific carried with them broad instructions of higher purpose and more momentous import than any mere commercial consignment to Hawaii. "You are to aim," Secretary Worcester solemnly charged them,

[11]Heman Humphrey, The Promised Land (Boston, 1819), 30-31.

[12]Panoplist, and Missionary Herald, XV (1819), 526-528.

"at nothing short of covering those islands with fruitful fields and pleasant dwellings, and schools and churches; of raising up the whole people to an elevated state of christian civilization; of bringing, or preparing the means of bringing, thousands and millions of the present and succeeding generations to the mansions of blessedness."[13]

The missionaries reached Kailua, Hawaii, in March, 1820. The story of their arrival and reception has often been told:[14] how the news of the old King's recent death and the subsequent destruction of the idols and the ancient system of tabus seemed to them a providential preparation for the Gospel; how after a series of conferences the chiefs and the young ruler, Liholiho, agreed to permit their settlement on the islands of Hawaii and Oahu for a probationary period of one year. Leaving Thurston and Dr. Thomas Holman and their wives at Kailua, Bingham led the others to Honolulu where they quickly established a mission in the seaport village where most of the foreign traders resided. A little later Samuel Ruggles and Samuel Whitney, unordained assistants, accepted the invitation of Tamoree and his father to settle on Kauai.[15]

From the beginning the mission was so successful in gaining the favor of the ruling chiefs, if not of the whole foreign community, that there was no question of departing at the end of the first year. Rather additional workers from America were welcomed, and the first of

---

[13]Instructions to the Sandwich Island Mission (Lahainaluna, 1838), 27.

[14]Recent scholarly accounts of the missionary establishment in Hawaii are found in H. W. Bradley, The American Frontier in Hawaii: The Pioneers in 1789-1843 (Stanford, 1942), 121-167; R. S. Kuykendall, The Hawaiian Kingdom 1778-1854: Foundations and Transformation (Honolulu, 1938), 100-116. There is a host of histories which treat this subject, of which two of the more recent are: Albertine Loomis, Grapes of Canaan (New York, 1951), 9-50, and L. B. Wright and M. I. Fry, Puritans in the South Seas (New York, 1936), 269-321.

[15]Tracy, History of the American Board, 99-100.

many large reinforcements sailed for the islands on a New Haven whaler in November, 1822.[16] As their colleagues in British India and among the Cherokees had already done, the Sandwich Islands missionaries began their attack upon heathenism by opening English-language schools, one of which enrolled chiefly the half-caste children of resident foreigners at Honolulu.[17] The mission turned to the use of the native tongue, however, as quickly as it could be mastered and reduced to writing. Bingham, who had visited John Pickering at Salem before embarking, was the first to preach in Hawaiian, and in the summer of 1822 the missionaries began serious efforts to organize the language in a simple written form.[18]

Their success made possible the printing of Hawaiian primers on the small hand press brought out from the United States, providing textbooks for an ambitious program of education at every station. With the cooperation of the principal chiefs, heathen Hawaii went to school, both adults and children. At first the enthusiasm for the new knowledge was so great that many of the islanders, according to critical European travelers at least, neglected their work, and the native economy suffered as a result.[19] Little beyond simple reading ability could be attained in these schools, for the Hawaiian teachers themselves knew hardly more than their pupils. In order to provide more and better-educated teachers, the mission established in 1831 a high school at Lahaina on the island

---

[16]Missionary Herald, XIX (1823), 11.

[17]Hiram Bingham, A Residence of Twenty-One Years in the Sandwich Islands (Hartford, 1847), 105-106.

[18]Pickering had not yet published his essay on the orthography of the Indian languages, but advised Bingham both personally and by letter. M. O. Pickering, Life of John Pickering (Boston, 1887), 291-292.

[19]F. W. Beechey, Narrative of a Voyage to the Pacific and Beering's Strait (London, 1831), II, 101-102; Otto von Kotzebue, A New Voyage Round the World in the Years 1823, 24, 25, and 26 (London, 1830), II, 261-262.

of Maui, and in the succeeding years various missionaries conducted other training institutes at their stations throughout the archipelago. By 1833 an estimated 40,000 students were enrolled in some 1,200 schools.[20]

The growth of the schools more or less paralleled the advance of nominal Christianity in Hawaii. Beginning with some of the most influential chiefs, a group of whom were baptized in December, 1825,[21] hundreds of the native population joined the churches. Hopu, one of the Hawaiian assistants from Cornwall, was so impressed that, remembering his New England training, he wrote, "It is Millennium." Citing this in 1830, the editor of the Missionary Herald remarked that the thousand years of Christ's reign might very well commence in the Pacific islands.[22] The missionaries grew so confident in their reports home that in 1833 the American Board announced that the Hawaiians had become a "Christian people." "Christianity," it was claimed in the pages of the Missionary Herald, "has preceded civilization, and is leading the way to it. Twelve years ago, that people were enveloped in thick pagan gloom; but the Sun of Righteousness has risen; . . . and the morning has come—the morning, it is believed, of a bright and happy day."[23] Although this pronouncement proved somewhat premature—for the thirties brought a reaction which nearly destroyed the mission's work[24]—the signal success in Hawaii cheered an American missionary public which found little to be optimistic about in reports from the rest of the world.

---

[20]American Board, Twenty-fifth Annual Report, appendix, 156-157.

[21]Missionary Herald, XXII (1826), 309-310.

[22]Missionary Herald, XXVI (1830), 179.

[23]Missionary Herald, XXIX (1833), 21.

[24]Lorrin Andrews, principal of the Lahaina Seminary, reported in 1833 that "it is apparent that our native schools have not accomplished what they are supposed to have done by our friends in America." American Board, Twenty-fifth Annual Report, appendix, 158.

Even the Unitarians recognized the value of what had been accomplished, though one spokesman in 1826 argued that the Orthodox exultation over Hawaii only demonstrated their lack of success elsewhere. "There is a formidable array of names and numbers belonging to the India missions; but when you ask for what has been done," he wrote, "you are always referred to the Sandwich Islands."[25] Chancellor James Kent, in the second edition of his great Commentaries on American Law, included a note on the "rapid transformation of the natives of those islands from being savages and heathen in 1820, to, in 1830, a civilized and Christian people," and gave due credit to the Board's evangelists.[26] The Board's prudential committee, following the strategy of directing the largest force at those points where the prospects of success were highest, favored the Hawaiian mission in the dispatch of reinforcements.[27] By 1852 thirteen missionary companies, numbering over one hundred and forty persons, had reached the Sandwich Islands from America.[28]

With regularly augmented numbers the mission was able to carry out an extensive program. Since the instructions of the prudential committee seemed to enjoin upon its agents the transfer of much of the total New England culture to the Sandwich Islands, the missionaries set out to effect a complete transformation of Hawaiian life. True, the first attempt to introduce American methods of agriculture did not succeed. When Daniel Chamberlain, a farmer from Brookfield, Massachusetts,

---

[25]Christian Examiner, III (1826), 119.

[26]James Kent, Commentaries on American Law (2nd ed., New York, 1832), II, 199n.

[27]The directors of the Board spelled out this strategy in some detail at the annual meeting in 1842 and announced their decision to increase the Hawaiian mission further. American Board, Thirty-third Meeting (Boston, 1842), 206-207.

[28]American Board, Forty-fourth Annual Report (Boston, 1853), 136-139.

resigned in 1823, no replacement was sent.[29] Some members of the mission encouraged silk and sugar culture, although nonmissionary groups carried on most of these experiments.[30] In 1836 the prudential committee engaged Miss Lydia Brown to teach the Hawaiian women spinning and weaving.[31] Two years later, however, the Board rejected the missionaries' petition for farmers and artisans to instruct the native population in their callings. The failure of large secular establishments among the Indians served as an example to the directors of missions. While clinging to the notion that Christianity and civilization must go hand in hand, they affirmed the primacy of evangelization and expected all other cultural attainments to follow in its train.[32]

Education was a different matter. With all the fervency of the New England faith in schools, the missionaries redoubled their efforts for the improvement of native instruction. The emphasis shifted, however, from adult education to the training of children. Boarding schools for boys sprang up at the various stations, and the high school at Lahaina became an institution of higher learning. In order to provide proper wives for the graduates of these academies, the mission commenced a girls' boarding school at Wailuku. In 1839 Mr. and Mrs. Amos Cooke organized at Honolulu a unique institution sponsored jointly by the mission and the Hawaiian rulers for educating the children of royal blood.[33]

[29]American Board, Fourteenth Annual Report (Boston, 1823), 107-108.

[30]Hawaiian Spectator, I (1838), 72-75; Reuben Tinker and others to Ladd and Company, Koloa, January 10, 1840, and Bingham and others to same, Honolulu, January 11, 1840, in Report of the Proceedings and Evidence in the Arbitration between the King and Government of the Hawaiian Islands and Messrs. Ladd & Co. (Honolulu, 1846), appendix, 43-44.

[31]Missionary Herald, XXXII (1836), 389-390.

[32]See the discussion of the whole question in American Board, Thirty-third Annual Report, 72-75.

[33]For an interesting account of this extraordinary school, see Mary A. Richards, The Chiefs' Children's School (Honolulu, 1937).

The common-school system which emerged from these endeavors was eventually taken over and extended by the government of Hawaii as part of the reform measures carried out under the constitution of 1840.[34] Provisions were made for schools in every village, the teachers to be supported by special lands set aside for the purpose and licensed by government inspectors and missionaries under the general supervision of the minister of public education, a post filled for many years by members of the Board's mission. In 1849 the A.B.C.F.M. also surrendered to the native government the academy at Lahaina, with the understanding that no "religious tenet or doctrine contrary to those heretofore inculcated by the mission" would ever be taught.[35] Thus American missionaries saw their work incorporated into Hawaiian society. Religious conversion also went on apace, after the brief reaction of the mid-thirties, and a series of revivals in the years 1838-1840 sparked the drive for the full evangelization of the islands.[36]

The Cornwall-trained youths proved to be the greatest disappointment of the work in Hawaii. After the death of his father, Prince Tamorre repudiated the religion of his American teachers and joined a revolt against the authority of the Hawaiian king, dying shortly after his defeat. William Tennooe, one of the three "pious" Cornwall students of the first company, was found guilty of intoxication and violating the Sabbath and was excommunicated a few months after arrival.[37] Some of their countrymen educated in New England assisted the mission greatly in

[34]Kuykendall, Hawaiian Kingdom, 347-351.

[35]American Board, Fortieth Annual Report (Boston, 1849), 198.

[36]Sheldon Dibble, the first missionary historian, called these the years of the "great revival." Sheldon Dibble, History of the Sandwich Islands (Lahainaluna, 1843), 341-354.

[37]American Board, Twelfth Annual Report, 84.

its commencement, but the missionaries finally came to the conclusion that American education unfitted the simple Hawaiians for the task of evangelizing their less-favored brethren. For one thing, the mission placed no emphasis on English-language instruction after its first essay in that direction and preferred to train assistants in their own vernacular schools on the islands.

At home the Cornwall academy itself suffered difficulties. The temptations of the outside world often attracted the heathen youths from the narrow path of evangelical rectitude, and many were dismissed. In 1823 the principal confidentially warned the prudential committee of the Board that boys of better character and greater ability must be obtained for the sake of the school's reputation.[38] William Ellis, moreover, the English evangelist who stopped over at Hawaii to assist the Americans in the early twenties, strongly recommended on his visit to the United States that native helpers should be educated on missionary ground, far from the allurements of a more advanced civilization.[39] The Board took Ellis's advice and closed the Foreign Mission School in 1826.[40]

II

In the Pacific the American Board came in close contact with the commercial and naval enterprises of the United States. The story of the Hawaiian mission is partly an account of the relations of these three aspects of American expansion in that region. At Honolulu in particular, and later at Lahaina and Hilo on the islands of Maui and Hawaii

[38]Herman Daggett to Evarts, Cornwall, December 17, 1823, ABC:12.1, II, no. 153.

[39]Evarts to Timothy Stone, Boston, August 26, 1825, ABC:1.01, V, 361.

[40]American Board, Eighteenth Annual Report (Boston, 1827), 150-151; Tracy, History of the American Board, 174.

respectively, the evangelistic band found a motley society of white
traders, sailors, and beachcombers, their numbers swelled by the whalemen who made the Sandwich Islands one of their chief resorts in the years
after the discovery of the important whaling grounds off Japan in 1820.
The missionaries added an alien element to this community which a large
part of the foreign residents, both American and European, did not welcome. Some of the chief trading concerns in Honolulu were Boston houses,
like the firm of Bryant and Sturgis, who freighted the first frame dwelling around the Horn free of charge for the Board's emissaries in 1821.[41]
Although one American trader called taking "Missionary Freight" for
eighteen dollars a ton an "unprofitable business,"[42] other New England
companies and even the whalers of Nantucket gave free passage to both
men and supplies for the mission.[43]

The chief complaint of the mercantile opponents at the islands
was that religion hurt business. John C. Jones, United States consular
agent in Honolulu and a Bostonian with Unitarian leanings,[44] pronounced

[41]When lack of cargo space prevented the first missionaries from taking
this "prefabricated" house with them, Bryant and Sturgis offered to carry
it out on a vessel embarking later in the season. Missionary Herald,
XVII (1821), 140n. That this gesture was not altogether altruistic may
be seen from a letter of the firm to the master of the ship: "Say to
the Missionaries that we shall bring the frame of the House in the Tartar
free of freight, and as we do so much for them they must aid you if they
can." Bryant and Sturgis to John Suter, July 18, 1820, Boston. Bryant
and Sturgis Papers, Baker Library, Harvard Graduate School of Business
Administration; also printed in Morison, "Boston Traders in the Hawaiian
Islands, 1789-1823," Massachusetts Historical Society, Proceedings, LIV
(1920), 29.

[42]J. C. Jones to Josiah Marshall, Oahu, June 15, 1826. Josiah Marshall
Papers, Houghton Library, Harvard University.

[43]Missionary Herald, XVIII (1822), 64. Captain Jonathan Winship of
Boston gave the first missionaries a letter authorizing them to use his
home in Honolulu in his absence. Ibid. XVII (1821), 131.

[44]In 1826 Jones wrote to Henry Ware and William Ellery Channing to ask
for a Unitarian missionary for Hawaii. Journal of Stephen Reynolds, I
(June 12, 1826), Peabody Museum, Salem.

perhaps the most severe condemnation upon the evangelists in a series of
letters to the Massachusetts firm of Marshall and Wildes. In 1823 he
wrote to his employers:

> Trade never will again flourish at these Islands until
> these emissaries from the Andover mill are recalled, they are
> continually telling the King and Chiefs that the white people
> traders are cheating and imposing on them, consequently have
> depreciated the value of most articles. I believe it is a
> fact generally acknowledged by all here, that the natives are
> fifty per cent worse in every vice since the missionaries be-
> gan their hypocritical labours here; these blood suckers of
> the community had much better be in their native country gain-
> ing their living by the sweat of their brow, than living like
> lords in this luxurious land, distracting the minds of these
> children of Nature with the idea that they are to be eternally
> damned unless they think and act as they do: O that Provi-
> dence would put a whip in every honest hand to lash such
> rascals naked through the world.[45]

In another communication the irritable trader portrayed Hawaii as a scene
of desolation and idolence because of the islanders preoccupation with
missionary affairs: "Nothing but the sound of the church going bell is
heard from the rising to the setting sun and religion is cramm'd down
the throats of these poor simple mortals whilst certain famine and destruction are staring them in the face."[46] A few years later, finding
business dull and experiencing difficulty in collecting old sandalwood
payments from the chiefs, Jones bargained with the Boston office: "If
you will get the missionaries removed, I will guarantee to get the debt."[47]

What most provoked the foreign colony was the growing influence
of the missionaries with the king and chiefs and the subsequent tightening
up of Hawaiian social legislation. When the rulers determined to prohibit
the commerce of native girls with the crews of visiting ships, the mission

---

[45]Jones to Marshall and Wildes, Woahoo, March 9, 1823. Marshall Papers;
printed with slightly different wording in Morison, "Boston Traders in
the Hawaiian Islands, 1789-1823," 46.

[46]Jones to Marshall, Oahu, May 5, 1826. Marshall Papers.

[47]Jones to Marshall, Oahu, August 13, 1829. Marshall Papers.

found itself fiercely denounced on nearly all sides for teaching the
Hawaiians the moral austerity of New England. The Board's agents became
embroiled in the twenties in two different clashes with foreign sailors,
one at Lahaina, where the crew of an English whaler threatened the life
and property of William Richards, and another at Honolulu, involving the
personnel and the prestige of the United States Navy. It was this latter
episode which incensed the religious community at home and eventually
improved relations between the mission and the American navy in the
Pacific. Lt. John Percival commanded the first United States naval vessel to touch at the islands, arriving in the Dolphin in 1826 at a time
when whalemen's tempers were high over the antiprostitution ban. After
a near-riot in which embattled sailors tried to wreak their vengence on
Hiram Bingham, Percival managed to persuade the chiefs to relax the unpopular edict. In this first test of power the mission had lost out.[48]

In Boston the Board decided to make an issue of the Dolphin
affair. The prudential committee sent a formal complaint to Washington
demanding punishment for the erring Percival. Secretary of the Navy
Samuel L. Southard ordered a court of inquiry, which met at Charlestown
Navy Yard in the spring of 1828. Though the tribunal sat in closed
sessions, the Board was permitted to have present an attorney, who questioned witnesses and took notes.[49] The case aroused intense interest in
New England. "The question," Rufus Anderson wrote during the progress
of the inquiry, "is made a party concern. The Unitarians are very
generally against us. And a very industrious effort will be made to

---

[48]American Board, Eighteenth Annual Report, 77-83. Percival clashed also
with other Americans in Hawaii, who brought charges against him in the
United States. Journal of Stephen Reynolds, I (March 24, 1826). See
also Nile's Weekly Register, XXXI (1826), 283.

[49]American Board, Nineteenth Annual Report, 60.

collect materials at the Islands to blind the eyes of our community."[50]
The court, moreover, brought in a sealed verdict, which the navy department never publicly disclosed, despite several efforts of the prudential
committee to force the secretary's hand.[51]

In regard to the Lahaina outrage, the Board had no recourse but
to public opinion. When a copy of the New York Observer containing the
missionary report of the incident reached Hawaii, the English whaling
captain and other foreign residents forced the native rulers to arrange
a farcical trial for Richards, which completely cleared him. In defending
its publication of the affair, the prudential committee argued the case
for evangelical censorship of immoral actions wherever they might take
place: "Neither the missionaries, nor their patrons, wish to bring the
private vices of individuals unnecessarily before the public. But one
of the important uses of the press is, that it can be made a powerful
instrumentality of restraining and punishing crime, where the arm of
civil law cannot reach."[52]

In the fall of 1826 the mission prepared a circular letter
answering its critics among the foreign residents and requested an impar-
tial investigation.[53] A group of foreigners accepted the challenge, but
Captain Thomas Ap Catesby Jones of the U.S.S. Peacock, who arrived in

---

[50]Anderson to Levi Chamberlain, Boston, June 4, 1828, ABC 2:01, I.

[51]In 1829 the secretary of the navy informed the Board privately that the
tribunal's verdict was that a court martial was "not necessary or proper."
John Branch to J. C. Smith and Stephen van Rensaelaer, Washington, October 14, 1829, ABC:13, I, no. 3. The prudential committee never saw fit
to publish this reply, and as late as 1842, Joseph Tracy, semi-official
historian of the Board, professed ignorance of the outcome. Tracy,
History of the American Board, 184.

[52]Missionary Herald, XXIV (1828), 281. Five years later, trader Stephen
Reynolds, often hostile to the mission, was angry with the Board's agents
in Honolulu over critical reports in the Herald and other "villanous Publications." Journal of Stephen Reynolds, III (March 18, 1833).

[53]Their petition is printed in the Missionary Herald, XXIII (1827), 241-
242, and in American Board, Eighteenth Annual Report, appendix, ix-xii.

Honolulu to settle commercial relations between Hawaii and the United States, championed the missionaries so effectively in public meeting that the trading community had little to say.[54] But the most significant vindication of the Pacific evangelists came in 1829, when Captain William B. Finch arrived in the _Vincennes_ bearing a message from President John Quincy Adams commending the mission's work in the highest terms. This unusual action in the closing months of the Adams administration was apparently intended as amends for the Percival incident, though a returned missionary, Charles Stewart, actively lobbied for the expedition in 1828 in Washington and received an appointment as its chaplain.[55]

The visit of the _Vincennes_ raised the prestige of the mission and silenced for the moment its more vocal critics. Captain Finch and Chaplain Stewart presented the remarkable communication addressed to the young King Kamehameha which stated that:

> /The President of the United States7 has heard, with interest and admiration, of the rapid progress which has been made by your people, in acquiring a knowledge of letters and of the True Religion—the Religion of the Christian's Bible. These are the best, and the only means, by which the prosperity and happiness of nations can be advanced and continued; and the president, and all men everywhere, who wish well to yourself and your people, earnestly hope that you will continue to cultivate them, and to protect these by whom they are brought to you. . . . He does not doubt that their motives

---

[54]Captain Jones, who negotiated a treaty which informally regulated American relations with the island kingdom for nearly twenty years, though it was never ratified by the United States Senate, remained a firm friend of the mission, and the Board published two letters from him in approval of its work in the _Missionary Herald_, XXIV (1828), 55-56. Some of the traders were nonplussed at Jones's advocacy of the missionaries. Just the year before one of them had suggested to his Boston office that if a naval warship could be sent to the islands it would help collect the sandalwood debts and at the same time lessen the influence of the mission. Eliab Grimes to Marshall, Woahoo, August 16, 1826. Marshall Papers.

[55]Stewart returned in 1827 for the sake of his wife's health. His lobbying activities are described in E. C. Tracy, _Life of Jeremiah Evarts_, 267-268, and in Stewart's letter to Evarts, Norfolk, Va., February 9, 1829, ABC:19.1, III, no. 148.

are pure, and their objects most friendly to the happiness of your people; and that they will so conduct themselves as to merit the protecting kindness of your government.[56]

This all but official endorsement of the Board's emissaries by the chief executive of the United States, accompanied by the sight of a former member of the Calvinist mission clothed in the authority and uniform of that country's navy, must have impressed upon both the native population and the foreign settlement the fact that the American flag followed the cross.[57]

At home the religious community watched closely the course of public opinion regarding Hawaii. In 1825 the Board had an opportunity to exploit the favorable report of an outsider, when William Ellis arrived in Boston en route to England from a London Missionary Society station in the South Seas and a two-year stint in Hawaii, where he assisted the Americans in acquiring the native language. The evangelist-printer, who later as secretary of the London organization provided a useful liaison between the British and American societies, lectured in New England churches on evangelistic successes in the Pacific and aroused wide enthusiasm. After hearing him on one such occasion Jared Sparks, scholarly Unitarian editor of the North American Review, called the next day at the Board's headquarters to secure further information from the British missionary.[58] The result was an extremely favorable account of the work of the mission in a review of Ellis's Journal of a Tour around Hawaii,

[56]Charles Stewart, A Visit to the South Seas in the U.S. Ship Vincennes, during the Years 1829 and 1830 (New York, 1831), II, 128-129. This document is also found in Bingham, Residence in the Sandwich Islands, 355-356, and Niles' Weekly Register, XXXVIII (1830), 295.

[57]Chaplain Stewart served in a double capacity on the voyage to Hawaii, for the prudential committee of the Board had appointed him a special agent to the mission. Missionary Herald, XXV (1829), 38.

[58]Anderson to Hiram Bingham, Boston, April 11, 1825, ABC:1.01, V, 223.

the narrative of an extensive reconnaissance of the largest of the Hawaiian Islands by several American missionaries and the English printer.[59]

It was the British press, however, that struck the first severe blows against the infant enterprise. In 1825 His Majesty's ship Blonde, commanded by Lord Byron, the poet's cousin and successor, brought back to the Sandwich Islands the bodies of King Liholiho and his queen, who had died in England on a visit to that country. When a journal of the voyage was published two years later, evangelical readers on both sides of the Atlantic were surprised and hurt to discover an outspoken criticism of the missionaries, based chiefly on their Sabbatarian austerity.[60] This was bad enough, but the Quarterly Review, an important London magazine often jaundiced in its American attitudes, promptly made matters worse by continuing the attack in a long review article.[61] Believing that charges from so formidable a source, in a periodical issued also in an American edition and much read in this country, must be answered, Jeremiah Evarts penned a stinging rebuttal in the pages of the now friendly North American Review.[62]

Charles Stewart, the missionary-turned-chaplain, published two works on Hawaii which brought before the public, both British and American, an extremely optimistic view of the mission's progress. The first achieved

[59]North American Review, XXII (1826), 334-364.

[60]/Maria G. Callcott, comp.,7 Voyage of H.M.S. Blonde to the Sandwich Islands, in the Years 1824-1825 (London, 1827), 145-148, and passim.

[61]Quarterly Review, LXX (1827), 419-445.

[62]North American Review, LVIII (1828), 59-111. Before this appeared, Evarts expanded his essay and published it separately as An Examination of Charges against the American Missionaries at the Sandwich Islands, as Alleged in the Voyage of the Ship Blonde, and in the London Quarterly Review (Cambridge, 1827). Abroad, William Orme of the L.M.S. wrote A Defence of the Missions in the South Sea, and Sandwich Islands, against the Misrepresentations Contained in a Late Number of the Quarterly Review, (London, 1827).

five editions and reached thousands of readers here and abroad.[63] Later

he issued an account of his experiences aboard the Vincennes in A Visit

to the South Seas, a lurid report on Hawaii and other Pacific islands

which influenced Herman Melville's treatment of the Marquesas in Typee.[64]

According to his former colleagues in the mission, however, Stewart's

volumes were a disservice to the cause, for he pictured the island king-

doms as already a veritable scene of heavenly glory, hardly requiring

additional evangelistic effort. Reuben Tinker angrily reminded the

Society of Inquiry at Andover Seminary that it is still "better to have

been born in a house top in New England than to be a native in a wide

house in the Pacific," and denounced Stewart for too sanguine an estimate.

"For who among you," he demanded, "will pray for a people so far on the

way to the millennium that they need their prayers less than they are

needed for themselves and their children."[65]

In the thirties and forties, however, a flood of adverse com-

mentary reached America when merchant captains, naval officers, and common

---

[63]C. S. Stewart, Private Journal of a Voyage to the Pacific Ocean, and Residence at the Sandwich Islands (New York, 1828; published also in London and in a second American edition with notes by William Ellis in 1828. A fifth edition appeared in Boston as late as 1839.

[64]It has been demonstrated that Melville made large use of Stewart's Visit to the South Seas in his descriptions of native scenery and customs in Typee. C. R. Anderson, Melville in the South Seas (Columbia University, Studies in English and Comparative Literature, 138, New York, 1939), 70-72, 98-100.

[65]Reuben Tinker to Society of Inquiry, Missionary Packet, Pacific Ocean, October 12, 1832. Society of Inquiry Papers, Andover-Newton Theological Seminary Library. A factual error in Stewart's first book, which was quickly picked up and widely disseminated in America, to the effect that all but one of the foreign residents in Hawaii opposed the landing of the first missionaries, provoked James Hunnewell, who was present at the time, to offer in rebuttal that the chaplain's exception, an Englishman, was the one who on the contrary used all his influence with the chiefs to prevent the settlement of the Americans. James Hunnewell to Anderson, Charlestown, October 23, 1832. James Hunnewell Papers, Houghton Library, Harvard University.

sailors, and adventurers hastened into print with narratives of months and years spent in the lush islands of the Pacific. Lt. Hiram Paulding of the Dolphin, defending his superior, Percival, published a highly unfavorable account of Hawaiian missionary life and suggested that the islanders be taught proper cultivation of their land rather than "a mysterious doctrine, which being beyond their comprehension, must resolve itself into a dark and intolerant superstition."[66] Commodore John Downes's visit in 1832 produced two books, in one of which his secretary, Jeremiah N. Reynolds, later a forthright advocate of a large-scale exploring expedition to the Pacific, criticized the evangelists' bigotry and "sectarian zeal."[67] In the second volume a naval officer painted a different picture altogether and found the society of the missionaries a happy reminder of his New England home.[68] A third visitor of the decade presented a sane, balanced view of the mission but described many of its members as "far behind the age in which they live," as well as "deficient in general knowledge." "I think," he wrote, "I can trace in them more of the lineaments of the Mucklewraths and Poundtexts of by-gone days, than is desirable in divines of the nineteenth century."[69]

These generally critical volumes received a wide audience in America. The more obscure publications of ordinary sailors, however, often told a different story. A whaleman who thought the missionaries

[66]Hiram Paulding, Journal of a Cruise of the United States Schooner Dolphin (New York, 1831), 223.

[67]J. N. Reynolds, Voyage of the United States Frigate Potomac, under the Command of Commodore John Downes, during the Circumnavigation of the Globe (New York, 1835), 418-419. One of Reynold's most effective efforts was a comic one, in which he reproduced the missionaries' rather ludicrous translation of a famous hymn. Ibid., 419-421.

[68]Francis Warriner, Cruise of the United States Frigate Potomac round the World, during the Years 1831-1834 (New York, 1835), 224-225.

[69]Ruschenberger, Voyage round the World, 475.

underrated their hearers in the seamen's chapel in Honolulu nevertheless paid tribute to their piety and good works.[70] A fellow hunter of the seas, George Lightcraft, who recorded the amusing story of his love affair with a mission-educated Maui girl, had nothing but good reports to give of the American evangelists.[71] After observing a native church service, a third asserted that even the atheistic Thomas Paine would have to agree that "the whole occasion was religiously sublime,--Nature's temple, worshipping the Christian's God."[72] The attitude of the United States Navy, at least since the Percival episode, was generally friendly. Lt. Charles Wilkes, who called at the Hawaiian Islands during his famous exploring expedition in the Pacific in 1840, took pains in his official narrative to answer the critics who charged the missionaries with luxurious living.[73] In 1843 James Jackson Jarves, who spent several years at the islands, published two influential volumes, one of them a history of Hawaii, in which he explained how his views had changed from antimissionary prejudice on his arrival in 1837 to active partisanship of the Board's labors.[74]

It was the publication in 1846 of Typee, the first production of the young and unknown Herman Melville, which raised the antimissionary argument anew. Melville, who was writing about Nukuhiva, an island in

---

[70]F. A. Olmstead, Incidents of a Whaling Voyage (New York, 1841), 243.

[71]George Lightcraft, Scraps from the Log Book (Syracuse, 1847), 78-91.

[72]James Oliver, Wreck of the Glide (New York, 1848), 69.

[73]Charles Wilkes, Narrative of the United States Exploring Expedition (Philadelphia, 1845), IV, 5.

[74]J. J. Jarves, History of the Hawaiian or Sandwich Islands (Boston, 1843), preface, vi-vii, and Scenes and Scenery in the Sandwich Islands, a Trip through Central America (Boston, 1843), 181-184. Fourteen years later, however, the vagabond art critic wrote a semi-allegorical autobiography in which he ridiculed the same missionaries he had earlier praised. Jarves, Why and What Am I? The Confessions of an Inquirer (Boston, 1857) 166-195.

the Marquesas, had spent several weeks in Honolulu and appended to his
widely read narrative some severe observations on the Hawaiian evangelists, their manner of living and their demoralizing effect upon the
natives.[75] Adverse reviews quickly appeared, some from religious journals, whose editors disliked not only the author's reactions to the
missionaries but also his frank pagan enjoyment of the primitive life of
the Marquesans and his dalliance with the lovely Typee maiden, Fayaway.[76]
The power of the evangelical public was made plain when Melville's American publisher, John Wiley, issued a second edition a few months later
omitting all the hostile references as well as the more lurid passages
describing uninhibited heathen customs.[77] Although the American Board
did not deign to notice the matter, members and friends of the Hawaiian
mission in Honolulu carried on a persistent campaign of abuse against
Melville.[78] Hiram Bingham, the controversial leader of the Honolulu

[75]Among other things, Melville spoke of missionaries dwelling in "pic-
turesque and prettily-furnished coral-rock villas" and their wives being
drawn around Honolulu in carts drawn by patient Hawaiian servants.
Herman Melville, Typee: A Peep at Polynesian Life (Constable edition,
London, 1922), 253-268.

[76]One evangelical reviewer discovered a subtle method of disparaging
missions in Melville: "If he meets a native female Islander, she is a
goddess;—if a missionary's wife, she is a blowzy looking, red-faced, fat
oppressor of the poor native—reducing him to the station of drudge."
New Englander, IV (1846), 449-450. See also C. R. Anderson, "Contemporary American Opinions of Typee and Omoo," American Literature, IX
(1937), 1-25. Omoo was also reviewed harshly in the New Englander, VI
(1848), 44.

[77]Meade Minnigerode, Some Personal Letters of Herman Melville and a
Bibliography (New York, 1922), 19-28, 109-123.

[78]David Aaron, "Melville and the Missionaries," New England Quarterly,
VIII (1935), 404-408. Mrs. Elizabeth Sanders wrote in 1848: "The missionary party prefer silence when no effective argument can be had. The book
written by Herman Melville, under the title of Typee, has received no
other notice than a strenuous endeavor to suppress the work, and persuade
the author to make another edition, leaving out the scandalous and wicked
transactions related of the missionaries at the Sandwich Islands." Remarks on the "Tour around Hawaii," (Salem, 1848), 34.

station, whom Stephen Reynolds called a "great Hypocrite,"[79] appended

this comment to his 1847 memoir of life in Hawaii:

> I have not altered my views of heathenism or Christianity since the uncivilized "Tipee" has sought, through the presses of civilization in England and America, to apologize for cannabalism, and to commend savage life to the sons and daughters of Christendom, instead of teaching the principles of science and virtue, or the worship of our Maker, among idolaters, man-eaters, and infidels.[80]

Whether applauded or condemned, the mission of the American

Board in Hawaii attracted much American interest to the Pacific archi-

pelago. Although missionaries still abominated the sale of New England

rum in barrels marked "paint oil,"[81] the hostility between commerce and re-

ligion gradually decreased. Popular books of Pacific travel noted the

convergence of trading and missionary influences in giving the United

States a preponderant position in Hawaii and concluded that both worked

for the future good of all.[82] Final testimony in this period came from

an unimpeachable source, lawyer Richard Henry Dana of Boston, who visited

Hawaii in 1860 and wrote a long descriptive letter to the New York Tribune.

Widely cited after their appearance in print, his observations, highly

favorable to the Board's enterprise, summed up the missionary accomplish-

ment of creating in Hawaii a Christian nation under American auspices.[83]

---

[79]Journal of Stephen Reynolds, I (December 12, 1825).

[80]Bingham, Residence in the Sandwich Islands, 466n.

[81]Letter of Dwight Baldwin, Lahaina, October 6, 1845, Missionary Herald, XLII (1846), 183-184.

[82]H. T. Cheever, Life in the Sandwich Islands: or, the Heart of the Pacific, As It Was and Is (New York, 1851), preface, 4; W. M. Wood, Wandering Sketches of People and Things in South America, Polynesia, California, and Other Places Visited (Philadelphia, 1849), 199-200. See also E. T. Perkins, Na Motu: or, Reef-Rovings in the South Seas (New York, 1854), 361-370.

[83]Much of this letter is quoted in Anderson, The Hawaiian Islands: Their Progress and Condition under Missionary Labors (Boston, 1864), 99-106.

III

From the outset the American Protestant mission in the Hawaiian Islands was implicated in internal political affairs and international entanglements in the Pacific. The first emissaries reported that the chief opposition to their landing in 1820 came from foreigners, apparently Englishmen who advised the rulers that the newcomers intended to acquire the islands for the United States.[84] Ever since Captain George Vancouver's visit in 1792 and 1793, when Kamehameha I informally placed his domain under the protection of the Crown, Great Britain exercised a nominal responsibility for the island kingdom. For this reason the American Board's agents were more than happy to welcome the endorsement of their work by a deputation of the London Society which arrived in 1822 with William Ellis, the English missionary printer from Tahiti, who remained two years in Hawaii helping organize the mission.[85]

From their central position in the Pacific the evangelists extended their views to outlying regions. In 1820, unsure of a permanent settlement at Hawaii in the face of both native and foreign opposition, Hiram Bingham wrote to the Russian authorities at Kamchatka for permission to carry the Gospel there. The governor courteously replied that he was willing to "see any missionaries, who would choose to visit the peninsula of Kamschatka /sic/, and offer them all the assistance in my power."[86]

[84]Missionary Herald, XVII (1821), 118. James Hunnewell, the Charlestown, Massachusetts, merchant who lived in Honolulu on friendly terms with the mission during the early years, later declared that British antipathy was directed toward his countrymen as Americans rather than as missionaries. Hunnewell to William Ellis, Charlestown, January 20, 1833. In his private diary the trader confided that "I am neutral for I sell Rum," when Anglo-American quarrels broke out in Honolulu. Journal of Hunnewell (May 11, 1820). Hunnewell Papers.

[85]Missionary Herald, XIX (1823), 97-105.

[86]Peter Reicord to Bingham, Kamchatka, September 5, 1820, in Bingham, Residence in the Sandwich Islands, 118-119.

Although this enterprise never matured the mission had other contacts with the czar's servants in Hawaii itself. Two ships of the Russian Navy landed at Honolulu in 1821 on a voyage of exploration. The officers—two of whom spoke English—visited the mission school and treated the Americans with the greatest respect. Bingham gave them a copy of Henry Obookiah's Memoirs and expressed his conception of the liberal czar's efforts at religious and political reform in Russia in writing to Boston: "We shall rejoice in the reign of Alexander, the patron of benevolent institutions, while his influence favors the increase of Evangelical light, and the enjoyment of universal liberty and peace."[87] The visit of a later Russian expedition was less auspicious. In 1825 Captain Otto von Kotzebue, a German in the czar's service, singled out Bingham for special denunciation on the score of his political interference in island affairs.[88]

The Americans, however, looked mainly to the English for guidance and support. In 1821 Prince Tamoree offered to send a vessel with two missionaries to the Society and Georgian Islands to the south, for conferences with the London Society's agents there, but the opposition of influential foreigners halted the project.[89] Not till 1832 did a delegation from Hawaii sail to Tahiti and other islands in the field of the L.M.S. Charles Stewart's Visit to the South Seas, which painted a glowing picture of the Washington or Marquesas Islands, inspired the American missionaries to return by way of those tropical isles, which they recommended to Boston as a mission field, in spite of the representations of the English society that its agents proposed going there.[90]

---

[87]Bingham to Evarts, Woahoo, July 7, 1821, Missionary Herald, XVIII (1822), 111-112.

[88]Journal of Stephen Reynolds, I (October 1, 1825). Kotzebue, New Voyage round the World, 254-262.

[89]Tracy, History of the American Board, 112.

[90]Missionary Herald, XXX (1834), 85-86.

While the Board, unwilling to enter a jurisdictional dispute with its trans-Atlantic brethren, advised delay, the Hawaiian mission hastened to dispatch three pastors and their wives, who in 1833 landed at Nukuhive Island, in the harbor Commodore David Porter named Massachusetts Bay during his famous expedition into these waters during the war of 1812. This was the place where Herman Melville deserted a whaleship a few years later and survived to describe his life among the savage inhabitants in Typee.[91] Unlike Melville, who enjoyed the free and easy life of the amoral Marquesans, the missionaries were quickly disenchanted and reluctantly returned to Hawaii after only eight months in what one of their number called "the suburbs of Hell."[92] In making this difficult decision they appealed to the overall evangelistic strategy, noting that Nukuhiva was "too small to justify the Board in sustaining a mission here, when such vast fields in other places are calling for their efforts.[93]

The instructions of the prudential committee to the first reinforcements of the Hawaiian mission admonished them to "abstain from all interference with the local and political views of the people. The kingdom of Christ is not of this world; and it especially behooves a missionary to stand aloof from the private and transient interests of chiefs and rulers."[94] But the Board's emissaries found it difficult to

[91]Melville's story about the missionary's wife whom the Marquesans shamefully humiliated by stripping off her clothes to discover her sex may have derived from the experiences of these Americans in Nukuhiva. Melville, Typee, 5-6. Anderson, however, has confused the actual missionary company with its predecessors, the delegation from Hawaii which remained only a few days. Anderson, Melville in the South Seas, 87.

[92]W. P. Alexander to Anderson, Nukuhiva, September 4, 1833, ABC:19.1, VI, no. 49.

[93]Missionary Herald, XXXI (1835), 227. Further accounts of the abortive mission may be found in M. C. Alexander, William Patterson Alexander in Kentucky, the Marquesas, Hawaii (Honolulu, 1934).

[94]Bingham, Residence in the Sandwich Islands, 282. Missionary Herald, XIX (1823), 100.

obey this precept, particularly in the light of their peculiar relationship to the island rulers, who sought their assistance not only as
spiritual but often as political advisers. In 1826, for example, the
Christian chiefs sought to enforce a code of laws similar to the Old
Testament Decalogue, which Bingham had presented to one of their number
earlier.[95] Through missionary influence the following years saw the issu-
ance of bans on prostitution, rum-selling, and Sabbath-breaking, which
greatly alarmed and angered many of the foreign residents and sojourning
sailors. Among the native islanders the mission attempted to discounten-
ance not only drinking, but also the use of tobacco, to which they were
much addicted.[96]

Although the missionaries themselves always denied any union
of church and state as a practical effect of their teaching in Hawaii,[97]
Rufus Anderson, Board secretary and historian of the mission, admitted
the situation to be one not unlike "what existed in the palmy days of the
Israelitish nation, and in the Puritan age of New England." [98]The first
important testing of church and state relations came when French Catholics
attempted to gain a foothold for their faith in Honolulu. The island
authorities expelled two priests who had arrived in 1827, and a number of
native converts to the alien faith suffered criminal prosecution.[99]

[95]Bingham, Residence in the Sandwich Islands, 282.

[96]General Letter of the Mission, June 23, 1832, Missionary Herald, XXIX
(1833), 165.

[97]Bingham, Residence in the Sandwich Islands, 278-280. Sheldon Dibble,
first historian of the mission, argued that this state of affairs arose
"notwithstanding the constant endeavors of Missionaries to prevent it."
Dibble, History of the Sandwich Islands, 35.

[98]Anderson, A Heathen Nation Evangelized: History of the Sandwich
Islands Mission, 117.

[99]Reginald Yzendoorn, History of the Catholic Mission in the Hawaiian
Islands (Honolulu, 1927), 34-75.

Opponents of the mission charged both the chiefs and their missionary advisers with bigotry, and an American naval officer, Commodore John Downes, took pains to persuade the rulers of the value of religious toleration. Jeremiah N. Reynolds, who accompanied the commodore to Hawaii, published this rebuke of the mission:

> Is this, then, the fruit of Christianity, in a place where we had reason to believe so much good had been done by the mild influence of missionary labours--where religion, and freedom, and knowledge had taken such deep root? where the gospel trumpet had been sounded, and the heathen had listened to its joyful notes?[100]

There can be little question but that the missionaries--with the same antipapal orientation so much in evidence among Protestant nativists at home--were largely responsible for the intolerant attitude of their charges.[101] Moreover, their actions brought international repercussions. Captain Cyrille Laplace, arriving in Honolulu in the French warship L'Artémise, forced a treaty upon the Hawaiian king which provided for religious freedom for Catholics and the importation of French wines and brandies. Adding national insult to evangelical injury, the French officer refused to accord the American missionaries the rights of neutrals, treating them as an integral part of the Hawaiian nation and subject to possible military action. The L'Artémise affair became a cause célèbre in mission circles at home and abroad. A sympathetic observer, Chaplain F. W. Taylor of the U.S. frigate Columbia, angrily denounced the proceedings in his popular travel memoirs:

> Behold then, citizens of the United States! Has it come to this, that the sealed protection of your country avails

---

[100]Reynolds, Voyage of the United States Frigate Potomac, 418.

[101]Yzendoorn, History of the Catholic Mission in the Hawaiian Islands, 44-75. Dr. William Ruschenberger, visiting the islands in 1836, was both convinced of missionary responsibility for expulsion of the priests and willing to condone the act as a wise policy. Ruschenberger, Voyage Round the World, 474.

you nothing? Behold the gathered band, who have left far
behind them privileges, and friends, and refinement, for a
life of benevolent action among a benighted people, who have
learned to appreciate their action, but are a small nation.
. . . Is this to be endured--this to be passed over? No!
there is not one of you, in whose bosom the pure blood of
American freemen courses, untainted in sentiment and alliance
with a foreign and popish hierarchy, but will kindle at the
insult, and ask due reparation for such measures in high disregard of the rights of American citizenship.[102]

In Hawaii the missionaries drew up a memorial to Congress, which a member

of the American Board, Peter D. Vroom, presented in May, 1840.[103]

This crisis only served to bind the mission closer to Hawaiian

state affairs, for William Richards of the Lahaina station, who had been

appointed interpreter and translator to the chiefs the year before, now

came out openly as their counselor.[104] Richards, whom the prudential

committee in Boston dismissed for the sake of appearances while regarding

him as "virtually connected with the mission and with us, though nomin-

ally separate", set about immediately to invigorate the native government,

helping to draft the first written constitution in 1840 and conducting

the first foreign negotiations of the island kingdom in Washington,

London and Paris.[105]

---

[102]F. W. Taylor, A Voyage Round the World, and Visits to Various Countries,
in the United States Frigate Columbia (9th ed., New York, 1850),II,260-261.

[103]The memorial, dated Honolulu, July 11, 1839, may be found in ABC:19.1,
VIII, no. 49. American Board, Thirty-second Annual Report (Boston, 1841),
151.

[104]William Richards to Anderson, Honolulu, August 29, 1839, ABC: 19.1,
IX, no. 86.

[105]Anderson to Richards, Boston, April 28, 1842, ABC:2.1.1, V, 95-96.
Samuel Williston has written a sketch of this missionary-statesman in his
"William Richards: The South Sea Solomon," New England Quarterly, X
(1937), 323-336, and more fully in William Richards (Cambridge, 1938).
Richards was the translator of the English edition of the 1840 constitu-
tion, a copy of which is preserved in the Harvard Law School Library, en-
titled Translation of the Constitution and Laws of the Hawaiian Islands,
Established in the Reign of Kamehameha III (Lahainaluna, 1842), and bearing on its flyleaf the inscription, "From His Majesty King of the Hawaiian
Islands to Harvard Law School."

Some British subjects in Hawaii believed that the growing success of the American mission constituted a real threat to England's Pacific interests. One of the most influential, Richard Charlton, who was consul from 1825 to 1842, constantly harassed the missionaries, supporting the competitive efforts of the French Catholics in the thirties and urging Westminster to more aggressive action in Pacific affairs.[106] Captain Edward Belcher, commander of a British warship, used force to liberate two Catholic priests seized by the chiefs, and heaped criticism upon the members of the American mission.[107] The activities of the Hudson's Bay Company, which had an agent in Honolulu by 1834, foreshadowed increasing English interest in Hawaii. Sir George Simpson himself appeared in Hawaii in 1842 and reported to the company's London office that the Calvinist mission could be considered a "political Engine in the hands of the Government of the United States."[108]

Great Britain, however, fearful of French designs, concentrated on insuring her rights by preserving Hawaiian independence rather than seeking to annex the archipelago. Simpson, in spite of his unfavorable impression of the American evangelists, played an important role in the appointment of William Richards as special envoy of the Hawaiian king and assisted him and his fellow ambassador, mission-educated Timoteo Haalilio, in securing recognition of the island kingdom's autonomy.in

[106]Bingham, Residence in the Sandwich Islands, 507-508; Jarves, History of the Hawaiian or Sandwich Islands, 268-269. Captain Thomas Ap Catesby Jones reported to Washington that Charlton tried to block Hawaiian acceptance of the commercial agreement he negotiated in 1826. J. I. Brookes, International Rivalry in the Pacific Islands 1800-1875 (Berkeley, 1941), 51.

[107]Edward Belcher, Narrative of a Voyage Round the World (London, 1843), I, 52-58.

[108]George Simpson to J. H. Pelly, Honolulu, March 10, 1842, in Joseph Shafer, ed., "Letters of Sir George Simpson, 1841-1843," American Historical Review, XIV (1900), 91.

1843 in London.[109] Shortly after the departure of these three men, a new crisis arose in Anglo-American relations in Hawaii. Charlton himself left the islands on a mysterious mission to England, leaving in his place as acting consul, the fur company governor's nephew, Alexander Simpson, who immediately used the prerogatives of his office to stir up trouble. In February, 1843, Lord George Paulet arrived in Honolulu Harbor on the warship Carysfort in response to the younger Simpson's urgent appeal in behalf of English rights in Hawaii. The demands of Paulet and Simpson proved so heavy that the Hawaiian king with the advice of Dr. Gerritt P. Judd, former medical missionary of the Board, made a provisional cession of the islands to Great Britain.[110]

Although the commander of England's Pacific fleet came on the scene and reversed his subordinate, and Westminster quickly disavowed Paulet's actions, the incident angered and surprised Americans.[111] The prudential committee of the Board, expressing astonishment that evangelical Britain could follow the example of papal France in the Pacific, deplored the event as unprovoked aggression.[112] England's joint declaration with France recognizing Hawaii's independence as a result of Richards's diplomatic mission to London and Paris in 1843 restored the confidence of the Board and its missionaries in Albion's good faith.[113]

---

[109]George Simpson, An Overland Journey Round the World, during the Years 1841 and 1842 (Philadelphia), II, 69. Simpson recognized the interest of both Britain and the United States in Hawaii, but commented severely upon the American missionaries. Ibid., I, 247-248; II, 33, 61.

[110]Bradley, American Frontier in Hawaii, 426-432.

[111]Herman Melville, however, who was present in Honolulu during the brief period of Paulet's rule, praised the British and accused the American public of misunderstanding the whole episode. Melville, Typee, 343-348.

[112]Missionary Herald, XXXIX (1843), 291-294; American Board, Thirty-fourth Annual Report (Boston, 1843), 159.

[113]See the letter of Richard Armstrong, Honolulu, August 1, 1843, Missionary Herald, LX (1844), 21-23.

Not until the sixties did the Calvinist missionaries' relations with the English suffer a second serious obstacle. In 1862 high-church Anglicans commenced a competing mission at Honolulu under Bishop Thomas N. Staley, and the Americans suspected that the Church of England was attempting to undermine the work of the New England Congregationalists at the islands.[114] In the same year Manley Hopkins published a book on Hawaii in London, endorsed by the Bishop of Oxford, which caricatured William Richards and criticized missionary "errors."[115] Anglo-American evangelical solidarity revealed itself, however, when William Ellis, secretary of the Nonconformist L.M.S. and an old friend of the Board, came vigorously to the Americans' support.[116]

Unlike the British government, France continued to pursue an aggressive colonial and commercial policy in the Pacific. English and American missionaries alike feared the advance of Gallic power, for it usually meant the introduction of a rival religion in islands already under Protestant tutelage. The French divided their attention almost equally in this period between the Marquesas and Tahiti, where the London Society was active, and the scene of the American Board's operations in Hawaii, the same naval commanders frequently appearing at each with exorbitant demands upon the native rulers for both trading and religious privileges. When Captain Abel du Petit Thouars, who had intervened in Honolulu earlier, annexed Tahiti and declared a protectorate over the

[114]Secretary Anderson of the Board gave a whole chapter to the development of the Anglican mission and its hostility to the American evangelists in his Hawaiian Islands, 331-359.

[115]Manley Hopkins, Hawaii: The Past, Present, and Future of its Island-Kingdom (London, 1862), 241-244; 384-393. In the second edition of his book, Hopkins in "the spirit of conciliation" withdrew some of his criticism, including the sketch of Richards. Ibid. (2nd ed., London, 1869), preface, IX.

[116]William Ellis, The American Mission in the Sandwich Islands; a Vindication and an Appeal (Honolulu, 1866).

Marquesas in 1842, the evangelical public in the United States and Great Britain protested loudly, and the prudential committee of the Board sent a strongly worded resolution to London in support of its sister organization.[117] The French still persisted in attempts to strengthen Catholic prestige at Hawaii, sending warships to Honolulu in 1842 and 1849.[118] The last of these occasions led directly to the naming of ex-missionary Dr. Judd and James J. Jarves as special envoys of the king abroad and to new treaties with both England and the United States which guaranteed Hawaiian independence.[119]

IV

In no part of the world did the American Board or its emissaries find it more difficult to resist the temptations of political action. In 1829 missionary efforts to remove the hostile United States commercial agent, John C. Jones, failed only for lack of a suitable candidate to replace him. The zealous Charles Stewart, who received a chaplain's commission in Washington at the time of these negotiations, declared just as he was preparing to depart for the Pacific on the Vincennes that he would try to secure evidence against Jones and, in any case, that he would inform that gentleman that unless "he does deport himself correctly he must and will be superceded."[120] The Hawaiian rulers joined the mission

---

[117]Missionary Herald, XXXIX (1843), 289-291.

[118]The French Catholic objective at this time was to secure certain privileges for the faith in the public-school system which the American missionaries had fathered. Missionary Herald, XXXIX (1843), 128-131. "What an exhibition have we," wrote one evangelist to Boston, "in all these transactions, of the true character of the church of Rome!" Letter of Richard Armstrong, Honolulu, September 23, 1842, ibid., 131.

[119]Kuykendall, Hawaiian Kingdom, 393-407. Brookes, International Rivalry in the Pacific Islands, 190-196.

[120]Stewart to Evarts, Norfolk, Va., February 6, 1829, ABC:19.1, III, no. 148.

in demanding the offending consul's removal, and in 1838 President Van Buren commissioned in his stead Peter A. Brinsmade, a New England merchant in the good graces of the Board.[121] That the prudential committee itself engaged in similar endeavors was revealed when Rufus Anderson recommended to an influential member of the A.B.C.F.M. in Washington that James J. Jarves--whose history of Hawaii delighted missionary supporters in Boston--be appointed United States commissioner in the islands.[122]

The fear of Roman Catholic advances under the aegis of France, which the L'Artémise affair in 1839 strengthed, stimulated unusual political efforts. Hiram Bingham, who left the islands in 1840 on account of health, interviewed President John Tyler and Secretary of State Daniel Webster on this subject in the summer of 1841. The latter appeared somewhat reluctant, according to the missionary, but promised to consider making a diplomatic protest to France over Captain Laplace's highhanded treatment of the Board's agents in Honolulu.[123] In Paris, the prudential committee's personal representative, Robert Baird, presented a memorial from the American Board to the French government.[124] The next year Richards and Haalilio appeared in Washington to negotiate a treaty between Hawaii and the United States.[125] Although Webster refused to commit the country to a written pact, he assured the envoys of the government's

[121]Kaahumanu to Martin Van Buren, Honolulu, January 12, 1839, ABC:19.1, VIII, no. 43.

[122]Anderson to T. S. Williams, Boston, January 2, 1843, ABC:1.1, XVII, 234-236.

[123]Bingham to Anderson, Washington, July 20, 1841, ABC:19.1, IX, no. 22.

[124]American Board, Thirty-second Annual Report, 151.

[125]The American Board kept in touch with Richards during this time, and Anderson sent him a copy of the House foreign relations committee report on China and the Sandwich Islands. Anderson to Williams, Boston, January 21, 1843, ABC:1.1, XVII, 235.

friendliness to the island kingdom and prepared Tyler's December, 1842, address to Congress which recognized Hawaiian independence. Whether or not Bingham's lobbying was effective in producing this strong expression of America's protective interest in the Hawaiian Islands, the Board was pleased with the result and printed large extracts from the presidential address in the Missionary Herald, as well as from ex-President Adams' report from the committee on foreign relations of the House of Representatives, which praised the mission for raising Hawaii to the level of a free and independent nation.[126]

In the meantime the agents of the A.B.C.F.M. in the islands had begun to enter the native government service. In 1838 the mission recognized the need of the Hawaiian rulers for political advice and asked Boston to send a layman to instruct the king and chiefs in "the science of christian government," but the Board declined. The Rev. William Richards, however, took the post himself after Lorrin Andrews, principal of the Lahainaluna Seminary, refused.[127] The prudential committee released Richards but urged him to continue his correspondence with the Boston office. In late summer of 1838 the new political adviser drew up a treaty between the United States and Hawaii and forwarded it to Attorney General Benjamin F. Butler enclosed in a letter to Rufus Anderson of the American Board in order, he wrote, to "prevent suspicion."[128] Nothing came of this premature effort, but Richards kept in touch with Anderson, who in 1842 advised strongly against the proposed embassy to the United States and Europe from fear that the former missionary's active role in

---

[126]Missionary Herald, XXXIX (1843), 90-92, 132. Adams's report was also reprinted in American Board, Forty-fourth Annual Report, 143-144, and Bingham, Residence in the Sandwich Islands, 588-589.

[127]American Board, Thirtieth Annual Report (Boston, 1839), 129.

[128]Anderson to Richards, Lahaina, August, 21, 1838, ABC: 19.1, IX, no. 84.

political affairs would not secure "a favorable public sentiment."[129]
In later years, after additional members of the mission had accepted
government positions, Gerrit P. Judd in 1842 and Lorrin Andrews in 1845,
the prudential committee grew regretful that the process had ever begun.
Anderson wrote the mission in 1846 that, while Richards's secular activities rendered him unfit for further service to the Board, he hoped that
divine Providence would direct the former evangelist to some course which
might relieve him from "the restless sea of political life."[130] Nevertheless, upon Richards's death a few years later the pastor of the Honolulu
church, Richard Armstrong, assumed the position of minister of public
education in the Hawaiian kingdom.

What most alarmed the Board was that white foreigners were taking into their hands complete control of the nation and thus destroying
the native government which decades of missionary labor had strengthened
and founded on Christian principles. This applied to both secular and
ecclesiastical life, for the Americans had as yet accorded little responsibility even to native pastors. "It certainly is incumbent on the mission," Anderson wrote, "to find, if possible, an immediate remedy for the
evil."

> The Hawaiian people are in danger of being excluded from all
> important offices, both in church and state. Foreigners are
> occupying all the offices about the king, and in the civil
> government, because they deem themselves more competent to
> fill the offices than the natives, and would fain believe that
> the natives are incompetent to fill them. . . . They cannot,
> indeed, perform the duties as well as foreigners, if the duties
> must be performed just as they are in foreign courts and govern-
> ments; but at the same time, it is better for the islanders,
> and it is essential to the continuance of their institutions as
> a nation, that the offices should be filled by natives. Better
> have the duties performed imperfectly, than not be done by them.

---

[129]Anderson to Richards, Boston, October 31, 1842, ABC:2.1.1, V, 249.

[130]Anderson to the Sandwich Islands Mission, Boston, April 10, 1846,
ABC:2.1.1, IX, 89.

I cannot help reasoning in a similar manner concerning the offices and duties of the native churches; and I feel bound to call your attention to the subject, because I believe that if the churches are officered by foreigners, the offices of the government will continue to have foreign occupants. Nothing will save the native government but a native ministry placed over the native churches.[131]

A year later Secretary Anderson continued his attack upon white supremacy in Hawaii: "What I fear is, that the foreign members of government will imperceptibly be so multiplied, that the young chiefs now in school, will never be able to rise to consideration and influence. As a missionary society, and as a mission, we cannot proceed on the assumption, however plausibly stated, that the Saxon is to supersede the native races."[132]

This was the key to much of the Board's policy in Hawaii at the middle of the century. On a few more occasions the prudential committee saw fit to intervene in behalf of its religious objectives there, writing to Ambassador George Bancroft in London in regard to Hawaiian attempts to secure a new treaty with England, and even asking Webster to send battleships, if necessary, to protect mission property from French aggression in 1851.[133] In 1849 the departing United States commissioner in Honolulu accused Secretary of State James Buchanan of attempting to advance "his own political interests with the American Board of Foreign Missions."[134] The A.B.C.F.M., however, had begun its withdrawal from Hawaiian affairs of both church and state.

The extraordinary success in evangelizing the islands created

[131]Anderson to the Sandwich Islands Mission, Boston, April 10, 1846, ABC:2.1.1, IX, 91-92.

[132]Anderson to S. L. Andrews, Boston, May 24, 1947, ABC:2.1.1, X, 78.

[133]Anderson to George Bancroft, Boston, March 6, 1849, ABC:2.1.1, XI, 152-153; Anderson to Webster, Boston, June 21, 1851, ABC:2.1.1, XV, 26-27; Webster to W. C. Rives, Washington, June 19, 1851, Foreign Relations of the United States, 1894. Appendix II. Hawaii (Washington, 1895), 97.

[134]A. Ten Eyck to James Buchanan, Honolulu, September 3, 1849, ibid., 71.

a difficult dilemma. The whole energy of the missionary enterprise had
been directed toward the Christian conquest of the world, but no one had
anticipated the time when the objective should have been attained in any
segment of the global effort. As early as 1839 the prudential committee
suggested the possibility of placing the Hawaiian churches on a self-
supporting basis, but this was motivated largely by a desire for economy.
In the forties, however, the Board foresaw the imminent destruction of
the mission in the increasing demand of the missionaries to return to the
United States for the sake of the education of their children. To meet
this emergency a whole new program was proposed in 1848, which provided
for the permanent residence of evangelists and their families as the
nucleus of a Christian community at the islands.[135] This decision reversed Anderson's position of only the year before, when he had advised
members of the mission not to think of themselves as settlers or colonists.[136] The missionaries responded favorably to the three main points
of the plan: (1) permission to become naturalized Hawaiian subjects;
(2) the right to purchase houses and lands presently occupied but owned
by the A.B.C.F.M.; (3) the outright grant of property to those who released themselves from the Board in order to seek local support.[137]

Members of the mission had earlier been allocated regular
salaries in place of the common-stock system originally employed, and
the superintendents who operated the Board's depository of supplies at
Honolulu turned this agency into a private business firm, Castle and

[135]"There will be an Anglo-Saxon community at the Islands," the prudential committee pointed out to the missionaries, "and it is doubtless a
part of your duty, as it is also your privilege, to see that it is a
religious community. American Board, Fortieth Annual Report, 195.

[136]Anderson to G. P. Judd (private), Boston, May 21, 1847, ABC:2.1.1,
X, 79.

[137]American Board, Fortieth Annual Report, 187-199.

Cook, one of the Big Five mercantile houses in Hawaii.[138] Although the prudential committee warned its agents against secular entanglements which might damage the mission's prestige, many of them began to invest in commercial enterprises, mostly in the years to come in sugar plantations. Others who had been printers or teachers took employment in those fields. It has often been remarked that the missionaries gave the islanders the Bible and took their land.[139] Except for the small tracts belonging to the Board which was divided among its agents relinquishing American support, the members of the mission received their land titles in the same way that other foreign residents did, by purchase from the Hawaiian government and individual owners. Their children, it is true, frequently came to occupy important positions in the management of plantations and in the commercial life of the archipelago. Others, however, left Hawaii for good, some following in their parents' footsteps and carrying the Gospel to other parts of the world. One of the most famous, General Samuel C. Armstrong, brought methods used in Hawaii's mission schools to the founding of Hampton Institute for freedmen after the Civil War.[140]

The Board solved the problem of the education of missionary children in the field by organizing in 1841 a separate school for them at Punahou, outside Honolulu. After the proposals of 1848 were accepted, it was determined to make this an institution of higher learning, and in 1853 Oahu College was chartered. The mission was now fully domesticated

[138]M. A. Richards, Amos Starr Cooke and Juliette Montagu Cooke: Their Autobiographies Gleaned from Their Journals and Letters (Honolulu, 1941),

[139]The whole question is dealt with fairly in H. B. Restarick, Hawaii 1778-1920 from the Standpoint of a Bishop (Honolulu, 1924), 107-115, and in Jean J. Hobbs, Hawaii: A Pageant of the Soil (Stanford, 1935), 83-101, 157-178.

[140]General Armstrong attributed his idea to the manual labor schools begun by missionaries in Hawaii in the little pamphlet, America. Richard Armstrong. Hawaii (Hampton, Va., 1887).

in the islands, its members permanently established on the soil and provided with the means of educating their posterity.[141]

    This process did not occur instantly. The Board continued to
support some evangelists completely and assisted others. The Hawaiian
Evangelical Association, formed by the island churches, co-operated with
the Boston society in commencing a new mission in the Micronesian Islands
in 1852 and later sent native Hawaiian missionaries to the Marquesas,
where the Americans had made an abortive beginning twenty years before.
These new ventures inspired the building of the Morning Star, financed
by the sale of ten-cent shares to children in the United States, which
carried the evangelists from island to island in the Central Pacific.[142]
In 1862 Rufus Anderson visited Hawaii to make final arrangements for the
transfer of the American Board's last responsibilities to the Hawaiian
Evangelical Association, an event which took place officially in 1863.[143]

    Meanwhile the continuing decline of the native population at
the islands raised fresh questions of Hawaii's destiny. As early as 1847
a member of the mission noted the "increasing class of the children of
foreigners by Hawaiian mothers." He reported them to be less religious
but more enterprising than the pure Polynesians, and predicted that they
would "succeed, or rather supersede, the aboriginal Hawaiian, though not
for a generation or two to come."[144] The prudential committee itself
reluctantly admitted in 1849 that in the future the Hawaiian race would
give way to a "mingled people, the descendents of Europeans."[145] But the

[141]Anderson, Hawaiian Islands, 202-206.

[142]J. S. Warren, The Morning Star: History of the Children's Missionary
Vessel, and of the Marquesas and Micronesian Missions (Boston, 1860).

[143]Anderson, Hawaiian Islands, 319-324.

[144]Letter of Artemas Bishop, Missionary Herald, XLIV (1848), 135.

[145]American Board, Fortieth Annual Report, 187.

Board was unwilling to hasten the process. It seemed to augur a peril
similar to that which had overcome its Indian missions in the United
States. Although the Cherokees and Choctaws had been Christianized, the
advance of white settlement brought demoralization, amalgamation, and
abridgment of Indian sovereignty. In Hawaii even the missionary policy
of vernacular education, which was directed toward the preservation of
the native tongue as essential to the survival of the nation, was lost
when the government legislated in favor of English-language instruction
in the schools in 1853 and 1854.[146]

In the fifties, moreover, Americans on the continent and in the
islands began agitation for annexation of the archipelago. Not only the
Democratic press and the secular expansionists, but some segments of the
evangelical community demanded the incorporation of Hawaii into the United
States as the final culmination of American commercial and missionary
enterprise in the Pacific. The Rev. Henry T. Cheever, popular religious
publicist of the time, spoke out boldly in the accents of Protestant
"manifest destiny" in 1851:

> Certain significant events of Providence, and the fact that
> the Hawaiian Islands are already a virtual colony of the
> United States, a missionary offshoot from the stock of New
> England, . . . give a strong probability to what might other-
> wise seem but a presumption, namely, that the lapse of a few
> years will find the Heart of the Pacific a twin heart with
> the great American Republic, organized under the same laws,
> and beating with the same Anglo-Saxon blood that shall ani-
> mate the united millions of all North America between the
> Atlantic and Pacific.[147]

The Board and most of the missionaries themselves dissented. In a letter
to his brother in 1853 William P. Alexander revealed the general attitude

---

[146]Kuykendall, Hawaiian Kingdom, 360-361.

[147]Cheever, Life in the Sandwich Islands, 340. As early as 1843 that
friend of the missionaries, James J. Jarves, termed it unwise to attempt
to preserve Hawaiian nationality and recommended that "the virtues,
language and knowledge, of the anglo-saxon race must be adopted."
Jarves, History of the Hawaiian Islands, 371-372.

toward the annexation for which Secretary of State William L. Marcy had

begun negotiations:

> Perhaps Hawaii may be the name of the 32nd star in our nation-
> al ensign. On some accounts I would like to have it so. We
> would then be out of the reach of the insults from the French.
> On the other hand, however, the native Hawaiian race would be
> trampled in the dust. Thus it has been with every tribe of
> Indians who have come in close contact with the whites. For
> the sake therefore of the aboriginal race, if we can be inde-
> pendent and enjoy peace, I wish not to be annexed and pray it
> may never be consumated.[148]

Although Hawaii remained an independent nation for the time

being, the mission was powerless to halt the process of native decline

and white supremacy. Whether the Board and its emissaries desired such

a consummation or not, the landing of Henry Obookiah and the subsequent

launching of New England's evangelical enterprise in Hawaii in 1819 had

wrought its effects in American-Pacific relations. Samuel Damon, seamen's

chaplain at Honolulu and intimate of the mission, declared in 1866 that

"the graves of the Puritan and polynesian will be side by side. It is

not possible to conceive of any social, political or religious revolution

which can separate them."[149] As for the American Board itself, great

satisfaction lay in the fact that its resources and its agents had brought

to birth a Christian nation out of heathen wastes. The secretary and

historian of the Board admitted in 1870: "The nation may, and probably

will, fade away. But the fact will remain concerning the success of the

gospel. It will be forever true, that the Sandwich Islands were Chris-

tianized by evangelical missionaries from the United States; and that,

---

[148]Quoted in Alexander, comp., William Patterson Alexander, 305-306.
Many evangelicals in America agreed with the Board. "The Islands may
be annexed; but with annexation comes ruin to all the labors of the
missionaries, and the extinction of the race," wrote a reviewer in the
New Englander, XIII (1855), 18.

[149]S. C. Damon, Puritan Mission in the Pacific: A Discourse Delivered
at Honolulu (Hiram Bingham, ed., New Haven, 1869), 34.

as a consequence of this, the people were recognized, by the leading
powers of Christendom, as entitled to the rank and privileges of a Christianized and civilized nation."[150]

---

[150]Anderson, A Heathen Nation Evangelized: History of the Sandwich
Islands Missions (Boston, 1870), 342.

CHAPTER V

THE GOSPEL IN THE NEAR AND MIDDLE EAST

After the customary religious celebrations at Old South and
Park Street Churches in Boston, the American Board's first envoys to
the Near East departed for Smyrna, Asia Minor, in November, 1819, just
a week and a half later than the embarkation of the maiden Sandwich Islands mission. Like their colleagues in the Pacific, these pioneers
followed a path of American commercial traffic that dated back to the
beginnings of the republic, for New England shippers did business with
Turkey under the protection of the English Levant Company long before the
Ottoman Porte recognized the United States as an independent nation.[1]
Even President Thomas Jefferson, whom the maritime gentry of Massachusetts
cordially hated, had sent the navy to deal with the piratical lords of
the Barbary States, and after the war with Algiers in 1815 an American
squadron regularly sailed the Mediterranean.[2]

I

Not mercantile, but characteristic theological factors aroused
the special interest of the New England religious community in the Levant.
The work of British groups for the conversion of Israel stimulated the
organization in 1816 of the Female Society of Boston and Its Vicinity for
Promoting Christianity among the Jews, a benevolent and pious sorority
which sent contributions to the London association of a similar name and

---

[1]Morison, "Forcing the Dardanelles in 1810," New England Quarterly, I
(1928), 208-225.

[2]C. O. Paullin, "Naval Administration under the Navy Commissioners,"
United States Naval Institute, Proceedings, XXXIII (1907), 624.

later assisted a Jewish school of the American Board in Bombay.[3] In millenarian thought the restoration of Israel was closely linked with the downfall of both Mohammedanism and the Vatican, identified respectively with the Biblical epithets, the "false prophet" and the "man of sin." Congregational ministers, like Isaac Knapp in Northampton in 1813, warned their listeners that the fifth vial (Rev. 16:10) was even then emptying and happily contemplated the early pouring out of the sixth and seventh, signaling the destruction of the religion of Mohammed and the overthrow of Antichrist.[4] Current events seemed to confirm this millennial prophecy, for not only did the Napoleonic struggle convulse Catholic Europe and reach into the Mediterranean, but also tumults within the Turkish empire showed evidence of the coming dissolution of Islam.[5]

The directors of the A.B.C.F.M. were also led to think of Western Asia as a mission field by their representatives in India and Ceylon. Only a few years before the arrival of the initial American company in Calcutta, a young chaplain of the East India Company, Henry Martyn, friend and co-worker of the celebrated Claudius Buchanan, had removed to Persia and earned martyrdom by dying in 1812 in Turkey.[6] His name was henceforward a symbol of Protestant evangelism on both sides of the Atlantic. Uncertain of their reception as American missionaries in British territory, Samuel Newell and Gordon Hall frequently recommended evangelistic efforts among the Persians and Arabians to the Board's prudential committee and even suggested the possibility of access to the

[3]Panoplist, XII (1816), 479; XIV (1818), 117.

[4]Isaac Knapp, The Zeal of Jehovah for the Kingdom of Christ (Northampton, 1812), 15.

[5]Griffin, Sermon in Sandwich, 25.

[6]Richter, A History of Protestant Missions in the Near East (New York, York, 1910), 93-94.

peoples of the Middle East by way of Russia.[7]

In October, 1818, the Board announced its intention of commencing a mission to Palestine—based in Jerusalem itself, if possible—and commissioned two young Vermonters, Levi Parsons and Pliny Fisk, both recent graduates of Andover, as its first evangelists in the eastern Mediterranean.[8] The religious public responded eagerly to the romantic prospect of establishing an American outpost in ancient Israel. In order to take full advantage of this enthusiasm the Board kept Parsons and Fisk traveling around the country a full year for the purpose of collecting funds and organizing "Palestine Societies" in support of the enterprise.[9] To American Protestants the Near East afforded a more particular interest than any other part of Asia, for it was there that were laid the familiar settings of Biblical history, lands "rendered almost sacred in the eyes of every Christian, by a thousand religious associations," as Fisk related in his farewell sermon in Boston in 1819.[10]

The Jews were the first objective of the mission. With the millennial hope of Israel's conversion in mind, the Board designated the City of David as the missionaries' ultimate designation, and evangelical Americans congratulated themselves that the United States, "the only Christian nation, which has never persecuted the descendents of Israel,"[11]

---

[7]Newell to Worcester, Colombo, Ceylon, December 20, 1813, American Board, Fifth Annual Report (Boston, 1814), 37-39; /Hall and Newell7, The Conversion of the World: or the Claims of Six Hundred Millions and the Ability and Duty of the Churches Respecting Them (Andover, 1818), 42-43.

[8]Panoplist, XV (1819), 92.

[9]In New York State a group of Indians gave Parsons $5.87 and sent a message to the Jews, "their forefathers in Jerusalem." D. O. Morton, Memoir of Rev. Levi Parsons, Late Missionary to Palestine (Pultney, Vt., 1824), 217.

[10]Pliny Fisk, The Holy Land an Interesting Field of Missionary Enterprise (Boston, 1819), 24.

[11]S. E. Dwight, "Address to the Palestine Society," in R. S. Storrs, A Sermon . . . at the Ordination of the Rev. Daniel Temple, and Rev. Isaac Bird (Boston, 1822), 44.

should have the honor of establishing the first permanent Protestant station in the Hebrew homeland. The restoration of the Jews, however, was not the only aim. Besides the Mohammedan Turks and Arabs, a multitude of other nationalities and religions dwelt in the Levant, including Greeks, Copts, Armenians, Maronites, and others of the so-called "Oriental Churches." Samuel Worcester's instructions to Parsons and Fisk as they set out for the Mediterranean indicated the far-reaching scope and nature of the mission:

> From the heights of the Holy Land, and from Zion, you will take an extended view of the widespread desolations and variegated scenes presenting themselves on every side to Christian sensibility; and will survey with earnest attention the various tribes and classes who dwell in that land, and in the surrounding countries. The two grand inquiries ever present to your minds will be, WHAT GOOD CAN BE DONE? and BY WHAT MEANS? What can be done for Jews? What for pagans? What for Mohammedans? What for those in Egypt, in Syria, in Persia, in Armenia, in other countries to which your inquiries may be extended?[12]

The two young men reached their destination in Asia Minor in January, 1820, going by way of Malta—held by Great Britain since 1800— where representatives of the English Bible and missionary societies in the Mediterranean gave them a hearty welcome and much advice.[13] At Smyrna they found a European community much like that at Bombay and Honolulu and made the acquaintance of the British consul, the chaplain of the Levant Company, and several friendly foreign merchants, including two members of the Perkins family of Massachusetts.[14] That part of the Ottoman domains

---

[12]Levi Parsons, The Dereliction and Restoration of the Jews (Boston, 1819), 47.

[13]William Jowett of the Church Missionary Society wrote for the Americans a long letter of suggestions. Missionary Herald, XVII (1821), 76-77.

[14]A loyalist member of the Perkins family removed to Smyrna after the Revolution and carried on a profitable trade in opium and figs with his relatives in Boston. Morison, Maritime History of Massachusetts, 181.

appeared free from religious and political restraints. "As to any moles-tation from government," the emissaries reported, "we feel almost as safe as we should in Boston."[15] Making that cosmopolitan port their head-quarters, they visited the sites of the Biblical "seven churches of Asia" and spent several months at Scio, an island off the Asian coast, where they studied Modern Greek, a language spoken by a large community in and near Smyrna. At the end of the year Parsons went on to Jerusalem alone, leaving his colleague behind to fill the temporarily vacant post of chaplain to the Levant Company.[16]

The first American pilgrim to the Holy City, Parsons wrote home detailed accounts of New Testament scenes which excited a great deal of attention in Boston, where a public meeting subscribed funds for a print-ing establishment in the Mediterranean.[17] In May, 1821, on his return from Jerusalem by sea, he also saw the new Greek flag, "black, with a white cross, the emblem of Christianity above the Turkish crescent," a portent of the future.[18] Unsettled conditions in Smyrna and its neighborhood created by the Hellenic revolt caused the Board to set up its press on the British-held island of Malta, where Daniel Temple of Massachusetts began printing tracts in Greek and Italian.[19] The death of Parsons in 1822 brought into the field Jonas King, whom Fisk invited to share the task of exploration. King, who held an appointment at Amherst College as professor of Oriental languages, had been attending the lectures of the celebrated Sylvestre de

[15]Pliny Fisk and Levi Parsons to Worcester, Smyrna, February 8, 1820, Missionary Herald, XVII (1821), 265.

[16]Tracy, History of the American Board, 101-102.

[17]American Board, Twelfth Annual Report, 96, and appendix, 200-204.

[18]Tracy, History of the American Board, 107.

[19]Ibid., 145.

Sacy in Paris, but gave up his Arabic studies to serve three years in the Near East, supported jointly by Protestant groups in France and the Netherlands and the American Board.[20] Fisk and King made an interesting tour up the Nile in Egypt, visiting the ancient temples and the recent excavations of European archaeologists, and traveled to Jerusalem through the desert by camel.[21]

The unstable situation in the Levant made permanent residence in any part of Palestine difficult. Unhealthful conditions took their toll also, and the pioneering Fisk himself died in 1825 while working on an Arabic and English dictionary.[22] On account of the supposedly hazardous nature of the work, the first evangelists in this region were all unmarried men. In 1823, however, the Board sent William Goodell and Isaac Bird with their wives to Beirut, Syria, where with King they established a mission in the midst of a polyglot population which included Arabic-speaking Maronites and Turkish-speaking Armenians, making a few converts among both of these groups. The most famous was Asaad el-Shidiak, whom the Maronite patriarch imprisoned and tortured for his alliance with the Protestant missionaries.[23] The infant mission in Syria suffered extraordinary difficulties during this period, as when a Greek fleet assaulted Beirut in 1826.[24] After the defeat of the Turks in the battle of Navarino the next year, some of the evangelists, fearing for their lives, called upon Captain John Downes of the American Mediterranean squadron for

[20]F. E. H. H/aines7, Jonas King: Missionary to Syria and Greece (New York, 1879), 65-74.

[21]Missionary Herald, XIX (1823), 343-350; XX (1824), 33-42.

[22]Tracy, History of the American Board, 164.

[23]In 1832 an English merchant obtained access to the convent where the imprisoned convert was held and discovered that he had died two years previously. J. Tod to Isaac Bird, June 26, 1832, Missionary Herald, XXIX (1833), 51-57.

[24]Ibid., XXII (1826), 354-359.

protection.[25] Jonas King had already returned to the United States after publishing his "Farewell Letter" explaining why he preferred Protestantism to Roman Catholicism.[26] In 1827 the remaining members of the mission took refuge on Malta, where with the aid of two friendly Armenian ecclesiastics whom they had attached to themselves in Beirut they continued their language studies, translated and printed tracts, and planned forays into the Mohammedan lands surrounding them.

In the same year the American Board broadened the designation of the Palestine mission to include all of the countries around the eastern Mediterranean under the rubric of "Western Asia."[27] The Jews were nearly forgotten in the tumultuous situation in which the Board's emissaries found themselves during those first years of the Hellenic revolt. Other inhabitants of the Near East, and particularly the Greeks themselves, seemed to offer a wider field for evangelism. As early as 1822 Fisk and Temple had sent two young refugees from Scio to the Cornwall Foreign Mission School in the United States.[28] When this type of training proved unsuitable, the prudential committee transferred the youths to private academies in New England, where others dispatched by the missionaries in Malta soon joined them.[29] Dozens of these Greek students came to American shores in the next several years, most of them finally graduating from either Amherst or Yale.[30] They excited an unusual interest

[25]American Board, Nineteenth Annual Report, 41-42.

[26]This influential letter was translated into many Oriental languages and was published in English in Jonas King's The Oriental Church and the Latin (New York, 1865), 5-33.

[27]American Board, Eighteenth Annual Report, 40.

[28]Missionary Herald, XIX (1823), 110-114.

[29]American Board, Seventeenth Annual Report, 98-99.

[30]Some assisted the American Board's missionaries in the Mediterranean upon their return home and one became United States consul at Athens. Others remained in America: Evangelinos Sophocles became a professor at

and elicited great compassion for their embattled fellow countrymen in Greece, while private individuals like Lydia Sigourney, the evangelical poet of Hartford, and organizations like the Palestine Society of Boston helped to underwrite their education.[31]

The growth of a popular movement in the United States in behalf of the rebelling Greeks reinforced the missionary sympathies of the Protestant community.[32] Edward Everett of Harvard, a leading "philhellene," who sounded the first appeal in the North American Review in December, 1823, demanded an extension of purely evangelistic assistance, but described the Greco-Turkish conflict in religious terms:

> America has done something for Greece. Our missionary societies have their envoys to the Grecian church, with supplies of bibles and religious tracts for their benighted flocks. But in the present state of this unhappy land, this is not the only succor they require. . . . We would respectfully suggest to the enlarged and pious mind of those, who direct the great work of missionary charity, that at this moment, the cause of the Grecian church, can in no way be so effectually served, as by contributions directed to the field of the great struggle. The war is emphatically a war of the crescent against the cross.[33]

Harvard and another, Photius Kavasales, who took the name of his benefactor, Fisk, was commissioned a chaplain in the United States Navy. Anderson, History of the Missions of the American Board of Commissioners for Foreign Mission to the Oriental Churches (Boston, 1872), 143; Pickering, Life of John Pickering, 326n. In 1829 the prudential committee successfully persuaded the United States Navy to give free passage home to two of these youths on board an American warship. Branch to Evarts, Washington, August 15, 1829, ABC:13, I, no. 2.

[31]G. S. Haight, Mrs. Sigourney: The Sweet Singer of Hartford (New Haven, 1930), 31-32; Daniel Thomas, A Sermon . . . before the Palestine Missionary Society (Boston, 1824), 22-24. Jonas King sent the last four Greek youths to the United States in 1835, when the Board called a halt to the process. Tracy, History of the American Board, 309.

[32]For the first phase of this movement, see M. A. Cline, The American Attitude toward the Greek War of Independence, 1821-1828 (Atlanta, 1930), 19-76, and E. M. Earle, "American Interest in the Greek Cause," American Historical Review, XXXIII (1927), 44-63.

[33]North American Review, XVII (1823), 420.

From evangelical quarters came new pleas for Greece. An appeal
signed by students in Andover Theological Seminary appeared in a New York
newspaper in the same month as Everett's article, linking the claims of
Hellas to both the classical and Biblical heritage of educated Americans.[34]
In April, 1824, Sereno Edwards Dwight of Park Street Church in Boston
joined the campaign in a sermon in which he described a vision of gospel
triumphs all through the Levant arising from the revolution. "How delightful," he said, "to overspread Greece with bibles, and to furnish her
with the chosen heralds of salvation.

> The downfal /sic/ of Turkey will remove that impassable
> barrier which has hitherto shut out christianity from Western
> Asia. The christian nations already there will open their
> eyes, at once, on the light of the Sun of righteousness.
> Missionaries loaded with bibles will feel their way into the
> farthest retreats of Mohammedan darkness.[35]

The victims of Turkish oppression in Greece called forth not
only relief vessels and the personal services of adventuresome Americans
like Samuel Gridley Howe, but also the special efforts of the religious
community. In 1827 a group of women in New York City, hoping to combine
spiritual with material aid to the suffering Hellenes, dispatched a food
ship to Greece in charge of Jonas King, newly returned from the Levant,
who resigned his position at Amherst and refused a similar offer from
Yale in order to become the New York Ladies' Greek Committee's missionary
agent.[36] Josiah Brewer, formerly the Board's emissary in Smyrna who had
visited the Aegean islands in 1827, accepted the commission of a similar
organization in New Haven to establish educational institutions for the

---

[34]Reprinted from the New York Commercial Advertiser in the evangelical
New York Observer, January 3, 1824.

[35]S. E. Dwight, The Greek Revolution. An Address Delivered in Park
Street Church (Boston, 1824), 27.

[36]H/aines/, Jonas King, 210-213.

Greeks in order to secure their "intellectual and spiritual, as well as political emancipation."[37]   Brewer, whose missionary career was a varied and colorful one, opened schools in Scio and Smyrna, where he represented American Protestantism for several years, both in the European community and on board the United States merchant ships which touched that point.[38]

Meanwhile the Board's missionaries were shut up in Malta with no very definite prospects of an opening for their labors. To clarify the situation the prudential committee sent Rufus Anderson on a special agency to the Mediterranean with directions to confer with the stranded evangelists at Malta and make an exploratory tour of the liberated parts of Greece.[39] His instructions contained a number of inquiries regarding the moral and religious condition of the country which revealed a curious probing by the American evangelical mind into the lives of a Christian people so recently emancipated from centuries of infidel rule:

> What is the state of morals among the people? How far truth and integrity prevail? What is the state of things, in regard to industry, temperance, chastity? How the female sex is treated? What is the state of morals among women? Whether the people are desirous of having their daughters well educated?
>
> How far there is a distinction of ranks among the people? What are the claims of birth? What the influence of wealth? . . . How far there is such a thing as political integrity among leaders? How far there is such a thing as moral integrity among eminent merchants? What is thought by the people of such vices as lying, cheating, lewdness, and drunkenness?[40]

Accompanied by Eli Smith from Malta and an American Episcopalian

---

[37]New Haven Ladies' Greek Association, First Annual Report (New Haven, 1831, 5-7.

[38]Brewer, who later returned to the United States after serving several societies as their agent in the Mediterranean for a number of years, was a significant American figure in the Near East during this time. See P. E. Shaw, American Contacts with the Eastern Churches, 1820-1870 (Chicago, 1927), 109-117.

[39]Missionary Herald, XXIV (1828), 394-396.

[40]Evarts to Anderson, Boston, November 24, 1828, ABC:8.1, I, no.1.

missionary, Anderson traveled through the Ionian Islands and the Peloponnesus and conferred with the American, Jonas King, and Count Capo d'Istria, newly chosen president of Greece. The latter agreed readily to the Board's proposal to supply much-needed textbooks for Greek schools from its Malta printing press and approved the use of the Bible in the Lancastrian classrooms arising all over the country under government and missionary encouragement.[41]

Out of Anderson's agency came a number of decisions: (1) as soon as practicable the missionaries on Malta were to seek access once more to the disturbed eastern Mediterranean world, in Greece, Syria, and elsewhere; (2) further explorations were necessary to find suitable mission fields, in pursuance of which Isaac Bird visited parts of the Barbary States in 1829;[42] (3) the immediate policy of Mediterranean missions was to stress "conversational" rather than formal preaching, the extensive employment of educational techniques, and cautious advances to the Greek and other "nominally" Christian communions of the Orient rather than a direct approach to Mohammedanism.[43] This first phase of the American Board's enterprise in the Near East, then, ended with large preparations for a broader attach upon the nonevangelical inhabitants of the eastern shores of the Mediterranean Sea. The close of the Greek war of liberation in 1830 made possible the commencement of these ventures.

---

[41]Capo d'Istria would have preferred the Board's assistance in the form of a loan, but the prudential committee rejected this proposal in favor of a policy of the outright gift of textbooks. Missionary Herald, XXVI (1830, 41-42; Anderson, Observations upon the Peloponnesus and the Greek Islands (Boston, 1830), 218-219.

[42]Missionary Herald, XXVI (1830), 207.

[43]Anderson, The Peloponnesus and Greek Islands, 317-321. Perhaps the best illustration of the Board's educational policy at this time is contained in the prudential committee's instructions of 1832 advising missionaries in the Near East to surround themselves with Lancastrian schools furnished with competent teachers and vernacular textbooks of an evangelical character. American Board, Twenty-third Annual Report, 153.

II

In the thirties the Board began reoccupation of the field. In Greece Jonas King re-entered its service and established two schools in Athens, where he purchased a site a few months before the final evacuation of the city by the Turks.[44] Although Secretary Anderson felt that by 1830 public opinion had "a good deal stagnated in respect of Greece,"[45] others came to the aid of the veteran King from America. Nathan Benjamin and the scholarly Elias Riggs assisted him at Athens and then opened a school in Argos; two Virginians, Samuel Houston and George Leyburn, established themselves at Scio and then, upon the invitation of the celebrated revolutionary patriot, Petros Mavromichalis, settled in Sparta.[46] In 1830 work in Syria was resumed by Isaac Bird and George B. Whiting, who were later joined by William M. Thomson, Eli Smith, and others. Civil disturbances in Palestine forced the missionaries to remain close to Beirut a large part of the time; nevertheless, they made several attempts to maintain a station in Jerusalem for its symbolic value if nothing more. Local rebellions and the pillaging of fellahin combined with the unhealthful sanitary conditions--the first medical evangelist to the Near East, Dr. Asa Dodge, died shortly after returning from Jerusalem to Beirut in 1835[47]--to defeat all efforts to establish a permanent settlement in the Holy City.

In 1830 Eli Smith and Harrison Grey Otis Dwight undertook an

[44]King, however, was disappointed in his project of an evangelical Greek university planned in New York before his recent agency to Greece. When the provisional government removed to Athens an official state university was established in the place of King's. H/aines_7, Jonas King, 260-261.

[45]Anderson to King, Boston, October 8, 1830, ABC:2.01, I, 260.

[46]Tracy, History of the American Board, 325, 341.

[47]Ibid., 311.

ambitious exploring tour into the interior of Asia Minor and as far as
northern Persia and Russian Georgia, with instructions from the prudential
committee to secure information about the various Christian subject-races
of Turkey and the Armenians in particular, to whom Parsons and Fisk had
recommended a mission during their early sojourn in Palestine.[48] As early
as 1826 King had visited Constantinople at the time of the downfall of
the Janizaries and witnessed the bloody repercussions of that event;[49]
the next year Josiah Brewer studied the city as a possible center for
Jewish missions and published an interesting account of his stay there.[50]
Smith and Dwight suggested that the Board commence stations in Smyrna and
Constantinople, in the latter of which William Goodell, formerly at Beirut
and Malta, took residence with his wife in 1831. When their rented house
in a city suburb burned to the ground shortly afterwards, destroying all
their family possessions, American merchants and shipmasters in Smyrna
showed their interest in the evangelical cause by contributing money and
clothing.[51] From the outset the Goodells enjoyed the friendly relations
of their fellow countrymen at the Sublime Porte. They resided briefly in
a large palace on the Bosphorus with a United States medical commissioner
sent to Turkey to study the Asiatic cholera, a New Yorker employed by the
sultan to supervise naval construction, and Charles Rhind, who had just

[48]Missionary Herald, XVIII (1822), 45; XXVI (1830), 75; Eli Smith, Researches of the Rev. E. Smith and Rev. H. G. O. Dwight in Armenia (Boston, 1833), I, Preface, v.

[49]Letter of King, Constantinople, June 23, 1826, Missionary Herald, XXII (1826), 359.

[50]Josiah Brewer, A Residence in Constantinople in the Year 1827 (New Haven, 1830). George Jones, an American schoolmaster in the United States Navy accompanied Brewer on a tour of Constantinople at this time and described the episode in his Sketches of Naval Life, with Notices of Men, Manners and Scenery, on the Shores of the Mediterranean (New York, 1829), II, 69-172.

[51]E. D. G. Prime, Forty Years in the Turkish Empire; or, Memoirs of the Rev. William Goodell (New York, 1875), 119-120.

negotiated the first American treaty with the Ottoman Empire.[52] Moreover, during the winter of 1831-1832 the newly appointed charge d'affairs, Commodore David Porter, put up the missionary family in his own home while Goodell assisted in the legation by copying dispatches to Washington.[53] In 1833 Daniel Temple and a printer brought the press from Malta to Smyrna where the Board established a second station in Turkey.[54]

An even more distant mission resulted from Smith and Dwight's travels in the heart of the Middle East. Their instructions included a brief notice of the Nestorian Christians living on the borders of Turkey and Iran, members of a sect famous in early church history but almost forgotten in the West in the nineteenth century.[55] Having reached Erzurum just as the Russian army was withdrawing into Georgia after an expedition against the Turks and Persians, the two missionaries crossed the border into Transcaucasia where they visited Tiflis and the German evangelical colonies in Georgia before going on into the Persian province of Azerbaijan.[56] A few weeks spent in Urumiah, an Iranian town with a large Nestorian population, convinced them that the Board should commence a

---

[52] /J. E. DeKay/, Sketches of Turkey in 1831 and 1832 (New York, 1833), 93; Prime, Memoirs of William Goodell, 121. The eccentric Rhind had assisted Smith and Dwight on their way through Constantinople to Armenia in 1830, procuring the necessary documents for travel, securing rooms for them in advance of their arrival, and permitting them to preach at his residence on Sundays. Eli Smith and H. G. O. Dwight to Evarts, Constantinople, May 15, 1830, ABC:16.9, I, no. 56; Smith, Researches in Armenia, I, 71.

[53] Goodell to Anderson, Constantinople, October 1, 1832, ABC:16.9, I, no. 149; Missionary Herald, XXVIII (1832), 246.

[54] Tracy, History of the American Board, 277.

[55] Secretary Anderson had included inquiries about the Nestorians in the instructions as a result of the casual reading of a brief account of them from the pen of an English chaplain at Constantinople. Missionary Herald, XXII (1826), 120-121; XXVI (1830), 75-76.

[56] Smith, Researches in Armenia, I, 224-278.

mission to that interesting Oriental communion.[57]

The prudential committee acted quickly upon their recommendation by sending Justin Perkins, a young tutor in Amherst College, as the first American missionary to Persia in 1833. His instructions stressed the importance of this region as a link between the Near and Far East—the Nestorians themselves being chiefly celebrated for their former missionary endeavors in India and China—and pointed out the significance for the eventual conversion of Islam of the occupation of the Turkish-Persian frontier, which served also as a dividing line between the two great Moslem sects, the Shiah and the Sunnah.[58] Perkins and his wife—"lonely, inexperienced adventurers," as the missionary noted in his journal[59]—made the long and arduous trip from Constantinople to the Black Sea port of Trebizond by English schooner and thence, where no American but Smith and Dwight had ever traveled before, to Persia overland through part of Russian Georgia and the mountains of eastern Turkey.[60] In the meantime the Board had dispatched a second representative to Iran, James L. Merrick, with directions to assess the possibilities of Mohammedan evangelism. Though unable to pursue the course suggested by the prudential committee of passing through the Middle East and crossing the Himalayas into India,[61] he visited Teheran, Isfahan, and Shiraz before

[57]Smith, Researches in Armenia, II, 263-265.

[58]Justin Perkins, A Residence of Eight Years in Persia, among the Nestorian Christians (Andover, 1843), 28-31.

[59]Ibid., 81.

[60]Perkins's experiences with the Russians on the Georgian frontier were less happy than those of Smith and Dwight and led him to make harsh observations on Holy Russia as an obstacle to the evangelization of the world. Ibid., 123-138.

[61]Missionary Herald, XXX (1834), 402-405. The Board's missionaries in Canton watched the progress of Middle Eastern evangelism in the belief that that region would provide access to central Asia. Chinese Repository, V (1837), 536-537.

settling at Tabriz in Azerbaijan, where he began his Moslem studies in
preparation for the evangelization of Islam.[62]

Although Merrick remained in Tabriz five years, he made no converts and the Board transferred him to the Nestorian mission, giving up
its efforts to evangelize the Moslems.[63] In both the Near and Middle
East missionaries had the greatest success among neither pagans nor infidels, but in the ancient Oriental Churches, which by evangelical Protestant standards had fallen to a low estate. The millennial notion that
Islam was decadent and nearing destruction slowly disappeared. Merrick
himself ridiculed "the general impression in Europe and America respecting
Mohammedanism . . . that it is such a flimsy, frost-work structure, that
a few rays of science, a smattering of literature, or a modicum of the
arts would annihilate it at once." His own studies led him to appreciate
the religion of the Koran as "in every joint and angle a master-piece of
skill and power."[64] The missionaries turned exclusively to non-Mohammedan
groups not because of their religious or moral superiority to the followers
of the Prophet, but in order to raise up the low level of their religion
and morality as an example to the infidels who surrounded and despised
them. Indeed, one of the Americans admitted that the Moslem Osmanlis
"in some respects exhibit better traits of character, than do the various
sects of nominal Christians."[65]

---

[62]Extracts from letters describing Merrick's Persian journeys were
printed in the Missionary Herald, XXXIII (1837), 61-66; XXXIV (1838), 63-66.

[63]American Board, Thirty-second Annual Report, 116. Merrick, however,
was interested only in Islam and returned to the United States where he
engaged in a long controversy with the Board over the transfer. J. L.
Merrick, An Appeal to the American Board of Commissioners for Foreign
Missions (Springfield, Mass., 1847).

[64]Letter of J. L. Merrick, Urumiah, June 19, 1837, Missionary Herald,
XXXIV (1838), 64.

[65]Goodell to Evarts, Beirut, September 15, 1826, ABC:16.5, I, no. 130.

Much of the energies of the Board's agents was directed to the
Greeks, not only in their liberated homeland but also scattered through
the Ottoman Empire, the largest communities of them being found in cities
like Constantinople and Smyrna. In 1834 two evangelists toured the island
of Cyprus and established schools for the Greek settlements there.[66] The
religious jealousies of the Orthodox clergy confined the mission's work
largely to the educational sphere. From the press at Malta and later in
Athens itself poured forth a stream of American textbooks for the schools
of Greece and Asia Minor, translated editions of Peter Parley's geographies
and histories and pious tracts like the popular "Dairyman's Daughter."[67]
In 1833 Jonas King urgently requested several copies of Webster's spelling
book,which he had used as a boy in New England.[68]

In Syria, however, the missionaries worked chiefly through the
medium of the Arabic language. Eli Smith took charge of a printing establishment in Beirut in 1834 and created a whole new typography more acceptable to Arabic taste than previous examples. The Board's lay printer in
Smyrna cut the punches, and a German firm in Leipzig cast the type under
Smith's personal direction.[69] An important element in the Syrian population was the large group of Maronite Christians, one of the Oriental
Churches in communion with Rome. In spite of intense opposition from the
patriarch and other ecclesiastics, the Board's agents organized a few
schools and churches in Beirut and in the mountainous region of Lebanon.

[66]Missionary Herald, XXXI (1835), 398-408, 446-452.

[67]Ralph Waldo Emerson found this tract particularly amusing in its
Hellenic dress when he visited the mission press in Malta in the early
thirties. R. W. Emerson, Journals (Boston, 1909), III (February 17, 1833),
33.

[68]King to Anderson, Athens, November 15, 1833, ABC:17.1, I, no. 73.

[69]American Board, Thirtieth Annual Report, 81. This typography, closely
modeled on the classical calligraphy, remained for years a standard form
of Arabic printing. S. B. L. Penrose, Jr., and C. J. Caldwell, "Ties that
Bind," in A. E. Christy, ed., The Asian Legacy and American Life (New York
1945), 121.

In the latter place they discovered the Druses, a wild, warlike people half pagan and half Mohammedanized, who began to respond in unusual numbers to Protestant teaching. Although the mission suspected that their motives were largely political in nature, since they obviously hoped to escape the harsh control and the military service of their Turkish rulers, several families presented themselves for baptism in the late thirties.[70] With stations begun in a few villages in the mountains, and later in Aleppo, Sidon, Damascus, and Tripoli, the missionaries ignored racial and religious backgrounds in their extremely heterogeneous field and gathered together into the same churches Greeks, Armenians, Maronites, and Druses.

But the Armenians of Turkey proved the most susceptible of the Board's subjects in the Mediterranean. King's "Farewell Letter," translated by a friendly bishop, had preceded the evangelists to Constantinople, where a group of Armenians under the leadership of a famous teacher, Peshtimaljian, had organized a seminary for the purpose of effecting evangelical reforms in the Gregorian Church.[71] From this school came the mission's earliest collaborators, including Hohannes and Senekerim, both of whom later came to the United States for additional education.[72] Despite the severe opposition of the Gregorian patriarch the mission attracted large numbers of Armenians, both priests and laymen. Such success encouraged the Board to send many additional reinforcements, who soon staffed new stations in other parts of Turkey: at Brusa, across the Sea of Marmora from Constantinople, in the east at Trebizond on the Black Sea and in Erzurum, and to the south at Aintab, which formed a link with

---

[70] *Missionary Herald*, XXXV (1839), 373-382.

[71] H. G. O. Dwight, *Christianity Revived in the East; or, a Narrative of the Work of God among the Armenians of Turkey* (New York, 1850), 10-18.

[72] Anderson, *History of Missions to the Oriental Churches*, I, 132; Tracy, *History of the American Board*, 342.

the Syria mission by way of its station at Aleppo. In each of these
cities and at smaller villages in between, the missionaries found Armenians willing to listen to Protestant preaching, sometimes at severe risk
of persecution, as at the hands of the bishop of Erzurum in the interior
of Anatolia.[73]

In Urumiah, Persia, the American Board's emissaries found a
group of Oriental Christians even more eager for evangelical assistance.
Unlike the Armenian high ecclesiastics, the Nestorian bishops welcomed
the Board's ministrations. One of them, the colorful Mar Yohannan, became a particular friend of the mission and accompanied Justin Perkins
on a triumphal tour of the churches of the United States in 1842.[74] Since
a majority of the Nestorian population lived to the west of Lake Urumiah,
in mountainous Kurdistan on the eastern border of Turkey, the mission
determined upon measures to reach this isolated field also. Though the
region lay within the jurisdiction of the Ottoman sultan, the fierce
Kurdish tribesmen and their Nestorian vassals maintained an independent
existence in the mountain fastnesses under conditions of dire poverty and
almost constant warfare. Dr. Asahel Grant, who had joined Perkins at
Urumiah, entered Kurdistan from the Turkish side in 1839 after a dangerous
journey through Mesopotamia disguised in Oriental garb and was enthusiastically received by the patriarch, Mar Shimon.[75] The American physician
made several subsequent visits to the mountainous region, becoming well
acquainted with both its Christian and Kurdish inhabitants, and published
a curious volume proving that the Nestorians were the lost ten tribes of

[73]Dwight, Christianity Revived in the East, 162-166.

[74]Perkins, Residence in Persia, 462-468, 492.

[75]Anderson, History of Missions to the Oriental Churches, I, 190-195.

Israel.[76]

In order to prosecute its work among the mountain dwellers of Kurdistan, the Board commenced a station at Mosul in Mesopotamia. Civil disturbances and Asiatic diseases aborted this endeavor, however, and three men, two wives, and two children perished in the first few years.[77] Their residence there, however, near the ruins of ancient Nineveh at the heart of the old Assyrian empire, raised an interest in another Oriental Christian communion, the Syrian Jacobites dwelling between the Tigris and Euphrates Rivers in modern Iraq. Perkins and William Stocking of the Urumiah mission made a reconnaissance of the area in 1849, and the prudential committee ordered the resumption of work in Mosul, sending Dwight W. Marsh from Boston and detaching William F. Williams from the Syria mission.[78] In 1851 Leonard Bacon, a widely known Congregational pastor of New Haven, who was traveling in the East with his son, accompanied Marsh to Mosul and surveyed the Mesopotamian field for the Board, which accepted his recommendation that a separate "Assyrian" mission be conducted there.[79]

The original "mission to Palestine" begun by Parsons and Fisk in 1819 had developed into a series of wide evangelistic operations in both the Near and Middle East. Working mainly among "nominal" Christians rather than pagans, the efforts of the Board's agents were more educational than pastoral, aiming at introducing evangelical concepts into the

---

[76]Asahel Grant, The Nestorians; or the Lost Tribes (New York, 1841). These views received a serious hearing in both Europe and America but were quickly disproved by other scholars. Cf. G. P. Badger, The Nestorians and Their Rituals (London, 1852), I, 185, 283, 287-288, and American Biblical Repository, VI (1841), 454-482; VII (1842), 26-68.

[77]C. H. Wheeler, Ten Years on the Euphrates (Boston, 1868), 29-30.

[78]Missionary Herald, XLVI (1850), 53-61, 83-97; American Board, Forty-first Annual Report (Boston, 1850), 110.

[79]American Board, Forty-second Annual Report (Boston, 1851), 82-84.

ancient churches of the Orient by means of schools, tracts, and the translation of the Bible into the vernacular languages. Missionaries at almost
every station labored at the task of rendering the Scriptures into Turkish,
Armenian, Modern Syriac, Arabic, Modern Greek, and even into the Spanish
and German variants of the Hebrew.[80] In a region where printing was all
but unknown, the American Board set up presses in strategic spots, even
transporting a specially assembled one in sections across the mountains
of Kurdistan into Persia in 1840.[81] Lancastrian schools arose everywhere
at the touch of the missionaries, Goodell even helping the Turks organize
several in army barracks near Constantinople.[82] Concerned for female
education in a land where the feminine half of the population had few
advantages, young unmarried women like Mary Lyon's Mount Holyoke protégée,
Fidelia Fisk,[83] opened girls' boarding schools in Persia, Syria, and
Turkey. The most important academy for boys was probably Babek Seminary,
founded by Cyrus Hamlin in 1840 at a beautiful site on the European side
of the Bosphorus.[84]

In 1844 Rufus Anderson visited the Levant on a second tour of

---

[80]This last was the work of German-born but Andover-trained William G.
Schauffler, who arrived in Constantinople in 1832 with a commission from
both the American Board and the Boston Female Society for Promoting
Christianity among the Jews. His lack of success in converting the
children of Abraham, as well as that of several other agents of the
Board who later worked among Jewish communities in Smyrna and Salonika,
led the prudential committee to halt that department of labor and transfer Schauffler to Mohammedan evangelism at the Turkish capital in 1856,
in a belated second effort to reach Islam directly. Anderson, History
of Missions to the Oriental Churches, II, 150-173.

[81]Ibid., I, 195.

[82]Prime, Forty Years in the Turkish Empire, 114, 164-165. The American
writer and traveler, N. P. Willis, visited one of these schools in the
company of Goodell and Dwight. N. P. Willis, Pencillings by the Way
(2nd ed., London, 1839), 277.

[83]Miss Fisk opened a Persian "Mount Holyoke" in Urumiah in 1843. /Thomas
Laurie_7, Woman and Her Saviour in Persia (Boston, 1863), 57-59.

[84]Anderson, History of Missions to the Oriental Churches, I, 122-123.

inspection. Entrenchment seemed necessary in view of the scattered efforts of the Board around the eastern shores of the Mediterranean and in the Middle East. Although Jonas King remained in Athens along with representatives of American Baptist and Episcopal mission boards, the prudential committee decided to close out its work in Greece and among the inhabitants of that nationality in Turkey. To Americans who had responded so eagerly two decades before to Hellenic pleas for assistance, the decision was a difficult one. Anderson himself reported that:

> I have sought earnestly . . . to find reasons for continuing the Greek mission. To turn away after having labored so long and done so much, has seemed like declaring a degree of reprobation. How can we shake off the dust of our feet against a whole nation! But we are not to close our eyes against facts and experience—against clear and providential indication.[85]

At the same time the Board surrendered its Jerusalem station, leaving as the only monument to twenty years of intermittent efforts in the city a Protestant burying ground.[86] The evangelical outlook upon the "lands of the Bible" had changed considerably under the pressure of missionary experience. Little was now heard of the restoration of Israel, and it was not to evangelize the Jews that American Protestants sent emissaries to the Mediterranean, but to assist to an evangelical rebirth communities of Armenians and Nestorians whom the religious public at home had hardly heard of at the beginning of the enterprise.

III

In a region where the inhabitants were acquainted with Europeans by a long association dating back at least to the time of the Crusades, the American missionaries found themselves the objects of a peculiar interest as representatives of the nearly unknown New World. A few commercial

---

[85]Anderson, <u>Report to the Prudential Committee of a Visit to the Missions in the Levant</u> (Boston, 1844), 7.

[86]Anderson, <u>History of Missions to the Oriental Churches</u>, I, 34-39.

products had entered even before them, as Smith and Dwight discovered when they stumbled upon a hogshead of New England rum in far-off Tiflis, Georgia.[87] Dr. James DeKay in Constantinople reported that in a single six-month period twelve million gallons of that beverage had been shipped from the United States to Turkey, where, he wrote, "'Boston particular' is much relished, notwithstanding the praiseworthy efforts of our pious and zealous missionaries."[88] The members of the Board's mission in Constantinople noted the fascination the American label had for Levantines in their journal:

> It is amusing to see how our country, on account of its being the New World, its distance from Turkey, and the general ignorance prevailing in respect to it, has the honor of giving name to whatever is curious, or particularly good. During the late festivities, the water-carriers would cry out among the people, "American water!" meaning good fresh water. The seller of cakes would call out as a wonderful recommendation, "Made of American butter!" while a man who kept an ostrich for shew, stood at the door of his stall, calling out from morning till night, "An American bird!" Even on ordinary occasions, the Jew is met at the corners of the streets, calling out at the top of his voice, "American cotton!" And it is a singular coincidence, that the American built frigate is now the flag-ship of the capudan pasha.[89]

Dwight commented in his history of the Armenian work how inquirers in Turkey commonly were more curious at first about "the manners and customs of the people in America" than matters "relating directly to the salvation of the soul."[90] In general, the fact that they came from the romantic Western Hemisphere gave the missionaries an initial opening wedge in the Levant.

During the thirties, however, the presence of the Protestant interlopers provoked an active reaction. This was especially violent

---

[87]Smith, Researches in Armenia, I, 215-216.

[88]/DeKay7, Sketches of Turkey, 185-186.

[89]Missionary Herald, XXXIII (1837), 156.

[90]Dwight, Christianity Revived in the East, 29-30.

in Greece, where the Board's agents were on the ground early and enjoyed close relations with the first government of the republic.[91] After the assassination of Capo d'Istria in 1831 and the naming of a Bavarian prince as king, the Greeks grew increasingly nationalistic. In Scio, for example, Houston encountered the suspicion that his "object was to train up their children for American soldiers."[92] In the year 1836 there was a great outcry against the "Americans," as all missionaries and Bible society agents came to be called, regardless of nationality. Mobs rioted in front of the mission school in Syra formerly operated by the Board but at that time under the direction of British emissaries. A letter published in Paris and widely circulated in Greece accused the evangelists of sealing children on the forehead to make them "Americans."[93] Similar excitement prevailed in Athens, King reporting that many feared the Greeks would all become "Presbyterians."[94] Even in Asia Minor where the Board's emissaries worked among the large Greek communities, Orthodox ecclesiastics forced the closing of mission schools.[95]

In the next decade further religious and political agitation in Greece made the position of the Board's emissaries extremely uncomfortable. King's bold stand for evangelical doctrines in Athens made him a special

---

[91]Anderson, however, warned in 1830 that "we should have no connection with the government in any of our proceedings, though we should aid them whenever we can thereby promote the great interests of Greece. We have no political, no sectarian, no party aims." Anderson to King, Boston, December 31, 1830, ABC:2.01, I, 270.

[92]Letter of S. R. Houston, Scio, August 24, 1835, Missionary Herald, XXXII (1836), 100.

[93]J. Wenger to King, Syra, May 2, 1836, ABC:17.1, I, no. 139; Missionary Herald, XXXII (1836), 422-424; Tracy, History of the American Board, 324.

[94]King to Anderson, Athens, August 16, 1836, ABC:17.1, I, no. 138.

[95]Letter of Daniel Temple, Smyrna, September 5, 1836, Missionary Herald, XXXIII (1837), 150-151.

target of Orthodox venom, assailed by the clergy, partisan associations, and the press. Though often a victim of religious persecution and finally tried for sedition in the fifties, the man whom an American woman tourist in Athens called the "modern Prometheus, . . . who has fanned into flame the unextinguished embers buried beneath the ashes of former Grecian glory,"[96] remained with his Greek wife and family at the capital of Hellas until his death in 1869--a lonely symbol of militant Protestantism in a stronghold of Eastern Orthodoxy.[97]

In Syria the Board's stations suffered unusual disturbances in the thirties arising from rebellions against Mehemet Ali of Egypt, who with his son, Ibrahim Pasha, wrested the province from the Ottoman sultan. Although Ibrahim, who controlled Syria from 1831-1840, was friendly to both French and American missions,[98] internal quarrels between the Catholic Maronites and the Druses further complicated a difficult situation. The Allied Powers of Europe having determined to bolster the Turks against the Egyptian usurper, an English fleet attacked Beirut in 1840, sending the missionary families fleeing to Cyprus on a United States warship. One of the evangelists returned to land with the assaulting troops and found the American flag still flying over the mission.[99] Ibrahim Pasha defeated, the Maronites, who had supported the British, conspired against the Board's missionaries and their Druse allies, who had recently shown

---

[96] /Sarah R. Haight7, Letters from the Old World (New York, 1840), II, 299.

[97] Shaw, American Contacts with the Eastern Churches, 82-84.

[98] When Ibrahim Pasha came to Beirut in 1835, Eli Smith of the mission called on him and described him as a "large, jolly, laughing, cunning man, with a very penetrating eye." Journal of Sarah Smith (October 24, 1835), in E. W. Hooker, Memoir of Mrs. Sarah Lanman Smith, Late of the Mission in Syria (Boston, 1839), 280.

[99] Letter of Samuel Wolcott, Beirut, October 13, 1840, Missionary Herald, XXXVII (1841), 63-64.

such an attraction to Protestantism.[100] The fighting which immediately ensued between the rival sects ended in the temporary victory of the latter, but the next decade was nearly as tumultous as the last. In 1845 a new war breaking out between Druses and Maronites endangered the lives of the evangelists in the Lebanon, where some of them witnessed the bloody massacre of Catholics in the village of Abeih. A French priest in a small convent there was murdered, but the Americans escaped harm and rescued many of the Maronite victims of the Druses' wrath. Once again a vessel of the United States Navy arrived in Beirut to offer asylum to members of the mission.[101]

The Board's representatives in the Near and Middle East seemed to have a penchant for landing in the midst of both international and internal conflicts in that strife-torn quarter of the world. In Kurdistan they encountered the unexpected competition of high-church Anglicans, who, becoming interested in the mountain Nestorians as a result of the report of the British government-sponsored Euphrates Expedition of 1837, commissioned an agent to explore the region at approximately the same time that the American Board was entering that field.[102] In 1842 the Anglo-Catholics sent a second emissary to open ecclesiastical relations with the Nestorian

---

[100]In a very complex position, the Americans apparently succeeded in persuading the English officers to show greater favor to the Druses than to the Maronite Catholics whom the mission looked upon as agents of France and the pope. At any rate the Druse mountaineers eagerly accepted the services of the missionaries and sent their children to mission schools in great numbers, relying in part, at least, upon informal guarantees of support from the British against their hereditary enemies, the Maronites. Tracy, History of the American Board, 441.

[101]Extracts from the journal of the eye-witness to these events, William Thomson, was published in the Missionary Herald, XLI (1845), 344-347.

[102]W. F. Ainsworth, Travels and Researches in Asia Minor, Mesopotamia, Chaldea, and Armenia (London, 1842), I, 1-8. Ainsworth, the joint agent of the S.P.C.K. and the Royal Geography Society, passed through Urumiah in Iran without even calling on the Board's mission. Ibid., II, 304-305.

patriarch, Mar Shimon, who was already on friendly terms with Dr. Grant of the Urumiah mission. This agent was George P. Badger, an Englishman formerly employed by the A.B.C.F.M. at Malta and Smyrna,[103] who succeeded in alienating the bishop from his American mentors just at a time when the political situation in Kurdistan approached a crisis. The Turks, determined to put an end to the independence of the mountaineers, sent troops to the area, and in 1843 the Kurdish chieftains descended upon the Nestorian villages, massacring hundreds and causing the rest to flee for their lives. Dr. Grant had escaped to Mosul, but the Kurds occupied the mission house he had built in the Tiyari region and converted it into a fortress. Though the missionaries succored the refugees in Mosul, Mar Shimon remained hostile to their efforts, and some British circles attempted to place the blame for the Kurdish uprising upon the American medical evangelist.[104]

The Board also met extraordinary difficulties in the Armenian mission, although the accession of a new sultan in 1840 raised hopes of political reform and a greater religious toleration.[105] But the chief opposition to the Protestants came not from the Turkish government but from the patriarch of the ancient Gregorian Church. Notwithstanding the missionaries' good intentions, they proved unable to work harmoniously with the established ecclesiastical authorities, and the Armenians who

---

[103]Thomas Laurie, Dr. Grant and the Mountain Nestorians (Boston, 1853) 282.

[104]This, the first large-scale Christian massacre in Turkey in modern times, shocked the West and brought accusations against both Badger and Grant for their alleged responsibility in inciting Mar Shimon to defy the Kurds. Badger, The Nestorians and Their Rituals, I, 189-191; Quarterly Review, LXXXIV (1848), 121-122; A. H. Layard, Nineveh and Its Remains (New York, 1849), I, 156-157. Edward Robinson, who wrote an introduction to the American edition of Layard's volumes, took the opportunity to refute the allegations against Grant. Ibid., I, vi-vii.

[105]General Letter, Smyrna, January 24, 1840. Missionary Herald, XXXVI (1840), 213-213).

came under their influence were estranged from their former priests and bishops. The patriarch resorted to physical persecution and religious excommunication, and many of the mission's followers were jailed or banished.[106]

The Board soon came under attack from an unexpected quarter. Horatio Southgate, an American Episcopalian missionary who had arrived in Constantinople in 1836, sided with the Armenian ecclesiastics in the struggle against Protestant heretics in their communion.[107] Although at first friendly to the agents of the Board, he soon took the high-church position of Badger and became an outspoken opponent of his Congregational and Presbyterian fellow countrymen.[108] The prudential committee censured his activities at the annual meeting in 1843,[109] an action which, when reported to Southgate in Constantinople, inspired a battle of pamphlets between the Episcopalian and the Board's missionaries in Turkey.[110] Some of the latter went so far as to accuse their antagonist of aiding the patriarch's persecution of evangelical Armenians.[111]

---

[106]Tracy, History of the American Board, 384-391.

[107]Southgate, who had been originally trained for the Congregational ministry at Andover, argued against the American Board's policy and in favor of direct evangelism among Moslems in a sermon before departure from the United States in 1836. Horatio Southgate, Encouragement to Missionary Effort among Mohammedans (New York), 1841, 8. Once in the field, however, he turned his attention to the Christian sects and wrote two vivid accounts of his travels among them, published as Narrative of a Tour through Armenia, Persia, Kurdistan, and Mesopotamia (2 v., New York, 1841), and Narrative of a Visit to the Syrian (Jacobite) Church of Mesopotamia (New York, 1844).

[108]See Shaw, American Contacts with the Eastern Churches, 36-39.

[109]New York Observer, November 18, 1843.

[110]Southgate wrote A Letter to the Members of the Protestant Episcopal Church in the United States (New York, 1844), which the Board's missionaries answered in A Letter from the Missionaries at Constantinople in Reply to Charges by Rev. Horatio Southgate (Boston, 1845). At least one additional pamphlet appeared on both sides.

[111]Dwight, Christianity Revived in the East, 210-213.

Opinion among Episcopalians at home, engendered by the tractarian controversy, brought the dissident enterprise to an end in 1850, and Southgate
returned to the United States leaving the American Board supreme in the
Armenian field.[112]

In the meantime the prudential committee's policy in respect
to the Oriental Churches came to a climax, when the Protestant Armenian
party seceded from the national church and formed independent congregations with the aid and advice of the American evangelists. The first was
organized in the Turkish capital in 1846.[113] In hopes of averting the
wrath of the patriarch, the Board's agents appealed to the American,
Prussian, and British diplomatic representatives to use their influence
with the sultan's court to gain recognition for the dissenting Armenians.
The English minister, Sir Stratford Canning, became their ardent advocate,
and his successor the next year was able to procure from the Porte a
promise to treat the Protestants as a separate body from the Gregorian
Church.[114] Three years later Canning returned to obtain an imperial de-
cree from the sultan himself guaranteeing permanent standing to the evangelical Armenian community, headed by its own representative like other
nations, or millets in the empire.[115]

The outbreak of the Crimean War in 1853 brought an understand-
able alarm not only to the missionaries on the scene but to their patrons
in the United States, anxious lest the hopeful gains of thirty years be
endangered or lost. The sympathies of the Americans in Turkey, familiar
with Russian maneuvers in behalf of the Armenian hierarchy, were undividedly

---

[112]Shaw, American Contacts with the Eastern Churches, 62-70.

[113]Dwight, Christianity Revived in the East, 229-230.

[114]Missionary Herald, XLIV (1848), 98-99.

[115]Ibid., XLVII (1851), 114-115.

against the czar. Even before the entry of the European powers into the conflict, H. G. O. Dwight expressed his strong conviction that Turkish rule was to be preferred to Muscovite. "Has God," he asked in October, 1853, "raised up free Christian churches in Turkey, and brought them thus far . . . merely to hand them over to the iron grasp of Russian despotion? For one I cannot believe it."[116] The issue was even clearer when Turkey was joined the next year by England, whose ministers had delighted the Board's laborers by championing so enthusiastically their Armenian proteges. The Protestant evangelists now saw in the war an opportunity to free the separate evangelical churches from both Holy Russia's self-proclaimed protection of the Oriental communions and the arbitrary interference of Moslem authorities.[117]

The religious community in the United States held largely the same sentiments, despite the current of anti-British prejudice which the war brought to the surface.[118] Editorials in Protestant newspapers almost unanimously denounced Nicholas I as an opponent of evangelical religion and argued that, though England might preserve the sultan his throne, the power of Mohammedanism would be broken.[119] On the other hand an articulate minority, chiefly among high-church Episcopalians who owned ecclesiastical ties with Russian Orthodoxy, pictured the conflict as a war between

---

[116]Letter of Dwight, Constantinople, October 8, 1853, Missionary Herald, L (1854), 15.

[117]Letter of H. J. Van Lennep, Constantinople, May 31, 1854, and Josiah Peabody, Erzurum, August 10, 1854, Missionary Herald, L (1854), 252; 346-347. The missionaries at the latter station were the only ones to come close to the scenes of warfare, when the battle of Kars took place several miles away.

[118]F. A. Golder, "Russian-American Relations during the Crimean War," American Historical Review, XXXI (1926), 462-476.

[119]Puritan Recorder (Boston), April 13, 1854, and November 2, 1854. Other examples of this anti-Russian sentiment are found in the crusading Independent, July 20, 1854, and the Methodist Christian Advocate, April 13, 1854. Only the Unitarian Christian Register urged neutrality in thought and action. Christian Register, August 19, 1854.

the Crescent and the Cross and asked American sympathy for a Christian nation struggling against Moslem infidelity.[120] One of these voices was that of the Board's old adversary, Horatio Southgate, who lamented that public opinion in the United States favored Turkey and suggested that Russian protection of the Oriental Churches in the Ottoman Empire was necessary to balance the power of Roman Catholicism in the Near East.[121]

The missionaries were justified in their support of England when the sultan, in compliance with Allied wishes, issued an imperial edict, the famous Hatti Humayun of 1856, which guaranteed religious liberty to all Turkish subjects.[122] During the conflict, moreover, the mission co-operated closely with the English, Cyrus Hamlin organizing both a laundry and a bakery to serve the troops which passed through Constantinople.[123] Out of these friendly relations arose the Turkish Mission Aid Society, formed in London in 1854 to assist the Board's work in the Ottoman Empire, contributing from two thousand to twenty-five hundred pounds annually for the support of native churches and schools.[124] This fraternal act so impressed American evangelicals that a speaker before the A.B.C.F.M. in 1855 could remark upon an anticipated improvement in Anglo-American relations: "Is not war between this country and Great Britain more improbable

[120]The most significant pro-Russian pamphleteer among the Episcopalians was William Giles Dix, author of The Doom of the Crescent (Boston, 1853) and The Unholy Alliance: An American View of the War in the East (New York, 1855). Even he nodded to the evangelical community by praising the work of the Board's Congregational and Presbyterian emissaries in Turkey. Unholy Alliance, 246-248.

[121]Southgate, The War in the East (New York, 1854), 18, 37-38.

[122]The Board agents immediately wrote a letter of gratitude to their old friend Canning, now Lord Stratford de Radcliffe. Missionary Herald, LII (1856), 184-185.

[123]Cyrus Hamlin, Among the Turks (New York, 1877), 226-243.

[124]American Board, Fifty-third Annual Report (Boston, 1862), 57-58; Richter, History of Protestant Missions in the Near East, 118-119.

by her union with us in our Turkish missions?"[125]

One result of this British aid was a final extension of the American mission into European Turkey. In 1857 an agent of the newly formed society accompanied Cyrus Hamlin on an exploring tour of Bulgaria.[126] The next year Charles F. Morse opened a station at Adrianople which was quickly followed by missionary settlements at Philippopolis and Eski-Saghra.[127] In spite of civil disturbances and international wars, the Board's enterprises in the East prospered exceedingly and in 1860 reached from the Caspian Sea almost to the Danube River.

IV

At a time when American diplomatic activities in the Near and Middle East were of meager extent and minor importance, it was the Protestant mission, even more than foreign commerce, which represented the nation in that quarter of the globe. Travelers from the United States rejoiced to discover their countrymen residing at distant exotic outposts ready to welcome them and act as guides and interpreters, as when Mrs. Sarah Haight of New York called with members of the Constantinople mission upon a leading Armenian family in order to taste thick Turkish coffee and smoke "chiboucks."[128]Some carried letters of introduction to the overseas evangelists, like the much-traveled John Lloyd Stephens, who enjoyed their hospitality in Jerusalem in 1837.[129] Pilgrims to the Holy Land and roving

---

[125]Nehemiah Adams, The Power of Christian Gratitude. A Sermon . . . before the American Board (Boston, 1855), 12.

[126]Letter of Hamlin, Constantinople, May 18, 1857, Missionary Herald, LJII (1857), 293-298.

[127]American Board, Forty-ninth Annual Report (Boston, 1858), 47; Fiftieth Annual Report (Boston, 1859), 58.

[128]/Haight7, Letters from the Old World, I, 46-47.

[129]/Stephens7, Incidents of Travel in Egypt, Arabia Petraea, and the Holy Land (3rd ed., New York, 1838), II, 156.

journalists helped publicize the missionary work at home by friendly references to the work of the Board's emissaries which they observed abroad.[130] Perhaps the most influential visitor in the Levant during this period, however, was General Lewis Cass, who took a Mediterranean vacation from his ministerial post in Paris in the summer of 1837. In a long, effusive letter to the corresponding secretary of the A.B.C.F.M. in Boston, the Middle Western politician described his pleasure at the contemplation of missionaries coming from the "banks of the Hudson" to the "pool of Siloam" and compared their work with the spirit of the Pilgrims.[131]

In Athens the first thing many Americans did was visit the schools kept by the Episcopalians and by "professor" Jonas King of the Board.[132] Journalist N. P. Willis thought this undertaking "a moral spectacle to which no thinking person could be indifferent."[133] Lloyd Stephens was impressed with the way in which citizens of a country which Plato and Aristotle had never dreamed existed were repaying the debt "the world owes to the mother of science."[134] A naval chaplain seized the occasion of a visit to King's school to praise highly the educational work of the Greek mission and denounce the "senseless clamor of those who would confine the missionary wholly to the work of the public preaching

---

[130]For example, see Stephen Olin, Travels in Egypt, Arabia Petraea, and the Holy Land (New York, 1843), II, 458-459; J. R. Browne, Yusef; or the Journey of the Frangi (New York, 1853), 272-274. One pilgrim to Palestine dedicated the profits, if any, of his publication to the American Board. Fisher Howe, Orient and Sacred Scenes from Notes of Travel in Greece, Turkey, and Palestine (New York, 1863), preface, vii-viii.

[131]Lewis Cass to Anderson, Paris, June 1, 1838, ABC:14, II, no. 47.

[132]Walter Colton, Visit to Constantinople and Athens (New York, 1836), 252. See also Francis Schroeder, Shores of the Mediterranean; with Sketches of Travel, 1843-1845 (New York, 1846), I, 89-93.

[133]Willis, Pencillings by the Way, II, 218.

[134]/Stephens7, Incidents of Travel in Greece, Turkey, Russia, and Poland (7th ed., New York, 1849), I, 61.

of the gospel."[135] Unlike their fellow countrymen in the Pacific, in the Near East American travelers seldom found an opportunity to criticize the work of foreign missions harshly.

The naval squadron in the Mediterranean was uniformly courteous and helpful to the evangelists, who often found themselves in danger from the wars and rumors of wars which infested many of the regions in which they resided. The first American warship to make port in Beirut was the Delaware, whose officers invited Eli Smith to preach on board and held open house on the vessel's deck for the curious inhabitants of the city in 1834.[136] In 1848, the commander of the naval expedition to the Dead Sea was grateful for the medical assistance of Dr. Henry A. De Forest when one of the official party fell sick.[137] As we have seen, the corvette Cyane carried members of the mission to safety in Cyprus during the seige of Beirut in 1840, and ten years later Commodore Charles W. Morgan sent a ship of his command to the Syrian coast with an assurance of his "willingness to serve you at all times, when not overruled by the pressing orders of the government."[138] In Smyrna and Constantinople, other regular ports of call of the American squadron, the missionaries frequently preached on board visiting warships as well as merchant vessels.

In spite of Commodore David Porter's initial friendliness to

---

[135]Charles Rockwell, Sketches of Foreign Travel and Life at Sea (Boston, 1842), II, 199-200.

[136]Letter of Smith, Mount Lebanon, September 27, 1834, Missionary Herald, XXXI (1835), 136-137; George Jones, Excursions to Cairo, Jerusalem, Damascus and Balbec (New York, 1836), 383-384.

[137]W. F. Lynch, Narrative of the United States' Expedition to the River Jordan and the Dead Sea (Rev. ed., Philadelphia, 1849), 506-507.

[138]Letter of C. W. Morgan, Bay of Naples, May 17, 1850, Missionary Herald, XLVI (1850), 379. In the same communication the commodore informed the mission that he was satisfied that the government in Washington had a deep interest in "the preservation and furtherance of your personal welfare and safety."

the Goodells, the minister's treatment of the missionaries' privileges
as American citizens residing in the Ottoman Empire was not satisfactory
to the Board. When he refused to uphold their right to evangelize freely
under the terms of the United States treaty with Turkey—a question raised
by the Maronite patriarch in Syria in 1841--Secretary Anderson angrily
wrote to Lewis Cass in Paris to ask his intervention with the old naval
hero, whom he termed "too feeble, physically at least, for the responsibilities of his station."[139] Since Cass proved unwilling to intercede
with Porter, an officer of the American Board met with President Tyler
and Secretary of State Webster, the latter of whom agreed to instruct the
careful minister to treat the evangelists as possessing the same privileges as American merchants in Turkey.[140]

The next diplomatic representative of the United States at the
Turkish capital, Dabney S. Carr, was a more outspoken advocate of the
mission than the aging commodore. In 1844 Rufus Anderson reciprocated
the minister's kind attentions during the corresponding secretary's tour
of inspection in the Levant by undertaking to advise and make recommendations to him in regard to American consular affairs in that part of the
world.[141] In the fall of 1848, moreover, Carr requested the prudential
committee of the Board to exert its influence at Washington to enable
the incoming administration to retain his services at the Porte.[142] Later

---

[139]Anderson to Cass, Boston, November 22, 1841, and February 10, 1842,
ABC:2.1.1, IV, 224-228; V, 11.

[140]Webster apparently offered to send this communication to Constantinople by the hand of the Board's officer, Ex-Governor Samuel T. Armstrong
of Massachusetts, as well as afford him every opportunity to study the
situation in the Levant at first hand; for some reason Armstrong did
not make the journey. S. T. Armstrong to Anderson, Washington, February 1,
1842, ABC:10, XXV, no. 92.

[141]Anderson to D. S. Carr, Smyrna, May 2, 1844, ABC:2.1.1, VII, 65.

[142]Carr to Anderson, Constantinople, November 4, 1848, ABC:14, III, no. 110.

ministers, while not so obliging to the missionaries as the unfortunate Carr, who was replaced despite Anderson's attempt to save him,[143] followed the spirit of Webster's earlier instructions to Porter in protecting the mission's interests.

In the early fifties Jonas King's difficulties with the Greek authorities brought a remonstrance from the American Board to Webster, once more secretary of state, this time in the Fillmore administration.[144] At the same time the navy sent a warship to Athens "for the purpose of protecting American interests in that city."[145] In 1852 George P. Marsh, the new minister of the United States at Constantinople, went to the Greek capital to make an investigation, which, though favorable to King, accomplished little. Three years later the state department dispatched a second agent, who secured the American missionary a satisfactory indemnity.[146] The Board did not require the direct intervention of the government again until 1862, when two of its emissaries were murdered, one in Bulgaria and another in central Turkey. Much concerned about outbreaks of anti-American fanaticism in the Ottoman Empire, the prudential committee wrote to Secretary of State William Seward, who offered the assistance of representatives of the United States in apprehending the slayers.[147]

In Persia and the rest of the Middle East, however, America had neither ministers nor consuls. From the beginning the Board's agents in

---

[143]Anderson appealed to Benjamin F. Butler for Carr's reappointment as "a great favor to our missionary brethren in the different parts of Turkey." Anderson to B. F. Butler, Boston, March 5, 1845, copied in Anderson to Dwight, Boston, April 28, 1845, ABC:2.1.1, VIII, 115-116.

[144]Anderson to Webster, Boston, June 21, 1851, ABC:2.1.1, XV, 27.

[145]W. S. Derrick to the American Board, Washington, July 21, 1851, ABC:10, XLII, no. 222.

[146]H. M. Wriston, Executive Agents in American Foreign Relations (Baltimore, 1929), 660-663.

[147]American Board, Fifty-third Annual Report (Boston, 1862, 13-14.

Urumiah relied on the good offices of the Russian and British legations, particularly the latter, which was located at nearby Tabriz during the first few years of the mission. His Majesty's officials granted the Americans full diplomatic protection.[148] Great Britain, long in a dominant position in Iran, suffered a diplomatic setback in the late thirties, and a new minister in 1843 refused to continue the usual privileges to the Board's missionaries. After an unsuccessful application to Carr in Constantinople,[149] the prudential committee approached Lord Aberdeen through Ambassador Edward Everett in London, who forwarded the guarded assurance that British protection would be extended to the property and persons of Americans in Azerbaijan.[150] A few years later, in a case involving the violent opposition to the mission of the Nestorian patriarch, Mar Shimon, Secretary Anderson expressed the Board's gratitude to Westminster for the aid afforded its evangelists by the British consul in Tabriz.[151]

In Mesopotamia the American missionaries also found English officials helpful. One of their number floated down the Tigris River on a raft to Bagdad to secure British assistance for the mission in the late fifties.[152] Their chief contacts with Europeans, however, were with the French and English archaelogists digging in the ruins of Nineveh, just outside Mosul, where the mission was located. As early as 1844 the Board's agents took an interest in the activities of the French scholars,

---

[148]Perkins, Residence in Persia, 219-220.

[149]Anderson to Carr, Constantinople, January 29, 1844, ABC:2.1.1, VI, 336-337.

[150]Aberdeen to Edward Everett, London, April 14, 1845, copied in Everett to Anderson, London, April 15, 1845, ABC:14, III, no. 178. Everett warned the Board's secretary not to publish the enclosed correspondence because of its unofficial character.

[151]Anderson to George Bancroft, Boston, February 20, 1849, ABC:2.1.1, XI, 206-207.

[152]Moses Tyler, Memoir of Rev. Henry Lobdell, Late Missionary of the American Board at Mosul (Boston, 1859), 367-375.

Paul Botta and Eugene Flandin.[153] Ten years later Amherst graduate Henry
Lobdell was directing excavations himself for American colleges in co-
operation with representatives of the British Museum.[154]

The traditional American policy of nonintervention in the internal affairs of other governments forced the Board's emissaries--resident
as they were for the most part in a religiously and racially alien, des-
potically ruled empire--to look to England for active protection in the
furtherance of their objectives. Whatever the missionaries in the field
thought, the directors in Boston conceived of the nation's isolationist
policy in this regard as "wise and just." While frequently calling upon
Great Britain to interpose its righteous authority in matters relating
to religious liberty in Turkey or Persia, the American Board rejoiced in
the free hand which the official position of the United States permitted
its agents in the same countries, free of any imputation of imperialistic
ambitions.[155]

American interests in the Near and Middle East in this period
were largely philanthropic and missionary in character; both commerce and
diplomacy played greatly subordinate roles. Moreover, because of the
nature of the Protestant missions, which were chiefly among nominally
Christian peoples rather than pagans, the program carried on by these
evangelical American ambassadors was more heavily educational than similar
ventures in heathen countries. It was this aspect of the Mediterranean
enterprise which gave it a special quality and created an enduring

[153]Letter of Thomas Laurie, Mosul, August 8, 1844, Missionary Herald,
XLI (1845), 40-42.

[154]Tyler, Memoir of Henry Lobdell, 243-244. Sir Austen Layard, the
British Museum's chief archaeologist at Nineveh, knew many of the American
missionaries and praised them highly. Layard, Discoveries in the Ruins
of Nineveh and Babylon; with Travels in Armenia, Kurdistan and the Desert
(New York, 1853), 424-425.

[155]American Board, Fifty-fifth Annual Report (Boston, 1864), 16.

monument in the institutions of higher learning which sprang up from these missionary stations---Robert College in Constantinople, founded by Cyrus Hamlin and a private benefactor in the United States after the Board decided to discontinue its English-language schools in the fifties,[156] and the American University at Beirut, which held its first commencement in 1870, just as the mission was being transferred from the A.B.C.F.M. to the Presbyterian Board.[157]

---

[156]Hamlin, My Life and Times (Boston, 1893), 415-484.

[157]Anderson, History of Missions to the Oriental Churches, 390-391.

CHAPTER VI

CHINA AND THE FAR EAST

Commercial enterprise preceded the Board's missionaries in many parts of the world, but the interval between the arrival in 1784 of the first American trading vessel to reach Canton, the Empress of China, and the initial evangelistic undertaking in the Far East by the churches of the United States was unusually long--forty-five years.[1] In the meantime, however, the evangelical community evinced considerable interest in the work of the Englishman, Robert Morrison of the London Missionary Society, who had resided in China since 1807 and had begun the translation of the Scriptures into Chinese. As early as 1816 an urgent appeal for contributions to this work, linked with American commercial interests, appeared in the religious press:

> Behold, fellow-christians of the U.S., what a field of usefulness, what scenes of blessedness are unfolding to your view. . . . American ships are soon to sail for Canton, to accumulate worldly treasure by the importation of the products of China: let them not depart without carrying with them some testimony, that American christians take an interest in the spiritual welfare of that nation, who have contributed so largely to the temporal wealth of the United States.[2]

The presence of a few natives of China who had somehow wandered to this country also drew attention to that ancient empire, and at least two of

---

[1]The Empress of China was a New York ship, but its supercargo was Samuel Shaw of Massachusetts, who became the first American consul in Canton and wrote a report for the government of the United States which stimulated commercial interest in the Celestial Empire. Morison, Maritime History of Massachusetts, 44-45.

[2]Boston Recorder, August 21, 1816. Morrison's name was a powerful symbol of missions to Americans. In 1821, Hiram Bingham in Hawaii wrote asking his advice in regard to reducing the native language to writing. Bingham to Morrison, Atooi, October 13, 1821, in /Morrison/, Life and Labours of Robert Morrison, II, 118.

them attended briefly the Cornwall Foreign Mission School in Connecticut. The Rev. William Jenks, one of America's first Orientalists, hoped to learn the language from a young Cantonese youth living in Boston and attempted to secure Chinese books from Canton.[3]

I

Commercial and evangelical influences combined to bring China to the notice of the American Board. In 1818 a pious Philadelphia merchant, Robert Ralston, who had assisted the first emissaries to India and corresponded frequently with Morrison in Canton, recommended that one of the Board's representatives in India spend four months of each year in Whampoa to preach to English-speaking seamen in that Chinese port.[4] Though this suggestion was impractical, the notion of making a beginning in an empire virtually closed to ordinary missions by instituting a sort of chaplaincy for American and other foreign sailors frequenting Chinese roadsteads lingered on. Six years later, in 1824, the prudential committee formally resolved to commence work in China, apparently encouraged by private communications from William Jenks and D. W. C. Olyphant, a New York merchant long a resident in Canton, as well as by the offer of a Philadelphia shipowner to transport missionaries free of charge.[5]

The Board, however, did not act upon this resolution immediately, perhaps because personnel was not available. In November, 1827, several

---

[3]William Jenks to Robert Morrison, Boston, May 15, 1821, in /Morrison7, Life and Labours of Robert Morrison, II, 126-129. The first American work on China was the ambitious but uncompleted book by the scion of a Quaker mercantile family doing business in Canton, Robert Waln, Jr., entitled China; a View of the History, Religion, Customs (Philadelphia, 1823).

[4]Robert Ralston to Worcester, Philadelphia, April 9, 1818, ABC:10, 1, no. 20.

[5]Evarts to Henry Hill, Philadelphia, January 12, 1824, ABC:11, I, no. 259; Prudential Committee Records, I (February 21, 1824), 272-273. American Board Archives, Congregational House, Boston.

American merchants and shipmasters, meeting with Robert Morrison in Canton, drew up a petition to the American churches asking that two missionaries be sent at once, to divide between them the tasks of preaching to seamen and preparing for the opening of China. Olyphant, the moving spirit in this enterprise, forwarded the memorial, with a separate letter from Morrison, to Gardiner Spring, a Presbyterian minister in New York, and Jeremiah Evarts of the A.B.C.F.M.[6] The prudential committee, still hesitating slightly, began to search for candidates and to prepare the public by printing long extracts from the writings of Morrison's colleague in China, John Milne, in the Missionary Herald.[7] Finally, Olyphant himself returned to the United States in 1829 and offered to provide free passage and a year's lodging in Canton for one missionary.[8] Accepting this proposal, the Board joined with the American Seamen's Friend Society in a plan to dispatch a marine chaplain to Whampoa and a medical missionary to Canton to learn the language and begin work among the Chinese.[9]

In October the prudential committee, unable to find a physician, commissioned Andover-trained Elijah C. Bridgman of Massachusetts to accompany the Seamen's Friend Society's David Abeel, who agreed to preach to

[6]The copies of the petition dated Canton, November 19, 1827, and signed by Olyphant, Walter Crocker, and Charles B. Brintnall, are enclosed in letters from Olyphant to Gardiner Spring and Evarts, December 5, 1827, ABC:16.3.3, I, nos. 145 and 150. The Canton merchant warned rather mysteriously against the publication of any of these documents. Not until 1847 did the Board make them fully public, in its Thirty-eighth Annual Report (Boston, 1847), 160-161.

[7]The editor included material derived from the Olyphant documents termed "recent and authentic correspondence in the possession of the Board." Missionary Herald, XXIV (1828), 326-330. Two years before Evarts had inserted extracts from Morrison's own writings in the same journal. Ibid., XXII (1826), 194-196.

[8]Olyphant to C. W. Talbot, New York, October 13, 1829, in Eliza J. G. Bridgman, The Pioneer of American Missions in China: The Life and Labors of Elijah Coleman Bridgman (New York, 1864), 38.

[9]Evarts to Joshua Leavitt, Boston, January 2, 1829, ABC:1.01, IX, 112-113; Sailor's Magazine, and Naval Journal, II (1829), 37-40.

mariners for one year before entering the service of the Board.[10] The committee's instructions to Bridgman were not very explicit beyond advising
him to consult closely with his English brethren in Canton, where he took
residence in the American consul's rooms in the foreign factories and set
out to learn the Chinese language, while teaching English to a small group
of Cantonese youths.[11] In 1832, when Olyphant's home church in New York
sent a printing press, Bridgman began publishing the Chinese Repository,
a monthly journal in English designed to disseminate a more intimate
understanding of eastern Asia.[12] The linguistic and literary studies
which thus predominated at the commencement of this mission also demanded
much of the time and energies of the first reinforcements--Peter Parker,
Yale-educated physician and minister, and a printer, S. Wells Williams
of Rensselaer Institute in Troy, New York.

Shut up as they were in the foreign factories outside the city
walls of Canton, the missionaries found support among English and American
merchants. Olyphant and his younger partner, Charles W. King, whose
quarters in the American hong were termed "Zion's Corner"[13] because of
their reputation for piety and their scrupulous abstention from the opium
trade, proved particularly helpful. Not all traders from the United
States looked kindly upon their countrymen's philanthropic venture. One

---

[10]Missionary Herald, XV (1829), 364-365.

[11]Ibid., XXVI (1830), 279-280; XXVII (1831), 228-229.

[12]Chinese Repository, I (1832), Introduction, 1-4.

[13]W. C. Hunter, Bits of Old China (2nd ed., Shanghai, 1911), 168. The
author of these reminiscences was a New York merchant who had studied
Chinese at the London Society's Anglo-Chinese College at Malacca and was
a fellow passenger with Bridgman on his way to Canton in 1829. One of
the few American traders to learn Chinese, Hunter gave the missionary his
introduction to the language on shipboard. Leavitt to Evarts, New York,
March 21, 1829, ABC:16.3.3, I, no. 154; Missionary Herald, XXVI (1830),
321.

New Englander, Augustine Heard, who, ironically enough, had commanded the Salem vessel which carried the Board's first envoys to Calcutta in 1812, wrote to his brother in 1833:

> From what I have seen of foreign Missionaries I do not think it incumbent on either of us to labour to support them; so far as my observation goes they are Christians only in speech, you get letters, reports, &c., which I know in many instances are false, to pay for which they are supported in luxury; both here and in Bengal they "clothe in fine linen and fare sumptuously every day" while many of our good hard working folks at home are credulous enough to believe that they suffer every privation and hardship.[14]

Many Canton residents, however, both British and American, joined with the veteran Morrison and the young representatives of the Board in evangelical enterprises. These organized themselves in 1830 as a "Christian Union" and later formed the Society for the Diffusion of Useful Knowledge in China, which furnished funds for the support of the Chinese Repository and the translation of Scriptural tracts in Chinese.[15] In 1835 the Morrison Education Society came into existence, named after the pioneer English missionary who had died the year before, and founded to provide English-language education for Chinese young men. But not until 1839 did the first teacher arrive in China, Samuel R. Brown, whom a committee of the Yale faculty selected at the society's request.[16] Two Chinese who had been students at the Cornwall Foreign Mission School made

---

[14]Augustine Heard to G. W. Heard, Canton, June 30, 1833, Augustine Heard Papers, Baker Library, Harvard Graduate School of Business Administration.

[15]K. S. Latourette, A History of Christian Missions in China (New York, 1829), 220-222. Olyphant himself apparently agreed to guarantee the Repository during its first year of publication before the Society for Useful Knowledge assumed responsibility. F. W. Williams, The Life and Letters of Samuel Wells Williams, LL.D.: Missionary, Diplomatis, Sinologue (New York, 1888), 77-78.

[16]This was perhaps the beginning, with Parker's enlistment as a missionary to Canton, of Yale's large interest in China. The committee was composed of Professors Benjamin Silliman, C. A. Goodrich, and J. W. Gibbs, Sr. Chinese Repository, VII (1838), 303; VII (1839), 550.

their appearance in Canton in the thirties, but neither attached himself publicly to the teaching of the missionaries.[17] Peter Parker, with an ophthalmic hospital at Canton, was a leading figure along with several British physicians in the organization of another important group, the Medical Missionary Society in China.[18]

Despite the fact that China was obviously not yet open to direct Christian evangelism—although Roman Catholic priests still operated covertly in many parts of the interior—the American public entertained somewhat extravagant notions of the empire and its importance to the strategy of missions. China's fabulous population on the mainland, and her colonization in Southeast Asia, together with the supposedly wide extension of the Chinese language, led the directors in Boston to envision exaggerated opportunities for Protestant endeavor, as these instructions to its agents in 1833 disclose:

> Your field of missionary labor is co-extensive with that great community which speaks, and with that still more extensive community which reads, the Chinese language—the language of at least a fourth part of the human race; a medium of thought, doubtless, long before the existence of any of the other languages now spoken in the world; printed and stereotyped ages previous to the invention of printing in Europe; singular in its nature, and difficult of acquisition. As she now rises to view, the Christian world is more and more impressed by the prospect. Her mountains, plains, rivers, and canals, are seen to be covered with people; while millions of the busy race are scattered over the neighboring countries and islands.[19]

But since the only open port in China, Canton, presented an extremely restricted field of labors, the Board attempted a flanking

---

[17]David Abeel, Journal of a Residence in China, and the Neighboring Countries, from 1829 to 1833 (New York, 1834), 96; Chinese Repository, IV (1836), 431; Missionary Herald, XXXI (1835), 413.

[18]Chinese Repository, V (1836), 370-373.

[19]Missionary Herald, XXIX (1833), 273.

movement, designed to reach Chinese settlers in Malaysia and the lands to the southwest. After his first year as seamen's chaplain, David Abeel undertook for the prudential committee a long exploring tour in this region, visiting Batavia on the island of Java and Bangkok, Siam, before returning to the United States to publish an account of his journey and arouse greater interest in that part of the world.[20] Two English evangelists, Walter H. Medhurst in Batavia and Jacob Tomlin in Siam, had already drawn the attention of the American Board to these points, and in 1830 the energetic Charles Gutzlaff, a German sent to China by the Netherlands Missionary Society who had accompanied Tomlin to Bangkok, wrote to Evarts inviting the prudential committee to enter the field.[21] Acting upon this stimulus, the Board agreed to commission two missionaries to Siam and two others to continue Abeel's explorations in Indonesia.[22]

When Stephen Johnson and Charles Robinson arrived in Bangkok in 1834, they found agents of the American Baptists there before them, for James T. Jones had transferred to Siam from Burma the year before, just as Edmund Roberts of Portsmouth, New Hampshire, was concluding the first Far Eastern treaty of the United States with the Siamese

---

[20]Abeel, _Journal of a Residence in China_, 143-331. Abeel, a member of the Reformed Dutch Church in the United States, hoped to find the Dutch clergy in Java willing to co-operate with their American brethren, but the Hollanders ignored him, according to the report of naval officer Francis Warriner who visited that island just after Abeel's departure. Warriner, _Cruise of the United States Frigate Potomac_, 147.

[21]Gutzlaff's correct name is Karl Friedrich August Gützlaff, but in the documents and publications of the A.B.C.F.M. appears simply as Charles Gutzlaff. Gutzlaff to Evarts, Bangkok, June 27, 1830, ABC:14, I, no. 33. Tomlin also issued a public invitation to American missionaries to enter Siam. Jacob Tomlin, _Journal of a Nine Month's Residence in Siam_ (London, 1831), 148-149. According to one authority, Tomlin and Gutzlaff sent one appeal to America on board the vessel which carried the "Siamese twins" to fame in the United States in 1829. G. B. McFarland, ed., _Historical Sketch of Protestant Missions in Siam, 1828-1922_ (Bangkok, 1928), 5.

[22]American Board, _Twenty-third Annual Report_, 35, 56-60.

ruler.[23] Although this envoy and his American attendants revisited Bangkok in 1836 and called on the missionaries of both societies, his treaty
had only commercial significance and did not effect the work of evangelism.[24] The Board's emissaries divided their labors between the Chinese
colonists and the Thai people of Bangkok and its vicinity, printing tracts
in both languages on a press sent from Boston. While hoping to extend operations into the neighboring countries of Southeast Asia, particularly
Cochin-China and Cambodia, the evangelists were largely confined to the
Siamese capital, except for a few excursions up the Menam River to outlying villages.[25]

The initial project of exploring the Netherlands East Indies,
however, ended in tragedy. Cannibalistic Batta tribesmen murdered Henry
Lyman and Samuel Munson during their tour into the interior of Sumatra in
1834.[26] Despite this shocking setback the prudential committee immediately dispatched a second agent, William Arms, recently returned from the
abortive Patagonian expedition, to continue the reconnaisance. Because
Dutch colonial officials prevented him from entering Sumatra, Arms spent
several months traveling through a part of Borneo, before his wife's death

---

[23]Edmund Roberts, Embassy to the Eastern Courts of Cochin-China, Siam and
Muscat (New York, 1837), 267-268. Roberts, the first American envoy in
eastern Asia, visited Bridgman briefly in Canton and employed Morrison's
son as an interpreter to the embassy. Ibid., 70, 169.

[24]Ruschenberger, Voyage round the World, 310-311; Journal of D. B. Bradley, April 13, 1836, in Missionary Herald, XXXIII (1837), 138.

[25]Joint letter of the missionaries, Bangkok, November 10, 1836, Missionary Herald, XXXIII (1837), 287-288. On one such excursion a few years
later, two missionaries of the Board brought news of her sons in America
to the mother of the "Siamese twins." Journal of Asa Hemenway, December 7,
Ibid., XL (1844), 403.

[26]Ibid., XXXI (1835), 101-103. The two missionary martyrs were recent
graduates of Andover Theological Seminary, whose death shocked the whole
New England evangelical community. Leonard Wood, one of the founders of
the American Board, preached their funeral sermon in the Andover chapel.
Wood, A Sermon . . . on the Death of Henry Lyman and Samuel Munson
(Andover, 1835).

in Batavia brought him back to the United States.[27] In order to take advantage of the fact that Indonesia was under the rule of the Netherlands, the Board determined to employ only Reformed Dutch communicants in the area. Accordingly, four ministers of that denomination with their wives and one unmarried woman teacher embarked for Batavia in 1836.[28]

In the meantime new restrictions upon their work in Canton caused the missionaries there to remove the printing of all Chinese tracts and other materials to British-held Singapore at the tip of Malaya, where Parker had earlier spent a few months in the study of the language. In 1834 Ira Tracy, who had arrived with Williams the year before, transferred to the new post to take charge of a press recently purchased in the name of the A.B.C.F.M.[29] Singapore, centrally located for operations in all of southeastern Asia, became an important station of the Board, with a dispensary, schools, and a press. After a single experiment with publishing Chinese tracts from stereotype plates in Boston, the missionaries in Singapore took over the printing of all vernacular materials while the Canton press produced the Repository and other English-language volumes.[30]

The press and the hospital proved to be the most effective means of approach to Far Eastern peoples in this early phase of American Protestant missions in that region. The Board, which had long employed several physicians in other fields, sent the first medical missionary to China--Peter Parker--and utilized the services of Dr. Dan B. Bradley in

---

[27]The journal of his Borneo tour was published in the Missionary Herald, XXXIII (1837), 114-115, 282-284.

[28]Ibid., XXXII (1836), 268.

[29]American Board, Twenty-fifth Annual Report, 98-99.

[30]From wood blocks sent by Bridgman from Canton, the Board manufactured stereotype plates to publish in 1834 what was certainly the first Chinese work ever printed in the United States. Ibid., 97-98.

Siam to obtain access to the ruling family of that proud nation. Although Bradley and his wife refused to get down on their hands and knees before the queen, explaining that "this was not American custom," she readily sought medical advice of "the famous American doctor," as she called him.[31] The physician's skill won the mission influential friends at the Thai court, especially after his successful introduction of inoculation against smallpox, a disease which ravaged the population year after year.[32] In the same way in Canton, Dr. Parker through his hospital made the acquaintance of several important imperial officers, the most significant of whom was Commissioner Lin, of Opium War fame.[33]

II

Unlike most of the previous enterprises of the Board in non-Christian lands, the early missionaries to the Far East suffered the great handicap of laboring in lands under pagan, and usually hostile, rule. As the prudential committee pointed out in 1841, the mission in Siam was peculiar in being situated in "the only country, under an independent heathen ruler and having an established and prevailing system of religion, which the missionaries of the Board have entered."[34] However, despite the fact that the government protected Buddhism as the official state religion in that kingdom, American evangelists found greater access there than in neighboring China, where imperial law prevented foreigners from residing elsewhere than the foreign factories at Canton.

---

[31]Journal of Bradley, January 8, 1836, Missionary Herald, XXXIII (1837), 135.

[32]Several unsuccessful attempts were made with vaccine shipped out from Boston before Dr. Bradley's inoculations proved effective. McFarland, ed., Historical Sketch of Protestant Missions in Siam, 17-18.

[33]G. B. Stevens and W. F. Marwick, The Life, Letters, and Journals of the Rev. and Hon. Peter Parker, M.D. (Boston, 1896), 175.

[34]American Board, Thirty-second Annual Report, 138.

Even in Dutch-ruled Indonesia the Board's emissaries encountered suspicion and outright hostility from the government. The colonial
officers not only refused them permission to settle in any of the islands
except wildest Borneo, but demanded also that they reside one year on
probation at Batavia, taking an oath to "refrain from instructing the
natives in such a manner as to weaken the passive obedience required by
the authorities placed over them . . . ."[35] In an effort to alter these
inconvenient restrictions, the Board requested Robert Baird, Paris agent
of the Evangelical Alliance, to apply for relief to the home government
in the Netherlands. At the Hague, in the fall of 1839, Baird saw both
the king and his minister for the colonies but could effect no change in
official policy.[36] Two years later, the A.B.C.F.M. joined with the Reformed Dutch Church, whose members conducted the Indonesia mission, in
sending to Holland a special representative, Isaac Ferris, who gained the
support of the Netherlands Missionary Society but received little satisfaction from the Dutch government.[37] The missionaries finally settled on
the western shores of Borneo among communities of Chinese and Malays;
moreover, finding the primitive Dyak tribes farther back from the coast
receptive to their work, they successfully induced the governor-general
of Netherlands India in 1843 to relax restrictions on travel into the interior.[38]

In China itself the outlook was unpromising in the thirties.
The prudential committee in its instructions to Parker in 1834 had warned

---

[35]American Board, Twenty-ninth Annual Report, 107.

[36]Baird to Anderson, Paris, November 14, 1839, ABC:14, II, no. 12.

[37]American Board, Thirty-third Annual Report, 167-168 and appendix, 221-223.

[38]American Board, Thirty-fifth Annual Report (Boston, 1844), appendix,
257-262.

against any attempt—as if that were possible with the Manchu emperors—to obtain governmental favor for the mission:

> The Christian missionary is not, therefore, to expect, and he is not to seek, the sanctions of heathen governments to his efforts to extend the gospel, but he is to go, with its heavenly message, directly to the people, wherever he can find them; and he is to proclaim its requirements and sanctions to them as individuals having souls for the salvation or loss of which they are themselves responsible, and who must hear and obey the gospel each for himself; expecting that if the truth is ever to reach and influence the governments under which he labors, it will be by its first being diffused through the community, extending its light and its reforming power through all ranks, till it rises to those who occupy the highest places in the state. And if he find a people willing to receive him, he is to persevere in proclaiming to them the message of salvation, though laws and magistrates forbid, and at the expense of liberty and life.[39]

But the problem in China was how to reach the teeming population that lay beyond the foreign factories, in the face of hostile bureaucrats and imperial decrees against Christianity. The Board's missionaries in Canton contended that they could only prepare for the future opening of the empire by close study of the language, while they spent the rest of their time in dispensing medical services to such Chinese as presented themselves and publishing a few vernacular tracts to be spread about cautiously. Liang A-fah, the first convert of Morrison and Milne, assisted the Americans in the preparation and distribution of these Chinese materials, some of which proved later, in the Taiping Rebellion, to be very combustible tinder.

The indomitable Gutzlaff, however, argued that China was already open to bold enterprise and proved his point by making celebrated voyages along the Chinese coast, distributing tracts and preaching to the inhabitants of villages along the banks of rivers near the shore. Speaking

[39]Instructions of the prudential committee to Peter Parker, May, 1834, ABC:8.1, II, 92.

some dialects fluently and passing as a native in his Chinese costume, the Prussian reached the northernmost shores of the country and even Manchuria and Korea.[40] "Blot it out from your missionary publications, that China is shut," Gutzlaff wrote to the prudential committee.[41] His enthusiasm was so contagious that Edwin Stevens, one of the Board's evangelists who had formerly been seamen's chaplain at Whampoa, accompanied him on one voyage up the Min River to the tea plantations of Bohea in 1835.[42]

As early as 1832, Gutzlaff had proposed to certain unnamed New Yorkers in the Canton trade a plan whereby Christian merchants would outfit commercial vessels for half-mercantile, half-missionary cruises in Chinese waters.[43] That such a curious project received serious consideration for a time is verified by a reference to it in an unpublished part of the prudential committee's instructions to Ira Tracy and S. Wells Williams the next year.[44] Likewise Abeel, an American Gutzlaff in many respects, appealed on his return from his exploring tour in Malaysia in 1834 for "missionary ships" sponsored by benevolent merchants.[45] Two years later, however, Secretary Anderson of the Board informed the Reformed Dutch evangelist that the project was abandoned for lack of support in

[40]Gutzlaff, a free lance after leaving the Netherland Missionary Society, enjoyed a friendly audience and perhaps monetary contributions in America, where he published the journal of one voyage in the Missionary Herald, XXIX (1833), 140-143, 174-178, 213-217, 249-252, 277-282. In addition, a New York firm published the first edition of the account of his earlier adventures: The Journal of Two Voyages along the Coast of China, in 1831 & 1832 (New York, 1833).

[41]Letter of Gutzlaff, Canton, November 24, 1833, Missionary Herald, XXX (1834), 308.

[42]Chinese Repository, IV (1835), 82-96.

[43]Letter of Gutzlaff, Macao, September, 1832, ABC:14, I, no. 33.

[44]Anderson and others to Ira Tracy and S. W. Williams, June 6, 1833, ABC: 2.01, II, 271.

[45]Abeel, Journal of a Residence in China, 37.

the New York commercial community.[46]

In China, however, the mission-minded Olyphant took up the scheme, but sought to exploit Gutzlaff's approach without incurring the opprobrium of sending missionaries on opium vessels, as the Prussian had sometimes done. In the fall of 1835, therefore, he lent the use of the _Huron_, an American brig chartered by his firm but lacking an immediate cargo, to William Medhurst of the London Society and Stevens of the A.B.C.F.M.[47] The Board bore none of the expense of the trip, Olyphant assuming nearly two thirds of the cost and the rest being carried by British societies.[48] These two evangelists, shipping a few bags of rice but no opium, sailed around the Shantung peninsula and on the return voyage distributed tracts at several points, including the harbor of the city of Shanghai.[49]

Although this venture did not produce any significant results, Olyphant sponsored an even more ambitious enterprise the next year, outfitting one of the company's vessels for an extended voyage through the Dutch East Indies and then northward to Japan. While Gutzlaff, Abeel and Bridgman had all mentioned the sealed empire of Nippon as a strategic point of attack in Asia, this was the first substantial plan to enter that country with Protestant emissaries.[50] Combining missionary with commercial

---

[46]Anderson to Abeel, Boston, January 6, 1836, ABC:1.01, XIV, 176.

[47]W. H. Medhurst, China; Its State and Prospects, with Especial Reference to the Spread of the Gospel (Boston, 1838), 296, 304-305.

[48]American Board, Twenty-seventh Annual Report, 69.

[49]Chinese Repository, IV (1835), 308-335; Missionary Herald, XXXII (1836), 197-202. This was probably the first appearance of Protestant missionaries at Shanghai, later to become so important a center of Chinese evangelism.

[50]Letter of Gutzlaff, Canton, January 14, 1832, Missionary Herald, XXVIII (1832), 256-257; letter of Bridgman, undated in ibid., XXXI (1835), 70; Abeel, Journal of a Residence in China, 376-377. As early as 1831, moreover, William Jenks of Boston had suggested that missionary societies of

objectives, the <u>Himmaleh</u> sailed in December, 1836, carrying articles of trade and two evangelists, G. Tradescant Lay of the British and Foreign Bible Society and the veteran Edwin Stevens. At Singapore the American Board's James T. Dickinson replaced Stevens, who died at that port, leaving the expedition without experienced leadership in such undertakings. The vessel touched at the Celebes and the Moluccas, and even Mindanao in the Philippines, but found a disappointing reception everywhere, both Dutch and Spanish rule proving inhospitable to either foreign trade or foreign religion.[51]

When the <u>Himmaleh</u> was delayed in returning to Canton in the spring of the following year, Olyphant's energetic partner, Charles W. King, fitted out for the second leg of the voyage another of the firm's ships, the <u>Morrison</u>, which had carried out to China so many of the Board's agents free of charge.[52] Special motivation for this trip to Japan was the presence in Macao of seven Japanese sailors, four of whom had drifted ashore on the American northwest coast.[53] With the solid pretext of restoring these men to their homeland, King stripped the <u>Morrison</u> of its armament, shipped some commercial cargo, but no religious tracts for fear

England and America draw up a joint memorial to the Japanese emperor setting forth the nature of Protestantism as opposed to the Roman Catholic teaching which was proscribed in that nation. <u>Spirit of the Pilgrims</u>, IV (1831), 534-535.

[51]Lay's account of the expedition was published as the first volume of G. T. Lay and C. W. King, <u>The Claims of Japan and Malaysia upon Christendom</u> (2 v., New York, 1839). Dickenson kept an interesting journal which is found in the <u>Missionary Herald</u>, XXXIV (1838), 171-179, 227-233, 241-244.

[52]The <u>Morrison</u> and other vessels of Olyphant and Company provided in all free passage to fifty-one missionaries and their families, both coming from and going to China. F. W. Williams, <u>Life and Letters of Samuel Wells Williams</u>, 77-78.

[53]Governor George Simpson of the Hudson's Bay Company arranged for the transportation of these castaways first to England and then to China, and was responsible for King's interest in them, having related their story to him while a fellow passenger on an Atlantic crossing in 1836. C. W. King to Anderson, Macao, July 2, 1827, ABC:14, I, no. 45.

of disturbing the anti-Christian Nipponese, and departed for Tokyo Bay in July with his wife, Dr. Parker, and S. Wells Williams, as well as the seven castaways.[54] At the Ryukyu Islands Gutzlaff, who was now in English government service, joined the company as interpreter, for he had learned something of the language from the Japanese seamen during their sojourn in Macao.

Despite its peaceful and even altruistic intent, the party received a cold welcome in Japan, where coastal batteries at Edo and in Kagoshima Bay fired upon them, and the frightened Nipponese sailors refused to stay behind among their hostile countrymen.[55] Charles King recommended that the United States government send a small naval force to rebuke this Japanese insult to the flag and perhaps force open the island empire.[56] Although there is no evidence that Washington ever took any note of this suggestion, the prudential committee of the Board apparently considered such action possible and instructed David Abeel to be prepared to take passage on the expedition if the opportunity presented itself.[57] The failure of this philanthropic mercantile venture, perhaps the boldest attempt to open Japan before Perry, brought to an end the

---

[54]Although this was a private venture, the American Board took a close interest in the voyage. Missionary Herald, XXXIV (1838), 77.

[55]All three Americans published independent versions of the voyage; King in the second volume of The Claims of Japan and Malaysia upon Christendom, Williams in the Chinese Repository, VII (1837), 209-229, and Parker in the Missionary Herald, XXXIV (1838), 203-207. The latter also published in London his Journal of an Expedition from Sincapore /sic/ to Japan, with a Visit to Loo-Choo (Andrew Reed, ed., London, 1838).

[56]King, who used the pages of the Repository to urge greater official interest in China and the whole Far East on the United States, not only demanded a naval expedition to Japan, but suggested that American influence be used to separate Korea and the Ryukyus from Japanese hegemony. Chinese Repository, VI (1837), 69-82; VII (1838), 9-32; 206-211. Lay and King, Claims of Japan and Malaysia upon Christendom, 180-186.

[57]Anderson and others to Abeel, Boston, October 15, 1838, ABC:8.1, II, 229.

sponsorship of missionary ships by China merchants. The indefatigable King, it is true, spoke of sending forth the Himmaleh and Morrison once more, and pressed upon the Board the urgency of preparing evangelists not only for Japan, but for Korea and Formosa as well.[58] In Canton Bridgman seconded the merchant's recommendation in respect to the dispatch of an American naval expedition and even mentioned the possibility of the occupation of the Bonin Islands as an approach to Japan.[59] In the meantime Williams employed two of the Japanese in his printing shop at Macao, where he and Gutzlaff continued their language studies, translating several books of the Bible into the language of Japan. Another pair shipped aboard the Morrison as common seamen on a voyage to the United States, but nothing is known of their reception there.[60]

Serious trouble between the British and the Chinese in Canton over the opium trade turned the Americans' attention to more immediate problems. Although some New England and New York firms dealt in this nefarious commodity, the East India Company supplied the bulk of it from British India.[61] In the Chinese Repository the Board's evangelists had long argued against the drug, while Charles King of opium-shunning Olyphant and Company took the English severely to task for their part in the drug commerce.[62] When Imperial Commissioner Lin confiscated the opium in the foreign factories in 1839, the Americans sympathized with China.[63]

[58]King to Anderson, Canton, November 10, 1838, ABC:14, II, no. 108.

[59]Chinese Repository, VI (1836), 390-391.

[60]Ibid., VIII (1839), 364; King to Anderson, Canton, September 6, 1837, ABC:14, I, no. 45.

[61]F. R. Dulles, The Old China Trade (Boston, 1930), 147-148.

[62]King published anonymously in England a pamphlet entitled Opium Crisis, a Letter Addressed to Charles Eliot, Esq., Chief Superintendent of the Trade with China (London, 1839).

[63]Bridgman accompanied Mr. and Mrs. King to Chunhow with the Chinese commissioner to see the opium destroyed. Chinese Repository, VIII (1839) 70-77.

In May of that year Williams wrote to Boston that "while partial distress must ensue upon the cessation of a trade worth sixteen millions of dollars annually, we cannot but rejoice at the check this traffic has received." Recognizing that the missionaries were implicated in Chinese eyes with the misdeeds of other foreigners, he added hopefully that the "moral sense" of the British would cause them to "applaud the firmness of the Chinese, and overlook any little breach of the so-called law of nations in considering their efforts to throw off such an incubus of death."[64]

But when Britain did not follow this philanthropic course and instead commenced military action against China in the early part of 1840, the members of the Board's mission quickly shifted their ground. "The time has come," Bridgman pronounced in the Repository, "when CHINA must BEND or BREAK."[65] In June Parker informed the prudential committee that he had also changed his mind:

> I am constrained to look back upon the present state of things not so much as an opium or an English affair, as a great design of Providence to make the wickedness of man subserve his purposes of mercy toward China, in breaking through her wall of exclusion, and bringing the empire into more immediate contact with western and christian nations.[66]

In spite of their distaste for the opium traffic, the missionaries, long straining against the restrictions upon their evangelistic operations, and firm in their conviction that the hand of God can "make even the wrath of man work for good ends,"[67] saw in the Anglo-Chinese struggle a vision of imperial China finally opened to the Gospel.

---

[64]Letter of S. W. Williams, Macao, May 17, 1839, Missionary Herald, XXXV (1839), 464.

[65]Chinese Repository, IX (1840), 2.

[66]Letter of Parker, Canton, June 24, 1840, Missionary Herald, XXXVII (1841), 43; also, significantly, quoted in American Board, Thirty-second Annual Report, 143.

[67]Chinese Repository, IX (1840), 5.

In the United States the "Opium War" brought the Celestial Empire into the news. Many if not most Americans looked upon England as morally wrong in the issue.[68] The Board, however, meeting at Philadelphia in September, 1841, discussed only the prospect of great missionary opportunities in the distressed nation.[69] Peter Parker, his medical work interrupted by the war, visited the United States at the end of 1840 to lecture on behalf of his Chinese hospital and to lobby for American intervention in China. After conferring at his alma mater in New Haven with President Jeremiah Day, the Rev. Leonard Bacon, and others, he decided, with their advice, to bring his views to the attention of the government in Washington.[70]

At the capital Parker met with members of the outgoing administration, including President Van Buren, and subsequently obtained interviews with Henry Clay, John Quincy Adams, Daniel Webster, and the newly elected chief executive, William Henry Harrison.[71] To Webster, as next secretary of state, he presented a long written statement which proposed that the government send an envoy—ex-President Adams, if possible, for his prestige would theoretically equal that of the Chinese emperor—to mediate between China and Britain; or, if hostilities ceased, to adjust American commercial relations with imperial officials.[72] According to Parker's report of the interview to Rufus Anderson of the Board, Webster

---

[68]Many argued as did the author of a magazine article on the China trade written after England had gained the advantage in the war: "The guns of a British fleet, although we conceive unjustly, have battered in the walls of their cities' chinks, through which will stream the light of Christianity and modern civilization." Hunt's Merchants' Magazine, XII (1845), 52.

[69]American Board, Thirty-second Annual Report, 35.

[70]Parker to Anderson, New Haven, January 6, 1841, ABC:16.3.8, II, no. 129.

[71]G. B. Stevens and W. F. Marwick, Life of Peter Parker, 253.

[72]Ibid., 184-188.

replied rather ambiguously that "a strong force would be sent to those seas."[73]   Adams, who was approached by other members of the foreign relations committee of the House in regard to accepting such a mission, told Parker he thought the whole scheme premature, if not unwise.[74]   The crotchety former president, however, may have been influenced by his talk with the medical missionary; for in November of the same year he aroused a hostile public opinion by an address in Boston justifying Great Britain's part in the war on the grounds of international law.[75]   Although the Board's emissaries in Macao—where they resided during the conflict—thought Adams laid too little stress on the role of the opium trade in the war, they printed the discourse—which the North American Review had rejected—in the Chinese Repository.[76]

Parker, meanwhile, having married a distant relative of Daniel Webster, returned from a lecture tour of England to Washington, where his wife's connections opened many doors to him.   He called upon President Tyler and Secretary of State Webster, both of whom assured him of their interest in China.[77]   Several months later, on the point of his departure to Canton, he called once more on Adams.   Now that the end of the war had set aside the question of American mediation, the former chief executive agreed that a commissioner should be dispatched to take advantage of any opportunity to negotiate with the defeated Chinese.[78]   Although other

---

[73]Parker to Anderson, New York, February 17, 1841, ABC:16.3.8, II, no. 130.

[74]J. Q. Adams, Memoirs (C. F. Adams, ed., Philadelphia, 1876), X (March 15, 1841), 444-445.

[75]Ibid., XI (December 3, 1841), 31.

[76]Chinese Repository, XI (1842), 274-289.

[77]Parker's journal, September 16, 1841, in Stevens and Marwick, Life of Peter Parker, 220-223.

[78]Adams, Memoirs, XI (June 2, 1842), 166-167.

influences were brought to bear upon the administration at this time, especially through the petitions of China merchants both in Canton and in this country, Parker's persevering presence at the capital may have been effective in the maturation of the first American embassy to the Middle Kingdom. In December, 1842, Congress heard Tyler's message, which Webster wrote, calling for the China mission, and in the spring of the next year Caleb Cushing of Newburyport, Massachusetts, accepted the appointment of United States commissioner to the Celestial Empire.

The American Board followed these events with cautious interest. In June, 1842, Anderson wrote to Macao: "I do not think there is any very confident opinion that great results will follow from this embassy at present, but it may be the beginnings of a series of advances on our part, that will result in something important at last."[79] A few days later, however, he informed the Board's missionaries that the "object of Mr. Cushing's mission, as we understand it, falls in with yours, though it be not the same, and it will contribute, we trust, in no small degree to facilitate the measures for the religious improvement of the Chinese empire, which we have specially in view."[80]

The prudential committee, moreover, offered Cushing the services of its missionaries. The corresponding secretary suggested that Bridgman—or possibly Williams, who knew Japanese as well as Chinese—act as interpreter, adding that Parker had not sufficient knowledge of the language, but might serve as physician to the embassy.[81] The latter was well known

---

[79]Anderson to the China mission, Boston, June 3, 1843, ABC:2.1.1, VI, 87.

[80]Anderson to Bridgman and others, Boston, June 8, 1843, ABC:2.1.1, VI, 89.

[81]This offer was made to Cushing through Governor Samuel T. Armstrong of Massachusetts, a member of the A.B.C.F.M. Anderson to S. T. Armstrong, Boston, June 8, 1843, ABC:1.1, XVIII, 105-106.

for his late activities in the United States, however, and was privately
recommended to Webster for the position by certain Boston merchants.[82]
At all events Cushing, whose chief assistant was Fletcher Webster, son of
the secretary of state, called upon Parker almost immediately after arriving at Macao and appointed him Chinese secretary.[83] Although Bridgman
was also attached to the mission, sharing the duties of translation and
interpretation as well as acting as chaplain,[84] it was his personable
colleague who made himself most useful to the American envoy.[85]

The friends of missions in the United States hailed the signing
of the treaty which Cushing and his aides negotiated just outside Macao
in the village of Wanghia in July, 1844. In Boston, however, the prudential committee was unhappy over the actions of the returned emissaries.
Fletcher Webster let it be known abroad that Parker, and not Bridgman,
had been their chief assistant in China, and neither he nor Cushing called
at the offices of the Board to extend thanks for the help of its agents.[86]
Furthermore, the New England Puritan, an evangelical weekly of wide influence, criticized the envoy for his alleged disparagement of the work

---

[82]In a petition to Webster written by John M. Forbes of Russell and Company for seven Boston firms in the China trade. Tyler Dennett, Americans
in Eastern Asia: A Critical Study of the Policy of the United States
with reference to China, Japan and Korea in the 19th Century.(New York,
1922), 136.

[83]Stevens and Marwick, Life of Peter Parker, 250.

[84]E. J. G. Bridgman, Pioneer of American Missions in China, 126-127. He
had earlier acted as interpreter for Commodore Lawrence Kearney. Chinese
Repository, XI (1842), 329-335. Williams also did some translating and
printing for the Cushing embassy. F. W. Williams, Life of Samuel Wells
Williams, 127.

[85]C. M. Fuess, The Life of Caleb Cushing (New York, 1923), I, 426-431.
Bridgman, who had discussed many of the questions covered in the treaty
in the Chinese Repository, recommending "firmness and decision" with
China, may have effectively aided Cushing with advice, however, as sug-
gested by Dennett, Americans in Eastern Asia, 48. See Chinese Repository,
X (1841), 47-48.

[86]Anderson to Parker, Boston, December 19, 1845, ABC:12.1.1, VIII, 337.

of foreign missions, reporting him as characterizing it "a humbug."[87]
Although Cushing had earlier granted public recognition of the services
of the missionaries,[88] he now wrote for publication another testimonial
to their work denying vigorously the accusations in the Puritan.[89]

The treaty itself, though chiefly commercial in nature, satisfied the missionaries in spite of their regret that Cushing did not insist
on being received at Peking.[90] Unlike the British pact, the American instrument included the principle of extraterritoriality and, apparently as
a special gesture to Parker, authorized the erection of hospitals and
churches in the five open ports.[91] Even before Cushing arrived in China,
the evangelists had noticed a change in the treatment of foreigners;
Parker, who had returned to his dispensary in Canton in late 1843 with
his wife, thought their military defeat by England had chastened the
Chinese.[92] The treaties did not, however, open China immediately to
large-scale missionary efforts. In Canton the inhabitants rioted against

---

[87] New England Puritan, March 14, 1845.

[88] Cushing to Rev. Septimus Tuston, Washington, February 17, 1845. Copied
from the Presbyterian in ibid., March 21, 1845.

[89] Cushing to Tuston, Washington, March 17, 1845, in ibid., March 28, 1845.

[90] Letters of Bridgman, July 18, 1844, and Parker, August 1, 1844, Missionary Herald, XLI (1845), 53. The next United States commissioner, Alexander Everett, was forced to remain at Macao also, a "disgrace" condemned
in 1845 by Bridgman. "I feel that it is a sacred duty on the part of the
U.S.A. to have a representative in China; and his residence should be at
the Emperor's court," he wrote to Anderson. Bridgman to Anderson, Canton,
November 24, 1845, ABC:16.3.3, I, no. 62.

[91] Stevens and Marwick, Life of Peter Parker, 254; Latourette, The History
of Early Relations between the United States and China, 1784-1844 (Connecticut Academy of Arts and Sciences, Transactions, 22, New Haven, 1917),
140-142.

[92] He noted first that "they appeared like a humbled nation." But he qualified: "Yet upon further acquaintance with the present state of the people
there is no doubt of the existence of the old feeling of superiority and
contempt, like a smothered flame, ready to burst forth should circumstances
favor." Letter of Parker, Canton, November 23, 1842, Missionary Herald,
XXXIX (1843), 257.

foreigners and refused to permit them into the center of the city for several years. Yet Bridgman and Williams, after spending three years in Hongkong when that island came under British rule at the end of the war, re-established themselves at their old station in 1845.[93] But the pattern of future Protestant efforts in China was foreshadowed when David Abeel, on his second tour of duty in the East, took passage in 1842 on a British warship to Amoy, where he commenced Christian worship on the outlying island of Kulangsu.[94]

III

The American Board conceived its new program in China to be twofold: the occupation of additional stations at the newly opened northern cities, and the replacement of much of the work of hospital, press, and school by more direct evangelistic means.[95] While Bridgman and the older evangelists lamented that "the tide of feeling has been setting strongly to the North,"[96] missionaries from other societies in the United States began settling in the treaty ports. The Baptists had been in Canton and Macao even before the war, but now Presbyterians, Episcopalians, and Methodists located themselves in China.[97]

The prudential committee dispatched reinforcements to the Far East and at the same time revised its strategy in regard to outlying posts in Southeast Asia. The Singapore station was closed out completely as having ended its usefulness, and the work among Chinese colonists in Siam

---

[93]American Board, Thirty-seventh Annual Report, 166.

[94]Missionary Herald, XXXVIII (1842), 465-469.

[95]American Board, Thirty-sixth Annual Report (Boston, 1845), 158-159.

[96]Bridgman to Anderson, Canton, 1845, ABC:16.3.3, I, no. 62.

[97]Latourette, History of Christian Missions in China, 248-257. The Opium War stimulated the Methodists to discuss sending emissaries to China. Christian Advocate, April 12, 1843; March 11, 1846.

and Indonesia liquidated. The Board ordered Elihu Doty and William J.
Pohlman of the Borneo mission to go to the aid of David Abeel in Amoy and
commenced a second northern station at Foochow, staffed by Lyman B. Peet
and Stephen Johnson from Siam.[98] The ailing Abeel, a little-sung missionary pioneer, returned home to die in 1846, but the Amoy mission prospered
as a special province of the Reformed Dutch Church, similar to the stations
at Arcot in India and on the island of Borneo.[99] At Foochow, a center of
the tea-growing region along the Min River explored briefly by Edwin
Stevens and Gutzlaff in 1835, the Board's agents were laboring long before
the advent of legitimate traders, if not before the opium dealers.[100]
Siam, which had not proved to be an avenue to the evangelization of China
after all, ceased to be a station of the Board in 1848, although another
society continued for a time to support the missionaries there.[101]

Shanghai became the chief literary headquarters of all missionary societies in this period, both British and American. As early as 1843
representatives from the two nations met in Hongkong to plan a joint translation of the Bible.[102] Four years later delegates from the various missions gathered at Shanghai, where they worked intensively for several

---

[98]American Board, Thirty-sixth Annual Report, 163; Missionary Herald,
XLIII (1847), 224.

[99]The Borneo station was surrendered in 1852 for lack of candidates, but
the Arcot and Amoy missions became separate Reformed Dutch enterprises
when that communion separated itself from the Board in 1858. Missionary
Herald, LIV (1858), 130.

[100]Justin Doolittle, Social Life of the Chinese: with Some Account of
Their Religious, Governmental, Educational, and Business Customs and
Opinions (New York), I, 19. Stephen Johnson reported in 1847 that all
foreigners there traded in opium. Letter of Johnson, Foochow, January 9,
1847, Missionary Herald, XLIII (1847), 225.

[101]Two of the evangelists developed divergent theological views which
made them unacceptable to the Board, though not to the American Missionary
Society, which undertook their support in 1849. American Board, Fortieth
Annual Report, 160-161.

[102]Chinese Repository, XII (1843), 448, 551-553.

years, finally emerging with two separate versions, differing somewhat in style and using variant expressions for the name of the supreme deity. The disagreement ran largely along national lines, the English preferring shang ti and the Americans shen, with the result that the Bible societies of the respective countries subsidized the publication of two different editions of the Chinese Bible.[103] Bridgman, who was chiefly responsible for the American translation, made the occasion of his labors in Shanghai an opportunity to organize a permanent station there after his return from a brief visit to the United States in 1852.[104]

The older phase of the Board's missions in China was drawing to an end, with the occupation of all the open ports except Ningpo. In 1851 the Chinese Repository issued its last number. Although the prudential committee had asked Bridgman to halt its publication as early as 1845, hoping he would have "less . . . to do with commercial and political China, and be exclusively devoted to her religious and spiritual interests,"[105] the editors maintained the journal as a private enterprise independent of the Boston offices. The discordance over Scriptural translation signaled the end also of perfect harmony among American and British societies. The Board's emissaries had long argued that England's record of colonial imperialism rendered her philanthropy less acceptable in China, though they were not unwilling to take advantage of Albion's aggressive action in prying open the Middle Kingdom. "The fact of our being Americans," wrote one of them from Foochow, "is no small recommendation to us in the eyes of the Chinese, and probably secures for us a much higher

---

[103]Chinese Repository, XX (1851), 216-224; Latourette, History of Christian Missions in China, 262-263.

[104]American Board, Forty-fifth Annual Report (Boston, 1854), 146-147.

[105]Anderson to Bridgman and Dyer Ball, Boston, July 17, 1845, ABC:2.1.1, VIII, 209.

degree of friendship, than we could hope to share did we bear any other name. There is no other nation on earth that is in circumstances more favorable for evangelizing China than the United States."[106] At mid-century, the predominance of American missionaries in the Middle Kingdom was definitely established. Out of one hundred and fifty Protestant evangelists in the field from the beginning, fifteen had come from Continental Europe, forty-seven from Great Britain and eighty-eight from the United States.[107]

In line with its conservative policy of keeping religion and politics separate—often, it is true, breached at Boston as well as in the field—the prudential committee advised its representatives to remain free of diplomatic maneuvering. In regard to the aid rendered the Cushing mission, the committee noted that "the benefits which incidentally grow out of a temporary connection of missionaries with secular embassies, rarely compensate for the serious interruption of their more appropriate labors, and the countenance which is thus given to the suspicions of the natives, that after all missionaries are agents of the governments of their own countries."[108] Peter Parker, however, whose preoccupation with his medical duties had already elicited Boston's disapproval, accepted an appointment from Secretary of State James Buchanan as secretary and Chinese

---

[106]Johnson to Anderson, Foochow, December 31, 1847, ABC:16.3.3, II, no. 137.

[107]Chinese Repository, XX (1851), 520.

[108]American Board, Thirty-fifth Annual Report (Boston, 1845), 185. At first willing to grant Cushing the services of one missionary, Anderson was angry when Bridgman and Parker both accepted positions: "Why does our Embassador /sic/ want two of our number? We cannot afford to swell his retinue merely for show." Anderson to King, Boston, September 28, 1844. Anderson's confidant in Canton, Charles King, testified that Bridgman had joined Cushing with great reluctance. "Dr. Parker," he wrote, "has none of these feelings and it is probable he will ere long quit the missionary side, for the political and surgical duties are more to his liking." King to John Dane, Canton, March 31, 1844, ABC:14, III, no. 265.

interpreter to the United States legation in April, 1845, and soon received the Board's dismissal.[109] At the death of Commissioner Alexander H. Everett in 1847, the former missionary became charge d'affairs, an office he held off and on, alternating with the post of Chinese secretary, for several years, during which time he attempted fruitlessly to negotiate with imperial officials concerning removal of the legation to Peking.[110]

Parker's defection was symptomatic of the impatience of many Protestant missionaries faced with a seemingly impervious barrier in China. Unsatisfied with their position in the treaty ports, the Board's emissaries sought a closer approach to the Chinese population and even looked with equanimity on further coercive action by the Western powers to open wider the partially unsealed empire. In the fifties, moreover, occurred the tremendous upheavals which encouraged friends of missions to think that the evangelization of China was near at hand. Civil war ravaged the land as a result of the Taiping Rebellion, a revolt against Manchu authority led by a visionary near-convert to Protestant Christianity, who had read one of Liang A-fah's tracts years before in Canton and organized a band of followers into a quasi-Christian religious and political society.[111] Though much of the fighting took place at a distance from the Board's missions, the insurgents seized Nanking in 1853 and captured both Shanghai and Amoy for a time, imperiling American missionaries in both places.[112]

---

[109]Stevens and Marwick, Life of Peter Parker, 258-269.

[110]Ibid., 279-296.

[111]For the religious character of the Taiping Rebellion and its relations to Protestant missions, see E. P. Boardman, Christian Influence upon the Theology of the Taiping Rebellion (Madison, 1952), 3-32.

[112]At Amoy the home of Elihu Doty was penetrated by "about one hundred balls of various sizes, from a few ounces to ten pounds." Letter of Doty, Amoy, January 18, 1854, Missionary Herald L (1854), 170. The Board's missionaries at Shanghai enjoyed the protection of the security forces of the Western powers. Letter of Bridgman, Shanghai, October 2, 1854, ibid., LI (1855), 61.

The first reactions in the United States were favorable to the rebellion, in secular as well as evangelical circles.[113] In 1853 the American Board saw in the allegedly religious character of the Taipings talismans of missionary success.[114] Alarmed by reports that the American commissioner in China planned to assist the British and French to put down the rebellion, the editor of the Puritan Recorder in Boston lamented that his own countrymen would aid in defeating "the insurgents who are about to achieve the most important revolution in the history of the human race."[115] Missionaries also tended to approve the rebels' course, at least in the initial phases of the struggle.[116] Bridgman, who visited the Taiping capital at Nanking with Commissioner Robert M. McLane on the U.S.S. Susquehanna in 1854, forwarded to the prudential committee a laudatory account of their doctrines and government.[117] Official representatives of the United States were generally unfriendly to the Taipings, however, as Humphrey Marshall, McLane's immediate predecessor, indicated in reporting to Washington the partisan zeal of his subordinate, Peter Parker: "He exhibits such enthusiasm for what he is pleased to call the patriots of China, as to make me apprehend that he may forget, in the sympathies of the missionary, the apathy necessary to a secretary of legation."[118]

---

[113]North American Review, LXXIX (1854), 158-200; De Bow's Review, XV (1853), 541-571; XVIII (1855), 1-15.

[114]American Board, Forty-fourth Annual Report, 123-125.

[115]Puritan Recorder, February 1, 1855.

[116]See J. B. Littell, "Missionaries and Politics in China—The Taiping Rebellion," Political Science Quarterly, XLIII (1928), 566-599.

[117]Letter of Bridgman, Shanghai, June 27, 1854, Missionary Herald, L (1854), 330.

[118]Humphrey Marshall to John Marcy, Shanghai, July 6, 1853, in House Executive Document, 33 Cong., 1 sess., no. 123, 198.

The growing fanaticism of the insurgents had begun to disillusion some of the Board's agents themselves. In December, 1854, S. Wells Williams wrote: "The hopes based on what was heard eighteen months ago of the Christianity of the rebels, are now seen to be delusive; and when that feature is gone, the sympathy felt will pass away from western minds." The missionary printer was not disturbed at the prospect of foreign intervention on the Imperialist side:

> It may be the channel by which the power of the enemy of true religion is to be held in check; and the gospel may also find an entrance amid the conflicting fears of the imperial government of a rising of its own subjects, on the one hand, and of offending powers whose aid it invoked when in danger, on the other. The civil war in China will take a new phase, if it brings in the nations of Europe and America as umpires.[119]

Williams apparently preferred to reside in China as an emissary of a foreign religion under the protection of treaties wrung from the emperor by Western powers than to see a native Christian dynasty—if so the Taipings could be considered—established in Peking. "The progress of Christianity in the Turkish empire," he wrote in a later letter, echoing the sentiments of his colleagues in Ottoman domains during the Crimean War, "would not be promoted by an Armenian Sultan or Emperor at Constantinople; and I think the time has not yet come for a Christian monarch at Peking, supposing Taiping to be a Christian, which I have strong reasons for doubting."[120]

During these troubles in China, the long-awaited American expedition to Japan was commenced. When Commodore Matthew C. Perry arrived in Canton in the spring of 1853, he invited Williams, who had been one of

---

[119]Letter of Williams, Canton, December 9, 1854, Missionary Herald, LI (1855), 118.

[120]Letter of Williams, Canton, February 1855, Missionary Herald, LI (1855), 168. Bridgman retained his enthusiasm for the movement long after most of his associates, reporting upon it in a friendly vein as late as 1860. Letter of Bridgman, Shanghai, August 2, 1860, ibid., LVI (1860), 369-370.

the Morrison party sixteen years before, to accompany him as Japanese interpreter.[121] With the approval of the Canton mission, Williams made two visits to Japan with the commodore, reporting unfavorably to Boston about that country as a field for immediate evangelistic endeavors. Noting that Perry's treaty said nothing about the residence of foreigners other than traders, he concluded that "it seems to be advisable to wait awhile before attempting a mission to Japan, and see how the trade progresses. Doubtless Russia, England and France will come for further facilities, and thus one step after another will be taken in the full opening of the long closed Land of the Rising Sun."[122]

The missionaries in China now became more rather than less involved in governmental and diplomatic activities. In 1855 Williams resigned permanently from the Board's service in order to succeed Dr. Parker as Chinese secretary to the legation. The latter, who received the appointment of United States commissioner to China from President Franklin Pierce in that year, proved to be an aggressive minister, preparing plans for the American occupation of Formosa and seeking to force an entry to the Chinese capital for the renegotiation of the old treaty.[123] But in the summer of 1857 a new administration in Washington superseded the former missionary just as hostilities between China and the British and French brought hopes of new and broader pacts. One of the Board's agents in Macao wrote an epitaph to his ex-colleague's career which pointed up the dilemna of the would-be missionary-diplomat in this period:

[121]Williams, A Journal of the Perry Expedition to Japan (1853-1854) (F. W. Williams, ed., Asiatic Society of Japan, Transactions, XXXVII, Yokohama, 1910), 1.

[122]Williams to Anderson, Bay of Yedo, April 4, 1854, ABC:16.3.8, III, no. 348. Williams, however, warned against publishing this letter.

[123]Dennett, Americans in Eastern Asia, 279-291.

I consider him a most unfortunate and unhappy man. He came
to China with an unusual reputation for piety, he soon acquired an enviable fame as a surgeon and philanthropist.
Then came the temptation of fame as a surgeon and public
position. After years of vexation and annoyance he at last
reached the summit of his desires and came to China no longer
Reverend and hardly revered, but with two lines of capitals
after his name. . . . And now just as the cup is filled to
the full, it is dashed from his lips, and Dr. Parker turns
from the shores of China more disappointed than if he had
failed in every previous step of his diplomatic career. . . .
Now his name will hardly be remembered unless as the first
missionary surgeon in Canton.[124]

In 1858 Williams accompanied the new commissioner, William B.
Reed, to Tientsin, where new treaties were signed under the guns of an
Allied expedition at the mouth of the Peiho River. The American document
contained guarantees against interference with either Christian evangelists or their converts in the so-called "toleration clauses," inserted at
the last moment through the personal intervention of the former missionary-
printer, who with a Presbyterian colleague conducted most of the inter-
mediary negotiations with the Chinese.[125] The Middle Kingdom was open at
last, partly at least through the efforts of the men sent to China by the
American Board. Like their fellow evangelists in Turkey, they were content to find support for their labors in the protective outreach of
Christian nations of the West. Evangelicals in their aspiration for the
Protestant conquest of a third of the heathen world did not cavil at
toleration clauses in a treaty extracted within sight of foreign gunboats.
Most missionaries undoubtedly agreed with Williams that "the chafing of
the Chinese will pass away in the ameliorated blessings of the Gospel."[126]

Townsend Harris's treaty with Japan in the same year was "very

---

[124]W. A. Macy to Anderson, Macao, August 8, 1857, ABC:16.3.8, III,
no. 230.

[125]F. W. Williams, Life of Samuel Wells Williams, 270-273.

[126]Williams to W. F. Williams, Yellow Sea, July 9, 1858, in ibid., 280.

wonderful and pleasant news" to the evangelists in China.[127] But though
Harris wrote Bridgman the next year, in reply to the latter's request for
information, that missionaries might find a not unfavorable reception in
that country, the Board did not commence operations there until 1869.
Williams revisited Japan in 1858, however, and Henry Blodgett of the
Shanghai mission in 1860. It was on his return to China that same year
that Blodgett took residence in the north at Tientsin to commence work in
the last station established by the A.B.C.F.M. in this period.[128]

Great changes had taken place in the missionary outlook upon
the heathen world since the organization of the American Board in 1810.
China, with the largest non-Christian population on earth, was now at the
west, not the east. With the acquisition of Oregon and California, the
United States faced the Middle Kingdom directly over the Pacific.[129] At
the annual meeting in 1852 a special committee announced: "Now we realize
the great vision of Columbus, and reach the Indies by the West. The bar-
riers of ages are broken; and the heart of China is now open to the direct
influence of Protestant America."[130] Fifteen years later another committee reminded the members of the Board of the earliest efforts in the Far
East, when "we were obliged to look across the entire eastern continent.

---

[127]Letter of Macy, Shanghai, August 21, 1858, Missionary Herald, LV
(1859), 13.

[128]American Board, Fifty-second Annual Report (Boston, 1861), 111-113.
The year before William Aitchison accompanied the American embassy to
Peking, thus attaining the long-sought goal of the Board's missionaries
in China. He died shortly afterward, however, and had no successor in
the Manchu capital for several years. Letter of Henry Blodgett, Shanghai,
September 1, 1859, Missionary Herald, LVI (1860), 25-26.

[129]The discovery of gold in California attracted hundreds of Chinese, most
of them from the Canton region. The Board's missionaries there, who
watched the departing shiploads of coolies to America and distributed pamphlets among them, recommended that the prudential committee employ evangelists among California's Chinese immigrants. Letters of Williams,
Canton, December 27, 1851, and S. W. Bonney, Canton, December 17, 1851,
Missionary Herald, XLVIII (1852), 125, 166.

[130]American Board, Forty-third Annual Report (Boston, 1852), 13.

The land of Sinim was to us the 'Ultima Thule.'" Yet the extension of
American population westward and the concomitant opening of China to the
world had made that nation an important neighbor. "Surely," the committee
added, "the God of missions has brought this empire, so populous, so
idolatrous, nearer and nearer, that we may accept the field which he has
assigned us."[131] American foreign missions, in more or less complacent
partnership with commerce and diplomacy, created a significant nexus between evangelical America and eastern Asia. For Protestants of the United
States, China was henceforward inexorably a market for religious as well
as more mundane merchandise.

[131]American Board, Fifty-seventh Annual Report (Boston, 1867), 30.

CHAPTER VII

AFRICA AND THE EVANGELICALS

Africa had been an object of American missionary ambitions since theologian Samuel Hopkins and his Newport, Rhode Island, colleague, Ezra Stiles, proposed in 1773 to evangelize that continent by means of Negro ex-slaves.[1] In this unrealized project were contained two elements of the evangelical concern for missions: the Hopkinsian notion of disinterested benevolence propounded in practice by its enunciator and the utilization for the purposes of evangelism of existing ties between the United States and a particular pagan domain. In 1801 a New York religious journal revived the idea, calling upon the missionary societies which had already begun operations among the North American Indians to colonize converted blacks under white leaders in Africa, in order to "practice and recommend Christianity in the sight of the heathen."[2]

Behind these proposals, early and late, lay a bad conscience about Negro chattel slavery which evangelicals sought to salve by making use of the nefarious institution to carry the Gospel to the homeland of the unfortunate bondsmen. The peculiar nature of America's relationship to the dark continent and its inhabitants placed missionary responsibility directly upon the United States. "We owe a greater atonement than any other nation to bleeding Africa," announced Edward D. Griffin in a sermon of 1817. "And it is more in our power to make it than in that of any other people. We have an immense population of the sable race at our

---

[1]Archibald Alexander, A History of Colonization on the Western Coast of Africa (Philadelphia, 1846), 48-55.

[2]New York Missionary Magazine, II (1801), 33.

door, and under our control, whom we could enlighten, and elevate, and convert into instruments of salvation to the millions of Africa."[3]

I

The evangelical approach to the problem of domestic slavery in the first decades of the nineteenth century combined Christianization and emancipation with the return of the Negro as an evangelist to his own-- or his ancestors'--native country. One of the explicit purposes of the American Colonization Society, founded in 1816 to facilitate the removal of the blacks from the United States, was to civilize and evangelize Africa through the agency of Christian emigrants.[4] It was Samuel J. Mills, founder of the Brethren and inspirer of overseas missions, whom the Society chose to explore the West African coast with Ebenezer Burgess in 1818. Having located a site to the south of England's Sierre Leone settlements, Mills died on the return voyage and was buried at sea, a martyr to a cause he never served in the role of foreign missionary.[5] With the establishment a few years later of a precarious colony at Cape Mesurado in what later became Liberia, various societies in this country employed agents to labor among both colonists and the surrounding tribesmen. The first were two Negro Baptist ministers from the South, who were followed by both black and white emissaries of the American churches.[6]

Not only did colonization and evangelism go hand in hand, but most evangelicals believed it impossible to carry Christianity successfully to Africa by other than colored missionaries, whose ancestral

---

[3]Griffin, A Plea for Africa. A Sermon Preached . . . at the Request of the Board of Directors of the African School (New York, 1817), 31.

[4]Alexander, History of Colonization, 93-94.

[5]Spring, Memoir of Samuel Mills, 224-229.

[6]William Gammell, A History of American Baptist Missions in Asia, Africa, Europe, and North America (Boston, 1849), 244-248.

heritage and pigmentation made them more acceptable to the native population than Caucasians, and provided adequate protection as well against the ravages of the tropical climate.[7] As a method of training such men, the American Board, which formally resolved in 1825 to commence a station on the African continent at the earliest opportunity, authorized the attendance of Negroes at the Foreign Mission School in Cornwall, Connecticut.[8] The next year the prudential committee corresponded with the American Colonization Society, offering to send evangelists to Africa but confessing the difficulty of securing "suitable persons among her descendants."[9] In 1827, the year in which the Cornwall academy closed its doors before enrolling a single such student, the Board appointed a colored Presbyterian minister from Tennessee, George M. Erskine, its first emissary to Liberia.[10] Erskine, however, preferring to become a pastor among the emigrants themselves, refused the commission, and the prudential committee announced its hope of yet finding "suitable colored men, to whom the climate is not unfavorable."[11]

After several years, during which time no Negro candidates appeared, the directors of the enterprise turned to the employment of white Southerners, in the belief that they would become more easily acclimated to Africa than New Englanders. When John Leighton Wilson of South Carolina offered his services, the American Board quickly accepted and in 1833 dispatched him with a Princeton classmate to explore the Guinea Coast

---

[7]See Leonard Bacon, A Plea for Africa; Delivered in New-Haven, July 4, 1825 (New Haven, 1825), 16-18.

[8]American Board, Sixteenth Annual Report, 23.

[9]Evarts to R. R. Gurley, Boston, June 28, 1826, ABC:1.01, VI, 161-162.

[10]Prudential Committee Records, II (November 21, 1827), 123-124.

[11]American Board, Nineteenth Annual Report, 111.

for a mission site.[12] The two young men sailed from Baltimore in company with a group of emigrants of the Maryland Colonization Society, recently organized to plant an independent community at some distance from the parent association's Liberian settlements.[13]

In its instructions to Wilson and his companion, the prudential committee outlined an ambitious program of evangelization utilizing the philanthropic colonies on the African West Coast as beachheads for conquering the interior when the great rivers like the Niger were opened.[14] In spite of some latent doubts about the expediency of associating missionary labors too closely with the colonizing efforts of other American societies, the Board's agents recommended the establishment of a station at Cape Palmas, the region selected for the Maryland Society's settlement.[15] In a confidential report never made public, the explorers presented a rather jaundiced view of the ex-slave colonies and of their potential influence upon African evangelism. Advising the Board to keep clearly distinct the two enterprises, they concluded that while the colored emigrants "will do very little in the way of communicating religious instruction," they may afford the missionary "a place of retreat and refreshment" and set an example to the native inhabitants of civilized life.[16]

After a brief rest in the United States, Wilson returned to Africa in 1834 with his wife and a Negro woman teacher as well, for the

---

[12]Stephen Wyncoop, a New Yorker, accompanied Wilson out of personal friendship, when it proved impossible to associate another Southerner with the enterprise immediately. Missionary Herald, XXX (1834), 73.

[13]The Maryland Society also planned to ban from its settlement the rum trade, which many complained of as the source of great troubles in Liberia. Alexander, History of Colonization, 405-407.

[14]Missionary Herald, XXIX (1833), 401-402.

[15]Ibid., XXX (1834), 212-213.

[16]Report of J. L. Wilson and Stephen Wyncoop, March 24, 1834, ABC:15.1, no. 6.

Board still hoped to employ persons of that race, if only in subordinate positions.[17] At Cape Palmas they found the frame house which the evangelist had brought out on the previous voyage constructed on land allocated to the mission by the Maryland Colonization Society.[18] In spite of his earlier doubts, Wilson found the settlers co-operative, and he acted as an informal advisor for a time to their white governor, James Hall.[19] Although the prudential committee had morbidly warned that "you may both die soon after entering the field,"[20] the South Carolinian and his wife defied the legend of the white man's vulnerability to the effects of the climate. "When I say good health, however," Wilson cautioned the committee, "you must not understand me as speaking of what you would call in America good health, but good African health. We have frequent attacks of chill and fever, but are not confined to our rooms for more than a few hours, and are able the next day to resume our duties."[21] Yet, of three members of the first reinforcement in 1836, only one, a Negro printer, survived the rigors of acclimation at Cape Palmas, David White of Massachusetts and his wife succumbing to "African fever" within the first month of residence.[22] This blow seemed to justify the fears of many Northerners about the danger of life in the tropics and discouraged candidates from volunteering to replace the victims, "nothwithstanding the interest that is felt in the colored race," as the prudential committee reported in

---

[17]Missionary Herald, XXX (1834), 465.

[18]American Board, Twenty-seventh Annual Report, 36.

[19]Alexander, History of Colonization, 409.

[20]American Board, Twenty-fifth Annual Report, appendix, 144.

[21]Letter of J. L. Wilson, Cape Palmas, August 24, 1836, Missionary Herald, XXXIII (1837), 36.

[22]Letter of J. L. Wilson, Cape Palmas, January 28, 1837, in ibid., 365-366.

1838.[23]

The mission began by setting up an English-language boarding school for native young men and women. But Wilson soon learned the speech of the Cape inhabitants, reducing it to written form so that printer Benjamin Van Rensselaer James was able to publish tracts and Scripture translations in the Grebo language, as well as a useful dictionary prepared by the white evangelist. For several years the missionaries followed the usages of their fellow laborers in Ceylon and the Sandwich Islands in designating boarding-school pupils by the American names selected by their benefactors in the United States.[24] Although the Board sent no additional Negro candidates from home, the mission employed several colonists and natives as assistants. The narrow limits of the colonial settlement at Cape Palmas, however, proved too restricted a field, in view of the prudential committee's ambitions to extend its operations inland from the colonies of the coast. One object was to reach the warlike Ashanti, who had defeated an English force on the Gold Coast fifteen years before. With the aid of Captain Richard Lawler, an American shipmaster and trader in African waters, Wilson commenced further explorations toward the south in 1839, seeking a point at which missionaries could penetrate to the interior.[25] The news the next year of a British expedition to be dispatched in 1841 to open the Niger to commercial navigation and philanthropic enterprise raised the little company's hopes of finding a pathway to the heart of Africa.[26]

In the meantime the Board established itself at another point

[23]American Board, Twenty-ninth Annual Report, 56.

[24]General letter from the missionaries, Cape Palmas, December 6, 1839, Missionary Herald, XXXVI (1840), 219-221.

[25]Journal of J. L. Wilson, in ibid., XXXV (1839), 352-359.

[26]Annual report of the mission, December 28, 1840, in ibid., XXXVII (1841) 356.

on the continent. A year before Wilson's exploring visit to the West Coast, John B. Purney, a member of the Society of Inquiry at Princeton Theological Seminary, had written to John Philip, the well-known superintendent of the London Missionary Society's stations in South Africa, for information concerning mission fields in that region.[27] In his reply, published in the Missionary Herald, the redoubtable Philip, celebrated for his advocacy of the rights of the native population of Britain's Cape Colony, invited Americans to evangelize the Zulus living just beyond the bounds of European settlement.[28] After further correspondence with the veteran missionary, the Board decided to send two companies to the Cape, one to work among the so-called Maritime Zulus in the area around Port Natal, and the other to attempt to reach a related tribe far in the interior—the Matabele, though neither Dr. Philip nor the prudential committee was aware of their proper designation and spoke of them as Zulus.

A month after Wilson's second departure for West Africa in 1834, six evangelists and their wives embarked at Boston for the Cape of Good Hope.[29] Three of the men came from south of the Mason and Dixon line— Henry I. Venable of Kentucky, Daniel Lindley, the Ohio-born pastor of a Presbyterian church in North Carolina, and his friend from the same state, Alexander E. Wilson, who was both a physician and an ordained minister. Two others, however, George Champion from Yale and Aldin Grout from Amherst, were New England Congregationalists, who with Dr. Newton Adams of New York were destined to the maritime mission in Natal. Although Wilson's experience at Cape Palmas had demonstrated the ability of white

---

[27]J. B. Purney to John Philip, Princeton, March 16, 1832, in D. J. Kotze, ed., Letters of the American Missionaries (Van Riebeck Society, Publications, 31, Cape Town, 1950), 21-27.

[28]Letter of John Philip, May, 1833, Missionary Herald, XXIX (1833), 414-420.

[29]Ibid., XXXI (1835), 32.

men to survive African conditions, the departing emissaries and their families at home were still apprehensive in this respect. On their arrival in Cape Town, however, Philip greeted them heartily and assured them of the healthfulness of the temperate climate of South Africa: "Tell your friends missionaries never die here."[30]

While the three families named to the Natal station were delayed at the Cape by the outbreak of war in Kaffirland, which lay in the direct path of their journey, Lindley, Wilson, and Venable set off with their courageous wives on a thousand-mile trek by ox-wagon into the northern wilds, where they hoped to gain the permission of the Matabele chieftain, Msilikatzi, for a mission.[31] Having spent nearly a year in travel, for the difficulties of the route through frontier country made it necessary to rest both men and oxen several weeks at two stations of the London Missionary Society, Griquatown and Kuruman, they reached Mosega, the capital of Msilikatzi's country in the summer of 1836. There, on the far side of the Vaal River and beyond white settlement, the missionaries prepared to establish themselves on the very site abandoned a few years previously by the emissaries of a French Protestant society.[32]

But events outside the reckoning of the Americans conspired against the pioneer undertaking. The Board's representatives had arrived at a critical juncture in the affairs of the Cape Colony. In 1835 the restless Dutch farmers, or Boers, disturbed by the recent emancipation of the slaves and the entire racial policy of the colonial authorities, were

---

[30]Journal of George Champion, Cape Town, February 26, 1835, Missionary Herald, XXXI (1835), 415.

[31]Ibid., XXXI (1835), 281. The story of this adventuresome trip has been fully related in E. W. Smith, The Life and Times of Daniel Lindley (1801-80): Missionary to the Zulus, Pastor of the Voortrekkers, Ubebe Omhlope (London, 1949), 65-92.

[32]E. W. Smith, Life and Times of Daniel Lindley, 87.

just beginning the Great Trek northward. At Mosega the mission collided
with the Voortrekkers in January, 1837, when a commando descended upon
the village to avenge earlier Matabele assaults upon the emigrants. In
the carnage and confusion that followed, the missionaries almost miracu-
lously escaped injury, though shots pierced their dwellings and terror-
striken Africans pursued by the merciless Boers sought refuge in their
compound. Caught up in the implacable hostility of Dutch farmers and
Matabele tribesmen, the Americans surrendered their post in the Transvaal
and accompanied the Boers back toward the coast.[33]

Meanwhile the second party of evangelists had procured ship
passage to the Bay of Natal, where they found a frontier settlement of
whites from whom they purchased oxen for the trek into the interior to
visit Dingaan, the Zulu ruler who had extended his authority over that
whole region.[34] With the African chief's permission secured, two members
returned to Bethelsdorp and brought in their wives and supplies by wagon
through the area recently desolated by the Kaffir War.[35] By the time
that their colleagues from Msilikatzi's country arrived after another
long and arduous journey that skirted the Drakensberg Mountains,[36] the
mission had commenced schools and begun publishing Zulu textbooks in its
press.[37]

At home the American Board, rejoicing that its emissaries had

---

[33]Joint letter of the missionaries, Grahamstown, May, 1837, Missionary
Herald, XXXIII (1837), 418.

[34]Letter of Aldin Grout, February 12, 1836, in ibid., XXXII (1836), 339-
342.

[35]Letter of Grout, Port Natal, June 16, 1836, in ibid., XXXIII (1837),
148-150

[36]Letter of Daniel Lindley, Port Natal, August 21, 1837, in ibid., XXXIV
(1838), 180-181.

[37]American Board, Twenty-ninth Annual Report, 58-59.

made two separate lodgments in Africa, was planning ahead. At the annual meeting in 1836 the prudential committee outlined a long-range project for the evangelism of the world which included an ambitious plan for the dark continent. According to maps of the time a great mountain chain extended across the center of Africa, giving rise to conjecture that somewhere in the unexplored interior south of the Sahara lay an elevated region which promised both a fertile soil and a salubrious climate. The committee proposed to advance toward this terra incognita from its stations on the southern and western shores of the continent, anticipating that its missionaries would some day meet and "keep a jubilee on the mountains of the centre."[38]

Two years later, moreover, Edmund Roberts' publication of his Embassy to the Eastern Courts drew attention to Africa's eastern coast and especially Zanzibar, an island under the tolerant rule of the sultan of Muscat, with whom Roberts had recently negotiated a commercial treaty for the government of the United States.[39] In 1839 three members of a reinforcement for the Bombay mission, who visited the island briefly, recommended a station there, and the American consul at Zanzibar, Richard P. Waters of Salem, Massachusetts, favored the scheme in correspondence with the Board.[40] Toward the close of the fourth decade of the century, the Board optimistically looked forward to an early occupation of a larger part of the African continent.

---

[38] American Board, Twenty-seventh Annual Report, 110.

[39] Missionary Herald, XXXVI (1840), 121.

[40] Letter of Ebenezer Burgess, September 11, 1839, in ibid., 118-121; American Board, Thirty-first Annual Report, 83.

II

Political conditions in Africa augured badly for the continuance, to say nothing of the extension, of missionary labors. As early as 1839 the Board considered breaking up the mission in South Africa and sending its agents to other fields, perhaps in nearby India.[41] The displaced evangelists from the Matabele country had hardly settled in Natal before the trekking Boers themselves determined to find homes in the same region. Discovering passes through the mountain barrier, the farmers crossed the Drakensberg and prepared to occupy the land.

In the spring of 1838, Dingaan, the Zulu ruler, treacherously slaughtered a deputation of fifty Dutch farmers headed by Piet Retief, who came to demand a grant of land from the powerful chieftain. Henry Venable arrived at the Zulu capital just a few hours after the bloody deed, in time to see vultures circling over the unburied bodies of the murdered men. This was merely a signal for further Boer-Zulu conflicts. Although Dingaan assured the Americans of his friendship, they looked upon the impending struggle as so great a threat to their work that they fled the country, leaving only Daniel Lindley to watch the course of events.[42]

At first the native Africans carried everything before them, and Lindley took refuge on board an English vessel, the _Comet_, which carried him to Port Elizabeth where he rejoined his family and associates.[43]

---

[41] E. W. Smith, _Life and Times of Daniel Lindley_, 147.

[42] General letter from the missionaries, Port Elizabeth, April 2, 1838, _Missionary Herald_, XXXIV (1838), 310-312.

[43] On the voyage the vessel touched at Delagoa Bay, which Lindley first surveyed as a possible mission site and later dismissed as impracticable by reason of the religious policy of the Catholic Portuguese who controlled the area. Letter of Lindley, December 31, 1838, in _ibid._, XXXV 193-195.

Some time after the British dispatched military forces to Port Natal near the close of 1838, Dr. Adams revisited the scene of the mission's interrupted labors, and the next year both he and Lindley reoccupied their stations.[44] In the meantime, the Boers, under the command of Andries Pretorius, had defeated Dingaan and were organizing a frontier republic while Britain's colonial authorities wavered unsteadily between firm action and conciliation. These uncertain conditions in Natal, moreover, so discouraged the mission that some of its members returned to the United States. The Venables retired permanently from the field; Dr. Alexander Wilson exchanged his post for one at Cape Palmas on the western coast; Aldin Grout, who like Wilson had lost his wife in Africa, returned to Cape Town after a brief American visit; and George Champion withdrew for the sake of his wife's health, only to die himself in the West Indies before he could resume his labors in Natal.[45]

The Board's missionaries had encountered, in a series of remarkable adventures, a situation not unlike the struggle between Indian and frontiersman in their own country. The Cherokee troubles in Georgia, fresh in everyone's mind, suggested a despairing parallel to the Boer's advance into Zulu territory. Lindley based his belief in the inevitable success of the Dutch farmers on this very analogy:

> All England's power on land and water will not prevent the emigration of her subjects from her territories. What can prevent the emigration of Americans to the west? . . . What has been said about the danger of natives destroying the government, is not worthy of much regard. It is just as probable that the abused western and southern Indians will destroy the United States. I now beg that you will not for a moment suppose that I defend any system of encroachments made by civilized on savage nations. I only think they cannot be stopped, while others seem to think they may.[46]

---

[44]American Board, _Thirty-first Annual Report_, 79.

[45]American Board, _Thirtieth Annual Report_, 52-53; _Missionary Herald_, XXVIII (1842), 75.

[46]Letter of Lindley, Port Natal, December 1, 1837, _ibid._, XXXIV (1838), 423-424.

The same evangelist expressed in a private letter to the prudential committee his wish that "Dr. Philip would let the laws of the land alone, and enlist the sympathy of British Christians to do a thousand times more, than can be done by legislation for the Hottentots."[47] Lindley went so far as to recommend that the Board employ evangelists among the Boers, whose efforts to establish a republic he admired, but his colleague, George Champion from New England, could only castigate the Dutch as "scourges of the natives." "Their ignorance, their parties, their ungodliness," he added, "make it improbable that they can unite in any good form of government. Far less are they prepared for independence, than the worst of the South-American States."[48] The prudential committee, unable to agree that it should shift its work from the native race to the European emigrants, described the task in Natal in terms of its experience in the Indian missions:

> If the pagan tribes in Africa and North America cannot be made christian and civilized communities, but must gradually melt away before the colonizing propensities of the white race, we must at least make the zealous and persevering endeavor to bring home the salvation of the gospel to as many individuals among them as possible.[49]

Lindley, who remained on the ground with Adams during the period of uncertainty, struck up a cordial friendship with the Boers in Natal, residing for a time in their camp and opening a school for their children.[50] Much of his concern was probably a matter of expediency. Taking the Board to task for publishing in the Missionary Herald an unfavorable comment on the Dutch by Champion, he wrote: "Should this extract come to

---

[47]Lindley to Anderson, Grahamstown, May 10, 1837, ABC:15.1, I, no. 58.

[48]Letter of George Champion, Port Elizabeth, April 9, 1838, Missionary Herald, XXXIV (1838), 425.

[49]Missionary Herald, XXXIV (1838), 307.

[50]E. W. Smith, Life and Times of Lindley, 170-171.

light here, it would ruin us--we would not be allotted a foot of land."[51]
But Lindley found the independent farmers friendlier to Americans than
to the British, "because we once asserted our rights from England," he
explained.[52] According to the leading historian of South Africa, the
Boer leaders at Pietermaritzburg fashioned their own government with the
aid of a copy of the Constitution of the United States which the missionary lent them.[53] After establishing their short-lived republic in Natal,
the Dutch turned to Daniel Lindley as their first regular pastor. In 1842
he accepted the office of predikant and for seven years ministered to
trekkers scattered throughout the region beyond the Orange and Vaal
Rivers.[54]

It was the harsh policy of the victorious land-hungry Boers
toward the Zulus which posed the most serious obstacles to missionary
labors. Suddenly, however, the situation altered when the British prepared to reoccupy Natal in 1842. "We may now consider the native population of this country as permanent and safe under the protection of the
English government," wrote Dr. Adams.[55] The prudential committee, after
having resolved to discontinue the mission in 1843, reversed itself the

[51]Lindley to Anderson, Port Natal, July 17, 1839, ABC:15.4, II, no. 85.
In an earlier letter, moreover, Lindley warned against publishing any of
their complaints against the Boers. "You see I expect to complain of
them," he wrote, "but only to you, and not to the world, so long as they
remain responsible to no government but their own." Lindley to Anderson,
Port Natal, December 1, 1837, ABC:15.4, II, no. 81.

[52]Lindley to Anderson, Port Natal, March 27, 1838, ABC:15.4, II, no. 49.

[53]E. A. Walker, The Great Trek (Pioneer Histories, London, 1938), 216.
Lindley, at any rate, asked Boston to send him such a copy in 1839.
Lindley to Henry Hill, Port Natal, July 14, 1839, ABC:15.4, I, no. 106.

[54]E. W. Smith, Life and Times of Daniel Lindley, 179-186. One of the
young Boers confirmed by Lindley during this period was Paul Kruger,
later first president of the South African Republic. Ibid., 195-196.

[55]Letter of Newton Adams, February 15, 1842, Missionary Herald, XXXVIII
(1842), 341.

the following year, authorizing further operations.[56] Aldin Grout had been on the point of returning to the United States when he was promised independent support at a public meeting in Cape Town sponsored by the American consul, Dr. John Philip, and others.[57] Moreover, the colonial authorities, anxious now to care for the native peoples of Natal, appointed him a government missionary on a salary of Ł 150 per annum, a position which he resigned, however, when the Board reinstated its work in South Africa.[58] When the British, after a brief skirmish with the Boers, raised the flag of empire in Natal, Daniel Lindley retained his pastorate with the Dutch but received his salary from the government. He did not resume his work among the Zulus until 1847, when the Board sent additional evangelists to the field.[59]

The chief problem facing the colony and the American missionaries was the disposition of the African population. With the advent of peace great numbers of Zulu tribesmen poured in from the north to join the thousands remaining through the wars. Although the Boer leaders of the abortive republic had discussed the possibility of creating native reserves as an alternative to black-and-white intermingling, which they abhorred, it was the British who saw in this policy of apartheid or segregation the surest method of preserving the Bantu race. The Americans had an opportunity to help shape this program in 1846, when the lieutenant-governor named Daniel Lindley and Newton Adams to a commission of five appointed to investigate land claims and submit recommendations. The next year the commission's report, setting the bounds of five native locations,

---

[56]American Board, Thirty-fifth Annual Report,

[57]Missionary Herald, XL (1844), 181-183.

[58]Letters of Aldin Grout, Cape Town, April 14, 1844, and June 19, 1845, in ibid., 286; XLI (1845), 419.

[59]American Board, Thirty-eighth Annual Report, 73-76.

in three of which the Board was then operating stations, was accepted.[60]

Just as the London Society earlier had approved complete segregation as a solution to racial conflict, planting their missions in areas set aside for native reserves, the Americans co-operated fully in a scheme two of their number had had a hand in drawing up. Although insufficient appropriations and the land hunger of both Boers and Britons prevented full implementation of the land commission's recommendations, which would have provided government support for agricultural and industrial education for the Zulus, the system laid a workable basis for missionary efforts. When the arrival of additional white settlers increased the pressure for diminution of the locations, the evangelists communicated to Boston their fears that the native reserves would eventually be destroyed, and with them, their missionary labors.[61] In the fifties, however, the Board occupied twelve stations in Natal, each in the midst of a large Zulu population. Because they were aliens, the Americans found it difficult to obtain legal title to the mission's holdings, and in 1855 sent a deputation to the English governor to secure adequate guarantees against removal. After a second meeting with government officials the next year the mission received satisfactory assurances of permanent rights to their five-hundred acre tracts in the native locations.[62]

During these same years the Board's emissaries in West Africa were entangled in their own special colonial and international problems. The partnership between evangelical missions and the colonization societies developed increasing friction as Liberia grew more and more independent

---

[60]Letter from the mission, December 4, 1847, Missionary Herald, XLIV (1848), 197.

[61]Letters of the mission and Lewis Grout, September 14, 1848, and March 19, 1849, in ibid., XLV (1849), 123-124, 373.

[62]Missionary Herald, LIII (1857), 27-28.

and nationalistic. An officer of an American naval vessel visiting the western coast suggested that the emigrants' jealousy of the white missionaries stemmed partly from the latters' attitude of racial superiority and their aloofness from the affairs of the colony.[63] The two enterprises clearly had become separate, particularly with the Board's continuing emphasis on the necessity of the subordination of Negro agents to Caucasian evangelists, a policy strongly advocated by Leighton Wilson himself. At any rate, the government of the Maryland Colony made several attempts to conscript both the native and emigrant assistants of the mission into its military forces in the frequent clashes with neighboring tribes.[64]

In the dual hope of escaping from the growing controls of the Cape Palmas settlement, and finding access to the interior, Wilson explored the coast afresh with newly arrived Benjamin Griswold. Traveling at no expense in the friendly Captain Lawler's trading ship, the evangelists arrived at the Gaboon River near the equator in June, 1841, and pronounced it a favorable place for a station.[65] Transferring their mission property at Cape Palmas to the Episcopalians, the little company, which included several native helpers, moved to the new location on the Gaboon, where they set up a press, opened schools, and began mastering another language.[66]

The river, which the Americans hoped would admit them to the heart of equatorial Africa, also attracted others. In the spring of 1844

---

[63] /Horatio Bridge7, Journal of an African Cruiser; Comprising Sketches of the Canaries, the Cape de Verds, Liberia, Madeira, Sierra Leone, and Other Places (Nathaniel Hawthorne, ed., New York, 1845), 72-73.

[64] J. L. Wilson and others to Anderson, Fishtown, August 24, 1841, ABC:15. 1, II, no. 26; American Board, Thirty-third Annual Report, 47-49, 99.

[65] Letter of Wilson, June 25, 1842, Missionary Herald, XXXVIII (1842), 497-498.

[66] American Board, Thirty-fourth Annual Report, 84-88.

French warships appeared off the coast. When the officers succeeded in obtaining somewhat unscrupulously a treaty of cession from the native ruler, King Glass, the missionaries lent their aid in drawing up a petition to the governments of both France and England, and in an interview with the French governor of Senegal attempted to gain assurances of the independence of the Gaboon.[67] Their efforts proved unavailing against the colonial ambitions of Louis Philippe, whom the representatives of the American Board at the Sandwich Islands had defied only five years before. In 1845 a French naval force dispatched to seize the region bombarded the native village, endangering the mission personnel and sending a thirty-two-pound shot through the chapel. Wilson immediately raised the American flag. "This," he wrote afterwards to the prudential committee, "if it had any effect at all, caused the fire to become more intense, and brought the balls still nearer to our dwelling."[68]

Like Captain Laplace at Honolulu in 1839, the French commander in the Gaboon River refused to recognize the neutrality of the American evangelists. In support of his raising the flag, Wilson argued that, if his government did not afford some protection to foreign missionaries, "they may well be afraid to go abroad, especially at a time when France seems bent upon adding to her realm every portion of the world, the inhabitants of which are incapable of resisting her power."[69] The mission received moral backing, however, from officers of the United States squadron cruising in those waters in enforcement of the slave-trade clause in

[67]Letter of William Walker, April 3, 1844, Missionary Herald, XL (1844), 349-351.

[68]Letter of Wilson, July 25, 1845, in ibid., XLII (1846), 29.

[69]Since the Gaboon River was the southern cruising point of the squadron, the mission was visited by American officers about every three months. Letters of Wilson, January 20, 1844, and July 25, 1845, Missionary Herald, XL (1844), 212; XLII (1846), 30.

in the Ashburton Treaty of 1842.[70]

Although a few Roman Catholic priests entered the territory
under the aegis of France, the work of the Americans went on without
serious interruption under alien rule. The corruptions of commerce rather
than empire-building most disturbed the evangelists. As the mission reported in 1849, "the foreign influence is not all political, neither is
it all French. American rum has done this people ten thousand times more
injury than French guns."[71] The slave trade that ravaged the entire
western coast was also a source of concern at the Gaboon, where Wilson
found on his first visit in 1842 a Spanish factory engaged in the unholy
business.[72] The part played by France, which abolished slavery in its
territories in 1848, in putting down the traffic brought about a friendly
exchange of letters between the mission and the commander of the French
naval squadron in 1851, serving to heighten their mutual good will.[73]

The missionaries, however, counted primarily on Great Britain
to eliminate the slave trade rather than on the French, who persisted in
shipping so-called "free emigrants" from the Gaboon to plantations in other
parts of the world. In 1850, when the English, discouraged with the meager results of their efforts, considered withdrawing their forces from
African waters, Wilson prepared a compelling argument against the move.
A wealthy merchant of Bristol, to whom the veteran evangelist had forwarded his statement, brought it to the notice of Lord Palmerston. Distributed in pamphlet form through the latter's agency, the document probably

---

[70]Letter of Wilson, September 21, 1846, Missionary Herald, XLIII (1847),69.

[71]Report of the mission for 1849, in ibid., XLVI (1850), 226.

[72]Letter of Wilson quoted in H. C. DuBose, Memoirs of Rev. John Leighton
Wilson, D.D., Missionary to Africa, and Secretary of Foreign Missions
(Richmond, Va., 1895), 217-218.

[73]Missionary Herald, XLVIII (1852), 58.

helped strengthen British sentiment favoring the continuation of the squadron.[74]

At the Gaboon Wilson and his colleagues labored chiefly among the Mpongwe, reducing their language to writing and printing the usual tracts and translations. Though they established out-stations at several points up the river, they were unable to penetrate far into the interior. But noting certain linguistic similarities, Wilson came near recognizing the basic unity of the Bantu peoples found in large numbers in all Africa south of the equator—a fact also apprehended by the missionaries in Natal, where the Zulus constituted another segment of the same racial stock.[75] The Board, however, never achieved its goal of reaching the heart of the continent. For reasons never stated, the mission to Zanzibar on the eastern coast never materialized. The special difficulties of the brethren to the south prevented any immediate accomplishments of the vision from that direction. It was David Livingston of the London Society's outpost at Kolobeng—where he also encountered the depradations of the Voortrekkers—who discovered in 1849 the fabled Lake Ngami, the rumored existence of which, far in the northern interior, the Board's agents in South Africa had reported to Boston as early as 1836.[76] The prudential committee rejoiced, however, in the news of the famous Scot's successful explorations in Central Africa, which opened up at last the inland pathway which the Americans had sought at the beginning.[77]

---

[74]DuBose, Memoirs of J. L. Wilson, 218-226; American Board, Forty-second Annual Report, 56, and appendix, 214-224.

[75]Missionary Herald, XLIII (1847), 260: Lewis Grout, Zulu-Land; or Life among the Zulu-Kafirs of Natal and Zulu-Land, South Africa (Philadelphia, 1864), 59-67.

[76]Joint letter from the missionaries, August 18, 1836, Missionary Herald, XXXIII (1837), 192.

[77]It was noted with some satisfaction that the noted missionary-explorer had a brother living in the United States, a clergyman in New York State. Missionary Herald, XVI (1820), 241-245, 481-494.

III

Colonization and foreign missions represented the conservative evangelical concern for the native population of Africa and her descendents in the United States. Not only did the A.B.C.F.M. employ Southern missionaries abroad but the churches of the South themselves, Presbyterian, Baptist, and Methodist, entered enthusiastically into the evangelistic enterprise. Although in 1820 Jeremiah Evarts had written two strong articles in the Panoplist "On the Condition of the Blacks in This Country,"[78] the American Board showed little interest in domestic slavery, and in its character as a national society attempted to avoid alienating its Southern constituency, even appointing a proslavery Virginian, William J. Armstrong, a corresponding secretary in 1835.[79] It was not long before abolitionist critics began demanding of the whole humanitarian movement a more particular regard to the "heathen" institution at home. In 1839 Gerrit Smith, wealthy New York State reformer who had recently left the Colonization Society for the more radical American Anti-Slavery Society, published an open letter to the A.B.C.F.M., condemning severely the prudential committee's complacent attitude toward the great domestic evil.[80]

The question came officially before the Board the next year when a group of New York clergymen petitioned against sending agents into the slave states for the collection of missionary funds.[81] In 1841 and succeeding year individual churches and clerical associations continued

---

[78]Panoplist, and Missionary Herald, XVI (1820), 241-245, 481-494.

[79]Armstrong served in this office, in spite of much opposition to him for his pronounced views against abolition, until his death in 1846 in the wreck of a trans-Atlantic steamer. Anderson, Memorial Volume, 218-220.

[80]Gerrit Smith, A Letter, Addressed to John Tappan, Esq. on Missions (Cazenovia, N. Y., 1839).

[81]American Board, Thirty-first Annual Report, 63-64.

to present memorials on the same subject, accusing the Board of "studied silence" on the issue.[82] In addition to the matter of accepting contributions from slaveholders, these petitioners pointed out that the well-known missionary to Africa, J. Leighton Wilson of South Carolina, was himself an owner of Negroes.[83] Wilson explained, in reply to the committee's hurried inquiries, that he had colonized in Liberia approximately thirty blacks belonging to him by marriage, but that two others inherited from his mother refused to accept manumission.[84] Although this answer did not satisfy his detractors, the Board defended its agent as morally blameless in the face of a crescendo of attacks from antislavery quarters.

While the directors of the enterprise in New England maintained a neutral attitude in their role as leaders of a national organization, missionaries in the field took sides in the abolitionist controversy. In Hawaii several of the evangelists corresponded with antislavery editors in the United States, one pointing out that the majority of Sandwich Islanders lived in a condition not far removed from that of Negro chattels in the South.[85] In 1841 they formed the Sandwich Islands Anti-Slavery Society, its members stating in the preamble to the constitution that "the fact of our separation from the land of our birth . . . does not weaken our obligations to co-operate with our brethren there, in averting the displeasure of heaven for national sins. . . ."[86] From as far away

[82]American Board, Thirty-second Annual Report, 59-60.

[83]American Board, Thirty-third Annual Report, 44-45.

[84]J. L. Wilson to Anderson, Gaboon River, January 23, 1843, in DuBose, Memoirs of J. L. Wilson, 100-102.

[85]Letter of Peter Gulick, June, 1837, in C. K. Whipple, Relation of the American Board of Commissioners for Foreign Missions to Slavery (Boston, 1861), 7.

[86]Union Missionary Herald, I (1842), 122.

as Urumiah, Persia, came the expression of similar sentiments from the pen of Justin Perkins.[87]

The gathering discontent at home was brought to a climax in the organization of rival missionary associations uncompromisingly based on antislavery principles. The first was the Union Missionary Society, formed in 1842 by delegates from Northern Negro churches who met in Hartford, Connecticut, and chose as white executive secretary Josiah Brewer, the subject of a controversial dismissal from the American Board several years before. At the same time the Amistad Committee, constituted to defend a group of natives of Mendi on the western coast of Africa who had come ashore at Long Island after a successful slave mutiny on a Spanish vessel near Cuba in 1839, planned to dispatch missionaries to accompany the Mendians to their homeland. In 1842 the two organizations joined in establishing a mission at Kaw-Mendi in West Africa.[88] Four years later, after the A.B.C.F.M. had declined to assume responsibility for the Mendian station, a convention of antislavery reformers at Albany, New York, brought to birth the American Missionary Association, which quickly absorbed the work of its predecessors and launched an ambitious program of foreign evangelism on abolitionist principles.[89]

Baptists and Methodists talked of similar action within their own denomination before the splitting of these two communions into Northern and Southern bodies made it unnecessary, but the A.M.A., drawing largely from the same Congregational and Presbyterian constituency as the American Board, took the leading role in opposing the more conservative

---

[87]Union Missionary Herald, I (1842), 33-35.

[88]Ibid., 71.

[89]Lewis Tappan, History of the American Missionary Association (New York, 1855), 8-24; A. F. Beard, A Crusade of Brotherhood: A History of the American Missionary Association (Boston, 1909), 31-32.

missionary societies. The issue raised questions concerning the whole
strategy of humanitarian benevolence. Although the new association carried on evangelistic work in various parts of the world, its members
located the immediate task of evangelicals in this hemisphere:

> We have heard much of Juggernaut, and what we have heard
> is true. . . . But we need not take a four months' voyage
> around the Cape of Good Hope to see Juggernaut. In our own
> country, within a distance of 50 or 60 hours, we may find many
> Juggernauts, and of the worst kind, in the shape of slave auc-
> tions and slave-breeding estates—where human hearts are
> crushed.[90]

In the fifties the struggle extended to other institutions of the "benevolent empire," creating dissatisfaction particularly with the tract societies, which distributed materials denouncing such evils as dancing,
smoking, and drinking, but ignored the sin of slavery. In opposing both
the American Board and the American Tract Society, one village parish in
Massachusetts called upon the rural districts to assume the lead in anti-
slavery pressures upon the conservative evangelical organizations, describing the metropolitan churches as "too near the fountain of commercial
and political influence . . . to take the first step."[91] The withdrawal
of churches on these grounds in New England and New York weakened the old
established societies, but did not alter their aims and practices before
the Civil War.

In this intraecclesiastical quarrel the actual African missions
were almost forgotten. New memorials to the Board raised the issue of
missionary-condoned slavery in the Choctaw and Cherokee Nations, and even
polygamy in India and Ceylon.[92] It was easily shown that the agents of

---

[90]American Missionary Association, Second Annual Report (New York, 1848),
26-27.

[91]Action of the Church in Franklin, Mass., in Regard to the American
Tract Society and the American Board (New York, 1854), 7-8.

[92]American Board, Thirty-fifth Annual Report, 66-67; Thirty-seventh
Annual Report, 72-74.

the society, after an uncertain beginning, had taken a strong stand against polygamous candidates for church membership, but the matter of Indian slaveholding was less easily solved. Not only did the Board's evangelists accept slave-owning Indians into full church fellowship, but they employed in the missions a number of Negroes belonging to Choctaw and Cherokee owners. Embarrassed by this disclosure, the prudential committee dispatched one of the corresponding secretaries on a tour of inpection of the Western stations. This agent recommended the discontinuance of the use of slaves, but in the long correspondence which ensued the missionaries demonstrated reluctance to alter practices of long standing.[93] Restrictive legislation passed in the fifties in both Indian nations prohibiting the education of blacks aggravated the Board's dilemma and led eventually to the cessation of evangelistic efforts among these tribes.[94]

At the annual meeting of the A.B.C.F.M. in 1859, the Rev. Henry T. Cheever presented a memorial addressed to the United States Congress condemning the African slave trade.[95] After some debate the question was postponed until the next year, when the petition was tabled on the advice of members of the Gaboon mission, who argued that the traffic did not directly affect their work in West Africa.[96] Thus on the threshold of the Civil War, the American Board persisted in its cautious neutrality in the face of the greatest controversy of the time. As a missionary society, it had a single aim, the evangelization of the world,

---

[93]American Board, Thirty-ninth Annual Report (Boston, 1848), 81-11; Fortieth Annual Report, 71-78.

[94]Missionary Herald, LVI (1860), 12, 332. The slavery question produced the most ardent debates in the annual meetings, requiring roll-call votes in 1845, 1854, and 1859. Anderson, Memorial Volume, 140.

[95]Missionary Herald, LV (1859), 336.

[96]Ibid., LVI (1860), 333-334.

just as Leonard Woods, one of the founders of the society, stated for the first committee to treat the question in 1841: "There are many forms of evil to be done away. But the evil which it is our object to do away, is the evil of idolatry, ignorance, and wretchedness among the heathen."[97]

In South Africa, however, the Americans came into conflict in the fifties with representatives of the Church of England over a moral issue which all considered related to the problems of evanglism. The Biblical scholar and newly appointed bishop of Natal, John William Colenso, who visited the Board's stations shortly after arriving in the colony in 1854,[98] soon announced that he planned no interference with the system of polygamous marriages. Once more overseas evangelists of the A.B.C.F.M. demonstrated an aspect of national divergence in the world-wide missionary crusade, when they took alarm at Bishop Colenso's loose interpretation of the application of Old Testament morality. The uncompromising American emissaries made a point of refusing church admission to Zulu males with more than a single wife and carried on a bitter pamphlet war with the Anglican bishop.[99]

Generally, American missionaries enjoyed friendly relations with both French and British secular authorities. By the time of the Civil War there was no connection between the Board's mission in Africa and the question of domestic Negro slavery in the United States. The evangelists stationed on the Gaboon and in Natal conducted their labors among pagan native peoples under the jurisdiction of European powers. With Liberia,

---

[97] American Board, Thirty-second Annual Report, 60.

[98] J. W. Colenso, Ten Weeks in Natal (Cambridge, Eng., 1855), 233-260.

[99] Letter from the mission, June 16, 1856, Missionary Herald, LIII (1857), 28-29. These opposing views were presented in a series of pamphlets, two of which were: Colenso, A Letter to an American Missionary from the Bishop of Natal (Pietermaritzburg, 1856), and /Lewis Grout/, An Answer to Dr. Colenso's "Letter" on Polygamy (Pietermaritzburg, 1856)

the only colony in Africa which had any ties with America, the Board was unable to co-operate successfully, proving to its own satisfaction, at least, that the early hope of evangelizing the continent by combined colonization and missions was an illusion. At the end of our period, stations in Africa were merely minor outposts of Anglo-Saxon Protestantism in its efforts to conquer the heathen world.

CHAPTER VIII

AMERICAN FOREIGN MISSIONS: SUBSTANCE AND SPIRIT

Under the spell of the millenarian conviction of the first
years of the nineteenth century, the projectors of American foreign missions aspired to Christianize the world in their own generation. This
was no grandiose expectation for men who had lived through the era of the
French Revolution and had seen Napoleon march undisputed across Europe—
all "signs of the times" which forecast the early advent of a new dispensation. No single society or nation could possibly effect so great a
transformation, however. "All the power and influence of the whole
Christian world," declared the prudential committee of the American Board
in 1812, "must be put in requisition during the course of those beneficent
labors, which will precede the millennium. . . . The utmost exertion of
every Christian now living, so far as his other duties will permit it, is
required in this glorious service."[1]

Protestants of the United States, then, were called to join
forces with a world movement in the grand final act of human history—the
gathering of the nations in preparation for the thousand years of peace.
Fortunately, the notion that "God has great things to be accomplished by
the men of this generation,"[2] could be extended almost indefinitely. In
1827, though the passage of time had dimmed somewhat the sanguine antici-
pations of the founders, Lyman Beecher informed the members of the Board
that within fifty years "every nation may be so far evangelized, as that

---

[1]American Board, Third Annual Report, 31.

[2]American Board, Fourth Annual Report, 33.

the work may move onward to its consummation, without extraneous aid."[3]

Almost twenty years later, when a third of a century had elapsed since the founding of the A.B.C.F.M., the prudential committee paused to measure its accomplishments and found them disappointing. Yet its statement in the annual report revealed the intrinsic optimism motivating the evangelical enterprise:

> It would almost seem as if a single missionary in a city, or a dozen in a kingdom, might speedily transform an ignorant, sensual, idolatrous, and selfish community into a nation of intelligent, moral, Christian freemen; or as if a hundred or two such laborers might, in a few years, put a British or American face on the whole Chinese empire.[4]

Despite the waning of chiliastic literalism and its abuse by the displaced Millerites, the vocabulary of millennial expectancy permeated the pronouncements of the Board for years to come. If nothing else, it developed a sense of men fashioning the forces of history in a working partnership with Providence.

I

In the propitious climate of the opening years of that evangelical age, the directors of missions marched toward Zion abreast of myriad sister organizations similar in outlook: the various benevolent societies formed to circulate religious literature, educate students for the ministry, promote temperance and other moral reforms, and ameliorate the circumstances of "the mariner, the imprisoned, the enslaved, and the neglected and outcast of every condition and character."[5] An unusual degree of co-operation marked the interrelations of Protestant enterprise in this period. Like the Bible, tract, home missionary and other

---

[3]Lyman Beecher, Resources of the Adversary and Means of Their Destruction (Boston, 1827), 31.

[4]American Board, Thirty-seventh Annual Report, 221.

[5]American Board, Thirty-first Annual Report, 195-196.

nondenominational agencies of the period, the American Board drew its strength mainly from the Presbyterians and Congregationalists who had been associated since 1801 in the Plan of Union.[6] Although the original program of unified action between these communions concerned only domestic missions in the new settlements of New York and the West, it spread an aura of interdenominational unity around other evangelical projects. The force of this solidarity was shown clearly when the United Foreign Missionary Society, representing chiefly Presbyterian and Reformed Dutch churches, disbanded in 1825, turning over its work to the American Board. The commissioners who negotiated the amalgamation announced that "the candid of the Christian public are all satisfied, that the same gospel which is preached in the Middle, and Southern, and Western States, is preached also in the Eastern States."[7]

This note of harmony sounded throughout the benevolent empire, with its interlocking purposes and leadership. When the American Society for the Promotion of Temperance was formed in Boston in 1826, it took its organizational model from the American Board of Commissioners for Foreign Missions.[8] Sunday schools became one of the important channels of missionary information and zeal, inspiring children to save pennies for the education of boys in China or Ceylon by abstaining from coffee, tea, and sugar.[9] Even the American Peace Society looked to missions to spread pacifist principles, sending to the Board copies of its tracts for distribution among the heathen.[10]

---

[6]See R. H. Nichols, "The Plan of Union in New York," Church History, V (1936), 49.

[7]Missionary Herald, XXI (1825), 333.

[8]J. A. Krout, The Origins of Prohibition.(New York, 1925), 108-109.

[9]John Scudder, Sabbath School Association (Boston, 1835), 18.

[10]In 1835 Rufus Anderson assured the Grimke sisters that his society always acted in the interest of peace, "never procuring arms, in any

In early decades the Board benefited from a stranger alliance: the co-operation of the Masonic order. In October, 1815, just prior to their embarkation from Newburyport, Massachusetts, four evangelists of the second company to depart from American shores were initiated into the mysteries of the fraternity and raised to the "sublime degree of Master Masons."[11] This ceremony, apparently never repeated, was obviously part of a campaign to promote interest in missions among members of the highly regarded secret society. Even at this date, however, not everyone in New England approved. One missionary candidate, who found a "deep solicitude" among Vermonters about the affair, questioned this unusual proceeding himself: "Will Masonry be a shield from the arrows of the enemies of God? Ought not missionaries to go to the heathen without a mask? Is it _expedient_ to blend Masonry with our holy religion?"[12]

The prudential committee persisted in its efforts to attract the order to its program and even commissioned a special agent to solicit contributions from local chapters under a plan endorsed by the Grand Lodge of Massachusetts and by Governor De Witt Clinton, master of the Grand Lodge of New York.[13] But the tide of anti-Masonry in the mid-twenties swept away these promising beginnings, although as late as 1826 the New Jerusalem Royal Arch Chapter in Wiscasset, Maine, donated the sum of thirty-one dollars to disseminate the Scriptures in translation.[14]

---

circumstances, for our missionaries to use against their fellow men, however savage." Anderson to S. M. and A. E. Grimke, Boston, September 26, 1835, ABC:1.01, XIV, 337-338.

[11] Manuscript notice in ABC:8.5, no.15.

[12] Parsons to Fisk, Burlington, Vt., January 20, 1818, ABC:16.5, I, no. 45.

[13] S. M. Worcester, _Life of Samuel Worcester_, II, 392.

[14] _Missionary Herald_, XXII (1826), 336. In part the response of Masons to the missionary appeal seems to have been an attempt to court evangelical favor in the face of rural antipathy to the organization. Worcester wrote that this alliance was a way of silencing "the tongue of reproach." Worcester to Henry Williams, Salem, May 2, 1820, ABC:1.01, IV, 120.

The principle of a division of labor made evangelical unity practicable and minimized rivalry in a common crusade. "Like the tribes of Israel," orated Lyman Beecher, "we may all encamp about the tabernacle of God——each under his own standard——and when the ark advances, may all move forward, terrible only to the powers of darkness."[15] Perhaps no better statement of the harmonious interrelationships of the many benevolent organizations of the time exists than that found in the instructions of the first secretary of the American Board to one of its domestic agents:

> While you powerfully display the urgent wants of the Pagan World, and press home to every heart, that a soul in India, in Africa, in the wilds of America, is as precious as a soul in our own land, or in our own state; yet your judgment and feelings will induce you to be particularly cautious of making any comparisons, or representations, which would seem to disparage other benevolent institutions, or to depress other charitable objects. Foreign Missionary Societies, Education Societies, Home Missionary Societies, Bible Societies, Tract Societies, are all of them important, are all of them of one great system; and should indulge no jealousies of each other, no spirit of invidious competition; but cultivate the best mutual understanding, act in the most perfect concord and rejoice each in the success of the other.[16]

The nondenominational character of the Board was threatened by the Presbyterian schism of 1837, when the Old School faction withdrew from all Plan of Union agencies. This group organized its own board of missions, while the New School Assembly continued to support the A.B.C.F.M. until the reunion of the two Presbyterian organizations in 1869. In actual fact the defection did not materially damage the work of the New England society. Many contributors and some churches belonging to Old School synods retained their former connections out of loyalty to the nonsectarian ideal. Moreover, none of the Presbyterian missionaries

[15]Beecher, Resources of the Adversary, 32.

[16]Worcester to Edward Payson, Salem, February 28, 1816, ABC:1.01, I, 68.

in the field resigned. The Reformed Dutch Church, which had supported
the Board since 1816, demanded an increasing degree of control over evangelists of its own communion, and finally withdrew from the co-operative
arrangement altogether in 1857.[17] Thus the first fifty years of the
American Board were the heyday of interdenominational unity. Within a
few years of the close of the Civil War unified efforts in foreign missions came to an end.

Since the benevolent institutions were "voluntary" associations
rather than ecclesiastical bodies, each depended upon its own network of
subordinate organizations and collecting agencies for funds. Rejecting
the methods of those societies which hired collectors on a commission
basis,[18] the Board paid regular salaries to its agents and organized hundreds of auxiliaries covering the larger cities and counties, as well as
local "gentlemen's" and "female" associations in each parish.[19] In 1848
the prudential committee divided the whole country into thirteen districts,
each headed by a general agent or secretary.[20] This was the complex structure typical of voluntary societies which the Unitarian, William Ellery
Channing, criticized so severely as "a kind of irregular government created within our Constitutional government."[21] An Episcopalian publicist
also denounced their financial organization:

---

[17]Anderson, Memorial Volume, 92-99.

[18]Secretary Anderson warned the Colonization Society in 1826: "Merchants,
lawyers, farmers, everyone in this part of the country will cry out a-
gainst the commission. It will tend also, powerfully to render agencies
for all benevolent societies unpopular, and thus will be injurious to
all." Anderson to Gurley, Boston, May 30, 1826, ABC:1.01, VI, 121.

[19]Missionary Herald, XIX (1823), 365-368.

[20]Anderson, Memorial Volume, 188. The number of districts was ultimately
reduced to eight.

[21]Christian Examiner, VII (1829), 106. Channing singled out missionary
societies for special attack. Ibid., 117-119.

> Their agents swarm over the land in clouds, like the locusts
> of Egypt; there is not a city, or town, or village, or settle-
> ment, from Georgia to Maine, from the Atlantic coast to the
> Rocky Mountains, which has not its minor and subsidiary con-
> tributions to the central treasury, resigning the entire con-
> trol of the affairs of these institutions, and the disposal
> of their funds, to a few individuals at their head, who are
> themselves, in the first place, and by their own enactments,
> well and independently endowed.[22]

The sums of money which flowed through these channels were not inconsequential. In the case of the American Board, the most heavily en-dowed of all, annual receipts which averaged $10,000 by 1815 had grown to over $250,000 by 1850. In their first half century, the directors in Boston had spent more than eight million dollars in sending out twelve hundred and fifty missionaries.[23] Dependent upon grass-root financial sources for the most part—although a few legacies provided some permanent funds—the Board's activities suffered from every financial fluctuation in the economy. The Panic of 1837 in particular was a severe blow, making necessary the withholding of candidates already appointed and cutting back allocations for established missions, a measure which reduced the effec-tiveness of presses and schools at every station.[24] Although the society often shouldered a large debt, its broad economic base, resting upon thousands of evangelical churches, insured its solvency. Incorporated under the laws of Massachusetts and its credit good in every quarter of the globe, the American Board was more than a benevolent enterprise; it was big business.

Moreover, though it drew its support from Presbyterian, Reformed Dutch, and some other churches, as well as Congregationalists, the Board never completely transcended its sectional character. By the forties,

---

[22]/Calvin Colton7, Protestant Jesuitism (New York, 1836), 132-133.

[23]Anderson, Memorial Volume, 18.

[24]Tracy, History of the American Board, 335-343.

after the Old School Presbyterians had formed their own missionary apparatus, the prudential committee estimated that half the constituency resided in New England and nine tenths of the remainder in New York, New Jersey, Pennsylvania, and the upper Ohio Valley.[25] The annual meetings took place mostly in New England and New York. In 1843 the anniversary was held as far west as Rochester, but not until ten years later did the Board meet beyond the Alleghanies, at Cincinnati.[26]

Prominent among the lay leaders were governors and former governors of Massachusetts, Connecticut, New Hampshire, and Rhode Island. Although several representatives in Congress and local political figures from New England played active roles, the outstanding national figures in the movement were John Jay and Elias Boudinot. In later years Senator Theodore Frelinghuysen of New Jersey served as president of the Board, an office frequently filled by prominent laymen. Everyone who contributed his mite was not admitted to voting membership. A self-perpetuating corps of commissioners or "corporate members," composed of both lay and clerical representatives and headed by a small executive or prudential committee, decided policy and directed the missionary enterprise. At the same time a much larger group of "honorary members," consisting of contributors and their beneficiaries, deliberated with the others in annual meetings without power to vote. The monolithic structure of the organization undoubtedly secured great efficiency in financial matters as well as permitted single-minded direction of a vast undertaking.

At the beginning a single secretary handled the clerical details—the venerable Samuel Worcester, one of the founding fathers and pastor of the Tabernacle Church in Salem. At his death in 1821 the prudential

[25]American Board, The Proceedings of the Special Meeting (Boston, 1842), 13.
[26]Anderson, Memorial Volume, 142.

committee chose a layman, Jeremiah Evarts, a lawyer and editor of the
influential Panoplist. The infant enterprise was fortunate in its early
leaders, though neither Worcester nor Evarts lived long in the performance
of their tasks. Both had taken part in the Orthodox-Unitarian struggle
in Massachusetts and represented the most aggressive segment of American
evangelicalism. Before the death of Evarts in 1831, the Board's affairs
had become so complex that additional secretaries were named, and the
work divided into home and foreign correspondence.

In 1832 Rufus Anderson, who had entered the missionary rooms
several years before fresh from Andover Seminary, assumed responsibility
for the overseas operations. The short careers of his predecessors mil-
itated against the development of a consistent implementation of policy;
Anderson, a member of the Andover Brethren who gave up the foreign field
because of threatened health, served continuously for over thirty years
and helped to lay broad and conservative foundations for the immense
undertaking. He corresponded with kings and ministers as well as the
scattered evangelists of the Board and exerted everywhere the influence
of his strong personality. Nor were his efforts confined to this country.
During his tenure of office he visited the Mediterranean twice, in 1828
and 1844, conferred at length with members of the India and Ceylon missions at the head of a special deputation in 1854, and finally toured
the Hawaiian Islands in 1862.

The Board's headquarters in Boston[27]—after 1838 housed in its

[27]Dr. Worcester had conducted the Board's business from his home in
Salem, and Evarts similarly worked in the basement of his own residence.
For several years the "missionary rooms" were located in a business
building in Cornhill and later in Lyman Beecher's Hanover Street Church
until the latter burned in 1830. In 1838 the Board built from permanent
funds the Pemberton Square "missionary house" which served as headquarters
for thirty-five years. W. E. Strong, The Story of the American Board:
An Account of the First Hundred Years of the American Board of Commissioners for Foreign Missions (Boston, 1910), 153.

own building in Pemberton Square—was the center of a tremendously active organization, collecting funds, editing, and publishing the <u>Missionary Herald</u>, and a host of other printed materials, locating candidates for the field, sending them abroad, and supplying and directing them at their distant stations in both hemispheres. With hundreds of representatives looking to Boston from all over the world for support and guidance, the prudential committee through its secretaries and staff constituted a small but potent "foreign office," radiating its effects in a larger circle than any other agency of the time, public or private.

II

Protestant overseas evangelism provided an inevitable extension of the notion of the "mission of America."[28] Missionary protagonists drew heavily upon the common conviction that the United States had a special destiny, religious as well as political, to fulfill. "The church in this country," one preacher stated in 1828, "must not only sustain herself, and purify the nation, but she must stretch out her arms, and make the whole world feel the strong embrace of her benevolence."[29] Linked closely with the domestic humanitarian crusade, foreign missions broadened the evangelical outlook to comprehend the moral reform of all of mankind, even if that meant modeling the rest of the globe on American conditions. President Francis Wayland of Brown University epitomized this sentiment in its simplest terms when he remarked in a famous missionary sermon: "In a word, point us to the loveliest village that smiles upon a Scottish or New-England landscape, and compare it with the filthiness and brutality

---

[28]See Gabriel, The Course of American Democratic Thought: An Intellectual History since 1815 (New York, 1940), 22-25.

[29]J. H. Rice, The Power of Truth and Love. A Sermon Preached at Philadelphia (Boston, 1828), 24-25.

of a Caffrarian kraal, and we'll tell you that our object is to render that Caffrarian kraal as happy and as gladsome as that Scottish or New-England village."[30]

From a nation which had neither colonial establishments nor imperial ambitions, the exportation of civil and spiritual values could only be accomplished by a kind of silent penetration which came to exemplify the American ideal of cultural expansion. Foreign missions illustrated this method perfectly, as John Quincy Adams noted in preparing a report from the House of Representatives committee on foreign relations in 1843. In this document he described the effect of missionary labors in Hawaii as giving the people of the United States a deeper interest than any other country in that island kingdom "by a virtual right of conquest, not over the freedom of their brother man by the brutal arm of physical power, but over the mind and heart by the celestial panoply of the gospel of peace and love."[31]

Thus patriotism as much as disinterested benevolence inspired the evangelistic enterprise. In an annual sermon before the A.B.C.F.M. the Rev. John Codman posed the question, "Do we love our country?"

> How can we better testify our appreciation of her free institutions, than by laboring to plant them in other lands? For, where the Gospel goes in its purity and power, there will follow in its train the blessings of civilization, liberty and good government. And, although it will not be the object of the devoted missionary to interfere, in any way, with civil government, but to confine himself exclusively to his appropriate work of preaching the Gospel, yet who can deny, or who would wish it otherwise, that his influence, when honorably obtained through the success of his labors, will in a greater or less degree, be felt in the relations of civil life; and,

[30]Francis Wayland, The Moral Dignity of the Missionary Enterprise (2nd ed., Boston, 1824), 17.

[31]"China and the Sandwich Islands," House Report, 27 Cong., 3 sess., no. 93 (January 24, 1843), 2. This passage was reprinted frequently by the Board and its agencies, notably in its Forty-fourth Annual Report, 143-144.

coming himself from a land of freedom, he will naturally
spread around him an atmosphere of liberty.[32]

This undoubtedly expressed a real conviction of the nature of the Protestant missionary program, which appealed to all who considered American
institutions worthy of imitation throughout the world.

Moreover, the very organization of the overseas work of the
Board conduced to this interpretation. At each station the missionaries
formed little colonies from the American religious community, designed
to practice evangelical ideals in the sight of the heathen. At the outset the prudential committee planned to include nearly all callings and
professions: "evangelists, pastors, directors of the press, physicians,
magistrates of colonies in their incipient state, teachers of children
and youth, husbandmen, mechanics of every useful occupation, and seamen
of every class, from the experienced navigator, who can guide his gallant
ship in unknown seas, to the hardy sailor, who is willing to buffet the
waves of every ocean, and run the hazard of every climate."[33] Although
similar plans for self-sufficient missionary settlements frequently appeared in later years, the Board, after experimenting briefly with such communities in the North American Indian missions, and to a lesser extent
in Hawaii, soon gave up this romantic conception.[34] Only a few physicians,
teachers, and printers remained to assist the work of the pastoral ministry.

---

[32]John Codman, The Duty of American Christians to Send the Gospel to the
Heathen (Boston, 1836), 15.

[33]American Board, Twelfth Annual Report, 106-107.

[34]In the thirties missionaries in Turkey and the Far East continued to
argue the utility of colonizing Christian laymen among the heathen.
Chinese Repository, IV (1838), 209-214; Goodell to Anderson, Constantinople,
January 16, 1833, ABC:16.5, I, no. 161. Anderson, rejecting the notion,
wrote in 1835: "It is difficult to secure union and peace and efficacy
to a numerous body of missionaries; how much more in a colony of different
trades, occupations, etc. etc." Anderson to Abeel, Boston, June 20, 1835,
ABC:1.01, XIV, 203.

Even this smaller community, however, conformed in its internal structure to patterns of American thought. Each mission was a compact unit, choosing its own officers, keeping regular records, and accounting for its funds.[35] Most evangelists received nominal salaries, but a few stations employed a common-stock system, furnishing individuals with supplies according to need; in Hawaii, where the members of the mission were scattered over several islands, the Board appointed a "secular superintendent" at Honolulu to handle disbursements. With all males over twenty-one voting, a majority decided all questions of local policy, subject to the revision of the Boston office.[36] "This system," the prudential committee pointed out, "is obviously more in accordance than any other, with the genius of our republican institutions, and with our habits as American citizens."[37] The Board took care, however, to insure that ordained ministers, the products of both liberal education and theological training, would bear the chief responsibility of representing the American evangelical community to the world. The instructions of a group of nonclerical "assistant missionaries" setting forth to Hawaii in 1836 stated clearly: "The pastors will be your natural advisors; and while you are not made subordinate to them in the sense of being placed under their authority, you will readily perceive the expediency and propriety of conferring with them in all cases before taking steps of importance."[38]

[35]Secretary Worcester advised the first mission in Ceylon to elect a treasurer, clerk, and a presiding officer, the last of which should rotate among the members. Worcester to James Richards and others, Newburyport, October 14, 1815, ABC:1.01, I, 41.

[36]American Board, Twenty-third Annual Report, 148.

[37]American Board, Nineteenth Annual Report, 28. According to Rufus Anderson "the missions derive their organization from the taste and habits of the American people; and persons of foreign birth and education have found it somewhat difficult to work happily and well in them." Anderson, Memorial Volume, 226-227.

[38]Missionary Herald, XXXIII (1837), 168.

The American foreign evangelist seldom lost his sense of nationality. "Had I nothing to do here but to make a fortune," cried Samuel Newell in India, "how quickly would I quit this land and fly across the ocean to my own country, my much loved America, that happy, happy land, which contains all that is dear to me on earth."[39] Another missionary of the Board wrote during a voyage to Constantinople from Smyrna: "Happy New England!"

> If we ever forget thee, let our right hand forget her cunning. Whenever we think of that good land, the land of our father's sepulchres, the land of hills, and vallies, and springs of water, the land of simplicity and purity of manners, the land of Sabbath's, and revivals, and benevolent institutions, the land of peace and plenty--we are ready to exclaim, "Happy art thou, O Israel: who is like unto thee, O people, saved by the Lord?"[40]

While gladly accepting their long exile from home, evangelists almost always considered themselves aliens and strangers wherever they resided, holding fast to their own citizenship and fastening it upon their children. Unwilling to see their offspring grow up denationalized in the midst of a pagan people in a strange land, parents parted early with young sons and daughters in order to send them to schools and careers in the United States.

Jonas King in Athens, married to a Greek woman of Smyrna, and fearful lest he lose his American citizenship during his long absence from home, begged the prudential committee to inquire of Daniel Webster "or some other one who will be able to give you an answer" concerning the legal status of missionaries.[41] This thorny question came before the Board at the annual meeting in 1841. A committee headed by Chief Justice Thomas S. Williams of Connecticut concluded that, although children born

---

[39]Newell to Worcester, Goa, February 26, 1814, ABC:16.1.1, III, no. 37.

[40]Journal of Goodell, June 3, 1831, Missionary Herald, XXVIII (1832), 35.

[41]King to Anderson, Athens, undated, ABC:17.1, I, no. 137.

abroad were in an ambiguous position in the absence of specific legislation on this matter, their parents remained citizens of the United States however long they were away.[42] In 1852 Secretary of State Webster endorsed this view completely, quoting in his instructions to the American ambassador in Constantinople the Connecticut jurist's comparison of the foreign evangelist to the merchant whose primary loyalty is to his native country.[43]

Exile from home was perhaps hardest for the wives, who left a comparatively sheltered family life for the sometimes extremely arduous career of helpmate and teacher on heathen shores. Henrietta Hamlin found in Turkey a "rude and semibarbarian look to everything, that carries us back an age from the advancement of the American world. Everything we see and hear gives an impression of ignorance, superstition and moral degradation, which disgusts as well as grieves us."[44] Another young missionary wife, accompanying her husband on a tour of European Turkey, recorded in her diary that she began to doubt her personal identity, "so recently a school girl, rambling amidst the quiet groves and villages of dear New England now gathering shells, and eating bread on the shores of the Black Sea."[45]

The Board's representatives created as far as possible a fair replica of life in the United States at their distant outposts. At Constantinople they held weekly meetings of the "American Lyceum" with

[42]American Board, Thirty-second Annual Report, 36-39.

[43]Webster to G. P. Marsh, Washington, April 29, 1852, in Senate Executive Document, 33 Cong., 2 sess., no. 9, 3-4.

[44]Letter of Henrietta Hamlin, Constantinople, September 11, 1839, in M. W. Lawrence, Light on the Dark River; or, Memorial of Mrs. Henrietta Hamlin, Missionary in Turkey (Boston, 1853), 152.

[45]Memoir of Mrs. Mary E. Van Lennep (Hartford, 1847), 301.

Commodore David Porter and attaches of the legation.[46] A visitor to

Honolulu in the thirties who was invited to tea with the missionaries

exclaimed that "the party was so much like one in America, that had I

been placed there by accident, or could I have forgotten the circumstances

of my visit, I should have fancied myself in New England. The dress and

the whole appearance was the same. We were in a framed house of one story,

similar to those in our country villages. The floor was carpeted, the

furniture was simple, provided by the liberality of their private friends

in America."[47] Except in parts of the Ottoman Empire where the first ex-

plorers affected the burnoose to render their Frankish appearance less

noticeable, the Board's emissaries seldom changed their garb or way of

life in foreign parts, as little tempted by exotic manners as by heathen

moralities or religions.

Food, clothing, and even furniture came in large part from the

United States. Nostalgic for accustomed household comforts, American

families in Constantinople and on the African veldt besought the Board to

send them "high-backed rocking chairs."[48] Like latter-day travelers they

found some productions of the countries in which they resided inferior to

their own; shoes and boots, William Goodell complained of in Malta as

"wretchedly made." "If convenient," his letter continued, "bring out a

barrel of beef tongues, of salt pork, of sour 'Crout,' a firkin of sweet

butter, some good cheese, pickled cucumbers, and pickled oysters."[49]

---

[46]Perkins, Residence in Persia, 74.

[47]Warriner, Cruise of the United States Frigate Potomac, 224-225.

[48]Lindley to Henry Hill, Port Natal, July 16, 1839, ABC:15.4, II, no. 82;
Anderson to Dwight, Boston, July 28, 1834, ABC:2.01, III, 101. While
visiting the mission in Turkey, Lloyd Stephens saw "scarcely a house in
which I did not find an article unknown except among Americans, a Boston
rocking chair." Incidents of Travel in Greece, Turkey, Russia, and
Poland, I, 221.

[49]Goodell to Anderson, Malta, April 5, 1823, ABC:16.6, I, no. 310.

It is interesting to note that for several years the prudential committee included wines in the commissary supplies regularly sent each station. In 1823 the secular superintendent at Honolulu asked for twenty gallons of rum, ten of brandy, and thirty of wine. "Some persons might be surprised," the conscientious steward wrote, "that missionaries should drink spirits, or that they should introduce so much tea and sugar into the list of their annual necessities: but in this enervating climate where no winter returns to brace up the relaxed system such articles are much needed, and almost indispensable. A much larger quantity of spirits than has been mentioned would be recommended by the physician."[50]

Even in New England evangelical circles wines were acceptable before the growth of a strong sentiment for total abstinence. But the full development of the temperance movement in the United States soon brought even this light beverage under the ban, and missionaries not only abstained themselves, but demanded the same of their converts and, where feasible, as in the Sandwich Islands, attempted to prevent the sale of liquor to all. Indeed, when a deputation from the Hawaiian mission visited the stations of the London Society in the South Seas in 1832, the Americans were aghast at both the lack of temperance societies among the native islanders and the moderate indulgence of the English evangelists, who had apparently never heard of the teetotalist principle.[51]

Mission families also endeavored to keep the New England Sabbath in far-away lands, even if, as Mrs. Sarah Smith at Beirut wrote, it meant their servants were idle all day long![52] Secretary Anderson, however,

---

[50]Levi Chamberlain to Evarts, Honolulu, October, 1823, ABC:19.1, I, no. 298.

[51]Report of the deputation to the Georgian, Society, and Marquesan Islands, ABC:19.1, IV, no. 40.

[52]Letter of Sarah Smith, February 12, 1835, in E. W. Hooker, Memoir of Mrs. Sarah Lanman Smith, 225.

found the missionaries in the Levant unaccountably lax during his official tour of inspection in 1844, and felt it necessary to warn his correspondents in Canton against loss of the religious meaning of the Lord's Day.[53] Perhaps even more unfortunate in its reverberations in the United States was the report of luxurious living at the A.B.C.F.M.'s stations around the world. A public outcry was heard when the young son of a Ceylon evangelist, returned to America for an education, innocently betrayed the fact that his parents and their associates employed native domestic servants.[54] In response to requests for higher salaries the prudential committee recommended "New England simplicity" as the "best style of living for missionaries everywhere."[55]

The American abroad often remained provincial in spirit in the most cosmopolitan surroundings, thinking it anomalous, for example, that he had seen Babylon before Niagara Falls.[56] A Virginian evangelist of the Board in the Mediterranean, overwhelmed by a confusing bedlam of tongues and nationalities on his arrival in Scio, sadly asked, "Is this the people . . . unto whom I am sent?"[57] In Syria Mrs. Sarah Smith expressed her delight at visiting the U.S.S. Delaware in 1834 in order to see Americans once more, contrasting the sailors' fair complexions and simple clean uniforms with the "tawny skin and fantastic dress" of the inhabitants of Beirut.[58]

---

[53] Anderson to Parker, Boston, October 3, 1846, ABC:2.1.1, IX, 218.

[54] Anderson to Daniel Poor, Boston, February 26, 1831, ABC:2.01, I, 305-307.

[55] Evarts to Allen Graves and others, Boston, July 31, 1830, ABC:8.1, IV, no. 69.

[56] Tyler, Memoir of Henry Lobdell, 377.

[57] Journal of S. R. Houston, November 8, 1834, Missionary Herald, XXXI (1835), 253.

[58] Hooker, Memoir of Mrs. Sarah Smith, 202.

Yet foreign residence provided a new and broader perspective for some. William Goodell in Constantinople confessed that much of his thinking was no longer "calculated for the Latitude and Longitude of Boston," and that he feared being called "a heretic, or a Jesuit at least."[59] One of his associates added that he had discovered that "America is one country and Turkey is another, and a very different country. And no man in America can decide what particular course of expedients is applicable to the state of things in Turkey."[60] Distance from home sometimes sharpened critical awareness, as when Mrs. Smith wrote that "my feelings and opinions have been changed since I left America. While I see much to admire and love, I also see faults that I wish might be corrected."[61] What this good missionary wife had discovered was the lack of family and social order which revealed itself in the "external deportment" of tourists to the Holy Land. "The plain, independent manners of some of our good republican citizens," she thought, "would be somewhat offensive to foreign taste; and were it not for the extraordinary talent of assimilation which Americans possess, they would err more often than they do now."[62]

Despite the expression of views such as these, the missionaries' partiality for the mores of American Protestant society led to a natural confusion of Christianity and Western culture. Not only did they consider

[59]Goodell to Anderson, Constantinople, December 9, 1834, ABC:16.5, II, 3.

[60]Dwight to J. B. Adger, Constantinople, December 20, 1834, ABC:16.5, II, 154.

[61]Letter of Sarah Smith, Beirut, March 19, 1835, in Hooker, Memoir of Mrs. Sarah Smith, 233.

[62]Ibid., 297. Justin Perkins remarked on the "stiffness and roughness of the American character" in the Mediterranean. "Even the tawny, degraded Maltese," he wrote, "are incomparably more respectful and polite than the mass in New England." Perkins, Residence in Persia, 50.

it a function of evangelical religion to inculcate among primitive peoples
a horror of idleness and a desire for decent clothing, but they also endeavored to mold social life and civil institutions. Where this proved
difficult or impossible, as in Syria under Ottoman tyranny, the evangelists grumbled.

> It is a great grief to us, that we can do nothing directly to
> diminish the political evils of the country; nothing to insure
> protection for the innocent, or to bring the guilty to justice;
> nothing to abate the national guilt by being instrumental in
> promoting a national reform. In this respect, our circumstances
> are widely different from those of our brethren at the Sandwich
> Islands, or among the Indian tribes of the West; whose labors
> have a direct and efficient bearing on the body politic, and
> who control the opinions and practices of others.[63]

The temptation to meddle with secular affairs was difficult to
resist, especially when Americans at home looked for concrete evidence
of the results of missions. In the case of Hawaii, many were disappointed
that the Board's representatives did not do more to democratize the arbitrary reign of kings and chiefs. Herman Melville, who visited Honolulu
in the early forties, severely criticized "republican missionaries" for up-
holding a corrupt monarchical government.[64] Yet the cautious policy of the
prudential committee prevented its agents from attempting to remodel
alien societies on their own. Whatever social and political effects resulted from missionary contacts were chiefly incidental to the enterprise
of preaching the Gospel to an unconverted people After the early failure
of the scheme of assimilation in the American Indian missions, the Board
rejected a mode of evangelism which laid too great stress on relaying

---

[63] Goodell to Evarts, Beirut, September 15, 1826, ABC:16.5, I, no. 130.

[64] Melville, Typee, 253-254. Just a few years earlier the members of the
mission, when asked to furnish an advisor to the king, stated that "we
are not politicians; and if we were, the work to be done does not come
into the appropriate sphere of a missionary laboring under the laws and
regulations of such a Board as ours." General letter of the mission,
June 20, 1838, Missionary Herald, XXXV (1839), 147. Those who entered
the king's service in Hawaii usually did so after resigning from the
mission.

cultural accessories. These were considered only the by-product of individual conversions, inevitable, perhaps, but not essential to the Christian message. Secretary Rufus Anderson, who had so large a part in defining the aims and methods of the American Board, summed up the official attitude at mid-century:

> It has seemed to be the mistake of some, that the great object of American missions should be to reproduce our own religious civilization in heathen lands, and just in the precise social and religious forms which that civilization has in this country. It may be that the Gospel will produce just these results, in process of time, all over the world; but that is not the proper object of Gospel missions. Their object is to proclaim salvation for immortal souls, through repentence and faith in the Lord Jesus. . . . It is no fault of the mission at the Sandwich Islands, that the social progress at those Islands, under the preaching of the Gospel, has resulted in a constitutional monarchy, rather than a republic. Nor is it the fault of the Armenian mission, that Protestant Christianity there adapts itself exactly to the constitution of the Turkish Empire, and pays tribute to Caesar. Nor is it the fault of the Cherokee and Choctaw missions, that slavery is not at once regarded by their mission churches in the same manner as it is by the churches in Massachusetts. . . . Our appropriate objects may be gained long before all these are, or can be.[65]

III

When the Rev. Joel Hawes returned from the Levant, where he accompanied the corresponding secretary of the American Board on a tour of the Mediterranean missions, he assured his congregation in Hartford, Connecticut, that "the salvation of our country is the hope of the world. If we fail in our great experiment of free institutions, the sun dial of time will go back for centuries, and despotism and superstition will hold a grand jubilee over the world." Having observed the degradation of the East and despairing of the puny results of missionary efforts, he called upon evangelical Christians to redouble their labors to hold this nation fast. "America is God's last dispensation towards the world. This act

---

[65]Anderson, The Missionary Age: A Half-Century Sermon (Missionary Tracts, no. 10, Boston, 1851), 20-21.

passed, the scene closes, the curtain of time drops, and the glories of eternity are revealed."[66] Although Hawes, who sent a daughter to the foreign field, was no detractor of missions, many persons skeptical of the movement expressed similar sentiments about the primacy of the domestic task.

Most other denominations in the United States responded more slowly than the Congregationalists of New England to the overseas enterprise. Only the Baptists, with a large following in the same Atlantic-oriented section, and stimulated by the defection of the Judsons and Luther Rice from the A.B.C.F.M., sent missionaries abroad within the first twenty years of the embarkation of the pioneer American company to India in 1812. Protestant bodies with constituencies largely outside New England were attracted more readily to the expanding West than to the larger heathen world abroad. A committee of the Methodist General Conference in 1819, for example, advised against commencing foreign missions when so much remained to be done at home. "Our own continent presents to us fields sufficiently vast, which are opening before us and whitening unto harvest. These, it is probable, will demand all the laborers and all the means which we can command at present."[67]

Those who would leave distant pagans to British and European benevolence pressed for a greater attention to the heathen aborigines at home as more properly within the sphere of American efforts—an argument which weighed heavily with the Board itself in sparing large numbers of its agents to staff expensive missions to the Indians. A preacher in New England, who hoped that Americans would not forget the red men while

[66]Joel Hawes, The Religion of the East, with Impressions of Foreign Travel (Hartford, 1845), 44-45.

[67]Cited in W. P. Strickland, History of the Missions of the Methodist Episcopal Church (Cincinnati, 1849), 37-38.

evangelizing "the Hottentot and Hindoo," ventured to call it a "false zeal, that professes to seek the salvation of souls in another hemisphere, and is utterly regardless of the welfare of the many precious immortals, who are perishing, on every side, for want of knowledge. . . ."[68] Although all the major communions of the United States eventually entered the overseas field, a residue of parochial thinking persisted throughout out the period. To men of this sentiment the religious responsibilities, like the political sympathies, of America should be restricted to this half of the globe. As late as 1854 a Presbyterian minister could write:

> As we are cutting ourselves off more and more from the old world, and /are/ likely to carry out the Monroe Doctrine, it seems to me that Christians in the United States are proportionately more bound to devise means of sending the gospel to Spanish America. Brazil is quite open, and New Granada nearly so. It seems to me that this, along with the black and red men, falls more justly to our share, than Hindoos, Nestorians, Druses, Arabs, or Turks.[69]

The antislavery reformers, however, presented the strongest argument for this isolationist view of the mission of America. In their minds Negro slavery was evidence enough of heathenism at home, upon the elimination of which evangelical forces ought to concentrate their efforts before seeking to transform the rest of the world. At the second annual meeting of the American Missionary Association in 1848, this forthright statement was put in the record:

> Here and in Europe is to be settled the destiny of the human race. If this American Empire or cluster of Empires shall come safely out of the probation to which it is to be subjected, then all is safe--China, India, and the World. But should this experiment through our mistakes and unfaithfulness fail, which God forbid, will it matter much what missions in Asia we planted or failed to plant? Not that Asia is unimportant or to be neglected. Far otherwise. Its destiny is great

---

[68] Codman, The Importance of Spiritual Knowledge. A Sermon . . . before the Society for Propagating the Gospel among the Indians and Others in North America (Cambridge, 1825), 23.

[69] J. A. Alexander, Forty Years' Familiar Letters, Constituting, with the Notes, a Memoir of His Life (John Hall, ed., New York, 1860), II, 204.

but distant, as we count distance; America first, then Asia.
. . . Nothing is more certain than that for a century to
come America rather than Asia should be the great missionary field.

The speaker, moreover, expressed his astonishment at observing

intelligent, Christian men, devoting all their enthusiasm to
the promotion of missions in Asia, while they turn their
backs upon the most promising missionary fields the world
ever saw, and not only so, but by their supineness, allow an
atrocious system to extend its heathenizing influences over
half of Mexico and ultimately perhaps over the whole. . . .
Surely this is giving attention to the mote in the Asiatic
eye, while we neglect the beam in our American eye.[70]

It has often been noted that English Evangelicals were quicker
to plead the case of the slave and oppressed native races overseas than
to improve the lot of the industrial masses in Great Britain.[71] The outpouring of American Protestant energies into distant evangelism may also
have tended to obscure the social evils of the time for the conservative
constituency of the Board. The neutral attitude of this and some other
great benevolent societies of the period toward slavery would seem to
bear out the conclusion that most of the churches in the United States
could identify remote pagan practices more easily than domestic. A few
contemporary critics of foreign missions, of whom Unitarian Elizabeth
Sanders of Salem was perhaps most articulate, pointed out that it was unnecessary to go so far from home to find objects of Christian charity.
"Had the wealth which flowed in such copious channels to foreign lands,"
she wrote in an anonymous tract of 1844, "been faithfully employed in the
suppression of crime, and in assisting the fallen to regain their independence by industry and economy, how great would be our triumph." Mrs.
Sanders was concerned chiefly about prostitution and its victims:

---

[70]American Missionary Association, Second Annual Report (New York, 1848),
26-27.

[71]K. L. P. Martin, Missionaries and Annexation in the Pacific (London,
1924), 2-3.

Let the benevolent missionary penetrate into the miserable
hovels, and damp cellars, the abode of those guilty outcasts,
who, with their helpless offspring, avoid the light of day,
and who subsist only by fraud and violence. . . . Assuredly
the darkness which surrounds them is far deeper than what is
felt by the benighted heathen, who excites so much sympathy
in the advocates for foreign missions.[72]

Most antimissionary criticism came from those who disparaged
the whole evangelical movement in the United States. A New England trader
in California in the early thirties called reports of the Board's doings
in Hawaii "a good example of what our country would be if those cropt
eared puritanical Rascals had the management of our Government, as they
have tryed to get by petitioning to stop the mail etc."[73] A sailor from
the same region visiting Indonesia hoped the time was far distant when
the "poor ignorant heathen" of that place would be "compelled to eat pork
and lace tight," and "when religious revivals and excitments shall be as
well known among them as with us, to the equal disorganization of society,
the destruction of domestic peace and harmony, and partial or total de-
rangement of all the weak heads in the community. . . ."[74] And even the
lofty Emerson spoke with scorn of the ministers who asked their parishes
to send money "a hundred or a thousand miles, to furnish such poor fare
as they have at home and would do well to go the hundred or thousand
miles to escape."[75] All this was a critique of American religious orthodoxy itself, pictured as more detrimental in its effects abroad than at
home.

Even within the evangelical community was heard some hint of

---

[72] /Elizabeth Sanders_7, Tract on Missions (Salem, 1844), 15.

[73] F. A. Thompson to Mrs. Lydia Thompson, Santa Barbara, October 27, 1832,
in D. M. Brown, ed., China Trade Days in California: Selected Letters
from the Thompson Papers, 1832-1863 (Berkeley, 1947), 7.

[74] /Ames_7, Mariner's Sketches, 40-41.

[75] Emerson, Complete Works (Boston, 1903), I, 140.

reproach. Horace Bushnell, liberal theologian of Hartford, expressed "salutary suspicions" of the whole benevolent crusade: "Piety," he wrote in 1844, "has become nearly, perhaps too nearly, synonomous with action." Preferring natural growth, what he later called "the out-populating power of the Christian stock," to quasi-military conquest, he argued against the whole paraphernalia of Bible, tract and missionary efforts: "As if God would offer man a mechanical engine for converting the world with the least possible expenditure of piety; or as if types of lead and sheets of paper may be the light of the world."[76] Home missions also was represented as a serious rival of overseas evangelism. In 1849 a secretary of the American Tract Society posed the question: "If the foreign missionary enterprise has been nearly stationary for ten years, is it not because we have so much heathenism in our own country? And would not the complete evangelization of America result in such an increase of men and means, as to give promise of the speedy diffusion of the Gospel among the heathen."[77] Yet most evangelicals agreed that the two enterprises were complementary: domestic purification only prepared this country for its special mission to the world. "With our inestimable civil institutions," the tractarian publicist concluded, "we only need the pervading influence of a pure, spiritual faith, and the baptism of the Holy Ghost; and the great family of nations may be moulded by our model for a Millennial day."[78]

To critics who urged the priority of domestic labors, the advocates of foreign evangelism replied that the United States was not isolated from the rest of the world. Although, unlike Great Britain, this nation had no political commitments overseas, the earth-circling

---

[76] New Englander, II (1844), 605-607.

[77] Home Evangelization, 149.

[78] Ibid., 157.

business enterprise of her citizens carried the flag to every sea. "Here lies the duty of the Church of America," announced Sereno Dwight before a missionary society in Boston in 1820.[79] Commerce broadened the horizons of men and opened a way for missions, many evangelicals argued; as one result of it, "the opinion is gaining ground in the church, that a man may be as much in the way of his duty, in supporting a preacher of gospel on the banks of the Tigris, or the Ganges, as in his own village."[80]

The relationship between foreign trade and foreign missions was a reciprocal one. American merchants often co-operated closely with the Board, transporting men and supplies gratuitously, and also contributing to their support in China, Hawaii, and the Mediterranean. Many captains and traders felt that missionaries aided business. "Every shipmaster," wrote Benjamin Morrell, adventurous and far-ranging skipper in the Pacific, "should say, God prosper their labours, unless indeed he prefer to obtain refreshments for a starving crew by force of arms."[81] But it was a naval medical officer, William Ruschenberger, who published the strongest argument for the commercial uses of missions. His visits to the Board's stations in Hawaii and the Far East in the thirties convinced him that the Christianization of "Asia, Polynesia, and indeed of all the world" was "sound policy":

> To what extent our trade in the East would be augmented by the conversion to Christianity of Siam, Cochin-China, China and Japan, it is impossible to conjecture. When the half naked millions of Asia shall attain Christianity, and with it, all the new wants which the necessary change in their social condition will produce, the soil of our country, as rich and vast as it is, will be scarcely adequate to supply them. A new and extensive mart must be opened for our manufacturers of all kinds, and even the literary will find an

---

[79] S. E. Dwight, Thy Kingdom Come; a Sermon . . . before the Foreign Mission Society of Boston and the Vicinity (Boston, 1820), 27-28.

[80] Eli Smith, Missionary Sermons (Boston, 1833), preface, viii.

[81] Morrell, Narrative of Four Voyages, 158.

increased demand for their labors. Hundreds of ships will spread their sails to the eastward of the cape of Good Hope, destined for the shores of Asia and the isles scattered in the southern ocean and commerce will pour her wealth, gathered in the old world, into the lap of the new.[82]

Missionaries' movements intersected the lines of American foreign commerce at many points. The Board's agents joined with the chaplains of the Seamen's Friend Society in ministering to "poor Jack" in distant ports, raising the Bethel flag in Smyrna, Canton, and elsewhere, and conducting English services aboard visiting ships and ashore. Prosecuting their labors thousands of miles from home, they spent months at sea in the company of rough sailors, boisterous whalemen, and scoffing or indifferent masters. They experienced a great variety of treatment at the hands of captains and crew. Daniel Chamberlain, misused on his return voyage to the United States in 1823, went to court and obtained four hundred dollars' damages from the shipmaster with the aid of attorney Daniel Webster.[83] Friendlier relations, however, generally prevailed. Officers often permitted preaching on deck and even attempts to convert common seamen, notorious for their irreligion. Most missionary travel in this period preceded the advent of steam, and the prudential committee apparently believed in the discipline of a long passage around the Horn, as Secretary Anderson told one group in 1851 who asked permission to take the newly opened Panama route to the Pacific.[84]

A prominent spokesman of the Board in 1850 found no anomaly in the mutual interaction of missions and commerce. "If the manufacturers

---

[82]Ruschenberger, Voyage round the World, 311.

[83]Missionary Herald, XXVI (1829), 30-31. In a similar case in later years the prudential committee of the Board exonerated the owner of a vessel on which missionaries were forced to cook their own food on a four months' voyage around the Horn, but not the captain. Ibid., 27-30.

[84]T. C. Bliss, Micronesia. Fifty Years in the Island World (Boston, 1906), 7.

of our country," he proclaimed, "find their way to Africa and China, to the Sandwich Islands and India, in increasing abundance, and produce correspondingly remunerative returns, it is because the herald of salvation has gone thither, seeking the welfare of the people, changing their habits of life, breaking down their prejudices, and creating a demand for comforts and wealth before unknown."[85]

To the evangelical public at midcentury, American commercial and missionary enterprise was the United States' contribution to the expansion of English-speaking civilization. A returned evangelist of the Board from India, Hollis Read, published a tract entitled The Hand of God in History in 1849 to show how the Lord of missions had given "an almost unlimited supremacy of the two most enlightened and Christian nations. England and America give laws to the nations; rather, I will say, the Anglo-Saxon race are extending an all-controlling influence over nearly the whole earth."[86] Even the Board's prudential committee, in its official instructions to missionaries sounded the same note: "We can suppose the Anglo-Saxon race to fill the myriads of sunny islands on the bosom of the board Pacific; and the genius of American and English enterprise to preside in great commercial cities, (other New Yorks, or even Londons,) reared on the Sandwich Islands, New Zealand, and Australia."[87] In his annual sermon before

---

[85]R. S. Storrs, Always Abounding in the Work of the Lord. A Sermon . . . before the American Board (Boston, 1850), 26.

[86]Hollis Read, The Hand of God In History; or Divine Providence Historically Illustrated in the Extension and Establishment of Christianity (Hartford, 1849), 159. Great Britain, the senior partner in this enterprise, was responsible for the political support of missions overseas: "Whenever English power is felt, there the arm of protection and assistance is extended to the missionary. No sooner is the roar of British cannon heard off the coast of Birmah, /sic/or at the Cape of Good Hope, than the captured missionaries are set free, and allowed to return to their work." Ibid., 160.

[87]Anderson to John Van Ness Talmedge, Boston, March 7, 1850, ABC:8.1, II, 273.

the A.B.C.F.M. in 1860, the Rev. Samuel Fisher reminded the supporters of
foreign missions that they constituted a "race which, informed by religion,
is prepared, yea necessitated, to lead the van of Immanuel's army for the
conquest of the world."[88] "What is to hinder us," he continued, "from as-
cending to a position where we shall command the markets of the world, and
give laws to commerce, and possess resources sufficient to sustain more
missionaries than we now have population?"[89]

Paradoxically, by proclaiming that "the field is the world,"
foreign missions contributed more than any other aspect of the evangelical
movement to nationalistic self-consciousness. Like the extended commercial frontier of the United States, the far-flung evangelistic enterprise
brought Americans into contact with other societies, projecting the
nation's vision beyond its territorial bounds. A people engrossed with
problems of internal growth and continental expansion stood in danger of
provincial isolation, which the outreach of militant evangelical Protestantism helped to circumvent. At one extreme this meant a heightened
sense of nationality and racial consciousness, which the promoters of an
Anglo-Saxon manifest destiny sought to exploit; at the other it developed
a more universal awareness and sensitivity. One of the Board's veteran
missionaries told the Yale Society of Inquiry in 1840: "We naturally
think our country the best in the world; the best in its soil, its
scenery, its climate, its government, its people. . . . But will you let
this American partiality bias your feelings and govern your deportment in
the Missionary field?" Rather, he asserted, the foreign missionary of the
churches of the United States should "feel himself a citizen of the world."[90]

---

[88]S. W. Fisher, God's Purpose in Planting the American Church. A Sermon,
before the American Board (Boston, 1860), 16.

[89]Ibid., 22.

[90]Eli Smith, The Missionary Character. An Address . . . before the Society of Inquiry (New Haven, 1840), 14.

CHAPTER IX

THE MISSIONARY IMAGE OF THE WORLD

Foreign missions helped to form the American attitude toward alien nations and peoples during an era when no other overseas relations seriously rivaled it in scope and importance. Stemming from the generation that grew to maturity after the Revolution, the benevolent undertaking expanded with the young republic, opening wider vistas to continent-minded Americans and at the same time stamping the national outlook with a peculiarly missionary character. While it was an international Protestant movement which revitalized an older Christian concept of the infidel world, the evangelistic enterprise in this country nourished the heathen image which during the greater part of the nineteenth century interpreted for many Americans the strange and distant peoples of the other half of the globe. In Protestant missions citizens of the United States found one satisfactory relationship with an Eastern Hemisphere largely beyond the diplomatic, if not the commercial, horizon.

I

Theology made an important contribution to the missionary perspective. Though conceived in provincial New England, Samuel Hopkin's consistent elaboration of Edwardean Calvinism opened men's minds to a compassionate view of a world of unsaved millions far removed in space yet potentially within American evangelical sympathies. The doctrine of original sin with its emphasis upon the universality of man's miserable condition without God's grace operated as a great equalizer of men and nations. It was mainly the application of Hopkinsian "disinterested benevolence" which inspired a Presbyterian divine in 1805 to announce

that "were there but one heathen in the world, and he in the remotest

corner of Asia, if no greater duty confined us at home, it would be worth

the pains for all the people in America to embark together to carry the

gospel to him."[1]

Christianity had always taught the brotherhood of man, but the

evangelical revival raised a fresh perception of this truth by dwelling

almost sentimentally on the thought that unnumbered multitudes departed

unsaved to eternity each year. One New England minister estimated that

at least one member of the human race expired every moment. What if that

dying soul were one's dearest friend? "And yet," he explained, "this

alters not the consideration."

> I am bound to call every human being, my neighbor, my friend,
> my brother; my Saviour has taught me to do so.--Whether he be
> the person, that is within the reach of my arm; or the man
> that treads the antipodes of the earth--he is my neighbor.
> The place or manner of his death, cannot change the question.
> Whether he is languishing in pain, without God and without
> hope, on the sultry deserts of Arabia, or breathing out his
> spirit, in the holy raptures of the christian death bed--it
> is enough for me to know, that a kindred soul to mine, is at
> this moment, departing.[2]

This altruistic spirit motivated many of the first evangelists

who left the farms and villages of New England to bring light to fellow

mortals dwelling upon the Ganges and the Euphrates. The unmistakable

note of Hopkinsian compassion appears in the sermon of a young Andover

graduate about to embark for India in 1815, who proclaimed that "the

soul of a Hindoo, or Hottentot, though thousands of miles distant, is

of as much value, and its salvation will cause as much joy in heaven,

---

[1]Griffin, _Kingdom of Christ_, 29.

[2]James Taylor, _A Sermon_ . . . _before the Hampshire Missionary Society
Society_ (Northampton, Mass., 1818), 12.

as the soul of an American."[3] Protestant leaders rejoiced that a growing knowledge of the world through discoveries and commercial enterprise enabled provincial Americans to adjust their vision. Referring to the dense non-Christian populations to whom the nation's trade provided access, the mission-minded Panoplist informed its readers that "the improvements of civilized society have made them our neighbors, and it is as easy for the people of America to do them good, as it is for the people of different states and communities to do good to each other.[4]

Missionary promoters in pulpit and press strove to drive home the geographical implications of the theology of disinterested benevolence. The Boston Recorder, the first religious weekly in the United States, underlined in its initial issue in 1816 the broad view of its editors by stating that their "constant regard will be to counteract and destroy local and national prejudices of every kind; and to cherish a more liberal way of thinking and speaking concerning the inhabitants of foreign countries than has hitherto been common . . . ." In general, the prospectus added, the paper would illustrate "the great truth, that all men are brethren."[5] In the Recorder and its sister publications[6]—especially the New York Observer and the New York Evangelist, founded in 1823 and 1830 respectively—missionary news and accounts of religious activities abroad filled a very large space, often as much as half the total. Representatives of the A.B.C.F.M. and other societies, moreover, acted as

[3]Horatio Bardwell, The Duty and Reward of Evangelizing the Heathen (Newburyport, 1815), 19.

[4]"Address to the Public," Panoplist, XIII (1817), 5.

[5]Boston Recorder, January 24, 1816, Prospectus, 16.

[6]Unlike the monthly journals, which followed a British prototype, religious weeklies originated in the United States, where by 1827 their number had grown to thirty-four. New York Observer, December 15, 1827.

foreign correspondents for these newspapers, describing faithfully in published letters the unfamiliar life of pagan races and recording the gradual advance of the Gospel throughout the world.

Evangelical Protestants of that era must have had an almost insatiable curiosity about remote non-Christian regions, to judge from the quantity of missionary journals and reports published in the religious press, both weekly and monthly. One of the most important of the latter type of publication was the American Board's own Missionary Herald, after 1821 the chief repository of information from its foreign outposts, of which Professor A. P. Peabody of Harvard wrote in 1848 that its "unobtrusive" numbers sent abroad through the churches "materials of knowledge which would be issued from the secular press with the longest and loudest flourishes of trumpets."[7] Other religious journals, moreover, drew freely upon its resources and multiplied the total impact of missionary intelligence many times.

The directors of foreign missions had no grand strategy for the Christian conquest of the heathen world. The first American missionaries proceeded to British India in 1812 without instructions specifically designating their field of exertions, except for the suggestion that they attempt to enter neighboring Burma. As a leading historian of American Protestantism wrote at the end of our period, "the comparative claims of the different benighted portions of the unevangelical world was a subject then but little understood."[8] All four hundred millions—the usual estimation—of the non-Christian population of the earth seemed to present an equal claim. The prudential committee confessed to an empirical strategy at the outset, announcing in 1812 that the members of the Board

---

[7] North American Review, LXVII (1848), 267.

[8] Robert Baird, Religion in America (New York, 1856), 605.

would not confine their efforts to any single region, but "may direct their attention to Africa, North or South America, or the Isles of the sea, as well as to Asia." "If unsuccessful in one place," the committee continued, they can turn to another; and can seize, (according to their means,) upon any promising opportunity to do good to any portion of the heathen world."[9]

The missionary program was conceived in terms of the subjugation of enemy territory and embodied in a phraseology of conquest which has survived to this day.[10] The Board's first emissaries went forth at a time when Bonaparte still convulsed Europe and his imperial ambitions filled the imagination of the whole civilized world. As late as 1834, in describing the need for thorough reconnaissance and careful planning to departing evangelists, the prudential committee likened the missionary contest to the "military enterprises of Napoleon."[11] If this martial language disclosed the temper of early nineteenth-century evangelical Protestantism, it also described rather realistically the methods pursued in advancing upon peoples beyond the pale. "In the process of subduing a country," read the annual report of the A.B.C.F.M. in 1842, "while portions of the grand army are employed here and there, the main force is usually directed to some one or two points. When these are carried, then one or two others are selected for the more concentrated movement; and so on till the country is subdued."[12] This principle guided the Board's gradual occupation of the heathen world, prompting its directors to exert

---

[9]American Board, Third Annual Report, 32.

[10]See E. C. Moore, West and East: The Expansion of Christendom and the Naturalization of Christianity in the Orient in the XIXth Century (New York, 1920), 66-67.

[11]Missionary Herald, XXX (1834), 13.

[12]American Board, Thirty-third Annual Report, 206.

greater efforts at points yielding higher prospects of early success and to regard the scattered stations as territorial bases for a spiritual warfare destined to overspread the world.

A careful regard to the means of increasing the interest of the evangelical community also motivated the statesmanship of the overseas enterprise. Secretary Anderson wrote privately in 1848 to agents of the American Board in South Africa that it was "good economy" to maintain stations in that part of the world. "A variety of fields is indispensable to the development of the missionary spirit in this country. . . . We never needed motives so much as now. There is a singular and not easily accountable want of impressibility in the Christian public, on all subjects."[13]

The Bible as the chief handbook of missions furnished, if not a strategy, at least assurance of ultimate victory. In the Old Testament --and particularly the messianic Psalms and the book of Isaiah--evangelicals found the rollcall of heathen nations which were to enter the Kingdom as well as much of the imagery which adorned missionary rhetoric in pulpit and press. American Protestants were able to interpret their overseas operations as the fulfilment of Biblical promises that "the isles shall wait for his law" and "Ethiopia shall soon stretch out her hands unto God."[14] If the Sacred Scriptures did not name all the regions which latter-day evangelical enterprise had marked out for itself, it seemed clearly stipulated that the Christian inheritance included the "uttermost parts of the earth."[15]

While the Bible afforded Protestants the dark image of heathen

---

[13]Anderson to the South Africa mission, Boston, August 31, 1848, ABC: 2.1.1, XI, 96.

[14]Isaiah 42:4; Psalms 68:31.

[15]Psalms 2:8.

nations which derived from Hebrew ethnocentrism, it also drew their attention to the geography of Palestine and the adjoining countries. It was not accidental that the American Board occupied the eastern Mediterranean decades before entering Africa or the Far East, and spent more of its funds and employed a greater number of evangelists in that area than in any other mission during the whole nineteenth century. No other segment of the earth's surface so stirred the evangelical imagination as that zone which inclosed the sacred scenes of the Old and New Testament. Americans rejoiced that missionaries from the New World were to carry the Gospel to the Holy Land once trod by patriarchs and prophets and to the eastern shores of the Mediterranean where Paul preached and John of Patmos saw his visions.

The Board's agents were the first American pilgrims to set foot in Jerusalem. Although this gained no significant evangelistic results, it was a moment of triumph for orthodox New England when Pliny Fisk reached the city of David in 1823 and resided for a time on Mount Calvary. "I have passed through the valley of Hinnon," he wrote back to the faculty of Andover Seminary, "drunk of the waters of Siloam, crossed the brook Cedron, and have been in the garden of Gethsemane."[16] To classically educated young men Greece and her many monuments in the Near East lent further interest to the same region. Missionary explorers in Asia Minor made note of the route followed in the retreat of Xenophon and the Ten Thousand.[17] But this was subordinated for the sake of the Gospel. "We never forgot," Rufus Anderson reported after his tour of 1828, "that we were sent to explore not ancient, but modern Greece, and that our inquiries were to be directed not so much to its natural, as to its moral

[16]Fisk to Porter, Jerusalem, April 23, 1823, in Bond, _Pliny Fisk_, 286.
[17]Perkins, _Residence in Persia_, 101, 117.

features."[18] Indeed, by the same token, the general evangelical outlook neglected cultural or historical differences among the various component parts of heathendom and tended to include all unevangelical peoples in a single appraisal.

II

If the brotherhood of man expressed the ideal of Christian compassion for a suffering world, nineteenth-century Protestants felt no uncertainty as to the religious and moral worth of paganism itself. "The heathen are neither holy nor happy," Lyman Beecher pontificated in an ordination sermon. He described them instead as depraved, ignorant, profligate, "debased by their superstitions," and "tortured by vain fears and useless penances."[19] The more tolerant, universalizing view of the men of the previous century was explicitly rejected. Samuel Worcester warned the Board's first emissaries to Hawaii against erroneous conceptions of the "noble savage." "It is a delirious dream of infidelity, that the various systems of paganism are only so many diversified forms of the true religion; that all nations acknowledge and worship the true God, only under different names, and with different rites. You will find the dream as false as it is delirious."[20] When the recently deposed high priest amicably greeted the Hawaiian missionaries in 1820 as brother clerics, he not only astonished but appalled the New Englanders.[21]

Supremely confident that a providential scheme assured the early conquest of the non-Christian world, neither the evangelists nor their

---

[18]Anderson, Observations upon the Peloponnesus, 32.

[19]Beecher, The Bible a Code of Laws (Andover, 1818), 50.

[20]Samuel Worcester, "Address to the Missionaries," in Moses Stuart, A Sermon Preached in the Tabernacle Church, Salem (Andover, 1818), 35.

[21]Journal of the Missionaries, April 5, 1820, Missionary Herald, XVII (1821), 117.

directors made thorough studies of the faiths they labored to supplant. Men who believed that Protestant Christianity had a mandate from on high to re-create the earth in its own image hardly took seriously such complex structures as Mohammedanism, Confucianism, or Buddhism, to say nothing of the animistic systems of the Sandwich Islanders or Zulus. Nor did they differentiate very clearly between primitive and highly developed religions. When the Board finally approached China, the prudential committee felt obliged to deny that the Chinese were "barbarians," pointing out that they possessed "arts and sciences." Lest any should doubt the need for missions among so enlightened a race, however, the committee added:

> We must distinguish between the excellent maxims contained in some of their sacred books, and the conduct of the people; nor must we suppose that their good maxims are understood in China in the same exalted and virtuous sense, in which they would be understood by a people enjoying the light of the Gospel. . . . Among that ancient people you will find, with some slight variations, the idolatry of Canaan, Egypt, Greece, Rome, Chaldea, and India.[22]

By emphasizing the "idolatrous" nature of pagan religion, evangelicals lumped together all the peoples outside Christendom. The accepted image of non-Christian morality provided the common denominator. Americans familiar with the catalogue of vices in the first chapter of Romans were ready to believe the worst of heathen morals and modes of worship, many of which were "too indecent . . . to be named," according to a sermon of 1792.[23] In publishing excerpts from Gordon Hall's notes on India in 1816, the editor of the Panoplist confessed that some passages were too improper to print: "The amusements of the Hindoos . . . are so scandalously obscene, as not to admit of description in a Christian country."[24]

---

[22]Instructions to China Missionaries, Missionary Herald, XXIX (1833), 273.

[23]Parish, The Excellence of the Gospel Visible in the Wretchedness of Paganism (Newburyport, 1798), 13.

[24]Panoplist, XII (1816), 505.

Despite this delicacy missionary letters circulating in private revealed vividly the reaction of the Puritan mind to a strange culture. In 1824 John Nichols wrote from India to his former classmates at Andover:

> Come over then, Brethren, and we will show you what idolatry is, in all its nameless abominations. Come over, and we will show you idolatry systematized, surrounded by all that is imposing in antiquity, by all that is wonderful in miracles, by all that is captivating to the senses, and by all that is gratifying to the depraved heart. . . . Come over, and we will show you . . . idols under every green tree; we will show you the great god of the land, a huge stone, in the form of the male and female organs of generation conjoined![25]

Although this was not the sort of thing which the _Missionary Herald_ could divulge to its readers, the Board and similar agencies managed to convey in pamphlet and periodical an impression of unutterable heathen depravity. Missionary promoters dwelt much upon the low standards of foreign sexual morality revealing an attitude of pruriency typical of contemporary evangelical ideas. When advance agents in the Marquesas described the islands as a "great brothel," the American Board hesitated to print a full report. "Perhaps we are sometimes too backward," the editors of the _Herald_ announced, "from motives of delicacy, to describe what our dear brethren and sisters, who go as missionaries to the heathen, are compelled to witness and endure."[26] But they printed an excerpt vivid enough to shock Protestant sensibilities and to suggest even more. "Chastity appears to be utterly unknown," Richard Armstrong wrote. "The gestures which the men practice before our eyes, are truly shocking; and wherever we have met native females, they have most unblushingly offered themselves for pollution!"[27]

American missionaries, in whatever part of the world they were

---

[25] John Nichols to Society of Inquiry, Bombay, August 15, 1824, Society of Inquiry Papers.

[26] _Missionary Herald_, XXX (1834), 90.

[27] Letter of Richard Armstrong, _ibid._, 91.

stationed, abhorred polygamy more than social evils like the caste system or even slavery. Conservative evangelicals who resisted the more radical movements for women's rights at home called loudly for female uplift abroad. Woman's degraded position in non-Christian lands became one of the chief emotional appeals for foreign missions. An important part of the moral stereotype concerning countries "wrapt in Pagan and Mahomedan darkeness" pictured wives and daughters treated as "beasts of the field" and "sunk to the lowest state of infamy and wretchedness."[28] For this reason the Board encouraged missionary wives to participate actively in the work of each station in order to obtain access to the feminine heart and mind. While raising up an educated body of young men in the field, the missions did not neglect the training of girls. A great corps of un-married women teachers as well as pastors' wives operated boarding schools for the maids of Asia and Africa. The plea for the elevation of their sex in distant lands helped tremendously to engage the sentiments and energies of American women in the missionary enterprise, an engagement they never suffered to lapse.

If the Calvinist image of the sinful condition of natural man made it possible to believe in the moral degradation of the heathen, the need for continuing missionary support made imperative its constant evocation. It created a whole literature. Besides the regular religious press, books, pamphlets, and broadsheets proclaimed the message. The A.B.C.F.M. published Monthly Papers and Quarterly Papers showing children sacrificed to devils,[29] as well as a series of Missionary Tracts dealing with various aspects of the foreign work. The American Tract Society

---

[28]Daniel Thomas, A Sermon . . . before the Palestine Missionary Society (Boston, 1824), 5.

[29]American Board, Monthly Paper, XV, September 1833.

circulated similar materials, one of which bore the title, Horrors of Heathenism.[30]

Much of this literature appealed particularly to children. One lady author described her book for the very young as drawing a "faithful and impressive exhibition of the ignorance, degradation and misery of the heathen world."[31] These writers held that the sympathies of Sunday school pupils were broadened by learning of "heathen children bereft of blessings they enjoy and subjected to every form of wickedness and wo . . ." "A generation of children thus educated," wrote John Scudder of the Madras mission, "would be better fathers and husbands, better members of every local community, better patriots, better Christians."[32] At the close of the year 1850, the American Board began publishing Youth's Dayspring for Sabbath schools in order that the young should "grow up active and warm-hearted in the cause."[33]

Through foreign missions the American people gained some knowledge of the individual personalities, if not the full scope, of alien cultures. The Sandwich Islanders, Indian aborigines, and other youthful foreigners at the Cornwall academy excited an unusual amount of personal attention among the orthodox of New England. The memoirs of the Hawaiian student, Henry Obookiah, who died in the odor of sanctity in the little

[30]H. B. Hooker, Horrors of Heathenism (New York, n.d.).

[31]Jane K. Welsh, A View of the Heathen World (Worcester, 1834), preface, v. Another purveyor of missionary tales to children was Sarah Tuttle, who wrote a series of Conversations on India, Ceylon, Burma, and China (Boston, 1830, 1833).

[32]John Scudder, Sabbath School Associations (Boston, 1835). Scudder, a medical missionary in India, published several books for children of this nature: Letters to Sabbath-School Children on the Condition of the Heathen (Philadelphia, 1843); Sermon to Children, on the Condition of the Heathen (Boston, 1845); and A Voice from the East to the Young (New York, 1859).

[33]Youth's Dayspring, I (1850), 177-178.

Connecticut town, went through dozens of editions to become an outstanding missionary best seller. "Peddlers and stationers mentioned it above the year's almanac. Ministers preached on it. Sunday school teachers read aloud from it and young ladies sobbed over it. Alive, Obookiah had been known to a few college boys, tutors and village pastors; dead, he was beloved of the whole Christian public."[34] Less well known but equally pathetic was the biography of a Marquesan boy, Thomas Patoo, who met a Christian death far from home and lies buried beside Obookiah in the Cornwall graveyard.[35] In the same vein were the narratives of the lives and deaths of youthful Indian converts--the first fruits of the Board's operations in the Old Southwest.[36]

The failure of the Cornwall Foreign Mission School illustrated one hazard of direct contact with alien races. Speaking particularly of the American Indians, but in terms equally applicable to other nonwhite pagans, the prudential committee explained that one reason for closing the academy was the difficulty of treating the students "in such a manner, as not to exalt them too high, or depress them too low." In the first place, large attentions to them turned their heads.

> At the same time, they are treated, in various respects, as though they were and must be inferior to ourselves. This results not merely from the differences of complexion, but from the hereditary feelings of our people in regard to Indians. These different kinds of treatment, which result from inquisitive curiosity, mixed with Christian benevolence on the one hand, and from established principles of prejudice on the other, make the young men feel as though they were mere shows, a feeling which is too accurate an index of their real situation.[37]

[34]Loomis, Grapes of Canaan, 12.

[35]/Harlan Page7, A Memoir of Thomas Hamitah Patoo, a Native of the Marquesas Islands (Andover, 1825).

[36]Anderson, Memoir of Catherine Brown, a Christian Indian of the Cherokee Nation (Boston, 1824); Elias Cornelius, The Little Osage Captive, an Authentic Narrative (Boston, 1822).

[37]American Board, Seventeenth Annual Report, 106.

More successful was the placing of a score or more of Greek students in the schools and colleges of New England during the philhellenic enthusiasm of the twenties and thirties. In the next decade, however, these were followed by several Armenians from Turkey, whose alien character and manners provided the greatest embarrassment to all concerned. One well-recommended couple made so little progress in the language and adapted so poorly to New England life that Secretary Anderson wrote to their sponsors in Constantinople that they damaged the missionary interest. "She is dressy, and they are both <u>childlike--exotic</u> plants. They will not grow in this soil; they ought both to be at home, and that soon."[38] Two bachelor compatriots arrived a few years later, whom the prudential committee of the Board established in menial jobs in Dorchester and Lowell, firmly requesting its missionaries in the Levant not to dispatch more.[39]

Returning missionaries occasionally brought with them living examples of redeemed heathenism. A native of Canton accompanied Dr. Peter Parker on his lecture tour through the nation in 1840 while he attempted to raise funds for medical work in China. A decade later Mrs. Eliza Bridgman carried to America a young woman from her Shanghai mission school --perhaps the first Chinese of her sex to be seen in this country--and afterwards published a book on the women of China.[40] But the figure who aroused the greatest attention was a Nestorian bishop from Persia, Mar Yohanna, who accompanied Justin Perkins to this country in 1842. Dressed in the bizarre costume of his native land and adorned with a heavy black

---

[38]Anderson to the Constantinople mission, Boston, February 28, 1845, ABC:2.1.1, VIII, 55.

[39]Anderson to Hamlin, Boston, January 8, 1849, ABC:2.1.1, XI, 181.

[40]Eliza J. G. Bridgman, <u>Daughters of China; or, Sketches of Domestic Life in the Celestial Empire</u> (New York, 1852).

beard and mustache,[41] the colorful ecclesiastic excited nearly as much interest as did the Hungarian patriot, Louis Kossuth, a few years later. An engraving of the good bishop in turban and flowing Oriental garb appeared in one of the religious giftbooks for the year 1843, along with an account of the Nestorian mission in Persia.[42]

The memoirs of native Christians converted on missionary ground through the instrumentality of the agents of the American churches also found a ready audience. These tracts, giving evidence of the first harvest of souls reaped through the efforts of American evangelists, treated chiefly the process of conversion itself and offered little insight into pagan life or thought. They enriched the devotional literature of the times by adding an exotic flavor to the conventional "pious lives" of the Protestant library: biographies of baptized Hawaiian queens, converted Brahmans, Burmese and Karens, "pious Nestorians," a blind Sandwich Islands preacher, and the Syrian Maronite, Asaad Esh Shidiak, who suffered martyrdom at the hands of his fellow religionists after embracing the Protestant views of the missionaries.[43]

But the missionary view of the non-Christian world did not completely prevail in the United States during this period. Critics from all sides brought in minority reports. In the first flush of the Board's evangelistic efforts in India, the Panoplist noted with horror that "a

[41]New York Observer, January 15, 1842.

[42]I. F. Shepard, ed., The Christian Souvenir (Boston, 1842), 296-303.

[43]/William Richards7, Memoir of Keopuolani, Late Queen of the Sandwich Islands (Boston, 1825); Anderson, Kapiolani, the Heroine of Hawaii (New York, 1866); Hollis Read, The Christian Brahman (2 v., New York, 1836); Deborah B. L. Wade, The Burman Slave Girl (Boston, n.d.); Francis Mason, The Karen Apostle (Boston, 1843); Sketches of Pious Nestorians Who Have Died at Oroomiah, Persia (Boston, 1857); Hiram Bingham, Bartimaeus, of the Sandwich Islands (Boston, n.d.); Isaac Bird, The Martyr of Lebanon (Boston, 1864).

certain doctor of divinity in New England"--probably the irrepressible William Bentley of Salem--had been heard to say that "he hoped, if the people of our country carry our religion to the Hindoos, they will bring back the morality of India."[44] The mercantile community of the Massachusetts seaboard, from long familiarity with foreign ports and products, afforded a large tolerance toward strange lands and their inhabitants which dated at least from the founding of the Salem East India Marine Society in 1799.[45] A seafaring member of the Ames family of Massachusetts, who frequently reproached the missionaries in the East, described the Hindus as "in the main, a virtuous, peaceable, and but for the infernal tyranny and oppression of the British East India Company, a happy people, however unreasonable and absurd their religion may seem in our eyes."[46] He added that he thought the Mohammedans in Calcutta the most honest men he had ever met.[47] In one of her anonymous pamphlets against missions Elizabeth Sanders of Salem praised Chinese society in terms reminiscent of eighteenth-century opinions of the enlightened Celestial Empire. She pointed out that the people of China had no need of Christian evangelists for even the masses were literate and endowed with political rights; no hereditary nobility or privileged classes ground down the poor. "And, moreover," she continued, "they are a moral and religious people, courteous and hospitable, and, of course, more civilized than the mass of Americans or Europeans."[48]

Nor did the protagonists of evangelical missions provide the

---

[44]_Panoplist_, XII (1816), 505.

[45]Morison, _Maritime History of Massachusetts_, 117.

[46]/Nathaniel Ames/, _Nautical Reminiscences_ (Providence, 1832), 60.

[47]_Ibid._, 63.

[48]_Tract on Missions_ (Salem, 1844), 4-5.

only American interest in exotic cultures in this era. An antithetical view of distant civilizations arose in New England literary circles, especially among Transcendentalists like Emerson and Thoreau, who read and were influenced by Oriental writings—the Bhagavad-Gita and the work of the Persian poet, Saadi, and the Chinese sages, Mencius and Confucius.[49] Although this highly appreciative attitude toward pagan thought must not be overlooked in appraising the total American outlook, it represented an intellectual minority with little influence upon the main body of American Protestants. In directing an exploration of Persia in 1834, the prudential committee of the Board noted that the city of Shiraz was chiefly interesting as being the scene of the labors of the English missionary, Henry Martyn. "What is it to you, that Sadi and Hafiz were born there, and that there are their tombs?"[50]

Orthodox spokesmen seized upon receptiveness to heathen literature in attacking religious liberalism. In a "Discussion with a Transcendentalist," published in the New Englander in 1843, an evangelical champion ridiculed the serious appropriation of Oriental wisdom. In response to the somewhat exaggerated praise of the religions of the East attributed to his Transcendental opponent, the speaker evoked the familiar missionary image of the heathen:

> Really, you must have a transcendental eye, for it is something more than a poet's to see so much beauty and true piety in those eastern idolaters. You doubtless see the same in the Chinese, in their worship of those half dozen fat hogs kept as gods at Canton. The funeral pile, the hook-swinging, the infanticides, and the thousand disgusting and horrible rites of Bramah, all must come up to your mind with peculiar attractions, in as much as you think them sincere acts of devotion.[51]

---

[49]See F. I. Carpenter, Emerson and Asia (Cambridge, 1930), and Arthur Christy, The Orient in American Transcendentalism: A Study of Emerson, Thoreau, and Alcott (New York, 1932).

[50]Missionary Herald, XXX (1834), 403.

[51]New Englander, I (1843), 511.

Even when face to face with a more secular--or more mystical--conception
of the non-Christian world, Protestant orthodoxy only reiterated and re-
affirmed the legacy of foreign missions. If the study of comparative
religion began with the Emersonians,[52] no such candid view of alien faiths
disturbed the missionary mind.

III

Foreign missions also thrust American Protestants into the
larger Christian world community. In part, it was the example of the
self-effacing Moravians, the Halle pietists, and the English Baptists and
Independents which drew the churches of the United States into the international missionary movement. In the early years of evangelistic ferment
in the colleges and seminaries of New England, members of the Brethren
and the Society of Inquiry corresponded fraternally with European students
with similar interests in Switzerland and Great Britain.[53] If home missions on the frontier tended to divert American attention from the Old
World, the foreign work involved American evangelicals in a global Protestant crusade in which the nations of Europe all played definite roles.
The corresponding secretaries of the A.B.C.F.M. communicated regularly
with individuals and societies abroad, giving and seeking counsel and
composing national and denominational differences in the occupation of
the field. Out of this friendly rivalry came mutual agreement upon a
principle of noninterference in each other's missions and a practical
division of labor in the task.[54]

England was, of course, the great Protestant champion in the
Old World to whom Americans looked for guidance and support. Protestant

---

[52]Carpenter, Emerson and Asia, 247-248.

[53]C. P. Shedd, Two Centuries of Student Christian Movements, 65-67.

[54]American Board, Twenty-ninth Annual Report, 32-34.

Germany, weak and divided, carried on no large-scale missions; Denmark's early efforts in India were drawing to a close; the rest of Europe was either predominently Catholic or unawakened to evangelical enthusiasm. From the outset the American Board enjoyed fraternal relations with its sister societies in Great Britain, maintaining an association which even the hostilities of 1812-1815 could not impair. William Wilberforce, M.P., Evangelical stalwart and a frequent correspondent of the Board, rejoiced publicly that the co-operative missionary endeavors of the two countries had the "blessed effect" of "cementing the mutual attachment of all good men, on both sides of the Atlantic, towards each other."[55]

With some exceptions, evangelists of England and the United States worked side by side in full harmony. On the invitation of the London Society's agents in those regions, the Board entered China, Siam, and South Africa. In Hawaii the English missionary-printer, William Ellis, helped establish the American mission before returning to London, where as secretary of his own society he strengthened the trans-Atlantic fellowship. Since the main axis of co-operation linked the A.B.C.F.M. with the Nonconformists of Great Britain and the Evangelicals of the established church, the rise of the Anglican Oxford Movement brought a disturbing element into the picture. The Board came into conflict with British high-church representatives in the Middle East, India, and the Sandwich Islands, a fact which damaged but did not completely destroy Anglo-American Protestant relations. Perhaps the best example of the continuing amity of the evangelical portions of the two nations can be seen in the strong support the Board's operations in the eastern Mediterranean elicited in England through the Turkish Missions Aid Society from the time of the Crimean War onwards.

---

[55]Letter of Wilberforce quoted in American Board, Fourteenth Annual Report, 12.

In the early years of the century enigmatic Russia appeared also on the side of the angels. The religious press in the United States lauded the pious-seeming Alexander I as the conqueror of the man considered by many as the incarnation of Antichrist, Napoleon Bonaparte, and hailed his proposal for a Holy Alliance in 1815 as laying the basis for a Christian state policy in Europe.[56] Protestants watched hopefully for the progress of evangelical principles under the reforming tsar and his minister of religion, Alexander Galitzin, who was also president of the newly formed Russian Bible Society.[57] Since British missionaries and colporteurs were already working in parts of Russia, some Americans saw an opportunity to reach the heathen nations of Asia on the borders of that empire. In their well-known appeal to the churches of the United States, Gordon Hall and Samuel Newell of the Board mission in India called upon their fellow countrymen to "make Russia the door to China, Persia and Turkey." "The friendly relation which subsists between this country and Russia," they wrote, "is a circumstance which calls the American churches in particular to embrace the new and extensive openings in that quarter of the globe."[58]

Alexander's last years, however, were reactionary ones, failing to fulfil the promise of an evangelical revival in his domains. With the accession in 1825 of the new tsar, Nicholas I, the Russian Bible Society and other evangelistic efforts came to an end. Nothing came of the hoped-for co-operation in the task of Christianizing the world. In Turkey

---

[56]Panoplist, XII (1816), 183-184; Boston Recorder, Wednesday, April 17, 1816.

[57]Panoplist, XIII (1817), 435-436; XIV (1818), 390; XV (1819), 452-454.

[58]/Hall and Newell7, The Conversion of the World, 42-43.

where the A.B.C.F.M.'s agents had looked to the sultan's powerful neighbor for aid in promoting the welfare of the submerged Christian minorities under Moslem rule, Russian policy in the Balkans and intrigue at Constantinople soon undeceived them. By the time of the Crimean War in 1854 the missionaries were calling for English victory over Nicholas as the only security for their Armenian charges against Russian Orthodox aggrandizement.

While officially deprecating direct communications with foreign governments, the American Board and its agents did enter negotiations of this nature from time to time. American evangelists in India and South Africa had frequent recourse to British colonial authorities, petitioning for special privileges as alien residents and even in some cases taking an active part in official questions, as in the land commission in Natal. When provoked by untoward incidents occurring in the missions in Hawaii and Indonesia, the prudential committee went so far as to authorize its representative in Europe to intercede immediately with the governments of Holland and France. Robert Baird, who undertook this task in 1839-1842, was received at both the French and Dutch courts almost as an ambassador of a foreign state. In Paris, in the manner of contemporary envoys, Baird managed to place in the French press articles favorable to the American version of Captain Laplace's insulting behavior toward the Board's missionaries in Honolulu in 1839.[59] The prudential committee's agent found the United States minister to France helpful in gaining access to Louis Phillipe, but disinclined to push the matter officially. "Mr. Cass," he wrote to Boston, "will do nothing himself but what is required by our government. He stands on etiquette more than he need do. But this we can not control. He is wholly a man of the world, and takes no

---

[59]Robert Baird to Anderson, Paris, April 22, 1840, ABC:14, II, no. 14.

interest in the Kingdom of Christ."[60]

In neither Paris nor The Hague did the Board succeed in its objects. It was difficult to understand the intransigeance of Protestant Holland, but American evangelicals scarcely expected Catholic France to reform its religious and political aggression, which the Board experienced both in West Africa and the Hawaiian Islands. This latter nation, a symbol of atheistic infidelity under the Directory, and once again "popish" after Napoleon, served as the archetype of the antievangelical forces to zealous Protestants in the United States. When the 1830 revolution raised hopes of the introduction of religious liberty, American churches organized the "French Association" to encourage the growth of Protestant congregations in that Romanist stronghold, employing as their emissary the same Robert Baird who later acted for the A.B.C.F.M. at the court.[61]

Even earlier, citizens of the United States residing abroad played a significant role in awakening evangelical sentiment in France. In 1822 a number of French, English, and American Protestants gathered at the home of the New England merchant, S. V. S. Wilder, to plan the formation of the Société des Missions Évangéliques de Paris.[62] The young Jonas King, who was studying Arabic at the Sorbonne to prepare himself for a professorship in Amherst College, participated in these meetings and became the French society's first missionary when he accepted the American Board's invitation to replace the deceased Levi Parsons in Palestine.[63] When the Paris group commenced a mission in South Africa in

---

[60]Baird to Anderson, St. Petersburg, September 11, 1840, ABC:14, II, no.18.

[61]H. M. Baird, The Life of the Rev. Robert Baird, D.D. (New York, 1865), 87-88.

[62]Jean Bianquis, Les Origines de la Société des Missions Évangéliques de Paris (Paris, 1830), I, 22-30.

[63]Records from the Life of S. V. S. Wilder (New York, 1865), 123-130; H/aines/, Jonas King, 69-74.

1829, its initial--unsuccessful--station was on the very spot chosen by American missionaries at Mosega among the Matabeles. The Board welcomed the efforts of its European brethren in the task of world evangelism, especially in view of the aggressive operations of French Catholics. In an attempt to counteract the Romanists in the Pacific, the prudential committee sought fruitlessly to persuade the Paris Society to send its own agents to the Sandwich Islands in the forties.[64]

Since the Board looked to evangelical England for protection against Gallic perfidy, the brief "annexation" of Hawaii by Lord Paulet in 1843 and his relaxing of missionary-inspired laws against rum shocked the supporters of missions in the United States. Melville, who had witnessed the short-lived British regime in the Islands, was so impressed with what he considered general American misinterpretation of Paulet's actions that he included an appendix in Typee justifying the proceedings.[65] The same issue of the Missionary Herald which recorded the prudential committee's abhorrence of a recent French attack upon Tahiti and the London Society's mission there, contained a stinging criticism of Great Britain's adoption of similar tactics at Honolulu.[66] But the magazine concluded, with a confidence which later events endorsed--for Westminster repudiated Lord Paulet almost immediately--that "the friends of religion and truth may reasonably anticipate a prompt and honorable disavowal of the wrongful acts of one of its servants."[67]

The missionary temper, like the whole evangelical atmosphere of the time, was strongly anti-Catholic. In part at least, the overseas work of the A.B.C.F.M. was an extention of the nativist campaign

---

[64]Baird to Anderson, Geneva, July 12, 1842, ABC:14, II, no. 25.
[65]Melville, Typee, 343-348.
[66]Missionary Herald, XXXIX (1843), 289-291.
[67]Ibid., 294.

and carried the attack upon papal institutions to the ends of the earth. The millenarian language in which so much of the early missionary objectives was phrased pictured the Roman Church as one of the great adversaries to be overcome in the world-wide struggle for men's minds. Since the Jesuits and other Catholic orders were before them in many fields, Protestant mission boards were forced to fight on two fronts at once. In its instructions to the men who were resuming their labors in Syria in 1830, the prudential committee warned that Rome and Islam both faced them in deadly battle:

> You must calculate, then, upon being opposed and frustrated to the full extent of his /the pope's7 power, and must not be dismayed, if the Beast and False Prophet occasionally unite their counsels in efforts hostile to the interests of your mission. Such an event is foretold as a prelude to the battle of the great day, when they are both to be overthrown and their power subverted.[68]

In a comment on Catholic missionaries in Southeast Asia--where France was gaining a foothold economically and politically as well as religiously--the Missionary Herald reminded its readers of the importance of entering "every heathen country as soon as providence opens a way of access, before the minds of the people shall be pre-occupied, and all entrance hedged up again by the introduction of papal doctrines."[69] Protestant emissaries--bottled up in the foreign factories of Canton during pretreaty days--felt particularly inadequate in China, where Catholic priests had long maintained establishments in the interior despite anti-Christian decrees. Partly in order to emulate the partisans of Rome, Gutzlaff and later Stevens and others of the A.B.C.F.M. made their valiant attempts to reach the Chinese by coastal journeys. To David Abeel of the Board it was a "painful circumstance" that Portuguese Macao, "the only

---

[68]Missionary Herald, XXVI (1830), 78.

[69]Ibid., XXVII (1831), 243.

spot under European control, in the whole empire of China, should exhibit

to the heathen the most gross and absurd notions of that holy religion,

whose name they attach to their worse than Pagan abominations."[70]

Tolerance of other faiths—pagan or "nominally" Christian—was

not a conspicuous characteristic of the American missionaries. A favorite

device was to compare Roman Catholic worship to the idolatrous practices

of the heathen.[71] In Hawaii, where the mission-influenced native rulers

at first proscribed Catholic proselyting on the grounds that it violated

laws against image-worship, the American Board and its agents almost always

followed the anti-Catholic stereotype in calling their competitors "Jes-

uits," although in fact they had no relationship to that order.[72] New

England missionaries who visited Malta en route to their Mediterranean

stations found the Old World Catholic atmosphere so exotic that one of

them offered to send the prudential committee a series of letters to be

published in the religious press describing in detail the evils of pop-

ery.[73]

It was only natural that missionary zeal, under these conditions,

---

[70]Abeel, Residence in China, 54.

[71]See Miron Winslow, A Memoir of Mrs. Harriet Wadsworth Winslow, Combining a Sketch of the Ceylon Missions (New York, 1835), 257-259.

[72]Letter of Coan, Hilo, May 3, 1844, Missionary Herald, XLI (1845), 86; American Board, Thirty-third Annual Report, 41.

[73]Anderson to Daniel Temple, Boston, December 31, 1830, ABC:2.01, I, 276, This was long before Samuel F. B. Morse's articles "exposing" the Catholic conspiracy appeared in the New York Observer in the latter months of 1834. The next year another note was struck when H. G. O. Dwight of the Constantinople mission, who had also visited Catholic Malta and Italy, wrote a letter published in the same journal denouncing current anti-Catholic intolerance. "To us, at this distance," he said, "it does seem sometimes as though the good people of America were perfectly crazy . . . ." In opposition to Morse and others, he argued that Catholic immigration was an ultimate good, removing such people from countries to which missionaries had little or no access to the United States, where Protestants could exert a powerful influence upon their poverty and ignorance. New York Observer, December 5, 1835.

would turn toward papal lands like France and Italy. As early as 1834, a small Presbyterian organization in Pittsburgh planned a mission to Austrian Trieste.[74] In the forties and fifties Presbyterians, Methodists, and the nondenominational American and Foreign Christian Union supported Protestant evangelists in Catholic Europe.[75] The American Board in the period before the Civil War did not follow this example, but in the 1870's began operations in Spain, Austria, and Italy on the same basis employed in its heathen missions.[76] The nineteenth-century Protestant image of the unevangelized world comprehended all the nations of the earth yet unvanquished by the evangelical teachings of the Reformation.

The question might well be raised how far the missionary outlook penetrated the popular attitudes of Americans and informed the nation's foreign policy. In general, it seems reasonable to assert that foreign missions contributed to American suspicion of the outside world and at the same time to a sense of benevolent superiority, the former directed at Europe, particularly the part which was neither English-speaking nor Protestant, and the latter coloring our relations with the "underdeveloped" nations of the earth. Caleb Cushing, who endorsed in a leading evangelical journal the missionary concept of a world divided into Christian and barbarous nations, later founded explicitly upon this very notion his reasoning behind the system of extraterritoriality introduced in China in the Wanghia treaty.[77]

---

[74] Western Foreign Missionary Society, Second Annual Report (Pittsburgh, 1834), 13-14.

[75] R. A. Billington, The Protestant Crusade 1800-1860: A Study of the Origins of American Nativism (New York, 1933), 264-275.

[76] Strong, Story of the American Board, 290-291.

[77] American Biblical Repository, s.s., I (1839), 180-205; Cushing to J. C. Calhoun, U.S. Brig Perry, September 29, 1844, House Executive Document, 28 Cong., 2 sess., no. 69.

From the time of President John Quincy Adams the United States
government recognized the importance of the missionary agency in Hawaii
and acknowledged the resulting ties between this country and that Pacific
archipelago.[78] The directors of the American Board often appealed to
Washington on behalf of missionary interests abroad and usually managed
to receive favorable assurances of official concern, if not succor, in
individual cases. The nature of the society's lobbying for overseas
interests is illustrated by the appointment of several members to visit
Washington in 1850, on the occasion of a French threat to Hawaii. Rufus
Anderson defined the aims of the group in a private letter as "bringing
the personal influences of the members of the Committee, and the prestige
of the Board, and of the highly respectable religious community it repre-
sents, to bear on the Government, and stimulate and encourage them in
doing what is incumbent on them for the protection of our mission, and
the institutions of the gospel we have been favored in planting at the
Sandwich Islands."[79] In general, however, the prudential committee,
thinking it "well to keep the missionary and political currents of the
world as distinct as possible,"[80] refrained from pressing for governmental
action except in fairly isolated instances. This derived largely from a
conviction of the necessity of strict separation of church and state as
well as a pessimistic attitude toward the latter. "I have seen enough,"

---

[78]See for example President Tyler's presidential message of 1842, reprinted in part and praised in the Missionary Herald, XXXIX (1843), 90.

[79]Anderson to T. S. Williams, Boston, September 23, 1850, ABC:2.1.1,
XIII, 253. In another letter Anderson confidentially informed the mission
that the United States government had agreed to prevent French seizure of
Hawaii. "Of course," he wrote, "all we had to present to our Government,
was the great interests which American missionary enterprise had at stake
in those Islands. They gave them a very respectful consideration."
Anderson to S. N. Castle, Boston, September 7, 1850, ABC:2.1.1, XIII, 248.

[80]Anderson to J. J. Jarves, Boston, October 24, 1849, ABC:2.1.1, XII, 43.

Anderson wrote in 1849, "of the political world,--the 'outer world' as I call it--to be sensible of the uncertainty attending the influence of motives such as we have to offer; in respect to which, there is not a great deal to choose between the two great parties which divide the nation."[81]

Missionary promoters were most successful in engaging the attention of the general public and of the official circles of government in situations where heavy American commercial commitments reinforced their demands. Thus a combination of trading and religious interests, running parallel rather than acting in collusion, operated to bring about closer relations with both China and the Hawaiian Islands. It is interesting to note that American philanthropic investment in foreign missions in some parts of the world--notably in the Ottoman Empire[82]--exceeded greatly the amount of commercial capital invested. Despite this fact, which was seldom duly appreciated, the missionary enterprise probably possessed no commensurate influence in diplomatic quarters. But the force of its action upon the evangelical community at large, in molding American habits of thought and attitudes toward the world, lies beyond exact calculation.

[81]Anderson to Carr, Boston, February 19, 1849, ABC:2.1.1, XI, 205.

[82]L. J. Gordon, American Relations with Turkey 1830-1930: An Economic Interpretation (Philadelphia, 1932), 246.

CHAPTER X

THE MISSIONARY AT HOME AND ABROAD

The central figure in this most ambitious of American evangelical enterprises was the missionary himself. In the young men and women
who so willingly left family and friends to execute their Christian duty
in remote parts of the globe was found the heroic model of nineteenth-
century Protestant piety. Looked upon almost as martyrs at the time of
their departure from this country's shores, they received a benediction
as saints of God when appointed to the overseas task. "We have consecrated you to God and the heathen," was the pastoral charge delivered
to the first emissaries to Hawaii in 1819. "You are, henceforth, dead
to the world, dead to the refinements of civilized society, and the en-
dearments of social ties in the bosom of your native land. Our eyes are
shortly to behold you no more."[1] In engaging the interest of the religious community, the foreign missionary enjoyed a distinct advantage
over his clerical brother at home whose more prosaic task could not
compare with the colorful struggle waged abroad against pagan principal-
ities and powers.

I

The image of the Protestant envoy to regions of darkness which
impressed itself deeply upon the American mind stressed self-sacrifice
and hardship, together with romantic adventure. At the beginning of the
enterprise preachers pictured "youth of both sexes . . . renouncing the

---

[1]D. L. Perry's charge to the missionaries, in Humphrey, The Promised
Land, 37.

comforts of civilized society, bidding farewell to father and mother,
to sisters and brethren, encountering the toils, sufferings and self-
denials, of a missionary life; the dangers of sickly and untried climate
. . . that they may redeem miserable pagans from pollution and ruin."[2]
Even more pathetic was the vision of "delicate young females, who have
been dandled in the lap of parental tenderness . . . tearing themselves
for the last time from the arms of trembling mothers and speechless
sisters, to encounter the dangers and the seas and the still greater
dangers of a torrid clime, in order to support their husbands by their
smiles and prayers in a foreign land, among sooty pagans . . . ."[3]

Orthodox New England demonstrated its profound interest by
turning out in large numbers for the ceremonies which marked the embarkation of missionaries in the decades when that event was still unusual
enough to command wide attention. Just before departure the great churches
of Boston often held special services. At one such meeting in 1819, the
Panoplist recorded that "the Old South was more crowded, than we almost
ever recollect to have seen any place of concourse. Not only the pews,
but the aisles, stairs, both galleries, and all the avenues, were throng-
ed, so that it was with great difficulty that the boxes could be circulated for the collection."[4] The final farewell took place at the wharf,
where tearful friends and relatives gathered about the departing company
on board ship to pray and sing a last hymn together on deck, weather

[2]Henry Davis, A Sermon, Delivered before the American Board of Commissioners for Foreign Missions (Boston, 1816), 30.

[3]Griffin, A Sermon Preached . . . before the American Board (Middletown,
Conn., 1826), 9-10.

[4]Panoplist, XV (1819), 576. Missionary sentiment at the time of the departure of the Board's first emissaries in 1812 was so uncertain that--
except for the ordination service several months before in Salem---there
was no ceremony, and the corresponding secretary was not even present at
the leave-taking.

permitting.[5]

Although these student volunteers usually went forth in a
spirit of true "disinterested benevolence," without thought of storming
heaven by displaying an unwonted devotion, the religious public surrounded them with an aura of special sanctity. The prudential committee was
not long in perceiving the danger to both the modesty and the motivation
of missionary candidates in elevating thus a single class of the churches'
servants. In plain-spoken instructions to a group embarking for India
in 1830 the committee advised:

> Think little of the mere fact, that you have devoted your-
> selves to the service of the heathen. Do not build upon this
> fact, as the foundation of your character, and a sufficient
> guaranty of your usefulness. We would be no means speak light-
> ly of the struggle, which is necessary to break the bonds of
> country and kindred, and to bid a final adieu to the home of
> your childhood, and the scenes of your youth. But all this
> may be done and much more, without possessing the true founda-
> tion of missionary character. It will be wise, therefore, not
> to count yourself to have attained, merely because you will
> have sailed on a mission.[6]

Evangelists in the field, moreover, often discovered that foreign residence involved great trials and temptations, presenting real
obstacles to saintliness. Gordon Hall confidentially reported to the
Board with much heaviness of heart the grievous contentions of missionaries and even the notorious adultery of one, "widely famed in his
native land, as something almost transcending human excellence." "How
humbling!" the American reflected. "No thanks to ourselves that we are
all whoremasters and rotting with that fatal disease."[7]

---

[5]In the Board's official manual, however, missionaries were instructed
not to sing a farewell hymn while the ship was getting under way, in
order to avoid interference with the crew. American Board, Manual for
Missionary Candidates (Rev. ed., Boston, 1849), 29.

[6]Instructions to the Rev. Messrs. William Harvey, Hillis Read, and
William Ramsay, August 1, 1830, ABC:8.1, I, no. 4.

[7]Hall to Worcester, Bombay, April 16, 1818, ABC:16.1.1, II, no. 75.

Early martyrdom came to several of the American Board's first
representatives overseas, and the accounts of their lives and tragic
deaths reinforced the popular conviction of missionary sainthood. The
pious biographies compiled to satisfy public curiosity about such personalities and augment evangelical zeal strikingly reveal the introspective
habits and religious intensity of New England youth affected by the Second
Great Awakening. Drawing liberally on personal diaries and letters, the
authors presented in somewhat idealized fashion the often highly sensitive
products of the evangelical revival, who created student organizations
like the Brethren and the Society of Inquiry and did not hesitate to carry
out their ideals in exile. In memoirs like that of Samuel J. Mills,
founder of the Brethren and promoter of so many missionary projects, and
those of the first two emissaries to Palestine, Pliny Fisk and Levi Parsons, the Protestant community--so long nourished on an inferior variety
of pious tracts--read the inspiring record of spiritual struggle in
school and college and the final commitment to the overseas work of the
churches.[8]

Later biographies gave a better picture of missionary life
beyond the sea and a fuller view of the lands and peoples to whom they
ministered. In addition, the Board's agents often published histories
and accounts of exploration in strange countries that opened realms of
romance to readers in the United States. To evangelical Americans, these
Gospel emissaries were the real heroes of modern history, who "contend

[8]Gardiner Spring's 1820 memoir of Mills was revised in 1829 by two
members of the Brethren who corrected parts of the account but kept
safe the secret existence of their fraternity. E. C. Bridgman and
C. W. Allen, eds., Memoir of Samuel John Mills (Boston, 1829). The
Andover Society of Inquiry published a collective account of the missionary careers of some of its own members as an illustration of collegiate
piety. /Elias Loomis, ed.7, Memoirs of American Missionaries, Formerly
Connected with the Society of Inquiry, in Andover Theological Seminary
(Boston, 1833).

against fearful odds, win bloodless battles, plant the standard of the cross on distant shores, and annex the farthest East with the remotest West to the dominions of the Prince of Peace."[9] While still much concerned with martyrdom and the tragedy of early death, both single and collective memoirs issued in large volume in this period portrayed the heroic character of the men—and women—of foreign missions.[10]

Eventually, as the century wore on and the missionary enterprise appeared less romantic, many voices spoke up against the current of overpious biography. In 1843 the art critic and editor, James Jackson Jarves, who had seen something of missionaries in Hawaii, denounced scathingly the popular devotional literature:

> There is . . . unfortunately a false curiosity abroad, which seeks to strip the missionary and expose his inmost thoughts. In many instances they have themselves pandered to this vitiated desire, and the reading world has been flooded to a nausea with works recording the thoughts, sentiments, speeches, feelings, and experiences of men, women, and even children, whose lives were all good and useful in their appropriate spheres, but whose biographies, even as prepared by admiring friends, are at best but an epitome of the life of every man, woman, or child with moderate pretensions to intelligence and religious hopes. The graveyards of our land contain myriads of such, and the stones that record their departure tell as briefly but appropriately their worth. Then let them rest.[11]

In the pioneer era of American missions it was perhaps natural to apotheosize the foreign evangelist as the ideal life of piety; for it was he who seemed to carry out most completely the theological commitments of New England Calvinism. The reaction against this image came not

---

[9]Tyler, Memoir of Rev. Henry Lobdell, 11.

[10]See E. H. Gray, The Christian Hero of the Nineteenth Century (Cambridge, 1851); H. W. Pierson, ed., American Missionary Memorial (New York, 1853); The Martyr of Sumatra: A Memoir of Henry Lyman (New York, 1856); L. D. Smith, Missionary Heroes and Martyrs (Providence, 1857); I. W. Wiley, The Mission Cemetary and the Fallen Missionaries of Fuh Chau (New York, 1858).

[11]Jarves, Scenes and Scenery in the Sandwich Islands, and a Trip through Central America (Boston, 1843), 194.

only from worldly laymen like Jarves, but also from the religious pam-
phleteers. George Cheever, clerical observer of the whaling industry and
tireless peddler of evangelical influence, noted in a Pacific travelogue
that missionaries were not necessarily saints, nor were they exempt from
"the ordinary infirmities and peccability of men." Condemning the type
of literature which Jarves had in mind, he added: "Nor do we find the
odor of sanctity, nor that imaginery halo of holiness with which certain
memoirs, and some other things that have been written, have surrounded
the missionary's person and office."[12]

In fact, as new values came to the fore in the middle years of
the century, we can discern a tendency in such literature to stress other
factors than early piety and consecration to converting the heathen.
David Coit Scudder, who died shortly after arrival in India, was pictured
as a promising Oriental scholar who had prepared himself by study of the
languages of southern India.[13] Professor William S. Tyler of Amherst
described his biography of his former student, Henry Lobdell of the
Assyrian Mission, as "the memoir of one who was at once a traveler and
an antiquarian, an Oriental scholar and a Christian missionary."[14]

At the same time nonclerical American travelers and men of
letters began to show considerably less hostility to missions. A politician and foreign diplomat, General Lewis Cass, concluded a Mediterranean
essay with a eulogy on the missionaries whose work he had observed: "No
American meets these little bands of pilgrims, which his country sends
forth to every benighted portion of the world, without an emotion of

---

[12]Cheever, The Island World of the Pacific, 135.

[13]H. E. Scudder, Life and Letters of David Coit Scudder, Missionary in
Southern India (New York, 1864).

[14]Tyler, Memoir of Rev. Henry Lobdell, v.

pride and patriotism as pure as it is profound."[15] Many travel writers
confessed that they had gone abroad with prejudices against the profession which personal acquaintanceship in foreign lands dispelled.[16] After
meeting with representatives of the A.B.C.F.M. in Syria, one noted adventurer was gratified "to find that there are a great many more sincere
people in the world than I had supposed in my younger days."[17] In 1850,
moreover, the ubiquitous Cheever declared that it was now "fashionable
and politic for travelers to speak well of missionaries and their work,"
suggesting that a book unfavorable to their character would not sell.[18]
Whatever the cause, the enterprise of foreign missions had by midcentury
established itself firmly in an honorable and honored niche in American
life.

II

The Earl of Shaftesbury, in a much-quoted passage, delivered
a high tribute to the quality of the American Board's missionaries in
the Ottoman Empire which would apply equally well to many in other parts
of the world:

> I do not believe that in the whole history of missions,
> I do not believe that in the history of diplomacy, or in the
> history of any negotiations carried on between man and man,
> we can find any thing to equal the wisdom, the soundness, and
> the pure evangelical truth of the body of men who constitute
> the American Mission. I have said it twenty times before, and
> I will say it again,—for the expression appropriately conveys

---

[15]Lewis Cass, An Historical, Geographical and Statistical Account of
the Island of Candia, or Ancient Crete (Richmond, Va., 1839), 12.

[16]See Jarves, History of the Sandwich Islands, vi-vii; J. R. Browne,
Yusef; or the Journey of the Frangi (New York, 1853). This phenomenon
was noted by the clerical tourist, Stephen Olin, in his Travels in
Egypt, Petraea, and the Holy Land, 105-106.

[17]J. R. Browne, Yusef; or the Journey of the Frangi, 272.

[18]Cheever, The Island World of the Pacific, 133.

my meaning,—that they are a marvelous combination of common sense and piety.[19]

The men who mastered difficult and unwritten languages, built educational systems where there was none, advised foreign governments and negotiated for their own, represented, as a modern historian has written, "some of the most vigorous material which came out of the New England colleges and seminaries.[20]

As noted before, the young men who responded to the missionary impulse came chiefly from the smaller towns and farm villages of New England and from the regions immediately to the west containing the constituency of the Presbyterian-Congregational coalition which fostered so much of the benevolent activity of the time. Few came from affluent families, but the majority were college trained, often at the expense of the American Education Society or other charitable organizations. It was in collegiate circles that missionary enthusiasm flamed high, creating societies like the secret Brethren and producing the sense of vocation that called forth the youthful evangelists to foreign lands. Not only the older institutions like Yale and Princeton, but the small new schools founded in the evangelical revival of the turn of the century—Middlebury, Amherst, Williams, and others—sent out scores of dedicated missionaries.

Amherst itself was founded in 1820 at least partly as a training place for overseas agents. "With what satisfaction," declared trustee Noah Webster, "will the sons of its benefactors hear it related, that a missionary, educated by their father's charity, has planted a church of Christ on the burning sands of Africa, or in the cheerless wilds of

---

[19]Cited in Mark Hopkins, "Historical Discourse," Anderson, *Memorial Volume*, 32.

[20]Greene, "A Puritan Counter-Reformation," American Antiquarian Society, *Proceedings*, n.s., XLII, 45.

Siberia . . . ."[21] In succeeding years the Society of Inquiry maintained
a high level of enthusiasm for the enterprise. In 1838 a leading Presbyterian divine confidently informed the students: "If other Lymans and
Munsons are to fall by the hand of violence, Amherst and other colleges
are to send forth those who will hail it as a privilege to tread in their
steps, and to die, if God so will it, as they died."[22]

Although the British pioneers like Carey and Marshman in India,
Morrison and Milne in China, Ellis and Williams in the Pacific often became celebrated scholars and interpreters of pagan civilizations, they
did not enjoy the same educational advantages as their American brethren.
Since the universities of England were virtually closed to Nonconformists
at the opening of the century, the first overseas evangelists were largely self-educated men—shoemakers like Carey and printers like Ellis.
This made for an important but often overlooked distinction between the
conditions of the evangelical movement in the United States and in England,
where except for one segment of the Anglicans it was the Dissenting Churches which provided the main missionary impulse. In America, Protestant
evangelicalism sat enthroned in the leading citadels of learning, Unitarian Harvard alone remaining isolated from orthodox religious currents.

The Board's agents had for the most part studied the ancient
languages, Hebrew as well as Latin and Greek, and in the mission field
were able to translate the Bible from the original tongues. So high was
the prestige of their calling that some of the best scholars of the colleges and seminaries entered missionary service. Jonas King, for example,

---

[21]Noah Webster, An Address, Delivered at the Laying of the Corner Stone
of the Building Now Erecting for the Charity Institution in Amherst
(Boston, 1820), 10.

[22]Albert Barnes, The Choice of a Profession. An Address before the
the Society of Inquiry in Amherst College (Amherst, 1838), 28.

gave up an important academic appointment at Amherst to spend a lifetime in Greece. In the earliest decades a sense of adventure and even the danger implicit in missions to the heathen seemed to make a natural selection of vigorous, talented youth, and filled the waiting list of the Board with names. In 1822, so many offered that most of them had to be refused.[23] The American Board attempted heroically to maintain high standards in the face of a decrease in the number of candidates volunteering. As early as 1838 the prudential committee noted a public demand for the acceptance of candidates less well trained and more moderately endowed. Domestic service also appeared to offer greater attractions to youthful talent than foreign. It seemed, the committee reported, as if the religious community expected the mission boards to send abroad "those whom want of health, or of mental discipline or vigor, or eccentricities of character rendered quite unfit to fill important stations at home."[24] The Boston society resolutely rejected this mode of selection, determined to send abroad only the best products of evangelical education, even if this meant fewer would go.

It was expected that missionaries would add to the scholarly knowledge of remote regions and people. The prudential committee of the A.B.C.F.M. reminded its first emissaries to the Levant that their religious duties need not suppress study and research: "There you will be on Classick Ground, and whatever of contribution or of service you can afford to Literature, or to Taste, with fidelity to your higher objects, will be interesting to many, and useful to the general cause."[25] Indeed, in the first half of the century, missionaries proved extraordinarily

[23]Tracy, History of the American Board, 113.

[24]American Board, Twenty-ninth Annual Report, 36.

[25]American Board, Instructions to Levi Parsons and Pliny Fisk, 5-6.

useful to American scholarship in the task of gathering scientific data from abroad, translating texts and preparing the tools for language study, and describing the religious and other customs of little-known races. John Pickering, pioneer philologist in New England, received aid from Cherokee and Greek students at Cornwall Foreign Mission School and even planned with Moses Stuart of Andover Theological Seminary to bring to this country by means of the Board's representatives in Palestine a native teacher of Arabic.[26]

From the first it was common practice to keep metereological journals at mission stations, recording daily temperatures and barometric readings over long periods of time.[27] Evangelists trained at Yale under Benjamin Silliman shipped back to New Haven geological and other specimens and published in the American Journal of Science detailed descriptions of natural phenomena observed in China, Africa, and the Sandwich Islands.[28] Joseph Goodrich of Hawaii is said to have applied himself with particular industry to mineralogy as a Yale undergraduate in order to prepare himself for greater usefulness as a missionary in a land so interesting to scientific observation.[29] Silliman, the pious editor of the Journal, not only printed long excerpts from the letters of his former students, but used the occasion to praise "the benevolent object of their perilous and noble enterprises."[30]

Other institutions in the United States also profited from the far-flung activities of their alumni. The natural-history cabinets of

---

[26]Pickering, Life of John Pickering, 283-284.

[27]See Missionary Herald, XXI (1825), 345-348.

[28]See American Journal of Science, X (1826), 21-29; XI (1826), 1-36; XX (1831), 228-248; XXIX (1836), 230-236; XXXVIII (1840), 301-306.

[29]Ibid., XI (1826), 1-2n.

[30]Ibid., X (1826), 29.

most of the New England colleges owed the diversity of their specimens to devoted missionary sons around the globe, who sent back everything from volcanic rocks in Hawaii to the Assyrian slabs and tablets reposing in the Nineveh Gallery at Amherst. There were other collections, too, like the museum of the American Board itself, which held miscellaneous items of anthropological interest, including heathen idols and the tools and clothing of exotic cultures.[31]

Their horror of pagan life and thought did not entirely inhibit the Board's emissaries in foreign lands from making some valuable studies. The twenty volumes of the Chinese Repository reveal the assiduous research of American and other missionaries in the languages and civilization of the Far East. In its pages and elsewhere S. Wells Williams published the results of his pioneer work on the almost unknown Japanese language.[32] The directors of the A.B.C.F.M. evinced special interest in the culture of the primitive peoples among whom their agents labored. In reply to the prudential committee's request for information about the religious thought of the Choctaws, Alfred Wright gathered many of the ancient Indian traditions, which the Missionary Herald published at some length.[33] In the papers of the Board's Cherokee mission may be found excellent descriptions of that tribe's social and religious life before its destruction under the impact of Christianity.

The Hawaiian Islands provided unusual opportunities for anthropological study, but the early repugnance to native customs prejudiced the missionaries' researches and caused many pre-Christian tribal practices

---

[31]In recent years the American Board broke up this museum and divided its contents between Hartford and Andover-Newton Theological Schools, where the missionary artifacts may be seen today.

[32]American Oriental Society, Journal, II, (1851), 55-60.

[33]Missionary Herald, XXIV (1828), 178-183; 214-216.

virtually to disappear--in particular, the hula, which the first evangelists characterized as "idle, time-killing, employment."[34] At the request
of the Board, Titus Coan, who had taken a post in the Sandwich Islands
after returning from an abortive mission to Tierra del Fuego, attempted
to compare the physical and mental characteristics of the Hawaiians and
the Patagonians.[35] Not until the late thirties did Sheldon Dibble,
Hawaii's first historian, make some effort to collect native traditions
through his students at Lahaina Seminary.[36] Although an English colleague
of the American missionaries, William Ellis, published a good survey of
island life as early as 1825,[37] it was left for a mission-trained Hawaiian, David Malo, to compile the best record of native customs.[38]

The men of the Board, however, were quite willing to employ
the gadgets of Western science to impress the heathen mind. In Urumiah
they exposed the workings of a Leiden jar received from America to a
large and startled audience.[39] Two Persian princes visited Constantinople
in 1837 to see the "fire-wonders" of the electrical experiments of William
Goodell.[40] Even more significant was the assistance rendered by Cyrus
Hamlin to an engineer from the United States who was demonstrating the

[34]Journal of the missionaries, April 10, 1820, Missionary Herald, XVII
(1821), 120.

[35]Ibid., XXXIV (1838), 34.

[36]Dibble, History of the Sandwich Islands, preface, iii-iv.

[37]Ellis's work was published in both Great Britain and America as A
Journal of a Tour Around Hawaii, the Largest of the Sandwich Islands
(Boston, 1825), and Narrative of a Tour through Hawaii, or Owhyhee; with
Remarks on the History, Traditions, Manners, Customs, and Language of
the Sandwich Islands (London, 1826).

[38]David Malo, Hawaiian Antiquities, Moolelo Hawaii (N.B. Emerson, tr.,
Honolulu, 1903).

[39]Perkins, Residence in Persia, 295-296.

[40]Missionary Herald, XXXIII (1837), 447.

Morse telegraph to the sultan's court at Constantinople in 1847. Obviously impressed, the Turkish ruler inquired "if that was one of those American missionaries who were turning the world upside down?" "He does not look like a dangerous man," he added.[41] The scientific and scholarly work of the Board's agents was probably more influential at home than abroad. Little that was translated into Asian, African, or Polynesian languages illustrated a higher level of Western thought than the pious sentimentality of the evangelical tracts of the day. The outstanding exception was Bridgman's two-volume History of the United States, which the mission press in Singapore published in Chinese in 1838--a work which must have provided many in China with some conception of this country.[42] The typical productions of missionary studies were books intended to inform Americans about the outside world: David O. Allen's India, Ancient and Modern, J. Leighton Wilson's Western Africa, and S. Wells Williams's monumental Middle Kingdom.

This last was perhaps the most significant piece of scholarship contributed by the American Board's agents in this period, a two-volume history of China which remained until recent times a standard work. After several firms rejected the book, a financial guarantee by a friendly Canton merchant enabled Putnam and Wiley to publish it in 1847.[43] Sympathetic to the Chinese and their culture, the Middle Kingdom exhibited representative evangelical attitudes toward a heathen nation. Williams wrote that his purpose was to "divest the Chinese people and civilization of that peculiar and almost undefinable impression of ridicule which is

[41]Hamlin, Among the Turks, 186-192.

[42]General letter from the missionaries, March 7, 1838, Missionary Herald, XXXIV (1838), 339.

[43]F. W. Williams, Life and Letters of S. Wells Williams, 163.

so generally given them . . . ."[44] Yet later he could pronounce that "the evangelization of the people of China is far more important than the form of their government, the extent of their empire, or the existence of their present institutions."[45]

At the first annual meeting of the American Oriental Society in 1842, the president, John Pickering, paid a handsome tribute to the scholarly labors of the nation's foreign missionaries, those "indefatigable men" who in addition to their religious duties make "lasting additions to our knowledge of the moral and social condition of those distant nations."[46] In setting up this organization, eighteen out of sixty-eight of whose charter members were missionaries,[47] the founders applied to the American Board for permission to hold meetings and house its library in the society's rooms in Pemberton Square.[48] Although this arrangement proved unfeasible, the two enterprises co-operated closely with each other in the succeeding years. At the initial meeting several mission boards reported on their facilities abroad, the A.B.C.F.M. putting into the record by far the largest establishment, which included seventeen printing houses with thirty-one presses and four type foundaries. Up to that date the Board's stations had printed four hundred million pages and issued publications in thirty-five languages, fourteen of which had been reduced to writing by its missionaries.[49] The degree of dependence of the Oriental Society upon missionary contributions can be seen

[44]S. W. Williams, The Middle Kingdom; a Survey . . . of the Chinese Empire and Its Inhabitants (New York, 1847, I, preface, xiv.

[45]Ibid., II, 604.

[46]American Oriental Society, Journal, I (1849), 2.

[47]Ibid., xi.

[48]John Pickering and William Jenks to the Prudential Committee of the American Board, undated, ABC:10, XXX, no. 204.

[49]American Oriental Society, Journal, I (1849), 61.

in the disproportionate number of articles published in its journal by representatives of the American Board and similar organizations.

James L. Merrick, who spent seven years in Persia for the Board, wrote the first study of Mohammed printed in this country, a work, however, which awakened little or no interest in the subject.[50]   Bible studies constituted the largest scholarly interest in religious circles, a branch of learning which the Board's emissaries in the Near East were favorably located to pursue. Eli Smith of the Beirut station, who contributed a great deal to American knowledge of the Holy Land in his frequent essays published in the theological journals of the United States, accompanied Edward Robinson of Andover and Union Theological Seminaries on an extensive tour of Palestine in the late thirties, from which resulted the latter's famous Biblical Researches. At a general meeting of the Board's agents in Jerusalem in 1838, furthermore, Robinson and the missionaries agreed upon a standard orthography for the romanization of Arabic names—based upon the Pickering system adapted for the Hawaiian language—which was employed by students for many years.[51]   In 1859 another member of the same mission published an influential handbook of Palestine in two large volumes entitled The Land and the Book.[52]

The interest in the geography and social customs of the Holy Land led to the disclosure of Palestinian practices which reacted upon the controversy in temperance circles in the United States over the use

---

[50]J. L. Merrick, The Life and Religion of Mohammed, as Contained in the Sheeah Traditions of the Hyat-ul-Kuloob (Boston, 1850). The manuscript was rejected when submitted to the Board in 1842. American Board, Thirty-third Annual Report, 130.

[51]Edward Robinson, Biblical Researches in Palestine, Mount Sinai and Arabia Petraea (Boston, 1841), I, x.

[52]W. M. Thomson, The Land and the Book; or Biblical Illustrations Drawn from the Manners, Customs, Scenes, and Scenery of the Holy Land (2 v., New York, 1859).

of fermented wine in the communion service. Some in America argued that the Biblical beverage was an unfermented one and thus sought to obviate the difficulties raised by those who pointed to the Scriptural condonement of supposedly alcoholic liquors. In an essay in the American Biblical Repository in 1836, William G. Schauffler of the Board's Constantinople mission used linguistic arguments and his observations of modern dwellers in the Levant to destroy the illusion.[53] His colleagues in all the lands around the eastern Mediterranean upheld him in similar articles and letters to deluded friends of temperance at home, helping to explode one of the popular myths of the evangelical community.[54]

The foreign missionary of this period, then, played many roles in the unfolding life of the American churches—preacher of salvation to the distant heathen, educator and carrier of civilization to a benighted world, and scholar and interpreter of that world to his fellow countrymen in the United States.

III

About half the number of those in the service of foreign mission boards were women. Despite early sentiments in favor of celibacy among some members of the Andover Brethren, most missionaries chose to go forth to heathen lands in the married state. All but two of the first company which embarked for India in 1812 procured wives before departure, and one of the bachelors, Gordon Hall, shortly afterwards married an Englishwoman in Bombay.[55] Perhaps recalling the unfortunate experiences

---

[53]American Biblical Repository, VIII (1836), 285-308.

[54]See Eli Smith in Bibliotheca Sacra, III (1846), 385-389. For a more complete survey of this controversy and the missionary role in it, see Thomas Laurie, The Eli Volume; or, the Contributions of Our Foreign Missions to Science and Well-Being (Boston, 1881), 430-441.

[55]Luther Rice, the other bachelor, returned to America shortly after his conversion to Baptist principles. The prudential committee initially

of the London Society—some of whose unmarried evangelists ran off with
Polynesian mistresses in the South Seas—the American Board committed
itself from the outset to wedded missionaries.[56] In 1815 the prudential
committee stated its reasons, arguing among other things that Christian
family life would set before the heathen the godly example of "pious
females" and obedient children.[57]

On several occasions some emissaries, assigned to particularly
perilous regions or duties, went out alone—as the first agents to
Palestine, or the pioneers who settled in 1830 in Canton, where foreign
women were forbidden residence by imperial edict. But most of these,
if they did not suffer early martyrdom or withdraw from the field, eventually married, either upon their return to the United States for this
purpose, or after finding a wife among the American or European community
abroad.[58]

From the beginning pious American women, organized in innumerable cent and mite societies, had faithfully supported the overseas
enterprise, an activity in which the officers of the A.B.C.F.M. agreed
they might take a "lively interest without overstepping the limits, which

---

proposed leaving the wives of agents behind for economy reasons, but
never regretted permitting them to depart with their husbands after
seeing the interest awakened at home by Mrs. Newell and Mrs. Judson.
Secretary Anderson later argued strongly for married missionaries.
"Among barbarians the wife, the mother, and children are, under God, a
defense," he wrote in his History of Missions to India, 55.

[56]"Remember, dear brethren," the first missionaries to Hawaii were warned,
"the sad downfall of Lewis, of Broomhall and of Veason." Humphrey,
Promised Land, 37.

[57]Panoplist, XL (1815), 179n.

[58]Sometimes marriages took place between single male and female representatives of the churches who found themselves engaged in the overseas
work together; often a widow married the colleague of her deceased
husband. Jonas King was probably unique, in uniting himself to one of
the subjects of the Board's benevolence, a Greek woman of Smyrna.

a sense of propriety has imposed on female exertion."[59] But actual participation in the conquest of the pagan world called for a new image of feminine character. Evangelicals who held a conservative opinion of the place of women at home considered that foreign missions opened to them "a sphere of activity, usefulness and distinction, not, under the present constitution of society, to be found else where." Continuing the same theme, this eulogist of the missionary wife asked:

> Who would not turn aside from a female advocate at the bar,
> or judge upon the bench, surrounded by the usual scenes of
> a court-house, even if she filled these offices with ability
> and talent, to render honor rather to her, who laying on the
> altar of sacrific whatever of genius, or acquirement, or
> loveliness she may possess, goes forth to cheer and to share
> the labors and cares of the husband of her youth, in his
> errand of love to the heathen?[60]

It was not an easy step to take to permit American women so unusual a role. A biographer of one of the pioneer wives has testified to the unfavorable state of public opinion at the time of the first Mrs. Judson's departure: "It was deemed wild and romantic in the extreme; and altogether inconsistent with prudence and delicacy."[61] The melancholy circumstances of the death of Harriet Newell, Ann Judson's Bradford Academy classmate and companion on the voyage to Calcutta, hastened rather than hindered the acceptance of the female missionary. The plaintive story of this nineteen-year-old Massachusetts martyr quickened the whole missionary impulse in New England. Expanded from a memorial sermon into a classic of American devotional biography,[62] the narrative

[59]American Board, Fourth Annual Report, 37.

[60]Arabella W. Stuart, Lives of the Three Mrs. Judsons (Boston, 1855), preface, iii.

[61]J. D. Knowles, Memoir of Mrs. Ann H. Judson (Boston, 1829), 36.

[62]Leonard Woods, A Sermon . . . in Remembrance of Mrs. Harriet Newell . . . to Which Are Added Memoirs of Her Life (Boston, 1814), This memoir went through numerous editions, one of which was that of the American Sunday School Union, entitled The Life and Writings of Harriet Newell (Rev. ed., Philadelphia, 1831).

of her short life made a powerful impact upon thousands of evangelical youth who read with sympathetic tears the account of Mrs. Newell's spiritual struggles and final dedication to a task she did not live to complete.[63]

Other American wives accompanied merchants to distant posts in these years and some even braved the high seas with husbands who commanded sailing ships, but their absence from home seldom exceeded a few years' duration. At the beginning, at least, it was quite otherwise for missionary helpmates, who anticipated lifelong exile and perhaps a martyr's grave on foreign shores. Harriet Newell herself expressed this mood when she wrote in one of her last letters before departure: "All will be dark, everything will be dreary, and not a hope of worldly happiness will be for a moment indulged. The prime of life will be spent in an unhealthy country, a burning region, amongst people of strange language, of a returnless distance from my native land, where I shall never more behold the friends of my youth."[64] In later years the prudential committee complained that "the brethren do not easily get wives; which is surprizing, when we consider how much stronger the missionary spirit is in the female sex, than in the male."[65]

Most young men appointed by the Board married shortly before their departure, sometimes at the very last moment. The prudential committee took the responsibility for determining the suitability of their choices, in at least one case rejecting the fiancee of a missionary sent

---

[63]See the reminiscences of Chaplain F. W. Taylor, in his Voyage Round the World, II, 15.

[64]Harriet Newell to H. B., Haverhill, August 23, 1811, in Life and Writings of Mrs. Harriet Newell, 129.

[65]Anderson to the South Africa mission, Boston, August 31, 1848, ABC:2. 1.1, XI, 96.

to the Mediterranean.[66] In 1836 Rufus Anderson suggested that evangelists' wives prepare themselves in the latest pedagogical methods: "Education is becoming a science, an art, a profession; and they must study the science, practise the art, and become interested in the profession. They should be familiar with the most approved mode of teaching with the best books, the choicest apparatus."[67] Some critics, however, thought too much was demanded of such persons on the mission field. Howard Malcom, who visited the Eastern stations of the Baptist board in the thirties, declared:

> The calculations which have been made on the labors of the wives of missionaries, are for the most part, much too large. Speeches, essays, and sermons have described the public usefulness of females in glowing terms. . . . Few missionaries' wives have acquired the language to such an extent as to enable them to be useful in this way in regard to finding access to heathen women. . . . She must find her principal sphere of usefulness in keeping her husband whole-hearted and happy; in being a good housewife; sustaining all the domestic cares; training up her children well . . . ."[68]

Although many hardworking wives succeeded in caring for their own home and children as well as attending to the education of the children of pagan parents, the prudential committee also dispatched large numbers of unmarried women to the field, chiefly as teachers. Students prepared for this task at female academies like Mount Holyoke. At this "Protestant nunnery," founded by Mary Lyon's unquenchable evangelical zeal, dozens of graduates already abroad corresponded with Miss Lyon and other teachers, and daughters of foreign missionaries from all over the

---

[66]A young woman affianced to Elnathan Gridley, who went to Smyrna unmarried, was refused in 1826 on the grounds that she had broken a previous engagement to someone else. Evarts to Martha T. Parker, Boston, September 4, 1826, ABC:1.01, VI, 275-276.

[67]Anderson, "On the Marriage of Missionaries," in Ellis, Memoirs of Mrs. Mary Ellis (Boston, 1836), xiv.

[68]Howard Malcom, Travels in South-Eastern Asia, Embracing Hindustan, Malaya, Siam, and China (Boston, 1839), II, 219-220.

world wore exotic costumes and conversed in strange languages for the edification of their classmates.[69] By 1850 forty former members of the school had gone to the mission field as wives or teachers, nine of whom had themselves served as instructors at South Hadley.[70]

Travelers from the United States rejoiced to find their charming countrywomen scattered about the globe at the various mission stations. Naval Chaplain Taylor marveled that a young woman, "with the intelligence, manners, and persons that would grace the halls of the noble as she moved among the elite of a court-levee," should leave "the happiest land in the world, and a circle of relatives and friends devoted to her, to seek a place among foreigners, and devote her life to the strange and dark people of eastern climes, who care not for the sympathies that are poured out in their behalf. . . ."[71] Other journeyers beside clergymen—awed at seeing supposedly fragile American women at such tasks—returned a similar verdict. That popular globe-trotter, Lloyd Stephens, who admitted that before going abroad he despised the only missionary he ever knew as a "canting hypocrite," made warm friends among members of the profession whom he met on his tours and spoke sentimentally of the wives:

> She who had been cherished as a plant that the winds must not
> breathe on too rudely, recovers from the shock of a separation
> from her friends to find herself in the land of barbarians,
> where her loud cry of distress can never reach their ears.
> New ties twine round her heart, and the tender and helpless
> girl changes her very nature, and becomes the staff and support
> of the man. In his hours of despondency she raises his droop-
> ing spirits; she bathes his aching head; she smooths his pillow
> of sickness; and after months of wearisome silence, I have en-
> tered her dwelling, and her heart instinctively told her that

---

[69]Edward Hitchcock, The Power of Christian Benevolence Illustrated in the Life and Labors of Mary Lyon (Northampton, 1851), 359-365; A. C. Cole, A Hundred Years of Mount Holyoke College: The Evolution of an Educational Ideal (New Haven, 1940), 118-119.

[70]Hitchcock, Life and Labors of Mary Lyon, 346.

[71]Taylor, Voyage Round the World, II, 14.

I was from the same land.[72]

Women suffered by far the greater mortality in the missionary service of this epoch, even in a country like China, where the climate was not particularly hostile to foreigners.[73] Surely the unaccustomed tasks imposed on mission wives and unknown to their gentle sisters at home, as well as the very real dangers of child-bearing in unhealthful climates, took a heavy toll. To appease the religious public, popular authors wove garlands of the lives of these modest saints, which issued from the press as: Heroines of the Missionary Enterprise, The Missionary Sisters, and Daughters of the Cross.[74] A great missionary patriarch like Adoniram Judson in Burma outlived a succession of wives, and each entered American hagiography, both singly and in series. The last Mrs. Judson, Emily Chubbock, before her marriage a popular writer under the pen name of "Fanny Forester," followed the taste of the period in composing a fitting memorial to her immediate predecessor.[75]

Included in the martyrology of foreign missions were some of the children as well. The narratives of promising lives cut short by an unprotecting environment added the color of exotic scenes to the perennial devotional literature centered around youthful piety, which dated back at least as far as Jonathan Edwards's portrayal of the

---

[72]/Stephens_7, Incidents of Travel in Egypt, Arabia Petraea, and the Holy Land, I, 192-193.

[73]Dean, China Mission, 167-169.

[74]D. C. Eddy, Heroines of the Missionary Enterprise (Boston, 1850), and Daughters of the Cross, or Woman's Mission (Boston, 1855); Mary C. Benjamin, The Missionary Sisters (Boston, 1860).

[75]Emily C. Judson, Memoir of Sarah E. Judson, Member of the American Mission to Burma (New York, 1848). Besides Knowles's biography of the first Mrs. Judson, there were Lives of the Three Mrs. Judsons both by Arabella W. Stuart and by D. C. Eddy (Boston, 1855), and finally a memoir of the last, A. C. Kendrick's Life and Letters of Mrs. Emily C. Judson (New York, 1860).

precocious Abigail Hutchinson in his <u>Faithful Narrative of the Surprizing Work of God</u>. Two of the best known were the American Tract Society's memoir of the daughter of a pioneer missionary to Hawaii and Justin Perkins's memento of a father's grief, which he entitled the <u>Persian Flower</u>.[76] After the Civil War a patriotic sentiment found expression in the biography of missionary sons who returned from abroad to give their lives on the battlefield.[77]

IV

The "romance of missions" contributed subject matter and a special flavor to the literature of a sentimental age. Although no American wrote so popular a hymn as Anglican Bishop Heber's "From Greenland's Icy Mountains," many put their pens to paper, from Samuel F. Smith, author of "My Country 'Tis of Thee," to Mrs. Lydia Sigourney, unofficial poet laureate of the evangelical movement, to produce missionary verses. Lowell Mason, moreover, who lent his musical talents to the enterprises by composing the tune for Heber's hymn, directed the Park Street Church choir in the first public rendition of his "Watchman, Tell Us of the Night," at a monthly concert for missions in 1830.[78]

Three themes predominated in this poetry: the martyrdom of missionaries, the sadness of parting from home, and the particular pathos of young wives embarking for pagan shores. An interesting example of this last is found in the verses copied into the red-leather album given a departing teacher by her pupils at Ipswich Female Academy:

---

[76]The Missionary Daughter: A Memoir of Lucy Goodale Thurston of the Sandwich Islands (New York, 1842); /Perkins/, The Persian Flower: A Memoir of Judith Grant Perkins, of Oroomiah, Persia (Boston, 1853).

[77]I. N. Tarbox, Missionary Patriots: Memoirs of James H. Schneider and Edward M. Schneider (Boston, 1867).

[78]Anderson, Memorial Volume, 354n.

Who'd be a missionary's bride,
Who that is young and fair
Would leave the world and all beside,
Its pomp and vanity and pride,
Her Saviour's cross to bear?

None—save she whose heart is meek
Who feels another's pain
And loves to wipe from sorrow's cheek
The trickling tear—and accents speak
That soothe the soul again.[79]

The missionary motif adorned much of the writing found in the annuals and gift books, especially the religious tokens which flourished side by side with the more purely secular ones. Besides the Religious Souvenir, edited by Mrs. Sigourney, there was also John A. Clark's Christian Keepsake and Missionary Annual, in both of which the pathos of parting from friends and family and an obsession with the thought of martyrdom provided the chief inspiration.[80] Even such well-known writers as Lowell, Whittier, and Poe furnished pieces for one annual called the Missionary Memorial.[81] An unusual gift book appeared in 1848 in commemoration of the great Baptist apostle to Burma, Adoniram Judson, who had recently visited the United States.[82]

The missionary and his works, however, did not figure largely in more serious literature. The chief exception before the Civil War was Charlotte B. Mortimer's Morton Montagu, a novel based on the life of a Moravian evangelist to the American Indians.[83] In 1856 John De Forest

---

[79]Mary D. Frear, Lowell and Abigail: A Realistic Idyll (New Haven, 1934), 22.

[80]Sigourney, ed., The Religious Souvenir (New York, 1838 et seq.); J. A. Clark, ed., Christian Keepsake and Missionary Annual (Philadelphia, 1837 et seq.).

[81]The Missionary Memorial: A Literary and Religious Souvenir (New York, 1846).

[82]John Dowling, ed., The Judson Offering, Intended as a Token of Christian Sympathy for the Living and Christian Affection for the Dead (New York, 1848).

[83]C. B. Mortimer, Morton Montagu; or a Christian's Choice (New York, 1850).

published his Oriental Acquaintance, compiled from his observations in the Levant, where his brother was a medical missionary for the Board, but not until the late seventies did he convert his experiences into a full-length novel which he called Irene the Missionary.[84] About the same time Horatio Southgate, one-time Episcopal bishop of Constantinople, issued his ambitious but unsuccessful novel, The Cross above the Crescent.[85]

The missionary, moreover, was not only a symbol of Christian heroism and romantic exile, but appeared in the flesh in the churches of America, a living bond between this country and far-off pagan lands. Not all foreign evangelists became martyrs; many returned to the United States for reasons of health or other personal affairs, bringing to the evangelical community fresh contacts with heathen peoples. The climate of religious opinion eventually permitted relaxation of the original conception of the permanent expatriation of missionaries.[86] Some came on extended furloughs, and others retired to their old homes to spend their declining years in the scenes of childhood. At annual meetings of the American Board and other benevolent associations grizzled veterans and younger men on leave spoke to hushed audiences of their labors on the frontiers of Christendom. America had many opportunities to see and hear those who brought back tidings from distant outposts: not only were the children of missionaries enrolled in the schools and colleges of the nation, but in many a town and village retired elders remained the

[84]John De Forest, Oriental Acquaintance; or Letters from Syria (New York, 1856); Irene the Missionary (Boston, 1879).

[85]Horatio Southgate, The Crescent above the Cross, a Romance of Constantinople (Philadelphia, 1877).

[86]In 1843 Secretary Anderson complained that there were so many returned missionaries in the country that interest in them was waning and criticism being provoked by the expense of traveling back and forth to the field. Anderson to Armstrong, Boston, August 8, 1843, ABC:2.1.1, VI, 149.

honored survivors of the heroic age of American foreign missions.

By midcentury the missionary enterprise was firmly established and had begun to create its own lore and legendry. Men turned to the past to reconstruct the history of its origins and to answer the question: What brought to birth this mighty engine of the evangelical movement? Filial piety as well as historical zeal motivated Samuel M. Worcester's two-volume biography of his father, the first secretary of the American Board. Published in 1851, this was the first work to reveal much about the Brethren, the secret organization of student volunteers formed by Mills and others at Williams College. Rufus Anderson, present secretary, and himself a prominent member of the fraternity, provided the author with the information that the Brethren had transferred intact to Andover Seminary in 1810, kept its records in cipher for many years, and still existed at the Massachusetts theological school.[87]

Worcester, who was perhaps the first to examine the early records critically and a few years later published an interpretive essay on missionary origins,[88] sought to divide the honor of inaugurating American missions among many figures, rather than add to the glory of Samuel J. Mills, whom popular tradition—influenced by Spring's widely circulated memoir—had cast as the founder and leading spirit. Nevertheless, the Mills legend lived on as an explanation in simplest terms of the genesis of the evangelistic crusade. Much of this was due to the work of President Edward D. Griffin of Williams, who in two sermons in 1827 and 1828 had firmly fastened the birth of foreign missions to alumnus Mills, the secret student society of the Brethren, and the little

[87]S. M. Worcester, Life and Labors of Samuel Worcester, II, 84-86.

[88]S. M. Worcester, "Origin of American Foreign Missions," American Theological Review, II (1860), 687-724.

college in the Berkshires. Dedicating the new chapel at Williams in 1828, Griffin reminded his hearers that this was the scene of Mills's endeavors, that under the haystacks in a meadow beside the Hoosack River he and his classmates had "prayed into existence the embryo of American missions."[89] In a footnote to the published sermon, he revealed that the Brethren was formed in 1808, in "the north west lower room of the east college."[90]

Although Gardiner Spring had also mentioned the "haystack meeting," the idyllic note struck no answering chord in rural New England, and not even Griffin made any attempt to locate the exact spot where the youthful students had prayed and planned their tremendous enterprise. In 1852, however, a Baptist layman passing through Williamstown registered a desire that the "sacred place" be properly identified and marked by a suitable memorial, leaving a gold dollar in care of Professor Albert Hopkins to be applied to that purpose.[91] Two years later an elderly alumnus appeared on the campus with the announcement that he was Byram Green, a member of the college at the time and in fact a participant in the haystack prayer meeting. "Can you identify the spot where that prayer meeting was held?" asked Hopkins. "I can," said Green, "if a certain grove is standing."[92] He located what he insisted was the correct position in a grove near the river and drove a cedar stake in the ground to mark it. More than this, Green volunteered a complete version of the whole episode and named Mills, James Richards, Francis L. Robbins,

---

[89]Griffin, A Sermon . . . at the Dedication of the New Chapel (Williamstown, 1828), 23.

[90]Ibid., 24n.

[91]A. L. Perry, Williamstown and Williams College: A History (n.p., 1904), 359-360.

[92]Proceedings of the Missionary Jubilee, Held at Williams College, August 5, 1856 (Boston, 1856), 21.

Harvey Loomis, and himself as the five persons present at the first gathering. They had intended to pray together in the grove, but a thunderstorm forced them to take shelter under a haystack conveniently at hand. It was there, Green vowed, that it was first proposed "to send the gospel to the Pagans of Asia, and to the disciples of Mohammed."[93]

Williams College alumni and officers went to work immediately to create a memorial of the event. Since Green named 1806 as the date of the original meeting,[94] preparations were made for a semicentennial celebration in 1856. The Alumni Society purchased the grounds where the grove stood and began its transformation into the Mission Park that remains to this day in Williamstown. At commencement that summer it was dedicated to "the memory of the Founders of American Missions, and to the missionary cause and spirit."[95] Very appropriately, a storm arose—the most severe since 1806, it was claimed—which drove the celebrants out of the park, furnished with genuine haystacks for the occasion. During the six-hour services conducted in a nearby church, Rufus Anderson of the A.B.C.F.M. named this site, "rather than any and all other places, the Antioch of our western hemisphere."[96]

The Andover Brethren authorized one of its members to represent the society at the Missionary Jubilee and to "use his judgment as to how far it is best to give publicity to the fact of the present existence of

[93]Byram Green to Albert Hopkins, Sodus, N. Y., August 22, 1854, in Proceedings of the Missionary Jubilee, 7-9.

[94]Both Spring and Griffin placed the haystack meeting in 1808, the date of the founding of the Brethren. The materials for idealizing a similar grove at Andover, where Mills walked arm in arm with other students talking about the missionary enterprise, were present in Spring's memoir, but this spot never succeeded in striking the popular imagination. Spring, Memoirs of Samuel J. Mills, 35.

[95]Proceedings of the Missionary Jubilee, 15.

[96]Ibid., 54.

the Society."[97] Scores of returned missionaries present in the country
attended the dedication of the shrine, and the next evening twenty-three
Hawaiian evangelists and their children held the first meeting of a
series of annual reunions to take place each summer.[98] It was a time
for remembrance and for stabilizing the American missionary tradition.
In 1861 the A.B.C.F.M. celebrated its own semicentennial with a series
of great meetings in Boston and a historical discourse by Mark Hopkins,
president of Williams and of the Board also.

Samuel J. Mills and his associates in the Brethren, together
with the haystack meeting, were now fairly fixed in the folklore of missions. At Williams the alumni were not yet completely satisfied with
their memorial. All over the country great monuments were being erected
to honor patriotic sites. In Boston the massive Bunker Hill monument
thrilled New England and renewed the memory of past deeds. A Cleveland,
Ohio, graduate came forward after the Civil War with an offer to build
on the spot Byram Green had identified a gray sandstone memorial, re-
sembling, he suggested, "in its size and form, a veritable haystack."[99]
President Hopkins approved the proposal, objecting only to the unesthetic
idea of reproducing a replica of the haystack in stone. On Sunday,
July 28, 1867, after the baccalaureate sermon, a large audience gathered
in Mission Park for the services of dedication. Some were reported to
have sat on haycocks brought in from the neighboring fields. To comply
with Hopkins's taste, the design of the monument was modified, but the
haystack symbol remained. Harvey Rice, the Cleveland sponsor, described
it at the time:

---

[97]Record Book of the Brethren, 169-170. Brethren Papers.

[98]Proceedings of the Missionary Jubilee, 102-103.

[99]Proceedings at the Dedication of the Missionary Monument, in Mission
Park, Williamstown, Mass., July 28, 1867 (Boston, 1867), 3.

It stands on the identical spot where the haystack stood. . . .
Its entire height is twelve feet; its shaft, cap and base
square; its surface polished; its color a silver blue. It is
surmounted with a globe, three feet in diameter, traced in map
lines. On its eastern face, and immediately below the globe,
are inscribed the words, "The Field is the World." The follows a similitude of the haystack, sculptured in bold relief,
and encircled with the words;--"The Birthplace of American
Foreign Missions, 1806." And beneath this, appear the names
of the five young men who held the prayer-meeting under the
shelter of the haystack.[100]

Professor Albert Hopkins brother of the president of the college, predicted that this was "destined to be more celebrated, probably,
than any other haystack in the universe.[101] His prophecy was correct.
This humble spot amid the rural surroundings of a small college in the
Berkshires became a powerful symbol in the foreign-missionary movement
throughout the world. A half century later, on October 10, 1906, over
two thousand persons collected for an open-air centennial service in the
beautiful tree-lined Mission Park in Williamstown. On the same day in
distant parts of the world similar meetings were held--at City Temple in
London, in Honolulu and Yokohama, in Shanghai and Bangkok, in Madras and
Bombay. Foreign representatives present in Williamstown completed the
international character of the event; eight Christian converts, fruits
of the American missionary enterprise, came to say, on behalf of "our
people who sat in darkness, but now see the light, we thank you Americans."[102] The president of the Board, Samuel B. Capen, compared this
"consecrated ground" with the battlefields of Waterloo, Bunker Hill, and
Gettysburg and concluded that the results of missionary inspiration went
deeper than any of the issues decided there. "So far as America is concerned, trusteeship for the world was here born."[103]

---

[100]Proceedings at the Dedication of the Missionary Monument, 14.

[101]Proceedings of the Missionary Jubilee, 21.

[102]The One Hundred Anniversary of the Haystack Prayer Meeting (Boston,
1907), 107.

[103]Ibid., 108.

BIBLIOGRAPHY

PRIMARY SOURCES

A. MANUSCRIPTS

American Board of Commissioners for Foreign Missions Papers. Houghton
Library, Harvard University.

> Over one hundred volumes of these papers cover the period
1810-1860, including original letters from the Board's missions and
letter-press copies of all correspondence issuing from the home offices
in Boston. Citations in the text are to volume and letter number for
the former and volume and page number for the latter category, as well
as the catalogue numbers as given in the typescript Index to the papers
deposited in Houghton Library and in the offices of the American Board
in Congregational House, Boston.

American Board, Records of the Prudential Committee. American Board
    Archives, Congregational House, Boston.

The Brethren and Society of Inquiry Papers. Andover-Newton Theological
    School Library.

Bryant and Sturgis Papers. Baker Library, Harvard Graduate School of
    Business Administration.

Capen, Edward W., American Board History. Typescript essay in American
    Board Library, Congregational House, Boston.

Clark, Calvin M., The Brethren: A Chapter in the History of American
    Missions. Thesis, Andover-Newton Theological School Library.

James Hunnewell Papers. Houghton Library, Harvard University.

Augustine Heard Papers. Baker Library, Harvard Graduate School of Busi-
    ness Administration.

Josiah Marshall Papers. Houghton Library, Harvard University.

Pierce, Richard D., A History of the Society of Inquiry in the Andover
    Theological Seminary, 1811-1920, together with Some Account of Missions
    in America before 1810 and a Brief History of the Brethren, 1808-1873.
    Thesis, Andover-Newton Theological School Library.

Journal of Stephen Reynolds. Peabody Museum, Salem, Mass.

B. MAGAZINES, NEWSPAPERS, AND OTHER PERIODICALS

The American Biblical Repository. New York, 1839–1850.

American Board, Monthly Papers. Irregularly published.

——————, Quarterly Papers. Irregularly published.

The American Journal of Science and Arts. New Haven, 1818–1850.

The American Missionary. New York, 1857–1860.

American Oriental Society, Journal. Boston, 1849–1860.

The American Quarterly Register. Andover and Boston, 1827–1842.

The Biblical Repository. Andover, 1831–1836.

Bibliotheca Sacra. Andover, 1844–1851.

The Boston Recorder. Boston, 1816–1849. Various titles. Continued as
the Puritan Recorder, 1849–1858.

Chinese Repository. Canton and Macao, 1832–1851.

Christian Advocate and Journal. New York, 1826–1860.

Christian Examiner. Boston, 1824–1850.

The Christian Observer. London, 1801–1820.

Christian Register. Boston, 1821–1860.

The Christian Spectator. New Haven, 1819–1828. Continued as the
Quarterly Christian Spectator, 1829–1838.

The Connecticut Evangelical Magazine. Hartford, 1800–1814.

De Bow's Review. New Orleans, 1846–1860.

The Friend. Honolulu, 1843–1860.

Hawaiian Spectator. Honolulu, 1838.

Hunt's Merchants' Magazine and Commercial Review. New York, 1839–1850.

The Massachusetts Missionary Magazine. Salem and Boston, 1803–1808.

The Missionary Herald. Boston, 1821–1860.

The New Englander. New Haven, 1843–1860.

The New York Evangelist. New York, 1830–1860.

The New-York Missionary Magazine, and Repository of Religious Intelligence. New York, 1800.

The New York Observer. New York, 1823-1860.

Niles' Weekly Register. Baltimore, 1811-1849.

North American Review. Boston, 1815-1860.

Oriental Christian Spectator. Bombay, 1830-1838.

Quarterly Review. London, 1808-1830.

The Panoplist. Boston, 1805-1808. Continued as the Panoplist and Missionary Magazine, 1808-1817, and the Panoplist and Missionary Herald, 1818-1820

The Piscataqua Evangelical Magazine. Portsmouth and Amherst, N. H., 1805-1808.

The Religious Intelligencer. New Haven, 1816-1831.

The Sailor's Magazine, and Naval Journal. New York, 1828-1840.

The Spirit of the Pilgrims. Boston, 1827-1833.

The Theological Magazine, or Synopsis of Modern Religious Sentiment. New York, 1795-1799.

The Union Missionary Herald. Hartford, 1842.

The Youth's Dayspring. Boston, 1850.

C. REPORTS AND MISCELLANEOUS PROCEEDINGS

American Board of Commissioners for Foreign Missions, Annual Reports. Boston, 1811-1862.

----------, First Ten Reports. Boston, 1834.

----------, Instructions of the Prudential Committee to the Sandwich Islands Missions. Lahainaluna, 1838.

----------, Manual for Missionary Candidates. Revised Edition. Boston, 1849.

----------, Statistical View of the Officers, Missions, and Missionaries of the American Board of Commissioners for Foreign Missions. N.p., n.d.

American Missionary Association, Annual Reports. New York, 1847-1860.

Anderson, Rufus, Report of the Prudential Committee of a Visit to the Missions in the Levant. Boston, 1844.

Deputation to the India Missions, Report Made to the American Board of Commissioners for Foreign Missions, at a Special Meeting, Held in Albany, New York. Boston, 1856.

Minutes of the General Meeting of the American Missionaries of the Bombay Presidency, Held at Ahmednuggar, December, 1854. Bombay, 1855.

Minutes of the Special Meeting of the Ceylon Mission, Held April and May, 1855. Madras, 1855.

Minutes of the Special Meeting of the Madura Mission, Held at Madras, February and March, 1855. Madras, 1855.

New-Haven Ladies' Greek Association, First Annual Report. New Haven, 1831.

Proceedings at the Dedication of the Missionary Monument, in Mission Park, Williamstown, Mass., July 28, 1867. Boston, 1867.

Proceedings, in July 1855, on Occasion of the Visit of a Deputation from the Prudential Committee of the American Board of Commissioners for Foreign Missions to the Madras Mission. Calcutta, 1855.

Proceedings of the Missionary Jubilee, Held at Williams College, August 5, 1856. Boston, 1856.

Semi-Centennial of the Litchfield Co. Foreign Mission Society, Celebrated at Litchfield, October 16, 1861. Hartford, 1861.

United Foreign Missionary Society, An Address of the Board of Managers to the Three Denominations United in This Institution. /New York, 1817/.

D. SERMONS AND ADDRESSES

Adams, Nehemiah, The Power of Christian Gratitude. A Sermon, Preached at Utica, New York, September 11, 1855, before the American Board of Commissioners for Foreign Missions, at Their Forty-sixth Annual Meeting. Boston, 1855.

Anderson, Rufus, The Missionary Age: A Half-Century Sermon (Missionary Tracts, no. 10). Boston, 1851.

Appleton, Jesse, A Sermon, Delivered at Northampton, September 18, 1817, before the American Board of Commissioners for Foreign Missions. Charlestown, 1817.

Bacon, Leonard, A Plea for Africa; Delivered in New-Haven, July 4th, 1825. New Haven, 1825.

Bardwell, Horatio, The Duty and Reward of Evangelizing the Heathen: A Sermon Delivered in Newburyport, Lord's Day Evening, October 22, 1815. Newburyport, 1815.

Barker, Joseph, A Sermon, Preached before the Massachusetts Missionary Society, at Their Annual Meeting in Boston, May 27, 1806. Salem, 1806.

Barnes, Albert, The Choice of a Profession: An Address before the Society of Inquiry in Amherst College, August, 1838. Amherst, 1838.

Beecher, Lyman, The Bible a Code of Laws; a Sermon, Delivered in Park Street Church, Boston, Sept. 3, 1817, at the Ordination of Mr. Sereno Edwards Dwight, as Pastor of that Church; and of Messrs. Elisha P. Swift, Allen Graves, John Nichols, Levi Parsons, & Daniel Buttrick, as Missionaries to the Heathen. Andover, 1818.

——————, Resources of the Adversary and Means of Their Destruction. A Sermon Preached October 12, 1827, before the American Board of Missions, at New York. Boston, 1827.

——————, A Sermon Delivered at the Funeral of Henry Obookiah, a Native of Owhyhee, and a Member of the Foreign Missions School in Cornwall, Conn., Feb. 18, 1818. New Haven, 1818.

Buchanan, Claudius, The Star in the East; a Sermon, Preached in the Parish-church of St. James, Bristol, on Sunday, Feb. 26, 1809, for the Benefit of the "Society for Missions to Africa and the East." 8th ed. New York, 1809.

Clark, Daniel A., A Plea for a Miserable World. A Sermon, Delivered in Amherst, Massachusetts, August 9, 1820, at the Laying of the Corner Stone of the Building Erecting for the Use of the Charity Institution. Boston, 1820.

Codman, John, The Duty of American Christians to Send the Gospel to the Heathen. A Sermon Preached at Hartford, Sept. 14, 1836, before the American Board of Commissioners for Foreign Missions, at the Twenty-seventh Annual Meeting. Boston, 1836.

——————, The Importance of Spiritual Knowledge. A Sermon, Delivered before the Society for Propagating the Gospel among the Indians and Others in North America, in the First Church, Boston, November 3, 1825. With the report of the Select Committee. Cambridge, 1825.

Collier, William, Sanctuary Waters; or, the Spread of the Gospel. A Sermon, Preached before the Massachusetts Baptist Missionary Society, at Their Annual Meeting, Boston, May 28, 1806. Boston, 1806.

Cooley, Timothy M., The Universal Spread of the Gospel. A Sermon, Preached at Northampton, before the Hampshire Missionary Society; at Their Annual Meeting, August 25, 1808. To Which is Annexed, the Annual Report of the Trustees of the Hampshire Missionary Society, at the Meeting of the Society, August 25, A.D., 1808. Northampton, 1808.

Cox, Samuel H., The Bright and Blessed Destination of the World: A Discourse Delivered at Pittsfield, Mass. on the Evening of Tuesday, Sept. 11, 1849, before the American Board of Commissioners for Foreign Missions. New York, 1849.

Davis, Henry, A Sermon, Delivered before the American Board of Commissioners for Foreign Missions, Which Was Held at Hartford, (Con.) Sept. 18, 19, and 20, 1816. Boston, 1816.

Dwight, Sereno Edwards, The Greek Revolution. An Address Delivered in Park Street Church, Boston, on Thursday, April 1, and Repeated at the

Request of the Greek Committee, on the Evening of April 14, 1824. Boston, 1824.

----------, Thy Kingdom Come; a Sermon, Delivered in the Old South Church, Boston, before the Foreign Mission Society of Boston and the Vicinity, January 3, 1820. Boston, 1820.

Dwight, Timothy, A Discourse, in Two Parts, Delivered August 20, 1812, on the National Fast, in the Chapel of Yale College. 2nd ed., Boston, 1813.

----------, A Sermon, Delivered in Boston, Sept. 16, 1813, before the American Board of Commissioners for Foreign Missions, at Their Fourth Annual Meeting. Boston, 1813.

Emerson, John, The Duty of Christians to Seek the Salvation of Zion, Explained and Urged. A Sermon, Preached at Northampton before the Hampshire Missionary Society, at Their Annual Meeting, August 31, 1809. Northampton, 1809.

Emerson, Joseph, Christian Economy. A Sermon, Delivered before the Massachusetts Missionary Society, at Their Fourteenth Annual Meeting, in Boston, May 25, 1813. Boston, 1813.

Fay, Warren, The Obligations of Christians to the Heathen World. A Sermon, Delivered at the Old South Church in Boston, before the Auxiliary Foreign Mission Society of Boston and Vicinity, at the Annual Meeting, January 3, 1825. Boston, 1825.

Fisher, Samuel W., God's Purpose in Planting the American Church. A Sermon, Before the American Board of Commissioners for Foreign Missions, at the meeting in Boston, Mass., October 12, 1860. Boston, 1860.

Fisk, Pliny, The Holy Land an Interesting Field of Missionary Enterprise. A Sermon, Preached in the Old South Church Boston, Sabbath Evening, Oct. 31, 1819, Just before the Departure of the Palestine Mission. Boston, 1819.

Griffin, Edward D., Foreign Missions. A Sermon, Preached May 9, 1819, at the Anniversary of the United Foreign Missionary Society, in the Garden-Street Church, New-York. New York, 1819.

----------, The Kingdom of Christ: A Missionary Sermon Preached before the General Assembly of the Presbyterian Church, in Philadelphia, May 23, 1805. Philadelphia, 1805.

----------, A Plea for Africa. A Sermon Preached October 26, 1817, in the First Presbyterian Church in the City of New-York, before the Synod of New-York and New-Jersey, at the Request of the Board of Directors of the African School Established by the Synod. New York,

----------, A Sermon Preached September 14, 1826, before the American Board of Missions, at Middletown, Connecticut. Middletown, 1826.

----------, A Sermon Preached September 2, 1827, before the Candidates for the Bachelor's Degree in Williams College. Williamstown, 1827.

Griffin, Edward D., A Sermon Preached September 2, 1828, at the Dedication of the New Chapel Connected with Williams College, Massachusetts. Williamstown, 1828.

----------, A Sermon, Preached October 20, 1813, at Sandwich, Massachusetts, at the Dedication of the Meeting House, Recently Erected for the Use of the Calvinistic Congregational Society in That Town. Boston, 1813.

Hall, Gordon, The Duty of the American Churches in Respect to Foreign Missions. A Sermon Preached in the Tabernacle, Philadelphia, on Sabbath Morning, Feb. 16, 1812, and in the First Presbyterian Church, on the Afternoon of the Same Day. 2nd ed. Andover, 1815.

Harvey, Joseph, A Sermon, Preached at Litchfield, before the Foreign Mission Society of Litchfield County, at the Annual Meeting, February 15, 1815. New Haven, 1815.

Holmes, Abiel, A Discourse Delivered before the Society for Propagating the Gospel among the Indians and Others in North America, at Their Anniversary Meeting in Boston, November 3, 1808. Boston, 1808.

Humphrey, Heman, The Promised Land. A Sermon, Delivered at Goshen, (Conn.) at the Ordination of the Rev. Messrs. Hiram Bingham & Asa Thurston, as Missionaries to the Sandwich Islands, Sept. 29, 1819. Boston, 1819.

Knapp, Isaac, The Zeal of Jehovah for the Kingdom of Christ. A Sermon, Preached at Northampton, before the Hampshire Missionary Society at the Annual Meeting, August 27, 1812. To Which is Annexed the Annual Report of the Trustees of the Hampshire Missionary Society, at the Annual Meeting of the Society, August 27, 1812. Northampton, 1812.

Lathrop, Joseph, The Angel Preaching the Everlasting Gospel. A Sermon Delivered in Springfield, April 21st, 1812, at the Institution of a Society for the Encouragement of Foreign Missions. Springfield, /1812/

Livingston, John H., A Sermon Delivered before the New-York Missionary Society, at Their Annual Meeting, April 3, 1804. To Which are Added an Appendix, the Annual Report of the Directors, and Other Papers Relating to American Missions. New York, 1804.

Mason, John M., Hope for the Heathen: A Sermon, Preached in the Old Presbyterian Church, before the New-York Missionary Society, at Their Annual Meeting, November 7, 1797. New York, 1797.

Mather, Cotton, India Christians. A Discourse, Delivered unto the Commissioners, for the Propagation of the Gospel among the American Indians. Which is Accompanied with Several Instruments Relating to the Glorious Design of Propagating Our Holy Religion, in the Eastern as well as the Western Indies. An Entertainment which They That are Waiting for the Kingdom of God Will Receive as Good News from a Far Country. Boston, 1721.

Miller, Samuel, A Sermon, Delivered in the Middle Church, New Haven, Con. Sept. 1822, at the Ordination of the Rev. Messrs. William Goodell,

William Richards, and Artemas Bishop, as Evangelists and Missionaries to the Heathen. Boston, 1822.

Morse, Jedidiah, The Gospel Harvest, Illustrated in a Sermon, Delivered at the Old South Church in Boston, before the Society for Foreign Missions of Boston and the Vicinity, at Their Annual Meeting, January 2, 1815. Boston, 1815.

——————, Signs of the Times. A Sermon, Preached before the Society for Propagating the Gospel among the Indians and Others in North America, at Their Anniversary, Nov. 1, 1810. Charlestown, 1810.

Norton, Jacob, Faith on the Son of God Necessary to Everlasting Life. A Sermon Delivered before the Massachusetts Missionary Society, at Their Eleventh Annual Meeting, in Boston, May 29, 1810. Boston, 1810.

Nott, Samuel, A Sermon, on the Idolatry of the Hindoos, Delivered Nov. 29, 1816, at the Annual Meeting of the Female Foreign Mission Society, of Franklin, Connecticut. Norwich, Conn., 1817.

Parish, Elijah, The Excellence of the Gospel Visible in the Wretchedness of Paganism. A Discourse Delivered December 20, 1797, Being the Tenth Anniversary of His Ordination. Newburyport, 1798.

——————, A Protest against the War. A Discourse Delivered at Byfield, Fast Day, July 23, 1812. Newburyport, 1812.

——————, A Sermon Preached at Boston, November 3, 1814 before the Society for Propagating the Gospel among the Indians and Others in North-America. Boston, 1814.

——————, A Sermon, Preached before the Massachusetts Missionary Society, at Their Annual Meeting in Boston, May 26, 1807. Newburyport, 1807.

Parsons, Levi, The Dereliction and Restoration of the Jews. A Sermon Preached in Park-Street Church Boston, Sabbath, Oct. 31, 1819, Just before the Departure of the Palestine Mission. Boston, 1819.

Porter, Ebenezer, A Discourse before the Society for Propagating the Gospel among the Indians and Others in North America, Delivered Nov. 5, 1807. Boston, 1808.

——————, A Sermon, Delivered in Boston, on the Anniversary of the American Education Society October 4, 1820. Andover, 1821.

Rice, John H., The Power of Truth and Love. A Sermon Preached at Philadelphia, Oct. 1, 1828, at the Nineteenth Annual Meeting of the American Board of Commissioners for Foreign Missions. Boston, 1828.

Richards, James, The Spirit of Paul and the Spirit of Missions. A Sermon Preached at New Haven, (Con.) before the American Board of Commissioners for Foreign Missions, at Their Annual Meeting. Boston, 1814.

Sabine, James, The Relation the Present State of Religion Bears to the Expected Millennium. A Sermon, Delivered in the Old South Church,

Boston, before the Foreign Mission Society, of Boston and the Vicinity, Jan. 8, 1823. Boston, 1823.

Smith, Eli, The Missionary Character. An Address Delivered before the Society of Inquiry in the Theological Seminary in New Haven, April 1, 1840. New Haven, 1840.

----------, Missionary Sermons and Addresses. Boston, 1833.

Spaulding, Joshua, The Burden and Heat of the Day, Borne by the Jewish Church. A Sermon, Preached at Shelburne, before the Auxiliary Society for Foreign Missions, at Their Annual Meeting, Oct. 12, 1813. Boston, 1814.

Storrs, Richard S., Always Abounding in the Work of the Lord. A Sermon, Preached at Oswego, New York, September 10, 1850, before the American Board of Commissioners for Foreign Missions, at Their Forty-first Annual Meeting. Boston, 1850.

----------, A Sermon, Delivered at North Bridgewater, Oct. 31, 1821, at the Ordination of the Rev. Daniel Temple, and Rev. Isaac Bird, as Evangelists and Missionaries to the Heathen. Boston, 1822.

Strong, Jonathan, A Sermon, Preached before the Massachusetts Missionary Society, at Their Annual Meeting in Boston, May 24, 1808. Boston, 1808.

Stuart, Moses, A Sermon Preached in the Tabernacle Church, Salem, Nov. 5, 1818, at the Ordination of the Rev. Messrs. Pliny Fisk, Levi Spaulding, Miron Winslow, and Henry Woodward, as Missionaries to the Unevangelized Nations. Andover, 1818.

Taggart, Samuel, Knowledge Increased by Travelling To and Fro, to Preach the Gospel. A Sermon, Preached at Northampton, before the Hampshire Missionary Society and Their Annual Meeting, August, 27th 1807. Northampton, 1807.

Taylor, James, A Sermon, Preached in Northampton, before the Hampshire Missionary Society, at Their Annual Meeting, August 20, 1818. Northampton, 1818.

Wayland, Francis, The Moral Dignity of the Missionary Enterprise. A Sermon Delivered before the Boston Foreign Mission Society on the Evening of October 26, and before the Salem Bible Translation Society on the Evening of November 4, 1823. 2nd ed. Boston, 1824.

Webster, Noah, An Address, Delivered at the Laying of the Corner Stone of the Building Now Erecting for the Charity Institution in Amherst, August 9, 1820. Boston, 1820.

Whitman, Samuel, Blessedness of Those Who Shall Ascend to Glory without Dying. A Sermon, Delivered before the Hampshire Missionary Society, at Their Annual Meeting in Northampton, August 21, 1817. Northampton, 1817.

Wisner, Benjamin, The Moral Conditions and Prospects of the Heathen. A Sermon, Delivered at the Old South Church in Boston, before the

Foreign Mission Society of Boston and the Vicinity, at Their Annual Meeting, Jan. 1, 1824. Boston, 1824.

Woods, Leonard, A Sermon Delivered at the Tabernacle in Salem, Feb. 6, 1812, on Occasion of the Ordination of the Rev. Messrs. Samuel Newell, A.M., Adoniram Judson, A.M., Samuel Nott, A.M., Gordon Hall, A.M., and Luther Rice, A.B., Missionaries to the Heathen under the Direction of the Board of Commissioners for Foreign Missions. Boston, 1812.

----------, A Sermon Delivered in the Chapel of the Theol. Seminary, Andover, Feb. 1, 1835, on the Death of Henry Lyman and Samuel Munson, missionaries, and of Aurelian H. Post, Luke Baker and Chester Lord, all recent members of the seminary. Andover, 1835.

Worcester, Samuel, The Kingdom of the Messiah: A Sermon, Preached before the Foreign Missionary Society of Salem and the Vicinity, on the First Anniversary, Jan. 6, 1813. Salem, 1813.

----------, Paul on Mars Hill: or, a Christian Survey of the Pagan World. A Sermon, Preached at Newburyport, June 21, 1815, at the Ordination of the Reverend Messrs. Samuel J. Mills, James Richards, Edward Warren, Horatio Bardwell, Benjamin C. Meigs, and Daniel Poor, to the Office of Christian Missionaries. Andover, 1815.

----------, The Wisdom of God. A Sermon Delivered before the Massachusetts Missionary Society, at Their Tenth Annual Meeting, in Boston, May 30, 1809. Boston, 1809.

E. PAMPHLETS, TRACTS, AND MISCELLANEOUS TREATISES.

Abeel, David, The Missionary Convention at Jerusalem; or an Exhibition of the Claims of the World to the Gospel. New York, 1838.

Action of the Church in Franklin, Mass., in Regard to the American Tract Society and the American Board. New York, 1834.

/Castle, Samuel N.7, An Account of the Visit of the French Frigate L'Artemise, to the Sandwich Islands; July, 1839. Honolulu, 1839.

Colenso, John W., A Letter to an American Missionary from the Bishop of Natal. Pietermaritzburg, 1856.

----------, Remarks on the Proper Treatment of Cases of Polygamy as Found Already Existing in Converts from Heathenism. Pietermaritzburg, 1855.

A Collection of Letters Relative to Foreign Missions: Containing Several of Melville Horne's "Letters on Missions," and Interesting Communications from Foreign Missionaries. Interspersed with Other Extracts. Andover, 1810.

/Colton, Calvin7, Protestant Jesuitism. By a Protestant. New York, 1836.

Correspondence Relative to the Prospects of Christianity, and the Means of Promoting Its Reception in India. Cambridge, 1824.

Dibble, Sheldon, A Voice from Abroad, or Thoughts on Missions, from a Missionary to His Classmates. Lahainaluna, 1844.

Dix, William Giles, The Doom of the Crescent. Boston, 1853.

——————, The Unholy Alliance: an American View of the War in the East. New York, 1855.

The Duty of the Present Generation to Evangelize the World: An Appeal from the Missionaries at the Sandwich Islands to Their Friends in the United States. Honolulu, 1836.

Ellis, William, The American Mission in the Sandwich Islands; A Vindication and an Appeal, in Relation to the Proceedings of the Reformed Catholic Mission at Honolulu. Honolulu, 1866.

——————, A Vindication of the South Seas Missions from the Misrepresentations of Otto von Kotzebue, Captain in the Russian Navy. London, 1831.

/Evarts, Jeremiah/, Essays on the Present Crisis in the Condition of the American Indians; First Published in the National Intelligencer, under the Signature of William Penn. Boston, 1829.

——————, An Examination of Charges Against the American Missionaries at the Sandwich Islands, as Alleged in the Voyage of the Ship Blonde, and in the London Quarterly Review. Cambridge, 1827.

/Grout, Lewis/, An Answer to Dr. Colenso's "Letter" on Polygamy. By an American Missionary. Pietermaritzburg, 1856.

——————, A Reply to Bishop Colenso's "Remarks on the Proper Treatment of Cases of Polygamy, as Found Already Existing in Converts from Heathenism." By an American Missionary. Pietermaritzburg, 1855.

Mr. Southgate and the Missionaries at Constantinople. A Letter from the Missionaries at Constantinople in Reply to Charges by Rev. Horatio Southgate. Boston, 1844.

/Hall, Gordon and Samuel Newell/, The Conversion of the World: or the Claims of Six Hundred Millions and the Ability and Duty of the Churches Respecting Them. Andover, 1818.

Home Evangelization: A View of the Wants and Prospects of Our Country, Based on the Facts and Relations of Colportage. By One of the Secretaries of the American Tract Society. New York, /1849/.

Hooker, H. B. Horrors of Heathenism. New York, n.d.

Hopkins, Samuel, A Treatise on the Millennium. Showing from Scripture Prophecy, that It Is Yet to Come; when It Will Come; in What It Will Consist; and the Events Which are First to Take Place, Introductory to It. Boston, 1793.

Horne, Melville, Letters on Missions, Addressed to the Protestant Ministers of the British Churches. Andover, 1815.

Merrick, J. L., An Appeal to the American Board of Commissioners for Foreign Missions. Springfield, Mass., 1847.

Pickering, John, An Essay on a Uniform Orthography for the Indian Languages of North America. Cambridge, 1820.

Plan of a College for the Literary and Religious Instruction of Tamul and Other Youth. Columbo, 1823.

Read, Hollis, The Hand of God in History; or, Divine Providence Historically Illustrated in the Extension and Establishment of Christianity. Hartford, 1849.

/Sanders, Elizabeth7, Remarks on the "Tour Around Hawaii," by the Missionaries, Messrs. Ellis, Thurston, Bishop, and Goodrich, in 1823. Salem, 1848.

————————, Tract on Missions. Salem, 1844.

————————, Second Part of the Tract on Missions. Salem, 1845.

Scudder, John, Letters to Sabbath-School Children on the Condition of the Heathen. Philadelphia, 1843.

————————, Sabbath School Associations. With an Address to Sabbath School Children in the U.S.A. on the Subject of Their Engaging in the Work of Foreign Missions. Boston, 1835.

————————, Sermon to Children, on the Condition of the Heathen. Boston, 1845.

————————, A Voice from the East to the Young, in a Series of Letters to the Children of the Reformed Protestant Dutch Church of North America. New York, 1859.

Smith, Gerrit, A Letter Addressed to John Tappan, Esq., on Missions. May 24, 1838. Cazenovia, New York, 1839.

Southgate, Horatio, A Letter to a Friend, in Reply to a Recent Pamphlet, from the Missionaries of the American Board of Commissioners for Foreign Missions, at Constantinople. New York, 1845.

————————, Vindication of the Rev. Horatio Southgate: A Letter to the Members of the Protestant Episcopal Church in the United States. New York, 1844.

————————, The War in the East. New York, 1854.

Speeches on the Passage of the Bill for the Removal of the Indians, Delivered in the Congress of the United States, April and May, 1830. Boston, 1830.

Thoughts on the Importance of Raising up a New Order of Missionaries. New York, 1838.

/Tracy, Joseph/, Refutation of the Charges Brought by the Roman Catholics against the American Missionaries at the Sandwich Islands. Boston, 1843.

/Tuttle, Sarah/, Conversations on the Bombay Mission. Boston, 1830.

——————, Conversations on the Burman Missions. Boston, 1830.

——————, Letters and Conversation on the Ceylon Mission. Boston, 1830.

——————, Prospective Missions in China. Boston, 1833.

Welsh, Jane Kirby, A View of the Heathen World: and of Light Dispelling the Darkness. With Questions, Adapting It to Sabbath Schools and Juvenile Associations. Worcester, 1834.

Whipple, Charles E., Relation of the American Board of Commissioners for Foreign Missions to Slavery. Boston, 1861.

F. MISSIONARY MEMOIRS AND LETTERS

Anderson, Rufus, Kapiolani, the Heroine of Hawaii; or, a Triumph of Grace at the Sandwich Islands. New York, 1866.

——————, Memoir of Catherine Brown, a Christian Indian of the Cherokee Nation. Boston, 1824.

/Armstrong, M. F. and S. C./, America. Richard Armstrong. Hawaii. Hampton, Va., 1887.

Bardwell, Horatio, Memoir of Rev. Gordon Hall, A.M.: One of the First Missionaries of the Amer. Board of Commiss. for Foreign Missions, at Bombay. Andover, 1834.

Benjamin, Mary G., The Missionary Sisters: A Memorial of Mrs. Seraphina Haynes Everett, and Mrs. Harriet Martha Hamlin, Late Missionaries of the A.B.C.F.M. at Constantinople. Boston, 1860.

Bingham, Hiram, Bartimaeus, of the Sandwich Islands. Boston, n.d.

Bird, Isaac, The Martyr of Lebanon. Introduction by Joel Hawes. Boston, 1864.

Bond, Alvan, Memoir of the Rev. Pliny Fisk, A.M., Late Missionary to Palestine. Boston, 1827.

Bridgman, Eliza J. G., Daughters of China; or, Sketches of Domestic Life in the Celestial Empire. New York, 1852.

——————, The Pioneer of American Missions in China: The Life and Labors of Elijah Coleman Bridgman. New York, 1864.

Bushnell, Albert, Memorial of Rev. Henry Martyn Adams, Missionary to Western Africa. Boston, 1859.

Campbell, William M., A Memoir of Mrs. Judith S. Grant, Late Missionary to Persia. New York, 1844.

Coan, Titus, Life in Hawaii: An Autobiographical Sketch of Mission Life and Labors (1835-1881). New York, 1882.

Cornelius, Elias, The Little Osage Captive, an Authentic Narrative. Boston, 1822.

Cox, Samuel H., Missionary Remains; or, Sketches of the Lives of Evarts, Cornelius, and Wisner. New York, 1835.

Damon, Ethel M., and Juliette M. Fraser, eds., Letters from the Life of Abner and Lucy Wilcox 1836-1869. Honolulu, 1950.

/Dwight, Edwin W._7, Memoirs of Henry Obookiah, a Native of Owhyhee, and a Member of the Foreign Mission School; Who Died at Cornwall, Conn., Feb. 17, 1818, Aged 26 Years. New Haven, 1818.

Dwight, Harrison G. O., Memoir of Mrs. Elizabeth S. Dwight, including an Account of the Plague of 1837, with a Sketch of the Life of Mrs. Judith S. Grant, Missionary to Persia. New York, 1840.

Eddy, Daniel C., Daughters of the Cross, or Woman's Mission. Boston, 1855.

—————————, Heroines of the Missionary Enterprise: or Sketches of Prominent Female Missionaries. Boston, 1850.

—————————, The Three Mrs. Judsons, and Other Daughters of the Cross. Boston, 1855.

Ellis, William, Memoir of Mrs. Mary Mercy Ellis, Wife of Rev. William Ellis. With an introductory essay by Rufus Anderson. Boston 1836.

Fiske, D. T., Faith Working by Love: A Memoir of Miss Fidelia Fiske. Boston, 1868.

Goodell, William, The Old and the New; or the Change of Thirty Years in the East, with Some Allusions to Oriental Customs as Elucidating Scripture. With an introduction by William Adams. New York, 1853.

Gray, Edgar H., The Christian Hero of the Nineteenth Century. With an introductory essay by S. F. Smith. Cambridge, 1851.

Grout, Lewis, Zulu-Land; or, Life among the Zulu-Kafirs of Natal and Zulu-Land, South Africa. Philadelphia, 1864.

Gulick, Rev. and Mrs. Orramel Hinckley, The Pilgrims of Hawaii: Their Own Story of Their Pilgrimage from New England and Life Work in the Sandwich Islands, Now Known as Hawaii. New York, 1918.

H/aines_7, F. E. H., Jonas King: Missionary to Syria and Greece. New York, 1879.

Hamlin, Cyrus, Among the Turks. New York, 1877.

—————————, My Life and Times. Boston, 1893.

Hitchcock, Edward, The Power of Christian Benevolence Illustrated in the Life and Labors of Mary Lyon. Northampton, 1851.

Hooker, Edward W., Memoir of Mrs. Sarah Lanman Smith, Late of the Mission in Syria, under the Direction of the American Board of Commissioners for Foreign Missions. Boston, 1839.

Judd, Laura F., Honolulu. Sketches of the Life, Social, Political and Religious, in the Hawaiian Islands from 1828 to 1861. With a Supplementary Sketch of Events to the Present Time (1880). Honolulu, 1928.

Judson, Emily C., Memoir of Sarah B. Judson, Member of the American Mission to Burmah. New York, 1848.

Kendrick, Asahel C., The Life and Letters of Mrs. Emily C. Judson. New York, 1860.

Knowles, James D., Memoir of Mrs. Ann H. Judson, Late Missionary to Burmah. Including a History of the American Baptist Mission in the Burman Empire. Boston, 1829.

Kotze, D. J., Letters of the American Missionaries, 1835-1838. (Van Riebeeck Society, Publications, 31). Cape Town, 1950.

Lathrop, A. C., Memoir of Asahel Grant, M.D., Missionary to the Nestorians. New York, 1847.

Laurie, Thomas, Dr. Grant and the Mountain Nestorians. Boston, 1853.

——————, Woman and Her Saviour in Persia. By a Returned Missionary. Boston, 1863.

Lawrence, Margarette W., Light on the Dark River; or, Memorials of Mrs. Henrietta A. L. Hamlin, Missionary in Turkey. Boston, 1853.

The Life and Writings of Mrs. Harriet Newell. Rev. ed. Philadelphia, 1831.

/Loomis, Elias, ed.7, Memoirs of American Missionaries, Formerly Connected with the Society of Inquiry, in the Andover Theological Seminary, Embracing a History of the Society, etc. With an introductory essay by Leonard Woods. Boston, 1833.

The Martyr of Sumatra: A Memoir of Henry Lyman. New York, 1856.

Mason, Francis, The Karen Apostle: or, Memoir of Ko Thau-Dyu, the First Karen Convert, with Notices Concerning His Nation. Rev. by H. J. Ripley. 1st American ed. Boston, 1843.

Memoir of Mrs. Mary E. Van Lennep, Only Daughter of the Rev. Joel Hawes, D.D., and Wife of the Rev. Henry J. Van Lennep, Missionary in Turkey. By her mother. Hartford, 1847.

The Missionary's Daughter: A Memoir of Lucy Goodale Thurston, of the Sandwich Islands. New York, 1842.

/Morrison, Eliza Armstrong/, Memoirs of the Life and Labours of Robert Morrison, D.D. Compiled by his widow; with critical notices of his Chinese works, by Samuel Kidd. 2 v. London, 1839.

Morton, Daniel O., Memoir of Rev. Levi Parsons, Late Missionary to Palestine. In Three Parts. I. Containing Sketches of His Youth and Education. II. Containing Sketches of His Missionary Labours in This Country. III. Containing Sketches of His Missionary Labours in Asia Minor and Judea; Together with an Account of His Last Sickness and Death. Pultney, Vt., 1824.

A Narrative of Five Youths from the Sandwich Islands Now Receiving an Education in This Country. New York, 1816.

/Page, Harlan/, A Memoir of Thomas Hamitah Patoo, a Native of the Marquesas Islands, Who Died June 19, 1823, while a Member of the Foreign Mission School, in Cornwall, Conn. /Andover/, 1825.

/Perkins, Justin/, The Persian Flower: A Memoir of Judith Grant Perkins, of Oroomiah, Persia. Boston, 1853.

Pierson, H. W., ed., American Missionary Memorial, Including Biographical and Historical Sketches. New York, 1853.

Prime, E. D. G., Forty Years in the Turkish Empire; or, Memoirs of Rev. William Goodell, D.D., Late Missionary of the A.B.C.F.M. at Constantinople. New York, 1875.

Read, Hollis, The Christian Brahmun; or, Memoirs of the Life, Writings, and Character of the Converted Brahmun, Babajee. Including Illustrations of the Domestic Habits, Manners, Customs, and Superstitutions of the Hindoos, a Sketch of the Deckan and Notices of India in General, and an Account of the American Mission at Ahmednuggar. 2 v. New York, 1836.

Records from the Life of S. V. S. Wilder. New York, 1865.

Richards, Mary A., ed., Amos Starr Cooke and Juliette Montagu Cooke: Their Autobiographies Gleaned from Their Journals and Letters. Honolulu, 1941.

----------, The Chiefs' Children's School: A Record Compiled from the Diary and Letters of Amos Starr Cooke and Juliette Montagu Cooke. Honolulu, 1937.

/Richards, William/, Memoir of Keopuolani, Late Queen of the Sandwich Islands. Boston, 1825.

Riggs, Stephen R., Tah-Koo Wah-Kan; or, the Gospel among the Dakotas. With an introduction by S. B. Treat. Boston, 1869.

Schauffler, William G., Autobiography. Edited by his sons with an introduction by E. A. Park. New York, 1887.

Schneider, Eliza C. A., Letters from Broosa, Asia Minor. Chambersburg, Pa., 1846.

Scudder, Horace E., Life and Letters of Davoid Coit Scudder, Missionary in Southern India. New York, 1864.

Sketches of Pious Nestorians Who Have Died at Oroomiah, Persia. By members of the mission. Boston, 1857.

Smith, Lucius B., Missionary Heroes and Martyrs. Providence, 1857.

Spring, Gardiner, Memoirs of the Rev. Samuel J. Mills, Late Missionary to the South Western Section of the United States, and Agent of the American Colonization Society, Deputed to Explore the Coast of Africa. New York, 1820.

----------, Memoir of Samuel John Mills. E. C. Bridgman and C. W. Allen eds. 2nd ed. Boston, 1829.

Stuart, Arabella W., Lives of the Three Mrs. Judsons: Mrs. Ann H. Judson, Mrs. Sarah B. Judson, Mrs. Emily C. Judson, Missionaries to Burmah. Boston, 1855.

Tarbox, Increase N., Missionary Patriots: Memoirs of James H. Schneider and Edward M. Schneider. Boston, 1867.

Temple, Daniel H., Life and Letters of Rev. Daniel Temple, for Twenty-three Years a Missionary of the A.B.C.F.M. in Western Asia. Boston, 1854.

Thompson, Joseph P., Memoir of Rev. David Tappan Stoddard, Missionary to the Nestorians. New York, 1858.

Thomson, William, Memoirs of the Rev. Samuel Munson, and the Rev. Henry Lyman, Late Missionaries to the Indian Archipelago with the Journal of Their Exploring Tour. New York, 1839.

Thurston, Lucy G., Life and Times of Mrs. Lucy G. Thurston, Wife of Rev. Asa Thurston, Pioneer Missionary to the Sandwich Islands. Ann Arbor, 1882.

Tracy, E. C., Memoir of the Life of Jeremiah Evarts, Esq., Late Corresponding Secretary of the American Board of Commissioners for Foreign Missions. Boston, 1845.

Tyler, W. S., Memoir of Rev. Henry Lobdell, M.D., Late Missionary of the American Board at Mosul; Including the Early History of the Assyrian Mission. Boston, 1859.

Wade, Deborah B. L., The Burman Slave Girl. Also, Narrative of the First Burman Inquirer, and of the First Converted Burman. Description of a Burman School. Mr. Judson's Visit to the Burman Emperor. Boston, n.d.

Wayland, Francis, A Memoir of the Life and Labors of the Rev. Adoniram Judson, D.D. 2 v. Boston, 1853.

Wheeler, C. H., Ten Years on the Euphrates; or, Primitive Missionary Policy Illustrated. Boston, 1868.

Wiley, I. W., The Mission Cemetary and the Fallen Missionaries of Fuh Chau, China. With an Introductory Notice of Fuh Chau and Its Missions. New York, 1858.

Williams, Leighton and Mornay, eds., Serampore Letters: Being the Unpublished Correspondence of William Carey and Others with John Williams, 1800-1816. New York, 1892.

Williamson, G. R., Memoir of the Rev. David Abeel, D.D., Late Missionary to China. New York, 1848.

Winslow, Miron, Memoir of Mrs. Henrietta Wadsworth Winslow, Combining a Sketch of the Ceylon Mission. New York, 1835.

Woods, Leonard, A Sermon, Preached at Haverhill, Mass. in Remembrance of Mrs. Harriet Newell, Wife of the Rev. Samuel Newell, Missionary to India. Who Died at the Isle of France, Nov. 30, 1812, Aged 19 Years. To Which Are Added Memoirs of Her Life. Boston, 1814.

G. MISSIONARY JOURNALS, TRAVELS, AND RESEARCHES

Abeel, David, Journal of a Residence in China, and the Neighboring Countries, from 1829 to 1833. New York, 1834.

Allen, David O., India, Ancient and Modern, Geographical, Historical, Political, Social, and Religious; with a Particular Account of the State and Prospects of Christianity. Boston, 1856.

Anderson, Rufus, The Hawaiian Islands: Their Progress and Condition under Missionary Labors. Boston, 1864.

----------, Observations upon the Peloponnesus and Greek Islands, Made in 1829. Boston, 1830.

Bingham, Hiram, A Residence of Twenty-one Years in the Sandwich Islands; or the Civil, Religious, and Political History of Those Islands: Comprising a Particular View of the Missionary Operations Connected with the Introduction and Progress of Christianity and Civilization among the Hawaiian People. Hartford, 1847.

Brewer, Josiah, Patmos, and the Seven Churches of Asia, together with Places in the Vicinity, from the Earliest Records to the Year 1850. Compiled by John W. Barber. Bridgeport, Conn., 1851.

----------, A Residence in Constantinople in the Year 1827 with Notes to the Present Time. New Haven, 1830.

Coan, Titus, Adventures in Patagonia. A Missionary Exploring Trip. Introduction by Henry M. Field. New York, 1888.

Dibble, Sheldon, History of the Sandwich Islands. Lahainaluna, 1843.

Doolittle, Justus, Social Life of the Chinese: With Some Account of Their Religious, Governmental, Educational, and Business Customs and

Opinions. With Special but not Exclusive Reference to Fuhchau. 2 v. New York, 1865.

Dulles, John W., Life in India; or, Madrass and the Neilgherries, and Calcutta. Philadelphia, 1855.

Dwight, Harrison G. O., Christianity Revived in the East; or, a Narrative of the Work of God among the Armenians of Turkey. New York, 1850.

/Ellis, William7, A Journal of a Tour around Hawaii, the Largest of the Sandwich Islands. Boston, 1825.

----------, Polynesian Researches, during a Residence of Nearly Eight Years in the Society and Sandwich Islands. 2nd ed. 4 v. London, 1831

Grant, Asahel, The Nestorians; or the Lost Tribes. New York, 1841.

Gutzlaff, Charles, The Journal of Two Voyages along the Coast of China, in 1831 & 1832; the First in a Chinese Junk; the Second in the British Ship Lord Amherst; with Notices of Siam, Corea, and the Loo-Choo Islands; and Remarks on the Policy, Religion, etc. of China. New York, 1833.

Hawes, Joel, The Religion of the East, with Impressions of Foreign Travel. Hartford, 1845.

Hunnewell, James, Journal of the Voyage of the "Missionary Packet," Boston to Honolulu, 1826. Edited by James F. Hunnewell. Charlestown, Mass., 1880.

King, Jonas, The Oriental Church and the Latin. New York, 1865.

Lay, G. Tradescant, and Charles W. King, The Claims of Japan and Malaysia upon Christendom, Exhibited in Notes of Voyages Made in 1837, from Canton, in the Ship Morrison and Brig Himmaleh, under Direction of the Owners. 2 v. New York, 1839.

Malcom, Howard, Travels in South-Eastern Asia, Embracing Hindustan, Malaya, Siam, and China; with Notices of Numerous Missionary Stations, and a Full Account of the Burman Empire; with Dissertations, Tables, etc. 2 v. Boston, 1839.

Medhurst, W. H., China; Its State and Prospects, with Especial Reference to the Spread of the Gospel; Containing Allusions to the Antiquity, Extent, Population, Civilization, Literature, and Religion of the Chinese. Boston, 1838.

Merrick, James L., The Life and Religion of Mohammed, as Contained in the Sheeah Traditions of the Hyat-ul-Kuloob. Translated from the Persian. Boston, 1850.

Munger, S. B., The Conquest of India by the Church. Boston, 1845.

Parker, Peter, Journal of an Expedition from Sincapore to Japan, with a Visit to Loo-Choo; Descriptive of These Islands and Their Inhabitants;

in an Attempt with the Aid of Natives Educated in England, to Create an Opening for Missionary Labours in Japan. Revised by Andrew Reed. London, 1838.

Parker, Samuel, Journal of an Exploring Tour beyond the Rocky Mountains, under the Direction of the A.B.C.F.M. Performed in the Years 1835, '36, and '37; Containing a Description of the Geography, Geology, Climate, and Productions; and the Number, Manners, and Customs of the Natives. Ithaca, 1838.

Perkins, Justin, A Residence of Eight Years in Persia, among the Nestorian Christians; with Notices of the Mohammedans. Andover, 1843.

Ramsey, William, Journal of a Missionary Tour in India; Performed by the Rev. Messrs. Read and Ramsey, Missionaries of the American Board of Commissioners for Foreign Missions. Philadelphia, 1836.

Read, Hollis, India and Its People, Ancient and Modern. Columbus, Ohio, 1859.

/Richards, William/, Translation of the Constitution and Laws of the Hawaiian Islands, Established in the Reign of Kamahameha III. Lahainaluna, 1842.

Robinson, Edward, Biblical Researches in Palestine, Mount Sinai and Arabia Petraea. A Journal of Travels in the Year 1838, by E. Robinson and E. Smith Undertaken in Reference to Biblical Geography. 3 v.

Smith, Eli, Researches of the Rev. E. Smith and Rev. H. G. O. Dwight in Armenia: Including a Journey through Asia Minor, and into Georgia and Persia, with a Visit to the Nestorian and Chaldean Christians of Oormiah and Salmas. 2 v. Boston, 1833.

Southgate, Horatio, Narrative of a Tour through Armenia, Kurdistan, Persia and Mesopotamia, with an Introduction, and Occasional Observations upon the Condition of Mohammedanism and Christianity in Those Countries. 2 v. New York, 1840.

———————, Narrative of a Visit to the Syrian (Jacobite) Church of Mesopotamia; with Statements and Reflections upon the Present State of Christianity in Turkey, and the Character and Prospects of the Eastern Churches. New York, 1844.

Speer, William, The Oldest and the Newest Empire: China and the United States. Hartford, 1870.

St rt, Charles S., Private Journal of a Voyage to the Pacific Ocean, and Residence at the Sandwich Islands, in the Years, 1822, 1823, 1824, and 1825. New York, 1828.

Thomson, William M., The Land and the Book; or Biblical Illustrations Drawn from the Manners, Customs, Scenes, and Scenery of the Holy Land. 2 v. New York, 1859.

Tomlin, Jacob, Journal of a Nine Months' Residence in Siam, London, 1831.

Warren, Jane S., The Morning Star: History of the Children's Missionary Vessel, and of the Marquesas and Micronesian Missions. Boston, 1860.

Wilder, R. G., Mission Schools in India of the American Board of Commissioners for Foreign Missions, with Sketches of the Missions among the North American Indians, the Sandwich Islands, the Armenians of Turkey, and the Nestorians of Persia. 3rd ed., New York, 1861.

Williams, S. Wells, "The Journal of S. Wells Williams, LL.D., Secretary and Interpreter of the American Embassy to China during the Expedition to Tientsin and Peking in the Years 1858 and 1859." F. W. Williams, ed. North-China Branch of the Royal Asiatic Society, Journal, XLII (1911), 3-232.

----------, A Journal of the Perry Expedition to Japan (1853-1854). (F. W. Williams, ed., Asiatic Society of Japan, Transactions. XXXVII, Part II). Yokohama, 1910.

----------, The Middle Kingdom: A Survey of the Geography, Government, Education, Social Life, Literature, Religion, etc., of the Chinese Empire and Its Inhabitants. 2 v. New York, 1847.

Wilson, J. Leighton, Western Africa: Its History, Condition, and Prospects. New York, 1856.

H. CONTEMPORARY MEMOIRS, JOURNALS, AND TRAVELS

Adams, John Quincy, Memoirs, Comprising Portions of His Diary from 1795 to 1848. Edited by Charles Francis Adams. 12 v. Philadelphia, 1876.

Ainsworth, William F., Travels and Researches in Asia Minor, Mesopotamia, Chaldea, and Armenia. 2 v. London, 1842.

/Ames, Nathaniel7, A Mariner's Sketches, Originally Published in the Manufacturers and Farmers Journal, Providence. Providence, 1830.

----------, Nautical Reminiscences. Providence, 1832.

Badger, George P., The Nestorians and Their Rituals: With the Narrative of a Mission to Mesopotamia and Coordistan in 1842-1844, and of a Late Visit to Those Countries in 1850; also, Researches into the Present Condition of the Syrian Jacobites, Papal Syrians, and Chaldeans, and an Inquiry into the Religious Tenets of the Yezeedees. 2 v. London, 1852.

/Bates, George Washington7, Sandwich Island Notes. By a Haole. New York, 1854.

Beechey, Frederick W., Narrative of a Voyage to the Pacific and Beering's Strait, to Co-operate with the Polar Expedition: Performed in His Majesty's Ship Blossom, under the Command of Captain F. W. Beechey, R.N., F.R.S., F.R.A.S., F.R.G.S. in the Years 1825, 26, 27, 28. 2 v. London, 1831.

343

Belcher, Edward, Narrative of a Voyage Round the World. 2 v. London, 1843.

/Bridge, Horatio7, Journal of an African Cruiser; Comprising Sketches of the Canaries, the Cape de Verde, Liberia, Madeira, Sierra Leone, and Other Places of Interest on the West Coast of Africa. Edited by Nathaniel Hawthorne. New York, 1845.

Brown, D. Mackenzie, ed., China Trade Days in California: Selected Letters from the Thompson Papers, 1832-1863. Berkeley, 1947.

Browne, John R., Yusef; or the Journey of the Frangi. A Crusade in the East. New York, 1853.

Callcott, Maria G., comp., Voyage of H.M.S. Blonde to the Sandwich Islands, in the Years, 1824-1825. Captain the Right Hon. Lord Byron, Commander. London, 1827.

/Cass, Lewis7, An Historical, Geographical and Statistical Account of the Island of Candia, or Ancient Crete. Richmond, Va., 1839.

Cheever, Henry T., The Island World of the Pacific: Being the Personal Narrative and Results of Travel through the Sandwich or Hawaiian Islands, and Other Parts of Polynesia. New York, 1850.

----------, Life in the Sandwich Islands: or, the Heart of the Pacific, as It Was and Is. New York, 1851.

Colenso, John William, Ten Weeks in Natal. A Journal of a First Tour of Visitation among the Colonists and Zulu Kafirs of Natal. Cambridge, Eng., 1855.

/Colton, Walter7, Ship and Shore: or Leaves from the Journal of a Cruise to the Levant. New York, 1835.

----------, Visit to Constantinople and Athens. New York, 1836.

Cooley, James E., The American in Egypt, with Rambles through Arabia Petraea and the Holy Land, during the Years 1839 and 40. New York,

De Forest, John W., Oriental Acquaintance; or, Letters from Syria. New York, 1856.

/DeKay, James E.7, Sketches of Turkey in 1831 and 1832. New York, 1833.

Foote, Andrew H., Africa and the American Flag. New York, 1854.

/Haight, Sarah R.7, Letters from the Old World. 2 v. New York, 1839.

Hodgson, Adam, Letters from North America, Written during a Tour in the United States and Canada. 2 v. London, 1824.

Hopkins, Manley, Hawaii: The Past, Present, and Future of Its Island-Kingdom. An Historical Account of the Sandwich Islands (Polynesia). With a preface by the Bishop of Oxford. London, 1862; 2nd ed. New York, 1869.

Howe, Fisher, Oriental and Sacred Scenes, from Notes of Travel in Greece, Turkey, and Palestine. New York, 1863.

Hulbert, Archer B. and Dorothy P., eds., The Oregon Crusade: Across Land and Sea to Oregon (Overland to the Pacific, V). N.p. 1935.

Hunter, William C., Bits of Old China. 2nd ed. Shanghai, 1911.

Ireland, John R., Wall-Street to Cashmere. A Journal of Five Years in Asia, Africa, and Europe; Comprising Visits, during 1851, 2, 3, 4, 5, 6, to the Danemora Iron Mines, the "Seven Churches," Plains of Troy, Palmyra, Jerusalem, Petra, Seringpatam, Surat. New York, 1859.

Jarves, James J., Scenes and Scenery in the Sandwich Islands, and a Trip through Central America: Being Observations from My Note-book during the years, 1837-1842. Boston, 1843.

——————, Why and What Am I? The Confessions of an Inquirer. Boston, 1857.

Jones, George, Excursions to Cairo, Jerusalem, Damascus and Balbec, from the United States Ship Delaware, during Her Recent Cruise, with an Attempt to Discriminate between Truth and Error in Regard to the Sacred Places of the Holy City. New York, 1836.

——————, Sketches of Naval Life, with Notices of Men, Manners and Scenery, on the Shore of the Mediterranean, in a Series of Letters from the Brandywine and Constitution Frigates. 2 v. New Haven, 1829.

Kotzebue, Otto von, A New Voyage round the World, in the Years 1823, 24, 25, and 26. 2 v. London, 1830.

Layard, Austen H., Discoveries in the Ruins of Nineveh and Babylon; with Travels in Armenia, Kurdistan and the Desert; Being the Result of a Second Expedition Undertaken for the Trustees of the British Museum. New York, 1853.

——————, Nineveh and Its Remains: with an Account of a Visit to the Chaldaean Christians of Kurdistan, and the Yezidis, or Devil-Worshippers; and an Inquiry into the Manners and Arts of the Ancient Assyrians. Introduction by Edward Robinson. 2 v. New York, 1849.

Lightcraft, George, Scraps from the Log Book; an Account of the Whale Fishery; with Many Thrilling Incidents in the Life of the Author. Syracuse, 1847.

Lynch, W. F., Narrative of the United States' Expedition to the River Jordan and the Dead Sea. Philadelphia, 1849.

Malo, David, Hawaiian Antiquities, Moolelo Hawaii. Translated by N. B. Emerson. Honolulu, 1903.

Melville, Herman, Typee: A Peep at Polynesian Life during a Four Months' Residence in a Valley of the Marquesas, with Notices of the French Occupation of Tahiti and the Provisional Cession of the Sandwich Islands to Lord Paulet, and a Sequel, the Story of Toby (Works, Standard Edition, I). London, 1922.

Minnigerode, Meade, Some Personal Letters of Herman Melville and a Bibliography. New York, 1922.

Minturn, Robert B., Jr., From New York to Delhi, by Way of Rio de Janeiro, Australia and China. New York, 1858.

Morrell, Abby Jane, Narrative of a Voyage to the Ethiopic and South Atlantic Ocean, Indian Ocean, Chinese Sea, North and South Pacific Ocean, in the Years 1829, 1830, 1831. New York, 1833.

Morrell, Benjamin, A Narrative of Four Voyages, to the South Sea, North and South Pacific Ocean, Chinese Sea, Ethiopic and Southern Atlantic Ocean, Indian and Antarctic Ocean, from the Year 1822 to 1831. Comprising Critical Surveys of Coasts and Islands, with Sailing Directions. And an Account of some New and Valuable Discoveries, Including the Massacre Islands, Where Thirteen of the Author's Crew Were Massacred and Eaten by Cannibals. To Which is Prefixed a Brief Sketch of the Author's Early Life. New York, 1832.

Morse, Jedidiah, A Report to the Secretary of War of the United States, on Indian Affairs, Comprising a Narrative of a Tour Performed in the Summer of 1820, under a Commission from the President of the United States, for the Purpose of Ascertaining, for the Use of the Government, the Actual State of the Indian Tribes in Our Country. New Haven, 1822.

Murrell, William M., Cruise of the Frigate Columbia around the World, under the Command of Commodore George C. Read, in 1838, 1839, and 1840. Boston, 1840.

Olin, Stephen, Travels in Egypt, Arabia Petraea, and the Holy Land. 2 v. New York, 1843.

Oliver, James, Wreck of the Glide, with Recollections of the Fijiis, and of Wallis Island. Edited by William G. Dix. New York, 1848.

Olmsted, Francis A., Incidents of a Whaling Voyage. To Which are Added Observations on the Scenery, Manners and Customs, and Missionary Stations, of the Sandwich and Society Islands. New York, 1841.

Paulding, Hiram, Journal of a Cruise of the United States Schooner Dolphin, among the Islands of the Pacific Ocean; and a Visit to the Mulgrave Islands, in Pursuit of the Mutineers of the Whale Ship Globe. New York, 1831.

Perkins, Edward T., Na Motu: or, Reef-Rovings in the South Seas. A Narrative of Adventures at the Hawaiian, Georgian and Society Islands. New York, 1854.

Reynolds, Jeremiah N., Voyage of the United States Frigate Potomac, under the Command of Commodore John Downes, during the Circumnavigation of the Globe, in the Years, 1831, 1832, 1833, and 1834. New York, 1835.

Roberts, Edmund, Embassy to the Eastern Courts of Cochin-China, Siam, and Muscat; in the U.S. Sloop-of-War Peacock, David Geisinger, Commander, during the Years 1832, 3, 4. New York, 1837.

Rockwell, Charles, Sketches of Foreign Travel and Life at Sea; Including a Cruise on Board a Man-of-war, as also a Visit to Spain, Portugal, the South of France, Italy, Sicily, Malta, the Ionian Islands, Continental Greece, Liberia, and Brazil; and a Treatise on the Navy of the United States. 2 v. Boston, 1842.

Ruschenberger, William S. W., A Voyage round the World; Including an Embassy to Muscat and Siam, in 1835, 1836, and 1837. Philadelphia, 1838.

Schroeder, Francis, Shores of the Mediterranean; with Sketches of Travel, 1843-1845. a v. New York, 1846.

Simpson, George, An Overland Journey round the World, during the Years 1841-1842. 2 v. in 1. Philadelphia, 1847.

Sparks, Jared, The Life of John Ledyard, the American Traveller; Comprising Selections from His Journals and Correspondence. Cambridge, 1828.

/Stephens, John Lloyd7, Incidents of Travel in Egypt, Arabia Petraea, and the Holy Land. By an American. 3rd ed. 2 v. New York, 1838.

-----------, Incidents of Travel in Greece, Turkey, Russia, and Poland. 7th ed. 2 v. New York, 1849.

Stewart, Charles S., A Visit to the South Seas, in the U.S. Ship Vincennes, during the Years 1829 and 1830; with Scenes in Brazil, Peru, Manilla, the Cape of Good Hope, and St. Helena. 2 v. New York, 1831.

Taylor, Bayard, A Visit to India, China, and Japan, in the Year 1853. New York, 1855.

Taylor, Fitch W., A Voyage round the World, and Visits to Various Foreign Countries, in the United States Frigate Columbia; Attended by Her Consort the Sloop of War John Adams, and Commanded by Commodore George C. Read. 9th ed. 2 v. New Haven, 1850.

Train, George F., An American Merchant in Europe, Asia, and Australia; A Series of Letters from Java, Singapore, China, Bengal, Egypt, the Holy Land, the Crimea and Its Battle Grounds, England, Melbourne, Sidney, etc. etc. Introduction by Freeman Hunt. New York, 1857.

Van Buren, Martin, Autobiography (John C. Fitzpatrick, ed., American Historical Association, Annual Report for the Year 1918, II). Washington, 1920.

Warriner, Francis, Cruise of the United States Frigate Potomac round the World, during the Years 1831-34. Embracing the Attack on Quallah Battoo, with Notices of Scenes, Manners, etc., in Different Parts of Asia, South America, and the Islands of the Pacific. New York, 1835.

Wilkes, Charles, Narrative of the United States Exploring Expedition during the Years 1838, 1839, 1840, 1841, 1842. 5 v. Philadelphia, 1845.

Willis, Nathaniel P., Pencillings by the Way. 2nd ed. 3 v. in 1. London, 1838.

Wood, William M., Fankwei; or, the San Jacinto in the Seas of India, China and Japan. New York, 1859.

——————, Wandering Sketches of People and Things in South America, Polynesia, California, and Other Places Visited, during A Cruise on Board of the U.S. Ships Levant, Portsmouth, and Savannah. Philadelphia, 1849.

Woodbridge, Timothy, The Autobiography of a Blind Minister; Including Sketches of the Men and Events of His Time. Boston, 1856.

I. NOVELS AND GIFT BOOKS

Clark, John A., ed., The Christian Keepsake and Missionary Annual. Philadelphia, 1837 et seq.

/De Forest, John W.7, Irene the Missionary. Boston, 1879.

Dowling, John, ed., The Judson Offering, Intended as a Token of Christian Sympathy with the Living and a Memento of Christian Affection for the Dead. New York, 1848.

The Missionary Memorial: A Literary and Religious Souvenir. New York, 1845.

Mortimer, Charlotte B., Morton Montagu; or a Young Christian's Choice. A Narrative Founded on Facts in the Early History of a Deceased Moravian Missionary Clergyman. New York, 1850.

Shepard, Isaac F., ed., The Christian Souvenir: An Offering for Christmas and the New Year. Boston, 1842.

Sigourney, Mrs. L. H., ed., The Religious Souvenir, for MDCCCXXXIX. New York, 1838.

Southgate, Horatio, The Cross above the Crescent a Romance of Constantinople. Philadelphia, 1877.

J. GOVERNMENT PUBLICATIONS

American State Papers. Documents, Legislative and Executive, of the Congress of the United States. Class II. Indian Affairs. 2 v. Washington, 1832-34.

House Executive Document, 26 Cong., 1 sess., no. 119 (February 25, 1840).

House Executive Document, 26 Cong., 1 sess., no. 170 (April 9, 1840).

House Executive Document, 28 Cong., 2 sess., no. 69 (January 24, 1845).

House Executive Document, 33 Cong., 1 sess., no. 123 (July 19, 1854).

House Report, 27 Cong., 3 sess., no. 93 (January 24, 1843).

Papers Relating to the Foreign Relations of the United States, 1894. Appendix II. Affairs in Hawaii. Washington, 1895.

Senate Executive Document, 28 Cong., 2 sess., no. 67 (January 28, 1845).

Senate Executive Document, 28 Cong., 2 sess., no. 138 (February 25, 1845).

Senate Executive Document, 33 Cong., 2 sess., no. 9 (December 19, 1854).

Translation of the Constitution and Laws of the Hawaiian Islands, Established in the Reign of Kamahameha III. Lahainaluna, 1842.

SECONDARY WORKS

A. BIOGRAPHY

Alexander, Mary C., William Patterson Alexander in Kentucky, the Marquesas, Hawaii. Honolulu, 1934.

Baird, Henry M., The Life of the Rev. Robert Baird, D.D. New York, 1865.

Bass, Althea, Cherokee Messenger. Norman, Okla., 1936.

       Critical biography of Samuel Worcester, a leading figure among the Board's missionaries to the Cherokees.

Damon, Ethel M., Father Bond of Kohala: A Chronicle of Pioneer Life in Hawaii. Honolulu, 1927.

——————, Koamalu: A Story of Pioneers on Kawai and of What They Built in That Island Garden. 2 v. Honolulu, 1931.

Doyle, Emma L., Makua Laiana: The Story of Lorenzo Lyons. Honolulu, 1945.

Drury, Clifford M., Elkanah and Mary Walker, Pioneers among the Spokanes. Caldwell, Ida., 1940.

——————, Henry Harmon Spaulding, Pioneer of Old Oregon. Caldwell, Ida., 1936.

——————, Marcus Whitman, M.D., Pioneer and Martyr. Caldwell, Ida., 1937.

       These three volumes by Drury are thorough studies based on manuscript sources of the lives of American Board missionaries to the Oregon Indians.

Eells, Myron, Father Eells or the Results of Fifty-five Years of Missionary Labors in Washington and Oregon: A Biography of Rev. Cushing Eells, D.D. Boston, 1894.

Frear, Mary D., Lowell and Abigail: A Realistic Idyll. New Haven, 1934.

       This volume, together with those by Ethel L. Damon and Emma L. Doyle above, is an example of the salvaging of the life records of the early missionaries to Hawaii by their descendants. Based on manuscripts and family traditions.

Gabriel, Ralph H., Elias Boudinot, Cherokee & His America. Norman, Okla., 1941.

Interesting historical account of the Cornwall Foreign Mission School and the Board's Cherokee missions, woven around the life of Boudinot and founded on family letters.

Hewitt, John H., Williams College and Foreign Missions. Boston, 1914.

Hulbert, Archer B. and Dorothy P., eds., Marcus Whitman, Crusader (Overland to the Pacific, VI, VII, VIII). 3 v. N.p., 1936-1941.

Pickering, Mary Orne, Life of John Pickering. Boston, 1887.

Restarick, Henry B., Hawaii 1778-1920 from the Viewpoint of a Bishop: Being the Story of English and American Churchmen in Hawaii with Historical Sidelights. Honolulu, 1924.

Valuable particularly for its observations on the missionary land question in Hawaii.

Richards, Thomas C., Samuel J. Mills: Missionary Pathfinder, Pioneer and Promoter. Boston, 1906.

This centennial publication is based on original research yet is eulogistic rather than critical.

Smith, Edwin W., The Life and Times of Daniel Lindley (1801-80): Missionary to the Zulus, Pastor of the Vortrekkers, Ubebe Omhlape. New York, 1952.

An excellent critical study of one of the first missionaries of the Board in South Africa.

Smith, George, The Life of William Carey, D.D., Shoemaker and Missionary, Professor of Sanskrit, Bengali, and Marathi in the College of Fort William, Calcutta. London, 1885.

Speer, Robert E., Studies of Missionary Leadership. Philadelphia, 1914.

Biographical sketches of the statesmen and administrators of foreign missions.

Stevens, George B., and W. Fisher Marwick, The Life, Letters, and Journals of the Rev. and Hon. Peter Parker, M.D., Missionary, Physician, and Diplomatist. The Father of Medical Missions and the Founder of the Ophthalmic Hospital in Canton. Boston, 1896.

Trumbull, Henry C., Old Time Student Volunteers: My Memories of Missionaries. New York, 1902.

Good profiles of many of the leading missionaries of the first half of the nineteenth century.

Williams, Frederick W., The Life and Letters of Samuel Wells Williams, LL.D.: Missionary, Diplomatist, Sinologue. New York, 1888.

Williston, Samuel, William Richards. Cambridge, 1938.

Worcester, Samuel M., The Life and Labors of Rev. Samuel Worcester, D.D.,
Former Pastor of the Tabernacle Church, Salem, Mass. 2 v. Boston,
1852.

B. HISTORY OF MISSIONS

Arpee, Leon, The Armenian Awakening: A History of the Armenian Church,
1820-1860. Chicago, 1909.

----------, A History of Armenian Christianity from the Beginnings to
Our Own Time. New York, 1946.

        Mr. Arpee's studies give full recognition to the work of the
American Board in revitalizing Armenian religious life.

Anderson, Rufus, A Heathen Nation Evangelized: History of the Sandwich
Islands Missions. Boston, 1870.

----------, History of the Missions of the American Board of Commissioners for Foreign Missions in India. Boston, 1874.

----------, Memorial Volume of the First Fifty Years of the American
Board of Commissioners for Foreign Missions. Boston, 1861.

----------, Republication of the Gospel in Bible Lands: History of the
Missions of the American Board of Commissioners for Foreign Missions
to the Oriental Churches. 2 v. Boston, 1872.

        These are all more or less official histories written by a
secretary of the Board of over thirty years' service, who had complete
access to the society's files and a desire to justify the methods and
results of his own and his colleague's efforts.

Bartlett, Samuel C., Sketches of the Missions of the American Board.
Boston, 1872.

Beard, Augustus Field, A Crusade of Brotherhood: A History of the
American Missionary Association. Boston, 1909.

Bianquis, Jean, Les Origines de la Société des Missions Évangéliques de
Paris 1822-1830. 3 v. Paris, 1930-1935.

        Scholarly treatment of French Protestant missions with due
mention of American influences.

Bliss, Theodora Crosby, Micronesia, Fifty Years in the Island World.
A History of the Mission of the American Board. Boston, 1906.

Cary, Otis, A History of Christianity in Japan. 2 v. New York, 1909.

        The first chapter contains a brief survey of American Protes-
tant attempts to open Japan before Perry.

Choules, John O., and Thomas Smith, The Origin and History of Missions;
a Record of the Voyages, Travels, Labors, and Successes of the Various

Missionaries, Who Have Been Sent Forth by Protestant Societies and Churches to Evangelize the Heathen; Forming a Complete Missionary Repository. 2 v. 4th ed. Boston, 1837.

Dean, William, The China Mission. Embracing a History of the Various Missions of All Denominations among the Chinese. With Biographical Sketches of Deceased Missionaries. New York, 1859.

General account by a Baptist missionary personally acquainted with the China missions.

Ellsbree, Oliver Wendell, The Rise of the Missionary Spirit in America, 1790-1815. Williamsport, Pa., 1928.

Doctoral thesis linking origins of missions closely to Hopkinsian theology and millennial doctrines.

Frear, Walter F., Anti-Missionary Criticism with Reference to Hawaii. 2nd ed. Honolulu, 1935.

Poorly organized, defensive treatment of an important subject.

Gammell, William, A History of American Baptist Missions in Asia, Africa, Europe, and North America. Boston, 1849.

Graves, William W., The First Protestant Osage Missions 1820-1837. Oswego, Kansas, 1949.

Green, Ashbel, A Historical Sketch or Compendious View of Domestic and Foreign Missions in the Presbyterian Church of the United States of America. Philadelphia, 1838.

Groves, C. P. The Planting of Christianity in Africa. Vol. I. London, 1948.

Broad survey of the subject in which the author treats cursorily the missions of the American Board in Africa.

Latourette, Kenneth S., The Great Century in Europe and the United States of America A.D. 1800-A.D. 1914 (A History of the Expansion of Christianity, IV). New York, 1941.

----------, A History of Christian Missions in China. New York, 1929.

Both standard scholarly studies by an expert in the subject, substantial contributions but not exhaustive.

----------, Missions and the American Mind. Indianapolis, 1949.

An exploratory essay into the effects of the missionary enterprise upon American attitudes.

Loomis, Albertine, Grapes of Canaan. New York, 1951.

Delightful narrative of the very early years of the mission in Hawaii, based on the papers of missionary-printer Elisha Loomis.

Lord, E. A Compendious History of the Principal Protestant Missions to the Heathen, Selected and Compiled from the Best Authorities. 2 v. Boston, 1813.

McFarland, George B., ed., Historical Sketch of Protestant Missions in Siam, 1828-1922. Bangkok, 1928.

McIntosh, Gilbert, The Missionary Press in China. Shanghai, 1895.

Martin, K. L. P., Missionaries and Annexation in the Pacific. London, 1924.

   Prize essay on the political influences of British missions without reference to American.

Moore, Edward C., West and East: The Expansion of Christendom and the Naturalization of Christianity in the Orient in the XIXth Century. New York, 1920.

   Scholarly interpretation by a university professor and one-time president of the American Board.

The One Hundredth Anniversary of the Haystack Prayer Meeting Celebrated at the Ninety-seventh Annual Meeting of the American Board in North Adams and by the Haystack Centennial Meetings at Williamstown, October 9-12, 1906. Boston, 1907.

Richter, D. Julius, Geschichte der Evangelischen Mission in Afrika. Gutersloh, 1922.

————————, A History of Missions in India. Sydney H. Moore, tr., Edinburgh and London, /1908/.

————————, History of Protestant Missions in the Near East. New York, 1910.

   Three solid historical studies by an outstanding German historian covering broad outlines of missionary history but lacking in detail.

Shaw, P. E., American Contacts with the Eastern Churches, 1820-1870. Chicago, 1937.

   A pioneering study of American Protestant missions to the Greek Orthodox, Armenian, Nestorian, and other Eastern Churches.

Shedd, C. P., Two Centuries of Student Christian Movements: Their Origins and Intercollegiate Life. New York, 1934.

   Excellent survey of student volunteer movements, with a good chapter on the Brethren and the Society of Inquiry.

Speer, Robert, Missions and Modern History: A Study of the Missionary Aspects of Some Great Movements of the Nineteenth Century. 2 v. New York, 1904.

Interesting but rambling discussion of the relations to missions of such historical crises as the Sepoy Revolt and the Taiping Rebellion by a prominent Presbyterian missionary statesman.

Strickland, William P., History of the Missions of the Methodist Episcopal Church, from the Organization of the Missionary Society to the Present Time. With an introduction by B. F. Tefft. Cincinnati, 1849.

Strong, William E., The Story of the American Board: An Account of the First Hundred Years of the American Board of Commissioners for Foreign Missions. Boston, 1910.

Well-executed centennial history by one of the officers of the Board.

Tappan, Lewis, History of the American Missionary Association; Its Constitution and Principles, &c. &c. New York, 1855.

Tracy, Joseph, History of the American Board of Commissioners for Foreign Missions. 2nd ed. New York, 1842.

Initially published in 1840 as part of a larger work, this first history of the American Board was written by the author of the Great Awakening, who covered the society's operations year by year, discussing many significant questions neglected in official publications.

Walker, Robert S., Torchlights to the Cherokees: The Brainerd Mission. New York, 1931.

Competent history of the Board's chief station among the Cherokees in the Old Southwest.

Winslow, Miron, A Sketch of Missions; or History of the Principal Attempts to Propagate Christianity among the Heathen. Andover, 1819.

Wright, Louis B., and Mary Isabel Fry, Puritans in the South Seas. New York, 1936.

Colorful study of English and American missions in the Pacific, with one chapter on the Board's work in Hawaii.

Yzendoorn, Reginald, History of the Catholic Mission in the Hawaiian Islands. Honolulu, 1927.

Irenic account of the Board's Roman Catholic rivals in Hawaii, with some stress upon the anti-Catholic episodes in the first half of the century.

C. SUPPLEMENTARY STUDIES

Anderson, Charles R., Melville in the South Seas (Columbia University, Studies in English and Comparative Literature, 138). New York, 1939.

Discusses briefly Melville's animosities toward Pacific missionaries.

Billington, Ray A., The Protestant Crusade 1800-1860: A Study of the Origins of American Nativism. New York, 1933.

        Useful for the background of anti-Catholicism in American foreign missions.

Boardman, Eugene P., Christian Influence on the Ideology of the Taiping Rebellion 1851-1854. Madison, Wis., 1952.

Bradley, Harold W., The American Frontier in Hawaii: The Pioneers 1789-1843. Stanford, 1942.

        Excellent—perhaps definitive—work on American influences in Hawaii, including the work of the missionaries, based on manuscript correspondence.

Bridgman, Howard A., New England in the Life of the World. Boston, 1920.

        Curious study of New England emigration and its effect upon the world, including the work of foreign missionaries.

Brookes, Jean I., International Rivalry in the Pacific Islands, 1800-1875. Berkeley, 1941.

        Treats missionary influences in the international quarrels in the Pacific briefly.

Christy, Arthur E., ed., The Asian Legacy and American Life. New York, 1945.

        A chapter entitled "Ties that Bind," by Stephen B. L. Penrose, Jr., and Oliver J. Caldwell, deals briefly with religious and philanthropic agencies in their effect upon American relations with Asia.

Cline, Myrtle A., The American Attitude toward the Greek War of Independence, 1821-1828. Atlanta, 1930.

Cole, Arthur C., A Hundred Years of Mount Holyoke College: The Evolution of an Educational Ideal. New Haven, 1940.

        An excellent college history which treats the missionary atmosphere of the early years of the school.

Danton, George H., The Culture-Contacts of the United States and China: The Earliest Sino-American Culture Contacts 1784-1844. New York, 1951.

        Disappointing study of American-Chinese relations with some interesting comments on missions.

Dennett, Tyler, American in Eastern Asia: A Critical Study of the Policy of the United States with Reference to China, Japan and Korea in the 19th Century. New York, 1922.

        Very useful volume with an unusual amount of attention to the work of missionaries.

Dulles, Foster Rhea, America in the Pacific: A Century of Expansion. Boston, 1932.

----------, The Old China Trade. Boston, 1930.

Dunbar, Seymour, History of Travel in the United States. 2 v. Indiana-polis, 1915.

        Contains an account of the Indian missions in the Old Southwest, with the spurious letter of President Jackson to the American Board.

Foreman, Grant, Indian Removal: The Emigration of the Five Civilized Tribes of Indians. Norman, Okla., 1932.

        The story of the tragic removal of the Cherokees and their neighbors to Indian Territory west of the Mississippi.

Foster, Frank H., A Genetic History of the New England Theology. Chicago, 1907.

        Good for the theological background of foreign missions and the whole benevolent movement.

Foster, John W., American Diplomacy in the Orient. Boston, 1903.

        An older account of American interests in the Pacific, with some attention to the missionary aspect.

Gabriel, Ralph H., The Course of American Democratic Thought: An Intel-lectual History since 1815. New York, 1940.

        Discusses American evangelicalism with little reference to foreign missions.

Gordon, Leland J., American Relations with Turkey 1830-1930: An Economic Interpretation. Philadelphia, 1932.

        Contains some materials on the work of the American Board in the Ottoman Empire.

Hobbs, Jean F., Hawaii: A Pageant of the Soil. Stanford, 1935.

        An excellent chapter on missionary land holdings explodes the older conception of expropriation by land-hungry Yankee evangelists.

Jarves, James J., History of the Hawaiian or Sandwich Islands, Embracing Their Antiquities, Mythology, Legends, Discovery by Europeans in the Sixteenth Century, Re-discovery by Cook, with Their Civil, Religious, and Political History, from the Earliest Traditional Period to the Present Time. Boston, 1843.

        An early history written by a former resident of Hawaii friend-ly to the missionary cause.

Keller, Charles R., The Second Great Awakening in Connecticut. New Haven, 1942.

Deals with foreign missions as an outgrowth of the religious renewal of the first years of the nineteenth century.

Kirk, George E., A Short History of the Middle East from the Rise of Islam to Modern Times. Washington, 1949.

A broad survey which discusses very briefly missionary influence, particularly in Syria and Lebanon.

Krout, John A., The Origins of Prohibition. New York, 1925.

A standard study of one of the allied benevolent associations of the evangelical crusade.

Krout, John A., and Dixon Ryan Fox, The Completion of Independence (A. M. Schlesinger and D. R. Fox, eds., A History of American Life, V). New York, 1944.

Brief but pertinent treatment of foreign missions found in one chapter.

Kuykendall, Ralph S., The Hawaiian Kingdom 1778-1854: Foundation and Transformation. Honolulu, 1938.

Sound historical account of Hawaii which relates missionary influences to the total picture.

Latourette, Kenneth S., The History of Early Relations between the United States and China, 1784-1844 (Connecticut Academy of Arts and Sciences, Transactions, 22). New Haven, 1917.

A pioneering study covering all aspects of American interest in China, including a large stress on foreign missions.

Miller, William, The Ottoman Empire and Its Successors, 1801-1927. With an appendix, 1927-1934. Rev. ed. Cambridge, Eng., 1934.

Good survey of the political conditions under which the missionaries of the Board operated in the eastern Mediterranean.

Morison, Samuel E., The Maritime History of Massachusetts 1783-1860. Boston, 1921.

A good picture of the New England commercial background of the activities of the American Board overseas.

Paullin, Charles O., Diplomatic Negotiations of American Naval Officers, 1778-1883. Baltimore, 1912.

Perry, Arthur L., Williamstown and Williams College: A History. 3rd ed. N.p., 1904.

Gives detailed account of Samuel J. Mills and the haystack prayer meeting, mildly debunking the legendary accretions to the story, and describing the religious background and college life out of which the missionary impulse sprang.

Robinson, David M., America in Greece: A Traditional Policy. New York, 1948.

       Reviews the history of American interest in Greek affairs, with copies of some significant documents.

Sakamaki, Shunzo, Japan and the United States, 1790-1853: A Study of Japanese Contacts with and Conceptions of the United States and Its People prior to the American Expedition of 1853-4 (Asiatic Society of Japan, Transactions, 2nd ser., XVIII). Tokyo, 1939.

Schlesinger, Arthur M., Paths to the Present. New York, 1949.

Starkey, Marion L, The Cherokee Nation. New York, 1946.

       Well-written narrative account of the Cherokees and their missionaries, based in large part upon the records and correspondence of the American Board.

Starr, Edward C., A History of Cornwall, Connecticut: A Typical New England Town. New Haven, 1926.

       Contains useful details about the Cornwall Foreign Mission School, its founders, students, and the social and religious environment in which it grew.

Stephenson, George M., The Puritan Heritage. New York, 1952.

       A broad survey of the American religious background, with little to say of foreign missions.

Stevens, S. K., American Expansion in Hawaii, 1842-1898. Harrisburg, Pa., 1945.

       Concerned primarily with economic and political expansion.

Stokes, Anson P., Church and State in the United States: Historical Development and Contemporary Problems of Religious Freedom under the Constitution. 3 v. New York, 1950.

       An encyclopedic work which, however, does not do justice to the political aspects of foreign missions as an element in church-state matters.

Thomas, B. P., Russo-American Relations, 1815-1867 (Johns Hopkins University, Studies in Historical and Political Science, Ser. XLVIII, 2). Baltimore, 1930.

Walker, Eric A., The Great Trek. 2nd ed. London, 1938.

----------, A History of South Africa. Rev. ed. London, 1947.

       Both standard historical accounts of South Africa, with some attention to the American missionaries.

Woods, Leonard, History of the Andover Theological Seminary. Edited by George S. Baker. Boston, 1884.

Wriston, Henry M., <u>Executive Agents in American Foreign Relations</u>. Baltimore, 1929.

D. MAGAZINE ARTICLES

Aaron, David, "Melville and the Missionaries," <u>New England Quarterly</u>, VIII (1935), 404-408.

Alexander, William D., "The Oahu Charity School," Hawaiian Historical Society, <u>Sixteenth Annual Report</u> (1908), 20-38.

Anderson, Charles R., "Contemporary American Opinions of Typee and Omoo," <u>American Literature</u>, IX (1937), 1-25.

Ballou, Howard M., and George R. Carter, "The History of the Hawaiian Mission Press, with a Bibliography of the Earlier Publications," Hawaiian Historical Society, <u>Papers</u>, no. 14 (1908).

Benz, Ernst, "Pietist and Puritan Sources of Early Protestant World Missions (Cotton Mather and A. H. Francke)," <u>Church History</u>, XX (1951), 28-55.

Brown, Ira, "Watchers for the Second Coming: The Millenarian Tradition in America," <u>Mississippi Valley Historical Review</u>, XXXIX (1952), 441-458.

Earle, Edward M., "American Interest in the Greek Cause, 1821-1827," <u>American Historical Review</u>, XXXIII (1927), 44-63.

----------, "Early American Policy Concerning Ottoman Minorities," <u>Political Science Quarterly</u>, XLII (1927), 337-367.

Ellsbree, Oliver W., "The Rise of the Missionary Spirit in New England," <u>New England Quarterly</u>, I (1928), 295-322.

----------, "Samuel Hopkins and His Doctrine of Benevolence," <u>New England Quarterly</u>, VIII (1935), 534-550.

Forsythe, R. S., "Herman Melville in Honolulu," <u>New England Quarterly</u>, VIII (1935), 99-105.

Fox, Dixon R., "The Protestant Counter-Reformation in America," <u>New York History</u>, XVI (1935), 19-35.

Gabriel, Ralph H., "Evangelical Religion and Popular Romanticsm in Early Nineteenth-Century America," <u>Church History</u>, XIX (1950), 34-47.

Gohdes, Clarence, "Gossip about Melville in the South Seas," <u>New England Quarterly</u>, X (1937), 526-531.

Golder, Frank A., "Russian-American Relations during the Crimean War," <u>American Historical Review</u>, XXXI (1926), 462-476.

Greene, Evarts B., "A Puritan Counter-Reformation," American Antiquarian Society, <u>Proceedings</u>, n.s., XLII (1932), 17-46.

Kuo, Ping Chuo, "Caleb Cushing and the Treaty of Wanghia, 1844," Journal of Modern History, V (1933), 34-54.

----------, "Canton and Salem," New England Quarterly, III (1930), 420-442.

Littell, J. B., "Missionaries and Politics in China--The Taiping Rebellion," Political Science Quarterly, XLIII (1928), 566-699.

Morison, Samuel E., "Boston Traders in the Hawaiian Islands, 1789-1823," Massachusetts Historical Society, Proceedings, LIV (1920), 9-47.

----------, "Forcing the Dardanelles in 1810," New England Quarterly, I (1928), 208-225.

Nichols, R. H., "The Plan of Union in New York," Church History, V (1936), 29-51.

Oliphant, J. Orin, "The American Missionary Spirit, 1828-1835," Church History, VII (1938), 125-137.

Paullin, C. O., "Naval Administration under the Navy Commissioners, 1815-1842," United States Naval Institute, Proceedings, XXXIII (1907), 597-641.

Shafer, Joseph, ed., "Letters of Sir George Simpson, 1841-1843," American Historical Review, XIV (1900), 70-94.

Steiner, Bernard, "Jackson and the Missionaries," American Historical Review, XXIX (1924), 722-723.

Williston, Samuel, "William Richards: The South Seas Solomon," New England Quarterly, X (1937), 323-336.

Worcester, Samuel M., "Origin of American Foreign Missions," American Theological Review, II (1860), 687-724.

INDEX

Abeel, David: as missionary in China, 174-175, 195, 196; Indonesian travels of, 178; appeals for "missionary ships," 184; on Japan, 185; on Catholicism, 286-287

Adams, John Quincy: his relations with missionaries, 64; praises Hawaiian missions, 105, 124, 243, 289; meets with Parker, 190, 191

Adams, Newton, 212, 217, 218, 219, 220

Advisor; or Vermont Evangelical Magazine, 16

Africa: mission work related to colonization in, 207-209, 221-222, 226, 232; mission education program in, 209, 211, 214, 222, 225; mission work in, 212-214 *passim*, 216-217, 219-221, 231; mission relations with Boers in, 213-214, 216, 218-219; apartheid established in, 220-221; permanent land rights granted missions, 221; mission relation with France, 223-224, 231; mission feeling on rum and slave trade, 224; rival American missions in, 228; mission relation with Britain, 231. *See also* Negroes

Alexander I, 282

Alexander, William P.: opposes annexation of Hawaii, 130-131

Allen, David O.: *India, Ancient and Modern*, 304

American and Foreign Christian Union, 288

American Anti-Slavery Society, 226

American Bible Society, 45, 77

American Colonization Society, 207, 208

American Education Society, 31, 298

American Home Missionary Society, 86

American Journal of Science, 301

American Missionary Association (A.M.A.), 228-229, 255

American Oriental Society, 305-306

American Peace Society, 235

American Seamen's Society, 174, 260

American Society for Encouraging the Settlement of the Oregon Territory, 81

American Society for Propagating the Gospel among the Indians and Others in North-America, 18

American Society for the Promotion of Temperance, 235

American Tract Society, 45, 229, 258, 273-274, 314

Ames, Fisher, 52

Ames, Nathaniel, 52

Amherst College, 28, 29, 298

Amistad Committee, 228

Anderson, Rufus: supports use of native language in mission work, 53; arranges for South American mission, 78; works with Hawaiian missions, 103-104, 116, 123-125 *passim*, 127, 129; on foreign encroachment in Hawaii, 125-126; is special agent to Greece, 142-143; on Greece, 144; tours Levant, 153-154; on closing missions in Greece, 154; on Porter, 167; his relations with Carr, 167-168; on "missionary ship" project, 184-185; on American commissioner to China, 192; his role in A.B.C.F.M., 241; concerned about missionaries' observance of the Sabbath, 249-250; on sole purpose of missions, 253; on need for missions, 268; on purpose of Greek missions, 269-270; on Turkish students in America, 276; on A.B.C.F.M.'s federal relations, 289-290; on missionaries' wives, 311; in Brethren, 317; on Mission Park, 319; mentioned, 169, 190, 260

Andover Theological Seminary: founded, 2; requests foreign mission service, 20-23 *passim*; Brethren fraternity at, 23-26 *passim*, 241, 307, 317; Society of Inquiry at, 27, 108; Cherokees at, 66; Hawaiian at, 90; appeals for help for Greece, 141

Andrews, Lorrin, 124, 125

Armenia: mission work in, 136, 139, 150, 154, 159-161

Arms, William, 78, 179-180

King, Charles W., 175, 186-188
    passim
King, Jonas: as missionary, 137-138,
    141, 154; his education program
    in Greece, 144, 149, 165; perse-
    cuted, 156-157, 168; questions
    legal status of missionaries,
    246; represents French mission
    society, 284; "Farewell Letter,"
    139, 150; mentioned, 143, 145,
    299-300
Kingsbury, Cyrus: works with Ameri-
    can Indians, 60-61; on difficul-
    ties of Indian evangelism, 61
Knapp, Isaac, 134
Kotzebue, Otto von, 114

Lancaster, John, 42
Laplace, Cyrille, 117, 123, 223, 283
Lawler, Richard, 211, 222
Lay, G. Tradescant, 186
Lebanon: missions in, 158; American
    University (Beirut), 171
Ledyard, John, 23
Lee, Jason, 82
Levant Company, 133, 136, 137
Leyburn, George, 144
Liang A-fah, 183, 199
Lightcraft, George, 110
Liholiho, 94, 107
Lin, Commissioner, 181, 188
Lindley, Daniel, 212-213, 216-221
    passim
Livingston, David, 225
Livingston, John H., 26
Lobdell, Henry, 170, 296
London Missionary Society (L.M.S.):
    founded, 13; early mission work
    of, 14; its relations with
    A.B.C.F.M., 32-33, 57; Pacific
    missions of, 106, 113, 114,
    121, 249, 285; China represent-
    atives of, 172, 185, 281; Afri-
    can missions of, 212, 213, 221,
    225, 281; Siamese missions of,
    281
London Tract Society, 14
Loomis, Harvey, 318
Louis Philippe, 223, 283
Lyman, Henry, 179
Lyon, Mary, 153, 311

Macauley, Thomas Babington: "Minute
    on Education," 44

McLane, Robert M., 200
McLoughton, John, 83
Madison, James, 14, 36
Malcolm, Howard: on missionaries'
    wives, 311
Malo, David, 303
Malta: missionaries on, 139, 142, 143,
    149
Mar Shimon, 151, 159, 169
Mar Yohannan, 151, 276-277
Marcy, William L., 131
Maronites: mission work with, 136,
    149, 150, 157-158
Marquesas Islands: American mission in,
    115, 272; French mission in, 121-
    122; Hawaiian mission in, 129
Marsh, Dwight, 152
Marsh, George P., 168
Marshall, Humphrey: on Parker, 200
Marshall, John, 72
Martyn, Henry, 134, 279
Maryland Colonization Society, 209,
    210, 222, 226
Mason, Lowell, 314
*Massachusetts Baptist Missionary
    Magazine,* 16
Massachusetts General Court, 36
Massachusetts Missionary Magazine, 16
Massachusetts Missionary Society, 19-20
Mather, Cotton, 17-18
Mayhew, Thomas, 17, 62
Medhurst Walter H., 178, 185
Medical Missionary Society in China, 177
Meigs, Benjamin C., 50
Melville, Herman, 110-111, 115, 252;
    Typee, 108, 110, 112, 115, 285
Merrick, James L., 147-148, 306
Mesopotamia: mission work in, 152,
    169-170
Methodists: mission work of, 5-6, 46,
    195, 226, 288; General Council
    of, 254
Micronesian Islands, 129
Middlebury College, 29, 298
Millennium, belief in: influenced by
    French Revolution, 8, 9, 233, by
    Napoleon, 8, 9, 134, 233, 267,
    282, 284; influences missionary
    work, 7-12, 233-234; Miller on,
    10; its relations to Mohammedanism
    and Vatican, 134, 135
Miller, Samuel: on millennium, 10
Millerites, 11, 234
Mills, Samuel J.: has call to be

HARVARD EAST ASIAN MONOGRAPHS

1. Liang Fang-chung, *The Single-Whip Method of Taxation in China*

2. Harold C. Hinton, *The Grain Tribute System of China, 1845-1911*

3. Ellsworth C. Carlson, *The Kaiping Mines, 1877-1912*

4. Chao Kuo-chün, *Agrarian Policies of Mainland China: A Documentary Study, 1949-1956*

5. Edgar Snow, *Random Notes on Red China, 1936-1945*

6. Edwin George Beal, Jr., *The Origin of Likin, 1853-1864*

7. Chao Kuo-chün, *Economic Planning and Organization in Mainland China: A Documentary Study, 1949-1957*

8. John K. Fairbank, *Ch'ing Documents: An Introductory Syllabus*

9. Helen Yin and Yi-chang Yin, *Economic Statistics of Mainland China, 1949-1957*

10. Wolfgang Franke, *The Reform and Abolition of the Traditional Chinese Examination System*

11. Albert Feuerwerker and S. Cheng, *Chinese Communist Studies of Modern Chinese History*

12. C. John Stanley, *Late Ch'ing Finance: Hu Kuang-yung as an Innovator*

13. S.M. Meng, *The Tsungli Yamen: Its Organization and Functions*

14. Ssu-yü Teng, *Historiography of the Taiping Rebellion*

15. Chun-Jo Liu, *Controversies in Modern Chinese Intellectual History: An Analytic Bibliography of Periodical Articles, Mainly of the May Fourth and Post-May Fourth Era*

16. Edward J.M. Rhoads, *The Chinese Red Army, 1927-1963: An Annotated Bibliography*

17. Andrew J. Nathan, *A History of the China International Famine Relief Commission*

18. Frank H.H. King (ed.) and Prescott Clarke, *A Research Guide to China-Coast Newspapers, 1822-1911*